AFRICA BEFORE THEY CAME

THE CONTINENT, NORTH, SOUTH, EAST AND WEST, PRECEDING THE COLONIAL POWERS

AFRICA

by Galbraith Welch

Member of La Société de Géographie

By the same author

NORTH AFRICAN PRELUDE
THE UNVEILING OF TIMBUCTOO

William Morrow & Company · New York, 1965

BEFORE
THEY CAME

THE CONTINENT, NORTH, SOUTH,
EAST AND WEST, PRECEDING THE
COLONIAL POWERS

Copyright © 1965 by Galbraith Welch
All rights reserved.
Published simultaneously in the Dominion of
Canada by George J. McLeod Limited, Toronto.
Manufactured in the United States of America by
Quinn & Boden Company, Inc., Rahway, N.J.
Library of Congress Catalog Card Number 65-22975

Design and decorations by Lynn Hatfield

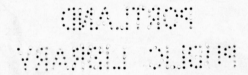

CONTENTS

AFRICA BEFORE THEY CAME

THE CONTINENT, NORTH, SOUTH,
EAST AND WEST, PRECEDING THE
COLONIAL POWERS

FOREWORD

THE AFRICAN CHARACTER AND THE "AFRICAN CLOCK"

· Thoughts do not die, though sometimes they change their forms of expression or fall into a long sleep—this, as of men and children and of continents. Africa's thoughts have alternately shone and dozed.

But the rest of us have almost ignored her ways of thinking and have concentrated on considering her ways of behaving or misbehaving, especially dwelling upon her contacts with European governments during colonization and, now that the continent has suddenly given birth to a vast family of new nations and nationettes, upon our own responsibilities and opportunities with regard to the newborn.

So in this book I have tackled what seems a new approach. I have attempted to discern what has been the continent's own manner of thinking, what this was previous to colonialism's brief interlude, what was—and probably in part still is—Africa's mental and emotional heritage, likely to emerge again as a strong influence now that colonialism is coming to an end.

Such hints as I can offer may have some practical value since the world today confronts the puzzle of a great continent which has been almost completely isolated through the ages, whose peoples are newly joining the nations and whose ways of thinking are practically unknown to us. Africa's own ideas, which she carries along, modified somewhat by colonial contacts, prophesy her thinking and her actions of tomorrow.

In considering Africa's ways of thinking it is significant that, though somnolent of late, Africa had mental equipment and the impulse to use her brains for purposes not purely utilitarian and protective a long time ago. Of this we have evidence in the hieroglyphs of the Nile Valley and in the figurines and rock art of other regions. Before most of our ancestors dreamed that there could be any other way of communicating a message than by talking Egypt began to write, to write in a literary sense. Egypt saw and recorded character and accomplishment. In the sensitive words of Professor Gordon Childe, there was carved on the famed Namer palette, "the oldest real portrait of a human personality." The portrait was presumably carved about five thousand years ago.

In Mediterranean Africa far to the west of Egypt were written pieces of literature which are still popular reading. About eighteen hundred years ago Algerian-born Apuleius wrote *The Golden Ass,* an almost modern sort of novel wherein mingle frank sex and fervent religion, of which as proof of its undying interest for the average reader two different English-language translations were recently simultaneously advertised. I wonder what novel of today will have corresponding longevity of interest and be making profit for the book publishers of the thirty-ninth century. In a nearby Algerian locality a couple of centuries later was born a writer of another type whose works, especially his *Confessions,* are equally popular with today's public—St. Augustine.

The Greeks curtsied to Egypt's brilliance in the days of old, permitting the Egyptian priest, imaginary character in the Atlantis story, to say patronizingly, "O Solon, you Greeks are children!" In science less fabulous we meet Eratosthenes of Cyrene, who really did put a girdle about the earth, and did it accurately, and Ptolemy, the geographical blunderer whose authority was respected till nearly modern times—involuntarily and inadvertently a true patriot for his invention of a hook-tailed Africa which hitched onto Asia discouraged attempts to circumnavigate the continent till da Gama went around the Cape of Good Hope and thus bequeathed prolonged prosperity to his native Alexandria as the transfer market between the Western and the Eastern world.

And there was Moses, too, a child of Egypt of revered wisdom. And Egypt shone briefly in an aborted effort at monotheism in the time of Akhnaton.

All these of which I remind the reader are blossoms of the brains of Mediterranean Africans. But in the rest of Africa are some traces of early briskness: proofs of skill and taste in the Sudan, delicate and wise art on Africa's West Coast and all across Africa rock pictures that are startlingly lively.

After all, if man did indeed begin his career in Africa it would seem natural that on the same continent he would come early to maturity. I have briefly mentioned a few indications of Africa's precocity to prove the outstanding vigor of the continent's brain in the days of old, when one might say that Africa was ahead of most of the world, that the "African Clock" ran fast. By this figure of speech I symbolize the ups and downs of Africa's thought processes in comparison with those of the rest of us who were her contemporaries. It was a clock which sometimes galloped and sometimes seemed almost to move backward.

In the pages that follow I shall try to tell something of what was Africa's way of thinking as time passed, what was her mental heritage, what Africa's character was when complete colonialism came suddenly across the continent, that short colonial passage which—being recent—seems longer to us than it really was, and which may not greatly have altered the continent's mentality in a lasting way. Europe taught some Africans new skills and brought scholarship to a few and installed countless items of modern civilization. The minds of Africa and Europe did not combine. Any attempt to estimate the value of colonialism is outside the scope of this book. And I may say incidentally that I sincerely have no opinion on this much discussed question.

What Africa thought and felt through the years before Europe took charge was the real Africa, the self which will emerge now that Europe is moving away. Such is the Africa that will determine the continent's future, and to some extent our own.

I do not suggest that Africa's behavior after some two generations of association with and control by the modern outside world will pick up in action where she left off. Many of her actions will be different. But the basic views are an influential and very old heritage.

In an attempt to reconstruct this heritage I have looked into many aspects. Let me list some of them briefly.

Prominently there figure the religions which Africa has known, those of importation and the indigenous African systems. The acceptance—sometimes but temporary—by sections of the continent's people of the three foreign faiths which came to them, Judaism, Christianity and Islam, and the religions which were of their own design all reveal the workings of their mind, their seeking, their questioning, their quarrelsome arguing, their eager curiosity and sometimes swift repulse or revamping of new thoughts and—in the pagan sections—an almost indistinguishable mingling of the social with the religious.

Africa's women—obviously they must have done the thinking for half of Africa—are an especially interesting study: the general attitude toward women and the attitude of the women toward themselves in a polygamous continent; the fact that the number of women who have gained a place in written and oral history is greater in Africa than among ourselves.

The arts in Africa are revealing and, along with the creative arts, sometimes leaping and active, sometimes exciting and hideously imaginative, and in the Ethiopian pictures, quaint and appealing in a childish simplicity—often on pious themes—there was that odd art of re-creation performed upon their own bodies, mutilations—sexual and otherwise—and queer cuttings and tooth hackings, as if, dissatisfied with nature's work, they sought to remodel themselves.

Then there is the continent's literature, the written works of the literate regions in Arabic by white and black Africans and in their own script by Christian Ethiopians, and the even more revealing oral history and symbolic legends of the non-writing regions.

Curious and puzzling has been the African very imaginative editing of what we call Bible incidents, attributing novel acts to personages named in the Koran and in the Old Testament and transporting these personages into an African setting.

Africa has had a unique chance to study race relations because she has possessed in her own territory native peoples of both colors. Their mutual reactions—the whites to the blacks and vice versa—have interest.

So has Africa's peculiar psychology about slavery, which has ranged from the sacrifice of a slave at crop ceremonies ("Customs") or funerals to the acceptance of a slave in high position, as king or ruler, even a eunuch slave. (The local effects of the slave trade with foreigners was another matter.)

Some characteristic items, threads in the African fabric, are puzzling and ugly to us, some handsome, some set us thinking, asking ourselves are they not—prejudice put aside—rather more shrewd than our own.

For cannibalism Africa has been regarded as headquarters, for both the ritual and the purely utilitarian. And human sacrifice was often a religious rite or part of a local ceremony.

Secret societies of immense potency and sometimes of great antiquity, the initiation systems and the special schooling of the young of both sexes—these were parts of a planned social system. So too was the frequent habit of destroying deformed babies, at which we wince.

And there was the omnipresence of magic across Negroland and the sentiment of animal association with mankind.

Part of the continent's psychology was the very definite and much regionally variegated notions and sentiments toward intoxicants and tobacco—toward the latter sometimes almost fanatical.

There was an early impulse to found universities; Cairo and Fez did this before Europe had any universities at all. There was later a renowned university in dark Africa at Timbuctoo. There was a time in the Middle Ages when Africa's culture in the Mediterranean section was in advance of our own, one indication being that the so-called Arabic numbers went from Algiers to Europe. In those days to some degree—not so great as in antiquity—the "African Clock" ran fast.

And the "African Clock" also ran fast in the early centuries of Christianity, when Alexandria and Carthage were theological centers, often named ahead of Rome. Discussion centers, too, disturbed by destructive Gnostic heresies and various debilitating schisms and the overinterference of politics and government, so that almost all of Africa which had been converted to Christianity had practically argued and talked itself into a stupor before Islam came.

In parts of Egypt, Christianity lived on. In Ethiopia it still glows. We hear vague rumors of Christianity's surviving influence deep into the continent. The reader will understand that I here refer to pre-colonial times and even to the times before the missionary effort which preceded the big rush of colonialism.

With the many things I have tried to tell I have thought it right to give special space to the religions of Africa (which, like colonialism, I view without personal prejudice)—the three faiths from the Near East: Judaism, Christianity and Mohammedanism, and the systems of paganism, sometimes horrid and sometimes wise and simple and touching. Religion is the mass expression of a group's point of view and of its philosophizing, that keyhole through which we can peep into their minds. Africa in her various religious experiences lays herself before us in mental and emotional nudity.

Since I wish to tell about the thinking and feeling and to try to reveal the continent's character through its behavior in pre-continental times I take much note of pre-continental sources, of the observations of early travelers and especially of the writings of Africans themselves in Arabic or by Ethiopian authors.

A selection of these is listed at the end of the book. This list also includes some of the recent observations and speculations that have appeared up to this date, 1965, and some historical and anthropological studies, and studies on the three religions—Judaism, Christianity and Islam as they affected Africa—and on the continent's paganism. Also mentioned are some writings which have been helpful in dealing with specific subjects: the position of women under Islam, in paganism and in Ethiopia; literature and legends, and the reappearance of Biblical and Koranic heroes in an African setting; definitions of cannibalism and meanings of human sacrifice; attitudes toward tobacco and intoxicants; the founding of early universities; racial relations, etc.

The List of Readings is not intended to be a bibliography in the usual sense of mentioning recognized authorities and the best available sources. It is a partial list carefully chosen from much reading over the years and naming items which have informed me or set me thinking or roused me to arguing in my own mind.

The world has been speculating and writing about Africa since classical times, when were attributed to the continent fantastic zoology, monstrous humans and localities which were playgrounds, love nests, gymnasiums and testing grounds of the gods. Something of a more sedate order which was written by one of the Roman writers in the first century B.C. seems surprisingly applicable to modern developments. To this author, Sallust, as to others of his day, the world was small and the extent of Africa unknown. He wrote, "In mapping the earth's surface most authors recognize Africa as a third continent, though a few admit only Asia and Europe as continents, including Africa in Europe."

If we take Sallust's two items in reverse order, his political geography was a correct prediction of what actually happened two thousand years later, when Africa, except for slightly over one three-hundredth part of the total continental area (Liberia's approximately 42,000 square miles), did indeed become a part of Europe, to re-emerge lately as a continent almost on its own.

So far as I know, nobody has been so rash as myself and attempted to speculate and try to discern what—in the days before Africa became for a brief while a part of Europe—was in the continent of Africa's heart and mind.

THREE BOOKS CAME
TO AFRICA

AFRICA HAS BEEN A RELIGIOUS CONTINENT, if we define religion as the imposition of special rules of conduct, intense imaginative reaching toward the intangible and an appetite for the supernatural, which last we call a belief in magic when it is manifested by people who are not of our own faith.

The Egyptians were "the first to broach the opinion that the soul of man is immortal . . . There are Greek writers who borrowed this theory and put it forward as their own. I could mention their names. I abstain from doing so." In this quaint fashion Herodotus chides his countrymen for appropriating without acknowledgment what he seems to regard as an Egyptian proprietorial idea, for committing an infringement of religious copyright.

There may have been immortality beliefs elsewhere in Africa at a yet more ancient time. The ancestor reverence of African paganism, the notion that the departed watches and supervises and criticizes, may well have been carried along from a very remote past. But it was dynastic Egypt which formulated the idea of immortality and perfected the luxurious baggage for their souls which was calculated to ensure an appreciative reception in the afterworld.

The religious appetite and consumption of Africa have been immense. No other part of the world has practiced so many religions, some indigenous and home-grown, some imported—witness the animal-faced gods of Egypt, Akhnaton's ephemeral monotheism, phallic idols, the gods of Punic Carthage drooling for the burnt bodies of little children, Greek and Roman genteel statuary. Then came "the book religions," so called—Judaism, homeless, Christianity in its precarious infancy and its African brilliant but short adolescence, tormented and weakened by heresies and schisms, and prancing disputative Islam. Most widespread of all was the sweep of native paganism. Africa has worshipped the sun and the moon and stars, the sacred tree or stone or a chosen animal, has seen in the mind's eye a multitude of spirits of mischief and little gods and sometimes the chief god of an unpretentious monotheism, and has been disciplined by reverence for dead ancestors and has accepted unflinchingly harsh and bloody practices.

Another possible item in Africa's spiritual life which I mention without comment as to its authenticity is the claim sometimes made that Freemasonry originated in Egypt and that the Great Pyramid of Gizah with its nearly two and a half million stone blocks, each weighing two and a half tons, was the world's first Masonic temple. Aside from this legend about Egypt's alleged precocity in a specialized spiritual field, I quote a practical tribute to the architects and workmen in a project which was motivated by a religious aspiration of some sort, "What architect of the present day would undertake to erect a building more than 400 feet high which would never need repairing for going on five thousand years?"

There have come to Africa those three books "which claim to rest their teachings on truth historically revealed by God not merely upon human reflection and discovery," to quote a thoughtful churchman. Africa knew the Old Testament in its gestation, participated in the New Testament's editorial struggles and met the Koran just as it graduated to parchment from scraps and fragments.

The three big books were not based on revelations or records made within Africa, but Africa was associated with the creation or assembling or earliest recognition of each of them. You might almost say that Africa glimpsed them in outline, in manuscript form or in advance copies.

The foundation of the oldest of them, the Bible of the Jews, the Old Testament, was mingled with the air and soil of Egypt. Africa had seen in person several of its greatest heroes. Africa had held Jews in her grasp during Judaism's infancy. It was in Egypt's adjacent possession, alongside the ancient turquoise and copper mines of Sinai, that Moses received the Commandments.

The New Testament went into its canonical form with Africa as one of its editors. In fact it was at Roman Carthage, near to modern Tunis, that in 397 a definitive list of the New Testament's contents was ratified by a Council under the leadership of that famous African, St. Augustine.

Many apocryphal documents which the official New Testament rejected have been preserved, and further such writings have recently been discovered in Africa. Some of what might be called the respectable ancient apocryphas were accepted by certain African Christians. The non-acceptables show us in a most interesting light the mental writhings, the discontent and the excited imagination of some of the African intelligentsia.

The earliest extant Christian prayer book, which turned up not so very long ago, is attributed to a fourth-century African bishop.

As for the Koran—when the Arab general Amr brought Islam to Egypt the book was just being collected and copied upon parchment from that pathetic and revered grab bag of flat stones, broken crockery, shoulder blades of sheep and camels and scraps of leather upon which his primitive Arab followers had written down their Prophet's words of revelation. The *doyen* of all Korans, supposedly the oldest surviving copy of the book, was discovered in Africa in 1963, according to a news report from Cairo—a Koran more than twelve hundred years old written on deerskin parchment and preserved in a metal box.

The three books were not composed in Africa, but it might be that the central idea, the backbone of all three of them—that there was one God, not a group of divinities—was contacted when the Jews were held in Egypt and was derived from memories of the Aten of Akhnaton, the sole and only god, or even from direct observation of Aten worship in action. A widely read book by Freud, *Moses and Monotheism*, suggests that Moses was in Egypt during Akhnaton's reign (1367–1350 in Sir Alan Gardiner's list of conjectural dates). This does not accord with the usual though uncertain Exodus date. Freud's hypothesis is that Moses carried out of Egypt the theory of one only God, then and long thereafter a dubious doctrine to the Jews. It is obvious that they had to learn and be convinced of monotheism. The Commandment ordering that there should be "no other gods before Me" proves that they had polytheistic flirtations.

Another possible African contribution concerns Christianity. It has often been suggested that the Trinity and the Mary cult are heritages, borrowings, reflections or vague influences from Isis of Egypt.

Along with the three books came men and women—Jews who were both victims and conquerors, and, so legend says, far-flung travelers to the Niger and beyond; Christians who made Africa the rival of Rome, squandered their force in bickering and established what now calls itself the oldest Christian nation on earth; and Moslems who fathered Moslem kingdoms beyond counting and, like their two predecessors, did much religious battling among themselves.

Of the influence upon the African mind and heart of the three books and their offshootings and heresies as told in history and legend I shall try to give some hint.

RETURN AFTER EXODUS

THE INFLUENCE OF JUDAISM ON AFRICA is something it is not possible to assess. There were a great many Jews, the original stock and descendants. They made a considerable number of converts while Africa was still in paganism, and history and legend tell us that they penetrated deep into the continent.

They gave Africa her first glimpse of one of three religious systems which, despite special prejudices and interreligious insults, are indisputably alike. They presented to the African mind a new form of religion—a religion which did not associate itself with or depend upon elements in nature, nor upon idols and statuary, nor upon those small objects sometimes called fetishes, and they showed Africa a new kind of intensity and integration based upon a faith and a code of behavior which amalgamated a group even when its members were widely split apart geographically.

The Jews' departure from Africa, the Exodus, seems to us the realest happening in Africa's antiquity, its elements of myth and mystery have become to us like a familiar adventure story. "The marks of Pharaoh's chariot wheels were distinctly visible on the shores of the bay where the children of Israel passed the Red Sea," according to author and traveler Baumgarten, who visited Egypt in 1507. Napoleon, perhaps inspired to emulate the feat of the Israelites and also deeply interested in the possibility of cutting that canal now called the Suez, went in 1798 to a place which had been designated as the likely site of the Exodus. It was a crossing some could wade across, but being a small man, Napoleon was nearly drowned. A discussion as to how many Jews actually left Egypt jolted the government of modern Israel in 1960, one side of the Knesset, the Israeli Parliament, insisting there were six hundred thousand Jewish men plus their families, the opposition maintaining that there were about six hundred.

History, which is sparse, and legend, which is considerable though it does not always inspire belief, tell us that the Jews moved across great African distances in their dispersion, from the Red Sea to the Atlantic, to Saharan oases and over the desert to the Niger and beyond.

Ample record about the Jews of Alexandria: how Alexander the Great himself apportioned to them a section of the new city he created—during the Ptolemaic period there were almost as many Jews as Greeks among the population, a big population for those days, said to have been three hundred thousand—how one of the Ptolemies authorized the construction of a sort of holy Jewish town which had the odd name of Onion. The name derived from Onias of the priestly family who was permitted to set up a combined fortress and sanctuary. Onias used as a part of the elegant Jewish building with its lamp hammered from a lump of gold—a detailed account is given by Josephus—a former temple of the Egyptian god Ra. Temples and churches and mosques in Africa frequently shifted their allegiances. Early Christians vaguely superimposed St. Peter on a wall fresco where once was the figure of a pagan god in a Nubian temple. The French turned a mosque into a cathedral, and after Algeria regained independence the cathedral became a mosque again.

Those were the good days for the Jews of Alexandria. Later came grievances, revolt and reprisal and near extermination. Yet when Amr, the Moslem conqueror, came there were no less than forty thousand Jews in the city.

Among Alexandria's intelligentsia stands out the still remembered philosopher Philo, who saw the Jews oppressed and sensed and expressed the potential influence of Judaism as he foresaw it. Proudly he said that the Jews were a people who had "received the priesthood for the whole human race." His vision was presumably a religious victory rather than the subtler effect of the Jews upon Africa's spirit which I have tried to suggest.

Philo himself headed a Jewish delegation to Rome when Alexandria rioted against Emperor Caligula's order that the Jews must recognize himself as co-divinity with their own God.

There was another and much smaller Jewish group up the Nile which had been there long before Alexander the Great welcomed the Jews to Alexandria and which had done little to give the influence or aura of Judaism to Africa. This was the military colony at Elephantine Island, near the First Cataract, maintained to protect the frontier which left us a sort of group autobiography in a collection of papyri discovered at the beginning of this century. These people far from home—they had probably been on their island for near two hundred years when they composed the documents in question —had forgotten the creed of a one and only God and caused "Yahu" to have several companions, notably a goddess concubine. Bultmann has remarked that there was with the Jews of the Diaspora a tendency to lessen the distinction between themselves and their non-Jewish neighbors.

Elephantine's isolated colony found it hard to put on spiritual evening dress in the pagan jungle year after year and century after century. One hears sometimes that modern Moroccan folk who call themselves Jews have fallen into beliefs that are near fetishism, and even that Jews in far parts in old times had drifted so far from their own traditions that they found the stories of the Flood and of Job, when told to them by a visiting rabbi, "fascinatingly new."

To the west of Alexandria is the region of Cyrene that was named after "the wild virgin Cyrene," who there spent her honeymoon with Apollo and there conceived the son who taught men to keep bees and thus endowed humanity with honey, and that started as a place of historically recorded habitation when a Greek went there with followers because the Delphic oracle told him he would there be cured of stuttering—which seems as odd a motive for African colonization as history can offer. Recently Cyrene was the summer residence of the King of Libya.

At the time of the dispersion Cyrene became an important Jewish settlement and at Cyrene the Jews met, indeed sought the disaster which again dispersed them and drove them—such as survived— farther westward and into the depths of the Sahara and beyond. It was the setting of one of the most horrid of massacres, if Dio Cassius, who gives us an almost contemporary report, told the truth, and an episode which stands pretty well alone in history, since it was the Jews who were the massacrers not the massacrees. It was a pogrom in reverse.

There were 220,000 victims of Jewish fury in the region of Cyrene. "They [the Jews] would cook their flesh, make belts for themselves of their entrails, anoint themselves with their blood and wear their skins for clothing. Many they sawed in two from the heads downwards. Others they would give to wild beasts." Rome's retaliation, after the rebels had swirled in bloody triumph and set up a brief Cyrenean kingdom and then been vanquished, was to massacre the Jews. Some thousands of the Jews escaped.

Less than a century before one Cyrenean Jew, then in Jerusalem, had made himself famous for kindness. He was Simon of Cyrene, who carried the Cross for Jesus according to the Bible, and who, according to the Gnostic fantasy, died by magic on that Cross in Jesus' place. Some variant of this story may have been believed by certain Christians as late as the sixth century and must have been in Mohammed's mind, for the Koran says, "They crucified him [Jesus] not; they had only his likeness."

Another version of substitution is that Judas was by a divine maneuver crucified in Christ's stead, having been magically transformed so closely into Jesus' image that even the Virgin Mary and the Apostles were deceived. This was included in the Gospel of Barnabas, allegedly written by a Christian renegade to Mohammedanism. The story traveled far. Chinese Moslems believed it. It was one of the apocryphas Christianity officially condemned. The kind man of the New Testament and the original basis for the substitution story was a Jew of Cyrene.

The revolt at Cyrene was the end of the big Jewish settlements in northern Africa, the end of "the continuation of Judea" for which they had hoped. It was more than dispersion. It was splintering. Minor Jewish groups were all across the top of the continent, some were refugees from Cyrene and farther east, some newcomers to Africa or perhaps very old settlers. They made converts. We read of whole tribes, then pagan—for the Arab-Moslem invasion did not come for many centuries—who accepted Judaism. Ibn Khaldun in his *History of the Berbers* says this, and lists seven such tribes by name.

We also find legends of vague reliability which nevertheless show wide and lasting memory of Jewish presence and prestige. There were supposedly synagogues "dating from the time of Solomon" and towns whose foundation Solomon had ordered; there was a synagogue with one of the doors of the temple of Solomon which a group of refugees had been able to carry away with them at the time of Nebuchadrezzar's attack on Jerusalem.

One item about Solomon's interest in northern Africa was taken seriously in relatively modern times. It was reported by an English explorer who had gone to Morocco in the hope of penetrating into the country—then a place of forbidden mystery to foreigners—and thence to cross the Sahara. He was told that there was in existence in southern Morocco a large Jewish community of great antiquity. This was communicated to him by a rabbi, and the explorer believed it and so informed his royal patron in England, saying he had offered the rabbi a sum of money for a promised copy of the actual record of the community, which he was told bore "the signet and seal of Joab," who was accustomed to visit the community as tax collector on Solomon's behalf. The rabbi told how the Jews had been sent by Solomon to the far West, "crossing the Great Sea to avoid Egypt."

Before the explorer could procure this strange document or could investigate the place for himself he was murdered by natives, as were many early explorers, for the African instinctively distrusted exploration as a prelude to conquest and colonization.

He was John Davidson, "a doctor and a man of learning," who was killed on December 18, 1836. His brother collected his correspondence and travel journal and issued them under the title *Notes Taken during Travels in Africa by the Late John Davidson*, of which only a few copies were printed.

Other personages whose names appear in the Old Testament and also in the Koran figure in a variety of legends found almost all over Africa, in some of which these heroes appear in person on African soil. Mention of some of these will be made later. Solomon was active in the way of colonization not only for Jews but also for a mysterious race called the jinn, for whom he is supposed to have founded a penal colony to which such jinn as did not work to his orders were sent—a sort of hell on earth. It was located at or near a place called Kalaa in western Algeria.

With the Arab conquest of Mediterranean Africa and very possibly earlier many Jews had gradually moved away from the coast and into the desert, to make their homes in one of the oases. It was a hard life. Sometimes unsympathetic persons have said that the Jews in their dispersion sought prosperous places, where by their shrewdness they could parasitically suck the local wealth. The Jews of the Sahara could at first suck only sand in a desert country so grim that it might not rain for twenty-five years running. Yet in the Sahara in one locality at least they eventually prospered.

They enjoyed many good years in the Tuat region. Tuat, a word which means "Oasis" in the Berber language, was taken as a geographical name for a strip of separated oases whose twelve-hundred-mile system of underground water conduits, sometimes two and three hundred feet below the surface, is a marvel of primitive engineering which has been justly compared to the miracle of the Pyramids.

Through the Tuat passed trans-Saharan trade: caravans from the south met caravans from the north; exotic things from Negroland were unloaded and camels recharged with the products of North

Africa's civilization. The resident Jews had a big part in the trans-actions. The sole European trader whose account of the Tuat ex-change business has come down to us, Malafante of Genoa in the end of the fifteenth century, says that the brokers charged 100 per-cent commission. The Arabs were the master race, but, says Malfante, "the life of the Jews goes along in peace."

A generation later there was a tragic change. A Moslem, one of those violent enthusiasts known in religious annals—not alone in Moslem annals—reared up in indignation against the Jews of the Tuat, those upstarts with their wealth and their handsome clothes who dared to set up a synagogue at their main center, Tamentit (translatable as "Perfection to the Eye"). His name, long in the Arabic manner, is usually abbreviated to al-Maghili. His campaign fired the Moslems, who were the Jews' neighbors and competitors in trade. Perfection to the Eye was no more. Some Jews escaped. The Moslems' report was complacent. "It is," they declared, "a merito-rious act to destroy a synagogue." Al-Maghili strode on into Negro-land beyond the desert, converting pagans to Islam and snarling against Islam's enemy, the Jews.

Jews had by then penetrated deep into the sub-Sahara. It was more than three centuries since the informant upon whom the great Arabic geographer Edrisi based his text had passed along word about Jewish settlements in the western Sudan, including the town of Mallel some twelve days beyond "the great city of Ghana."

About simultaneously with the anti-Jewish campaign of al-Maghili a Sudanese history, *Tarikh el-Fettach*, told in detail about a real Jewish kingdom which had recently flourished alongside the Niger, citing as authority a living person who had been told about the place from his grandfather, and even a very aged slave who claimed that he had worked there.

The place was civilized to a degree that amazed the *Tarikh el-Fettach*. It possessed over three hundred wells the like of which had never been seen—prodigiously deep with a lining of clay and stone into which logs of wood had been dropped. Then shea (vegetable) butter had been poured in and a fire set. The result was a well inte-rior like cast iron. The place, whose name according to the old slave had been Bako and whose importance was known in far-off Morocco according to the *Roudh el-Kartas,* a fourteenth-century Arab history, was governed by seven princes "descended from the King of the Jews." But local tradition would have it that these "Beni-Israel" were the descendants of some female slaves of Noah who had mated with a giant. This piece of fantasy need not cast doubt on the story as a whole. In fact modern exploration is said to have discovered traces of Bako.

There are many legends and speculations about the Jewish presence in the sub-Sahara. Here are a few:

At Atar in Mauretania (now a republic) there was a Jewish king who was something of a regional conqueror and who protected his capital with a pack of savage dogs and thus would have blocked the way of the Almoravid campaign to enlist all men under the banner of Islam had not a saintly person in the Islamic army announced that he possessed a special power to subdue wild dogs. He marched ahead of the troops, and the savage dogs at the sight of him were quelled to gentleness. So Islam conquered the Jews of Atar, but the saintly dog-tamer was killed in the final combat by an arrow shot by a blind Jew. This happened in the eleventh century, and was carried along by local storytellers till a modern regional historian, Siré-Abbas-Soh, included it in his chronicles of the Senegalese Fouta.

South of a great river, presumably the Niger, was "a territory of immense extent which is reported to be inhabited by one of the lost or missing tribes of Israel," wrote James Grey Jackson in 1809, a student of Africa then unexplored and mysterious. We hear of the lost tribes of Israel all across the continent, including their spectacular establishment in East Africa, which will be mentioned later. At Yoruba, Nigeria, today certain of the population like to think they descend from one of the lost tribes which made the long trek across Africa to the Atlantic, not in itself an unusual notion for some have seriously theorized that the lost tribes were the forebears of the British, while others have suggested they were the ancestors of the North American Indians.

What one might call unproven Jewish presence in Africa also includes a possibility which has attracted some historians and ethnologists of standing: that Ghana, the ancient empire and gold trade center in Mali—no connection with modern Ghana—was first ruled by Jewish kings. The *Tarikh es-Soudan,* a history written in Arabic at Timbuctoo which, like the *Tarikh el-Fettach,* contains many of the legends conserved with the pious care which non-writing peoples give to oral history, says that Ghana's first masters were men "of the white race." Were they Jews? No evidence to prove or to disprove.

A really grandiose theory about possible Jewish penetration has been that the many million Fulani race of West Africa, which includes part of the population of both Nigeria and the Guinea Republic and which some call and many insistently deny to be a Negro branch, are descended from Jews. The Fulani are a thin-featured people with a reddish skin tone, which however is getting darker as they absorb more black stock, a skin tone so noticeable that they used locally to be called "The Red People." The question of who they once were and where they came from has filled stacks of printed paper, the Jewish possibility—yes or no—being the leading argument, though other theories are suggested that are excessively queer, for instance that the Fulani proceeded from the fathering performed by a Roman legion which got lost in the sub-Sahara.

In contrast Mediterranean Africa after the Moslem push saw the Jews with no romanticized view, but took them in a prosaic and bitter fashion, regarding them as displaced persons who insistently, and to the local people objectionably, carried along their special codes of religion and behavior. They displeased the Moslem population and they were too clever and competent to despise. So they were tormented. There were few large-scale persecutions in the pogrom sense, nothing to resemble our modern misbehavior, but continuous discrimination, humiliation and cruelties and sometimes the equivalent of serfdom.

Moslem prejudice became almost absurd in some of its manifestations. Medieval Arabic writers customarily put a phrase like "God damn the Jews," or "May God curse them," after any historic reference to Jews. Leo Africanus stated that they were responsible for venereal disease in Africa. There was reportedly a tribe of Jews who were one-half dog. At times of drought the Jews in some Moroccan cities would be driven out of town to howl, forbidden to return till the rain came. In addition to such absurdities were the well-known humiliations as to dress and conduct that were forced upon their Jews.

The post-colonization situation of Jews in North Africa does not concern this book but is of interest. After the French conquest of Algeria their position was favorable. During the Algerian struggle for independence it was dubious, and since independence many Jews have fled.

Despite the ill use of Jews in groups, individual Jews in Africa have been honored and many have made money. We hear how sultans would employ Jewish doctors and how Saladin and Richard Coeur de Lion competed for the services of Maimonides, who was a physician merely on the side, his real work being philosophy.

In trade they were brilliant and tireless. Here is an appreciation from a Moslem source: the ninth-century geographer Ibn Khordad-beh told of them, "These merchants speak Arabic, Persian, Roman [i.e. Greek and Latin], the Frank, Spanish and Slav languages. They journey from West to East, from East to West, partly on land, partly by sea. They transport from the West eunuchs, female slaves, boys, brocade, castor, marten and other furs, and swords." The first three items seem rather oddly listed as Western trade goods, but Ibn Khordadhbeh centered his compass in the Middle East and to him the West was wide. Perhaps the Jewish traders picked up these fancy wares along the way. There follows his account of the Jewish traders' route across the whole world—as the world was then—as far as India and China, and he tells of the goods brought on the return: "musk, aloes, camphor, cinnamon and other products of the Eastern countries." He tells of their trading along the southern route: Spain to Morocco, then walking across North Africa to Kairwan and Alexandria.

I have tried to give a notion of the Diaspora in Africa, widespread geographically but thinly spread, occasional wise men whose counsel kings accepted, and legends where Jews themselves were kinglets—all against that ill will and persecution for which modern Europe cannot criticize Africa.

From it all, the good and the mean, there was left an effect upon the African brain. It was the continent's first encounter with a widespread foreign influence. If it did no more it opened the door of the mind for influences to come—Christianity, Islam and what we call "modern civilization."

As specific examples and proofs of Jewish influences the following pages will tell of two striking Jewish individuals, both women, who by the power which they wielded showed the vigor of Judaism to Africa—one a Berber, the other a native of Ethiopia. And I shall tell about a woman who, legend says, brought Jewish blood to Africa three thousand years ago, which heritage it claims still flows in an emperor's veins. And finally I shall tell of Africa's Jewish glamour story, which roused Europe's jealousy and rivalry and so launched more ships than ever Helen did.

In the Arab effort to conquer Africa and in Africa's effort to resist, two romantic figures stand out. One is the seventh-century Arab leader Sidi Okba. The other is his contemporary, the African Jewess queen and general called The Cahena, her name deriving from the Hebrew word for "Priest," as is recognizable in the modern name of Cohen. She was a Berber whose forebears had been converted to Judaism.

The Arabs had sliced through Christian Egypt as if it were molded jelly; "it was like a conquest that was expected, almost hoped for, with the tacit consent of the conquered." Alexandria fell to the Moslems, who destroyed its walls so that, as the Arab commander remarked, "men could go in on every side as to the house of a harlot." The resistance of Christian Carthage seems to have been flabby. In due course Okba reached the Atlantic, rode into the ocean and cried out to Allah that but for the waves he would ride on and on, "fighting always for Your religion and killing all who did not believe in You!" It was dramatic but, as it turned out, overconfident. Berbers under a Christian leader defeated and killed him.

Now came Cahena's turn to fight the invaders. She was not one of the generals of modern warfare who plot and plan and risk not their lives but their reputations, but a general who charged with her men and finally died in battle. She vanquished the Arab army and chased it back to Libya. For some time the Arabs licked the painful wound of pride at having been defeated by a female general, but Cahena knew that they would come back for a return match, and knowing that they were too strong for her, she conceived a strange and tragic plan. She decided to burn and chop and sack the countryside so that the Arabs would turn back and go home in disgust, and being a creature of immense power in the land, she was able to carry her plan into execution, but even such a one as she could not make men accept the destruction of their vineyards and olive groves and grain crops. They turned against her and she died, the still fighting leader of a faithful few. The Arabs, who had at last won a victory over her, sent her head as a triumphant trophy to the caliph.

She had held back the Arab invasion for five years. She had postponed the rush of Islam to and across Gibraltar to conquer Spain and threaten France. She was the heroine of the first Arab-Jewish conflict.

A Jewish queen fought and vanquished the Christians in tenth-century Ethiopia. She drove out the long-established Christian monarchy and disturbed the country from its pattern for the next three hundred years. Not only were Ethiopia's Christian churches and its capital, Axum, destroyed, but all the members of its reigning family were assassinated except one child, who was smuggled away to safety and one of whose descendants eventually came back to the Ethiopian throne. Such is the tradition. This wild female fighter for Jewry left no diary, and the records of her exploit are scanty and unsure.

Judith was the name by which she is best known though she is mentioned by several others, the most striking of which is "The Fire." This last she well deserved, as also she deserved the name of Judith for, like the heroine of the apocryphal Book of Judith, she was an ardent fighter for the cause she believed in. (Judith of the Apocrypha, to save her city from Nebuchadrezzar, seduced his general and cut his head off.)

The fact that the Ethiopian Judith succeeded in crushing Christian power established over the centuries proves that Jews were numerous and strong in the land: the long line of Christian kings of the Axumite dynasty—their coins each marked with a cross, their prosperous and civilized capital—this was not something which an ardent Jewish enthusiast could destroy without the backing of an army of devoted Jews. These she had.

In all Africa the Jewish influence was nowhere so vigorous and so lasting as in Ethiopia. Even today Jews exist there as an integral group, known as the Falashas, who are the only independent long-surviving Jewish community in Africa. Indeed they were unique in the world till Israel's debut.

In very early times many Jews from the neighboring Jewish land of South Arabia made the easy leap across the Red Sea, which at the narrow strait was less than twenty miles wide, and implanted Judaism in Ethiopia as a lasting spiritual crop, a perennial which still lives. Alternate legends attributed many more romantic explanations of Jewish beginnings in the land. One which was cherished by the Falashas was that they descended from certain of the Jews in Egypt who instead of following Moses in the Exodus preferred to invent an exodus of their own and made their way into Ethiopia. A more realistic modern view of the Falashas is that they were probably remnants of the Jewish-via-Arabia emigrants who had declined conversion to Christianity.

In contrast to other Jewish groups in Africa, who lived as humiliated members of hostile settlements, the Falashas established a community, almost a little country of their own. They took refuge in a locality called Semien, which means "High." Its mountains rise to fifteen thousand feet. It looks southward toward Lake Tsana, near which James Bruce thought he had identified the source of the Nile. It was a homeland fitted to produce communal longevity and religious tenacity and it has done so.

They were a peculiar variety of Jews, whether because of their origin or because of their isolation. They did not know Hebrew. Their Bible was in Gheez, the Ethiopian classical language. Though described as not orthodox they were insistently Jewish to such a degree that one of them who had been reckless enough to set foot in a Christian house had to be purified before he was fit to return to normal Falasha society.

With this they combined some elements which resemble paganism. They transformed the Sabbath, for which Judaism has an especial reverence, into a personality, a deified being, a sort of goddess. Sabbath has a seat in Heaven and speaks to God with authority; among other remarks she states her expectation that she will be at the entrance of Hell to advise God in his judgments upon the children of

Adam. These items are in the Commandments of the Sabbath (*Te'ezaza Senbat*). A translation of this is included with other curious matters in *Falasha Anthology*, edited by Wolf Leslau. Their goddess Sabbath would seem to suggest that African paganism had smeared something of its symbolic idolatry across their Judaism. The same pagan contagion affected the Jews who settled on Elephantine Island.

Christian Ethiopia, when it got back on its feet, battled the Falashas with weapons and with insults, calling them black magicians and sorcerers with hypnotic powers. An Italian rabbi, Obadiah da Bertinoro, who traveled in the fifteenth century, wrote of Ethiopia's interreligious wars and of the human booty taken by the victorious Christians—Jews sold into slavery: "I saw two of them in Cairo; they were black, but not so black as Negroes."

A royal lady who had Jewish associations—very intimate associations—is claimed by Ethiopia to be one of theirs. This is the Queen of Sheba, who visited King Solomon. That she was an Ethiopian is legendary. Marib in Yemen—southern Arabia near Aden—is stated to have been her home town. But to Ethiopia she is an indubitable and sacred national possession. She plays her part in modern Ethiopian diplomacy, commerce and politics. She gives her name to Ethiopia's Order of the Queen of Sheba, which the Emperor of Ethiopia confers on important or beloved foreigners. She is a part of the Ethiopian national advertising; Ethiopian Airlines says that it carries passengers to "The Land of the Queen of Sheba." And her name is mentioned in the modern Constitution of Ethiopia, wherein it is stated with solemnity that the imperial line "descends without interruption from the son of the Queen of Ethiopia, the Queen of Sheba and King Solomon of Jerusalem."

Some two thirds along the road the Solomon-Sheba descendants lost government control for some centuries following the violence of Judith The Fire, but Ethiopia today takes pride in the belief that the blood flowed honorably from the time of their romantic national mother some three thousand years ago to the day of Emperor Haile Selassie, who regained Ethiopia from Italy. The point is not whether the story is true historically. The point is the inspiring effect it has had upon an isolated land in Africa.

The legend of the Ethiopian Queen of Sheba is one of three different stories about this adventurous woman who literally embraced Judaism, the three being officially told in Jewish, Arabic and Ethiopian records. Few women, and certainly no woman of such remote antiquity, aroused such variegated inventiveness and religious imagination.

The Old Testament story is brief and dignified, dwells on the financial and intellectual elements of her encounter with King Solomon and contains no statement of a sexual character, but the average person infers that Solomon and the Queen of Sheba had a love affair.

It has tickled many to think that the beautiful physical phrases in the Song of Solomon, which the Authorized Version of the Bible says are allegorical references to Christ and the Church, were Solomon's passionate tribute to the Queen of Sheba's charms. This is a romantic fancy, but impossible since the composition of the Canticle is dated by students some six hundred years after Solomon and Sheba's queen had their idyllic meeting.

The Arabic account of our heroine, given in part in the Koran and supplemented by Arabic legends, is ungallant and impish and is detailed in several ways, most of them unpleasant. Solomon heard of the land of Sheba with "a woman reigning over them, gifted with everything and she has a magnificent throne." She and her people worshipped the sun. This information stirred Solomon in a variety of ways, rousing male curiosity, greed and religious wrath. He summoned this woman to come humbly before him.

The queen (called in Arabic tradition Balkis) was alarmed, fearing military attack if she refused. She endeavored to avoid trouble by sending Solomon a present—a thousand young slaves, half of them boys, half of them girls, five hundred "bricks of gold," plus other valuables.

Solomon indignantly sent her another message. If she did not come to him he would attack in force and drive her people out of their country, "humbled and contemptible." So Balkis, the queen, obeyed. While she was on her way to Jerusalem, Solomon played a trick upon her—a trick which failed. He ordered one of the jinn who were his servitors to go to her city and steal and fetch to Jerusalem her throne, which was indeed "magnificent," being made of gold and silver and covered with precious stones and of vast dimensions, so that it was more like an outsized dais than a mere throne to sit upon. The jinnee told Solomon to look up to the sky and before he could cast his eyes down again the throne would appear before him. And that is what happened, certainly an example of superb service.

Solomon then had the appearance of the throne altered so as to be unrecognizable, and when the Queen of Sheba arrived he asked her as a test of her intelligence whether it was like her throne at home. The queen snapped back, "As though it were the same!"

Then he played another trick upon poor Balkis which succeeded. It was a shabby trick. Solomon had heard a rumor that Balkis had hair on her legs or a deformity of the feet. In advance of her coming he caused the courtyard of his palace to be paved with transparent glass under which was running water with fish swimming about. She took this to be a lake and pulled up her dress, baring the calves of her legs. Sneered Solomon, "It is glass!"

The incident shocked the Queen of Sheba and, oddly enough, caused her to announce her conversion to the religion of Solomon.

After he had converted the Queen of Sheba by this mean piece of trickery, legend says that Solomon, who was then getting along in years—he died seven years later—had thoughts of marrying the lady but could not resolve to do this till his jinn had taken the hair off her legs by a magic depilatory, and it is uncertain whether the marriage subsequently took place. Some say she decided to marry an Arab prince instead.

The Ethiopian version has a smiling but roguish, even smoking-room tone: Solomon shows as a man of the world who suspects that the pretty lady will readily slide into his bed if he greases the route. The name of the young Queen of Sheba-in-Ethiopia was Makedda. Her country was a primitive place whose king until the time of her father had been a gigantic snake named Arwe ("Serpent" in Gheez) and whose people worshipped the sun. Makedda's father killed Arwe and became ruler, and under certain conditions Makedda was now the queen.

Reports about Solomon came to Makedda via a trader, and presently the brave young woman set out for Jerusalem to see his grandeur and hear his wisdom. She carried gifts. Solomon received her with cordiality and set her up in large and luxurious quarters. One day he gave a banquet in her honor, put her at his right hand in a sort of private box with curtains so that she might see but not be seen by the male guests, a distinguished company made up of gentlemen of Solomon's family, nobles and army officers. Along with the well-seasoned food Solomon at her side pressed upon her highly spiced wine.

The royal banquet with stylish servants and special officers with "silk-handled fly switches" delighted Makedda, who was used to simple home ways. She told Solomon that he was twenty times greater than she had been led to expect. She then attempted to go back to her own quarters.

Solomon protested, saying it was late and that she had best spend the night in his palace.

Makedda's reply was of a frankness which accorded with her simple upbringing. "I am a virgin," she said, "and I do not dare spend the night near you, for if I lose that flower I shall lose my kingdom." She explained that it had been her father's oath on taking power that chastity was obligatory upon his daughter—he had no son—who would succeed him, which does not seem a very practical way of establishing a dynasty.

Solomon smiled and encouraged her with a joking reply. He would not endanger her throne provided she would promise not to take anything which was a possession of his. Angrily she answered that she had plenty of treasures at home—"gold in big basketfuls." She accepted his hospitality. Evidently there was no guest room in Solomon's palace, or the wily king preferred not to offer one to his attractive guest. Ethiopian art—for the country's artists have delighted to show serial representations of the episodes of her trip—picture two beds so close that Solomon could and did reach across and grab Makedda by the wrist.

Do not think that Solomon broke his promise. It was Makedda who did this, and she did so unaware and in innocence. Because of the spiced food and wine Makedda was thirsty during the night. She whispered to her maidservant to bring her a drink of water. Solomon, who had been feigning sleep, reached out and seized Makedda's arm.

"You have broken your word!" he cried. "You have taken something of mine!"

"It is only water!" she protested.

"What is more precious than water?" he demanded.

At the end of Makedda's sojourn in Jerusalem she informed Solomon that she expected the birth of a baby. She went away converted to Judaism and very happy. Subsequent events prove that her people forgave her for breaking the oath of her father, the serpent-killer, as to perpetual virginity. Instead they found therein cause for three thousand years of racial pride, and were still displaying the site of her capital when Father Alvarez of Portugal visited Ethiopia in the sixteenth century.

A rather touching variant of the Ethiopian story tells that one of Makedda's feet had been turned into the hoof of an ass because a drop of serpent Arwe's blood had spattered it, nine saints having saved her from further injuries. It was in the hope that in his wisdom he could cure her deformity that she had gone to Solomon.

This legendary omelette which combines Jewish, Moslem and Christian ingredients around Ethiopia's treasured heroine seems especially characteristic of the mixed religious influences in Africa. It even introduces a time mix-up which is rather Gnostic by involving around one personage the prehistoric myth of an animal king, the power of a Jewish monarch of the tenth century B.C. and Christian saints of our own era.

The child of Makedda's mating with Solomon was a boy; his name was the equivalent of Son-of-the-Wise-Man. When he came of age he went to present himself before his father. King Solomon, who in this version of the romance was still alive and reigning in Jerusalem received him with enthusiasm and renamed him Menelik, meaning "How handsome he is!"

Handsome Menelik was not the only Ethiopian king said to have had a distinguished Jewish father. A dynasty which held power during a part of the eclipse of the Sheba descendants thought they also were sired by Solomon, the maternal side plebeian, Solomon having taken a fancy to one of Makedda's attendants (five hundred virginal girls had been in Makedda's entourage when she set off to visit Solomon) and the maidservant, like the queen, had returned home pregnant. To one interim king, a very pious Christian, was ascribed descent from Moses, whose marriage to an Ethiopian woman is mentioned in the Old Testament. And a highly revered Ethiopian Christian saint was said to descend from Zadok, great priest in Solomon's time.

It seems strange that such very Christian people and a people who battled with the Jewish part of their population so bitterly should have taken pride in supposed Jewish associations in the past. Consider this prayer, part of the church services at old-time ceremonies honoring the Virgin Mary:

May the Jews, who are doomed to perdition, whose name stirreth up wrath, go down and have their habitation in the lowermost depths of the place of judgment. Amen.

It seems as if when they boasted of Jewish ancestors while hating contemporary Jews they did not let the right side of their brains know what the left side was thinking.

A story which broke suddenly in the Middle Ages stirred Jewry's delight and roused anger, jealousy and even emulation among Christians.

It was the story of Eldad the Danite, which told of the existence of a large and important Jewish empire in eastern Africa dating from antiquity. Naturally Jews were eager to believe a report that their people had a flourishing home country which dated back to long before the fall of Jerusalem and that the Jews were not therefore a dispersed lot of stateless individuals grouped together in little bunches here and there under usually humiliating conditions. Eldad the Danite's story of a secret happy land in a remote region was one of that series which has charmed the world, a dream which never dies. They are the Atlantis heritage.

The Jewish state Eldad the Danite told about was a duplicate affair. One part was rich and belligerent and the other part was rich and idyllic. The former consisted of the kingdom of the tribe of Dan and three other Jewish tribes. The latter was a group of Levites living in luxurious privacy in a tract of land surrounded by a non-traversable river, so that "they see no man and no man sees them except those four tribes," and even the four tribes could communicate with them only by shouting across the river. They had "glorious houses and fine buildings and castles and they trained elephants for themselves in their times of joy." In their happy land there were no flies, fleas, foxes, scorpions, serpents or dogs. None were servants, all were equal and they lived to be a hundred and a hundred and twenty years old. Of course precious stones, gold and silver were part of the story. So much for the Levite section of the Jewish empire in Africa, to which place they had been transported miraculously from exile in Babylon in the time of Nebuchadrezzar upon a cloud by night.

The tribe of Dan and the rest who lived in the adjoining but separated kingdom had arrived in two groups some three centuries before the Levites. They were fighters, all year round and every year, battling and plundering neighboring lands in a system of rotation, each of the four tribes fighting and pillaging for three months and resting for nine. Their fighting banner was white, and thereon written in black was, "Hear, O Israel, the Lord our God is one God," and they were said to go into battle 120,000 strong, all with little white bannerettes. And they, like the Levites, had treasure and gold. And, indeed, why not? for the land where these tribes had made an empire was Havilah, a noble name since it was the first territory except Eden to be mentioned in the story of the Creation, and a glittering name—"the land of Havilah where there is gold."

Geography does not help us to locate this empire, nor to place the remarkable river which enclosed the private domain of the Levites. It was the Sabbation, that river which listened to the Commandment and worked only six days a week. "On the seventh day it rests and is tranquil until the end of the Sabbath," said Eldad, and during its holiday it was so covered by mist that the Levites' seclusion was undisturbed.

It was a fairy story which compensated for the actuality of Jewish tribulations. Verisimilitude was given to it by the ritual details included therein about such matters as the slaughtering of food animals, but it was not such prosaic items as these that kept Eldad the Danite's story alive, copied and recopied and discussed from the later part of the ninth century to the end of the fifteenth, when it was printed. (And one doubts that any book was printed in those early days of printing unless there was a real demand.)

In the processes of copying and translating and oral reporting into different languages variations developed in the story. The partial résumé I have given is based on Elkan N. Adler's *Jewish Travellers,* from Epstein's critical edition. There was endless argument about Eldad: Was he an adventurer and a liar? Was he a missionary for a form of Judaism, using a tall tale to gain attention? Was his story a grandiose fancy picture of the Falashas? Was it true?

At the conclusion of the story Eldad the Danite's full name is given and could not well be fuller. It takes up ten printed lines and includes thirty-eight forefathers.

Whatever was the motive of this author with the ten-line name, his account of a Jewish empire in hidden Africa seems to have inspired a counterblast. It is widely believed that the Prester John myth, which eventually came to roost in Africa and which excited the medieval world almost beyond bearing, originated as an imitation of Eldad's boastful yarn. Prester John might well have been Eldad's progeny. Prester John, the marvelous Christian king of a gorgeous hidden country, became the romantic, tempting and almost sacred carrot before the nose of exotic travelers and early explorers. Columbus dreamed of Prester John, a son of Vasco da Gama's was tortured to death in his cause in Ethiopia, Marco Polo told about him, Shakespeare mentioned him, Henry the Navigator found him an inspiration for his African expeditions. As to the part which Prester John played in Ethiopia, I shall speak later.

Indeed this Jewish fairy tale may be said to have punished Africa for its harshness toward the Jews in that it inspired and hastened the exploration which, after ships had doubled the Cape of Good Hope and made their way to India, was the ruin of Africa's overland trade with the East. Alexandria was no longer the unique Market of the Two Worlds.

THE THREE PHASES OF AFRICA'S PRE-COLONIAL CHRISTIANITY

EXUBERANT CHILDHOOD ·
BLACK SHEEP · POCKETS

EXUBERANT CHILDHOOD · Africa from Gibraltar to the Nile was ready for new thoughts and some new religious philosophy. Religions Africans had known in plenty, some imported in older days, some home invented. They had observed and perhaps they remembered with horror what Carthage had brought, those gods like cruel and rapacious tax collectors screaming for the sacrifice of children. The religion of the Greeks and the Romans had become like the installments of an uncensored novel, featuring the series of erotic adventures of a band of voluptuous, perverse and useless divinities. The Egyptians, who had cut their religious teeth on gods with strangely imagined animal faces and had obediently accepted the temporary reign of Aten, saw their religion degenerate into what

Breasted described as merely "elaborate and insistent punctiliousness," and now submitted to Serapis. Serapis was the result of artificial insemination for political purposes in the time of the Ptolemies—an invention which combined the Greek and the Egyptian.

In these religions there was no comfort or encouragement or material on which the curious mind could gnaw. And the African mind must have been most especially curious. The Africans must have sensed their own peculiar destiny, for theirs was the most mysterious and puzzling part of the small world of those days. It was strangely framed and strangely inhabited. To the west was nothing but the River Ocean, which encircled the earth—or to those who suspected the earth was global it slipped away to a place of no return. To the east was the dark Nile, which came from none knew where and had a yearly surge like the heat of some great female animal. They had human beings of two different colors and monstrous strange beasts. It was indeed a very special land, a land to breed groping thoughts in the minds of its people.

So Africa's appetite sampled new things, new explanations of the world's creation, of the stars and of death.

Some who were scattered here and there, largely primitive pagans, tried Judaism, but the appeal was hampered by the insistent proprietorship of a special foreign group of unhappy exiles. Some tried Mithra or the Great Mother or the cult named after Mani. Some tried Gnosticism, which straddled between a Christian heresy and a religious philosophy of multiple inspirations.

It was a generously laden smörgåsbord of religions, the like of which we do not see in modern times.

And there was Christianity.

Christianity had bounded into Africa. It was important in Africa when our ancestors were pagans, meaning the ancestors of such of us as lived in England or in the major part of northern Europe. The word "important" is used with intent. Africa was a center, possibly the greatest center of Christian thought in its young and very vital days as a new faith.

But Christianity's life in the African sun was short. It bloomed with vigor—a tremendous fighting vigor and much internal quarreling and an almost insane devotion—and faded soon. A few centuries—five, six—and Christianity had almost disappeared.

Africa welcomed Christianity with enthusiasm, almost boisterously, like a dog greeting the beloved, jumping and leaping and barking, so that the beloved, the welcomed one, was soon disheveled and tattered. Africa was too enthusiastic and its worship seemed sometimes to approach hysteria and even masochism.

From this turbulence there survived after Islam came some Christian pockets, some Christians in amber here and there across the continent. Some pockets are familiar to us all: Ethiopia and the Coptic Christians of Egypt. Others lived hidden for centuries and were discovered in the Middle Ages, when Europe attacked the Mediterranean coasts. Others, deeper in Africa, in the Sahara and far beyond, are semi-fabulous.

Though most of Africa and the Christian religion parted company only to meet again with the coming of colonialism, Christianity during its short early sojourn had stimulated the African brain. For one thing, it had taught Africans theological arguing, an accomplishment which, carried along and applied to the Moslem faith, they practiced assiduously, with considerable effects upon African history and much bloodshed.

Just how and when Christianity cautiously tiptoed into Africa —for in those days the avowed Christian beckoned to death—we do not know. From Carthage came news of martyrdom in the late second century, tragic proof of Christianity's progress across the top of the continent. The uncertainty as to the African debut of the new faith was described by Harnack as "a most unfortunate gap" in our knowledge. Africa does not figure in St. Paul's missionary itinerary. Egypt was near Jesus' homeland. Egypt and Libya (Cyrene) had a large Jewish population. These facts provided a geographical and a psychological approach, but who it was that did the approaching, who was Africa's first missionary we cannot tell.

This discounts the romantic legend that it was St. Mark who converted Egypt, with the legendary sequel of a remarkable robbery of his supposed tomb at Alexandria long afterward and the carrying away of his remains by a band of fervent Venetians inspired by that gruesome fascination which famous bones seem to have possessed, especially in the Middle Ages. The rape of the holy bones was allegedly performed in the ninth century, a treasure to the Venetian adventurers because of St. Mark's traditional association with their own city.

The legend that Egypt learned of Christ from St. Mark, which many take seriously, was first recorded, insofar as we know, by Eusebius, the great Christian writer who lived in the third and fourth centuries after Christ—and after St. Mark—that is to say a very long time after the supposed event. It has been suggested that "The Father of Christian History" was merely speaking symbolically. The recent (1960) discovery of a seventeenth-century copy of a supposedly ancient document concerning St. Mark's association with Alexandria might seem to confirm the legend. Perhaps the pious grave robbers from Venice were right.

Another tradition has in a muddled fashion associated another of the disciples with work in the missionary field in Africa. St. Matthew supposedly tried to convert "the city of the cannibals" in Ethiopia and eventually became the traditional apostle of Nubia, the ancient country up the Nile beyond Egypt. But the legend managed to confuse both the man and the place. The heroic missionary of the legend was not Matthew, whose name is applied to the first Gospel, but Matthias, he who was chosen by lot to fill the place among the Twelve left vacant by Judas, and the place of the cannibals which Matthias pluckily sought to gain for Christianity was not Ethiopia in Africa but a vague locality of the same name near the Caspian Sea. So neither this tradition nor that which Marco Polo records, that "Messer Thomas" (St. Thomas) converted Abyssinia, can help us to deduce the facts about Christianity's first arrival in Africa.

But we do know of a really charming incident, authenticated in the New Testament, which happened in Palestine but associates itself with Christian beginnings in Africa, although any effect it had upon Africans at large is unproved. It, too, uses the confusing name of Ethiopia. It concerns Philip and a eunuch, and is told at some length in the eighth chapter of Acts.

Philip, who was not the disciple but one of a group of men "of honest report and wisdom" chosen by the disciples as helpers, encountered on the road from Jerusalem to Gaza "a man of Ethiopia, a eunuch of great authority," the treasurer of "Candace, queen of the Ethiopians." The eunuch was on his way home from a pious pilgrimage to Jerusalem and, as he rode along in his chariot, was reading aloud a passage from the Book of Isaiah.

Philip ran toward him and asked the eunuch whether he understood what he was reading.

The eunuch frankly admitted that he did not, which is not surprising for the verses in question (53:7 and following) are puzzling. They are part of the famous "Suffering Servant" passage, supposedly prophetic of Jesus and thus dear to early Christianity. It seems a strange coincidence that the eunuch, presumably a Jewish convert, was reading this particular passage and suggests that while in Jerusalem he became intrigued by rumors of the new faith of the Christians and was attempting some research reading. If so it explains the swiftness of his conversion by Philip.

At the eunuch's invitation Philip had mounted into the chariot, and as they rode along he preached about Jesus—a noble instance of hitchhiking. The eunuch was convinced and uttered the first formal creed of which we have record: "I believe that Jesus Christ is the Son of God."

At a spot along the way which Christian pilgrims with pious imagination later sought and which an early sixth-century Christian geographer, Theodosius, who was perhaps a North African, confidently identified, the eunuch spied a pool or rivulet and cried out, begging to be baptized. So he and Philip got down out of the chariot and he received baptism and "went on his way rejoicing."

The homeland toward which the eunuch drove off in his chariot was not the country which now calls itself Ethiopia (formerly Abyssinia), but Nubia in the Sudan. This is proved by the New Testament's statement that he was treasurer of "Candace, queen." "Candace" was a royal title exclusively used in Nubia, not a proper name. (A similar custom of calling all the kings of the country "Kabyl" is recorded by the Arab historian Makrizi.) We get glimpses of these dominant females in classical literature. There was the earlier Candace who, Strabo says, was "a masculine woman who had lost one eye." Her army—or at any rate the Candace is credited as the prime force in the adventure—drove down the Nile just after Rome had vanquished Cleopatra and become master of Egypt. Her soldiers captured Syene (Aswan), enslaved its inhabitants and threw down in contempt the statue of Augustus. Rome responded by razing Napata, the onetime Nubian capital where the Candace had "her royal seat," as Strabo puts it.

The later Candace, whose treasurer, the eunuch, was converted by Philip, resided at Meroe, two cataracts farther up the Nile.

It was one of the many cases of Ethiopian name confusion. The names "Ethiopia" and "Ethiopians" have been as bothersome terms as could be found in geography and ethnology. "Ethiopia" might mean almost anyplace in the Eastern Hemisphere. And all that one could be sure about with regard the term "Ethiopian" was that it was used as applying to a human being. He might be black. He might be white. He might be red-faced or yellow. And his home might be anywhere from the Atlantic to China.

The familiar "burnt skin" (dark) derivation is pleasant etymology, but it does not fit the many usages to which the word has been put. In ancient geography (Herodotus, Pliny, Ptolemy) there is mention not only of black or dark Ethiopians, but of white folk of that name (Leucoethiopians, from *leukos,* meaning "white") and of red Ethiopians, and some Ethiopians—the Chinese who were called by that name—were presumably yellow.

They were sometimes called the tallest and handsomest of men, and they were described as "the virtuous Ethiopians." There was a group of diet experts living up the Nile known as the "long-lived Ethiopians" who attributed their longevity to "not eating dung," that is, food raised in fertilized soil. There were other Ethiopians who were not fastidious at all. The term "Ethiopian" was used as almost a synonym for "cannibal." Origen wrote, "Ethiopians who are cannibals . . ."

To these many hued peoples of assorted habits there was assigned a variety of homes. Homer called them "the most remote of mankind." Classical geographers sometimes located them on Africa's Atlantic shores, sometimes splashed them right across the continent or placed them far to the south. Relatively modern geographers have done the same. For instance Marmol in the sixteenth century has a section on "Lower Ethiopia" in which he includes Guinea, Timbuctoo and Mozambique.

Arabic geographer Ibn Khordadhbeh (ninth century) included China under the elastic term. So far as I know, the name did not stray across the Channel or over the Atlantic.

When the eunuch reached his Nubian home, so runs a very doubtful legend, he converted his royal mistress and all her kingdom to Christianity, a remarkable achievement when we remember how vague must have been the doctrine he had to communicate—being but things quickly told to him while on a ride with the evangelist Philip. But this eunuch was evidently a remarkable person, one of those slaves of importance we meet through the ages in the annals of Africa.

So far as history tells us, Nubia went on in its same old idolatry and star worship for some five hundred years after the eunuch's spiritual adventures.

The historical account of Nubia's conversion is comical, if we may venture to apply this adjective to the Christianizing of a nation. The Emperor Justinian and his interesting spouse, the Empress Theodora, favored different forms of Christianity, it being at the time one of Christianity's many passages of controversy. Justinian was orthodox. Theodora favored the Monophysites. The outstanding difference between the two philosophies concerned the nature of Christ: Was He both God and man, or had He but one nature? Theodora sponsored a Monophysite by name Julian on a missionary expedition. Justinian sponsored an orthodox rival mission. The two missionary bands raced toward far-off Nubia, traveling through Egypt, and Theodora sent in advance a threatening message to the effect that her protégé, Julian, must be hustled forward and his orthodox rival tricked and impeded. (It must have pleased this self-made empress to give orders to officials in that land of Egypt, where in her girlhood she had, according to history's scandals—such especially as Procopius' *Secret History*—been poor and of low repute.) Her commands were obeyed and the Monophysites stole the race.

In Ethiopia—real Ethiopia, ex-Abyssinia—Christianity had already been accepted and had also been the subject of an intersectarian dispute when Constantinople's emperor of the moment shifted

to Arianism, a doctrine based on still another aspect of Christ's personality, and tried to jerk Ethiopia into the Arian fold. Ethiopia was so averse to the Arian theory that for centuries thereafter she viewed Arianism with loathing.

Nubia received Christianity with a touchingly practical adaptability, not only transforming pagan temples into churches, but putting the old pagan decorations to naïve new uses. There has survived to modern times a certain quaint instance of this economical redecoration wherein the figure of an Egyptian god was plastered over and St. Peter, with halo and key painted into his place, while the rest of the original design was left unaltered, so that Rameses II is shown deferentially offering a tribute of flowers to the Apostle. Thus was Christianity retroactively and unintentionally conferred upon the most famous of Egypt's Pharaohs.

Another rather sweet piece of innocence was the enshrining in a Nubian church of a stone ram, once symbol of Ammon-Ra, it having been mistaken for the Christian Lamb. On the other hand Nubia developed certain religious sophistications. It is interesting to read of a Nubian prince who, when traveling, carried with him a demountable wooden church which could be set up at each stopping place.

In the days when to be a Christian was to be a criminal Mediterranean Africa and Egypt had their martyrs. Indeed almost the earliest documentary indication that sections of Africa had been converted is found in the records of martyrdom. There is a story of how twelve—seven men and five women—were killed in Carthage in the year 180. A Carthaginian girl of twenty-two, remembered as St. Perpetua, perished in the amphitheater a few years later.

Christian teachers like Tertulian of Carthage and Origen of Egypt preached anti-militarism and sometimes soldier converts—one even in the farthest west of Africa at Tangier—listened and refused to serve and were executed. We read of Christian virginal girls condemned to life in a brothel or publicly violated for the entertainment of a pagan crowd and as a warning. A deacon was tortured by "scourging and scraping."

It was very ugly, and we who look back at the persecutions may think it was all senseless cruelty. Cruelty, yes—spectacular cruelty that was intentionally spectacular. But senseless, no. The intellectual

and government elements of those days were afraid of Christianity and sought to terrify it out of existence. Christianity, they thought, angered the gods and made them vengeful against the world, causing the calamities of the time—a period of especial uncertainty and disaster; Christianity made men disloyal to the state; Christianity was a mysterious danger. All this was the expression of the instinctive fears of a regime, already weakening, when confronted with a new idea.

It seems oversimplification to attribute the fall of this old regime primarily to Christianity. Perhaps it was ready to fall.

Said Gibbon, "I believe that the propagation of the Gospel and the triumph of the Church are inseparably connected with the decline of the Roman monarchy." Frazer in *The Golden Bough* speaks of the gradual undermining of the whole fabric of ancient civilization, a "halt in the march of civilization."

It was the end of an epoch. Smelling its doom, the imperiled pagan world was frightened and, as frightened people do, turned to cruelty. The darkness of the Middle Ages lay like a black tunnel ahead. Perhaps they were right to be afraid. The suave paganism of classical days was through.

As for Africa, she had seen everything classical paganism offered and was bored. Africa welcomed Christianity emotionally and clutched the new faith so tightly that eventually it was crushed and almost destroyed. No place was so ardently Christian as Africa. None so burning with curiosity and itching with questions. None so shaken with asceticism and hysteria and bitter arguments. None more inventive of Christian novelties in dogma and conduct.

Fascination seems to have been added to the new religion by the attendant risks. To become a Christian in those early days was both a spiritual experience and a tremendous physical adventure, a thrilling test of courage. Arrest, torture and martyrdom might always be around the corner from the meetinghouse. Certain Christians of renown managed to avoid danger and were criticized. For example, St. Cyprian, Bishop of Carthage, went into hiding during a period of persecution, and when it was over returned to his see. When another persecution broke a few years later he became a martyr. Avoidance of risk by flight was condemned, and there rose a cult of hatred for such as "lapsed," who went back to idolatry under threat of torture.

Africa's earliest Christians were presumably a humble lot socially. The snobbery of the day is shown in the novel *The Golden Ass,* in which the Algerian-born author, Apuleius, chooses a peculiarly vulgar female character to represent a typical member of the "fantastic and blasphemous cult of an 'Only God' " in whose honor she daily gets drunk and whores. Later the intellectuals joined the movement. Christianity came from the shadows and out of hiding in back streets. Africa became a center for Christian thinking, and Christianity acquired something new—social prestige.

One memorable African maiden of high degree who allegedly charmed and repulsed a Roman emperor was a martyr. She was St. Catherine of Alexandria, the subject of many traditions, including the startling anachronism that she was the daughter of Moses and another and miraculous tradition that her saintliness shattered the wheel on which she was to have been broken. St. Catherine became the patron saint of unmarried girls, and her memory is celebrated every year by Paris *midinettes.* Her name was given to the renowned and isolated monastery at Sinai.

After the official approval of Christianity the historian Eusebius, whose life dramatically overlapped the change to tolerance—he had survived by artful dodging the years of the so-called "Great Persecution" (starting in 303), so cruel that it is still commemorated in the dating system of the Copts and Ethiopians as "The Era of Martyrs," drew a high-flown picture of the new Christian temporal grandeur. It was, he declared, in the name of Jesus that the greater part of the earth was for the first time under the sole control of Rome. God had chosen Constantine and had put the vision of the Cross in the sky. It was the Kingdom of Heaven upon earth, ruled by Constantine.

St. Augustine, looking back about a century later at the dramatic recognition of Christianity, seems in *City of God* rather more reserved in his estimate of the emperor. Augustine, who lived from mid-fourth to well into the fifth century, is the one completely unforgettable African of Christian times whose name is as familiar to us today as it was to those who founded the first town in the United States and named it after him.

Two of the Popes also were Africans and so, incidentally, was the very non-Christian Emperor Septimius Severus of the "harsh nature" (to quote the phrase of Bede, called "The Venerable"), who was born in Tripolitania (Libya), so thoroughly African that he had to learn to talk in Latin, and who spent his last three years fighting in England, dying at York and thus giving a vaguely African association to an English and to an American city.

Now that their religion was safe and honored certain especially brave and vigorous people set out to see for themselves the places where they had been told Jesus lived. Some of these were Africans, and many people from other lands passed through Africa on their pilgrimage way.

So Africa heard many strange things, for the baggage of the returning pilgrims was stuffed with extraordinary tales, but it seems ungallant to laugh at the absurdities allegedly observed and included in the reminiscences of these credulous travelers. They had suffered much hardship with such lofty motives and in many cases were in an exalted or hysterical mood from the start, which would have hampered observation and critical judgment. Take, for instance, the Breton Frotmund, who, having committed a crime, set out in penance barefoot with a heavy chain around his arms and waist and after praying at Jerusalem arrived still in chains at the tomb of St. Cyprian at Carthage. Could such as he have been in the state of mind to pass a competent judgment on the extravagant tales he may have heard, like the alleged existence near Jerusalem of "a cave to which in one night a lion had conveyed the bodies of twelve thousand martyrs"?

St. Helena's pilgrimage to "Christe's Patrimonie which they call the Holy Land" made news in Africa, as it did in all the Christian world. Some three hundred years after the Crucifixion, St. Helena succeeded in finding the Cross near the site on which mischievous paganism had erected a statue of Venus. Her discovery has been rather curiously called "The Invention of the True Cross." The subsequent beautification of the place reached the pages of Bede, whose praise of "the magnificent regal style of the church" contrasts with the spiteful little account Africa was to hear later from the medieval African, Ibn Khaldun, written in the days of tension between Christian and Moslem. Helena found, said he, that the Cross "had been thrown on the ground and had been covered with excrement and filth. She built 'The Church of the Excrement' over the place." There is a Christian legend that it took nearly six months to shovel away the filth.

Presumably these two so different pictures each gave satisfaction to Africa, which shows how completely African sentiment changed as Christianity waned and Islam rose.

In Africa was born Christianity's triumphant self-tribute—the worship of chastity combined with monastic celibacy. It was then something which was in the African, the Egyptian air, for contemporary Gnosticism also hated sex as a physical condition, though sometimes accepting lustful sexual practices. It would look as if the intellectual of those days resented the sex difference because it made man the animal's brother and so discounted the grandeur of the immortal soul.

It was a period of intense self-consciousness. We are told that there is a large proportion of people with mental difficulties in modern society. It would seem that the proportion must have been even higher among the thinking public in northern Africa during the opening centuries of the Christian era.

In religious writings which have come down to us we find preachings on chastity, virginity and sex asceticism. St. Cyprian urged women to remain virginal—always virginal—showing at the same time a worldly understanding of temptation when he suggested that they best avoid cosmetics, wedding parties and the baths. There were at that time no nunneries in Carthage to whose protective care he could direct them. Other writers of the day were sterner: wives were advised to abandon their husbands, marriage was condemned as fundamentally evil. A special place "with couches of gold" was reserved in Paradise for "men who had never known women," according to a divine communication made to the Virgin Mary—or such was a very ancient Coptic belief.

The so-called Gospel of the Egyptians, a work which attracted wide interest in those days but which did not gain a place in the canonical New Testament and now survives only in fragments, contained the prophecy that someday the distinction of sex would come to an end, a statement being attributed to Jesus which looked forward toward eventual hermaphroditism.

This was the expression of an idea on which mankind had been speculating for a very long time. In ancient Egypt there was a belief that the god Re had bred the world's population from himself alone, "joining his seed with his body to create the egg within his secret self," and a similar creation myth was widespread: the mythical ancestors of humanity were androgynous; to be at once male and female symbolized the supreme being; even Adam, some maintained, was originally androgyne.

This admiration for hermaphroditism with its implied contempt for the normal sex relation comes into The Gospel According to Thomas, a second-century work that lay hidden in a crockery pot in the sands of Upper Egypt till it was discovered in 1945, now translated and widely published. In this work Jesus is quoted—or misquoted—as foreseeing that women must become men to enter the Kingdom of Heaven and as blessing "the womb which has not conceived."

Of the sex sentiment which preoccupied the thoughtful there is a strange and shocking proof.

The greatest Christian thinker of his day, the renowned Origen of Alexandria, castrated himself.

This was no maniac or follower of some perverse religion, but an exceptionally active man and a brilliant scholar, the "intellectual giant," who was, Harnack has said, "the most distinguished and most influential of all the theologians of the ancient church." He worked with fierce energy. His literary production was enormous. He performed an astonishing editorial exploit when he compared word for word the various then existing Greek manuscripts of the Old Testament which differed greatly with the Hebrew, which he had learned for the purpose. He invented the system of a sixfold version in columns: the Hebrew, Hebrew in Greek characters and four different Greek texts. It was the vast work of twenty years, estimated as having equaled more than sixty-five hundred pages, now lost except for some scraps.

The self-mutilation performed by this man so that he might avoid sexual temptation and the fact that his action was at the time "rather admired than censured" (I quote Bury's footnote to Gibbon), and the fact that he was not Christianity's sole self-made eunuch of the times, though the most famous—these facts are significant. But they are less significant than they would have been in another age, for the frenzied incitations of the Great Mother public displays—similar in physical result though different in motive—had created a certain tolerance toward the unnatural act. The Emperor Elagabalus, according to a fourth-century Roman writer (Aurelius Victor, cited by Professor Hadas), "lopped off his genitals and dedicated himself to the Great Mother."

It was in such a mood that the Christian monastery system was launched. Its place of launching was Upper Egypt. It happened at the beginning of the fourth century. It was a simple person, an ex-conscript soldier who had just graduated from paganism who invented and put into successful operation this system which was to sweep across Europe and is still with us in numbers today. He organized the first cenobitical (community) monastery. His sister established a nunnery. When we reflect upon the wide influence which the monastic way of life has had upon our society it is interesting to realize that it was an African mind that contrived it and made it work.

Without entering into any question of the merits or demerits of monasticism we have to recognize that it has altered the lives of millions of men and women during the ages all across the Christian world. Monasticism was Africa's outstanding export. Africa is the source for various raw materials, and she supplied millions of slaves. But nothing of African origin has had such a powerful effect on the world over the centuries—sixteen of them—as the Christian monastery system for men and women, invented in Africa. That was a spiritual export, a moral attitude, a way of life. Its force has been incalculable.

Oddly the designer of monastic rules and the founder of the first monastic order is a man with a practically forgotten name. How many of us have ever heard of St. Pachomius?

There were already individual Christian recluses or monks—Pachomius himself was one before he conceived the idea of grouping ascetics under a sort of regimentation. One famous anchorite was St. Antony, also an Egyptian, whom other ascetics imitated and followed. But the executive leader of monasticism was Antony's contemporary, Pachomius. Antony was an individualist. Pachomius stands as a professional—the first professional organizer of Christian monastic society.

His discipline was harsh. Upon the cornerstone of that mood and emotion of the day and place which was early Christianity in Africa —the exaltation of chastity and lifelong negation of sex—he piled other deprivations which though hard perhaps helped in the self-discipline which the main rule demanded. There was a near starvation diet, prolonged silences, rough labor, severe punishments and no bathing of the body except in case of illness. "The Rules of Pachomius" were renowned and translated into the Christian-used languages of the times. They came from Europe to study his methods.

His fellow Egyptians flocked by thousands to submit to his austerities, not only males but females. His sister, an ex-pagan renamed the Coptic equivalent of Mary, founded a convent to shelter feminine devotees, who till then had either been isolated in their virginal piety or had got together informally in groups. Mary prudently located her convent on the opposite side of the Nile.

A conservative estimate is that the inmates of Pachomius' several monasteries numbered altogether seven thousand. Some enthusiasts put their number at fifty thousand. Perhaps the latter estimate was based on pious crowds which every year at certain seasons joined the permanent members like pilgrims. A contemporary devout traveler from Italy is quoted as saying that the region "so swarmed with monks that their chants and hymns by day and night made the whole country one church of God."

Here is a curious proof of the interest Egypt took in its monasteries. To a certain archbishop of Alexandria in office about a half century after Pachomius is attributed an ancient work telling how the Virgin Mary recounted to the archbishop the story of the Holy Family's visit to Egypt. It is one of the many Coptic legends giving alleged direct communication from the Virgin Mary. Mary, after telling at length of hardships and miraculous things which befell them on a long march into Upper Egypt, said to the archbishop that she desired he should dedicate a church to Pachomius at a certain place to which little Jesus had pointed His finger and where they had found water to wash the Child.

Mary promised that she *and her Son,* whose career on earth was then three centuries in the past, would come to the consecration of the Pachomius church.

The good archbishop (or the scribe who used his name in the ancient manuscript) expressed in his visionary fashion the sentiment of his period when he attributed to the Virgin Mary a promise to honor so splendidly Pachomius, the founder of monasticism.

The mobilized regiments of monks and nuns under Pachomius were only a part of Africa's army of those who chose chastity for their souls' sake. There were, especially in Lower Egypt, uncounted individual anchorites living apart in caves or here and there in the hills or in the desert, and presently these hermits were organized into groups by Macarius—"Father Macarius the Great," Egyptians sometimes called him, saying of him affectionately and with reverence that he was "an earthly God, for as God overshadoweth the world so also did Father Macarius cover the shortcomings which he saw, as if he did not see them, and the things he heard, as if he heard them not." I quote from very early Christian comments compiled by 'Anân Ishô of Bêth' Abhê in Budge's translation, which go on to tell how a maiden had come to Father Macarius "to be healed of a devil." One night while Father Macarius was pondering over her problem he chanced to find a certain monk was with her, "committing sin." Father Macarius did not rebuke the monk. He merely said, "If God who fashioned him seeth and is long-suffering—for if He so desired He could consume him—who am I that I should rebuke him?" It is no wonder that such personal humility and so tolerant an attitude made Macarius renowned. His tolerance was unusual; a long section of 'Anân Ishô's compilation is devoted to the horrors of "the war against fornication."

The monks of Macarius settled in the Natron Valley, deep in the desert to the south of Alexandria, and there, "in the frightful solitudes of Nitria," as a startled eighteenth-century observer said, "where the water of the lakes is tinged with the hue of blood from the Natron," their numbers so increased as the centuries passed that there were one hundred monasteries. Being relatively near to that intellectual center of the day, Alexandria, certain of the intelligentsia came to Nitria and the worship of chastity mingled with the worship of books. Their libraries must have been for those days enormous, judging by what survived, for despite the Arab invasion and all the medieval mishaps a European visitor in the seventeenth century stated that he saw there some eight thousand manuscripts.

This intense verbosity was typical of African religious expression during the Christian (pre-Islamic) period. It was an avalanche of writing, of arguing, of re-interpretations and contentious theorizing, of imaginative flights which sometimes followed, sometimes ignored and sometimes insulted what would eventually be adopted as the canonical Testaments. Charming pious fancies were invented. Sacred figures were presented in startling guise and as sponsoring amazing doctrines, and heresy snarled and clashed against heresy.

It was an era of complex discord. The leaders wrangled and the plain folk were bewildered.

BLACK SHEEP · It was by wrangling that Christianity in Africa committed suicide and left the door open to Islam, whose coming was the beginning of Africa's isolation from our own world —and of Africa's greatest military brilliance.

With what seems like perversity Christian leaders invented new approaches, so that arguments took the place of comfort and of the kind and friendly teachings of a new faith. Africa saw the religion it had welcomed in its childhood racked by a series of heresies and schisms which afflicted Christianity elsewhere but were especially virulent—fatal even—in Africa.

Mediterranean Africa was a religious arena. When the lions had eaten their fill of Christian meat, a gang of fighting theories rushed in. Perhaps the persecutions had had a psychological effect and, once ended, there was an emotional void. Self-confident and fight-prone people began to wonder exactly what was this religion of theirs, to speculate about details and to define their theories and to call one another heretics. There was a fury of words, bloodshed and varying government rebukes, and eventually a glum fatigue.

Africa had gulped down Christianity and felt it ferment within herself. Before much of Europe had ever heard of Jesus, Africa—most of Africa—had lost her appetite and was ready to shove Christianity aside.

Of the black sheep which disfigured the Christian flock in Africa the *doyen* was the philosophical religion of the Gnostics, "the people who knew." This disturber of Christianity was a hybrid of mixed breeding which plagued and shocked and fascinated the orthodox of those days—and of today. Our present-day interest was stimulated and piqued by the discovery in 1945 at Nag Hamadi by the Nile of a whole Gnostic library, written in the Coptic dialect of Upper Egypt, which had been buried there some fifteen centuries ago in a crockery pot. These are slowly being translated and published and represent to specialists a find as exciting as the Dead Sea Scrolls.

Nag Hamadi, where for reasons we do not know the Gnostics buried their treasured documents, was in the immediate neighborhood of the Pachomius monasteries, so that religious opponents—some thousands of ultra-fervent Christians and a body of heretical fantasts—lived side by side in an atmosphere of strain. It was a typical instance of the harm which Africa suffered from the religious antagonisms of early Christian times.

Africa's encounter with Gnosticism was one of the big intellectual adventures of her career during the period when Africa's mental address was at the center of the world, and an adventure which almost overturned Christianity in its infancy.

It was a psychological attack. It was like fighting a floating mist across the intellect, creating doubt whether supposed facts were actual or mythical. The mental air was thick with Gnostic myths and allegories. They wrapped themselves around personages of the Bible, clung to God the Father and to Jesus, and in this fog of myths people began to ask themselves whether anything spiritual was true, whether it was not all mythical. This came at a time when Christians were still seeking to formulate and put in canonical order the New Testament narrative. Gnosticism was a subtle enemy, a sort of brain washing. Christianity, says Jung in his study of psychology and religion, "had to fight for its life."

To many, especially in Africa, Gnosticism was irresistible. It was no obscure faith with crankish followers. It attracted "the most polite, the most learned and the most wealthy," according to Gibbon. It chewed into Christianity like a termite and it mingled its ideas with Christian ideas. The New Testament recognized the Gnostic danger, broadly hinted at it in Timothy, and in Acts gives an account of Peter's angry encounter with a sorcerer and would-be briber, whose name gave us the dictionary word "simony" and who was allegedly the same individual as the strange Simon Magus, the earliest Gnostic of Christian record. In the Book of Revelation one of the Gnostic sects, the Nicolaitans, is mentioned, Jesus threatening to fight them "with the sword of my mouth." Readers of Bultmann note that he believes that Gnostic influences entered deeply into the thought of the New Testament.

Incontestably, individuals of importance were influenced. St. Augustine in his pre-saintly period soaked for years in the Gnosticism of the Manichees before he became a Christian. Valentine, the most important of the Egyptian Gnostics, started his career, so they say, by an attempt to become pope. Alexandria was particularly affected. The Egyptian scholar Origen seems at times to be straddling between the two so different and yet in some ways similar faiths. He argued brilliantly against a certain Gnostic writer. He vigorously repudiated the apocryphal Gospel of Thomas, known in his day, lost and now found again at Nag Hamadi, which had been trying to sneak into the New Testament. Yet certain of his ideas, as recorded and as guessed at by manuscripts of his discovered recently, seem on the borderline. He is quoted as insisting that at the Resurrection women will become men; he had a theory as to the plurality of worlds and —this is a queer item—he elaborated a doctrine which gave great offense: that stars have souls.

Paganism had so familiarized people with the notion that stars were the home of human souls in the afterlife that sometimes, Franz Cumont tells us, a symbolic ladder for use on the climb would be placed alongside the defunct. But Origen's idea was far more sweeping and had a Gnostic smell. It was disturbing to the theologians of antiquity and the Middle Ages. Indeed it is rather a disturbing suggestion to us today!

Much has been written about Gnosticism, considerable before and a lot since the Nag Hamadi finds. Modern studies in English or translated into English include an anthology of Gnosticism edited by Robert Grant, other titles by Grant, Doresse, Professors Puech, Quispel and van Unnik, plus other writings, some of which I list at the back of this book. A revised edition of Hans Jonas' *The Gnostic Religion* is an interesting treatment of the philosophy which underlay the imaginative, often bizarre mythology some call "mere ravings."

It had many sects, a variety of parentage and a mass of cousins— sects like Sethians, Ophites and, some have estimated, fifty more; parentage, Greek or Eastern or Christian or Jewish; cousins that included Manichees and Mandaeans, both old religions of the Near East, both having had African associations, the former very strong in Europe in the Middle Ages, the latter still surviving in a small way in the East. The Mandaeans (also known as Sabaeans or Nasoraeans) were once so important and learned a group that the Koran mentions them with respect. They had ancient traditional ties with Egypt; ancestors of theirs allegedly helped the Pharaoh chase Moses at Exodus time, and till recently modern Mandaeans held religious observances every year in memory of their drowned co-religionists. The Sabaeans or Mandaeans may well have had evil sentiments toward Moses, whose military campaigning in his pre-Prophet days had led him into Nubia, where, according to a local very old Arabic source, he destroyed their town called Tafa, a day's journey south of Aswan.

Gnostics were dissatisfied with the philoso[...]
about them. They were religious revolutionarie[...]
selves to possess special wisdom which their ne[...]
self-confidence has modern interest. It has bee[...]
by Professor Grant: "The Gnostic is a Gnosti[...]
by revelation who his true self is. Other relig[...]
measure God-centred. The Gnostic is self-centr[...]
thing many moderns can understand. It might see[...]
mon sense attitude. Perhaps some of us are Gnostic[...]
it.

But the mythology in which the various sects w[...]
cealed their thoughts was to ancient Christianity a[...]
tling. They have seemed like a lot of dissatisfied [...]
bolstered with self-conceit, ran away from their vari[...]
instead of going empty-handed they each took wit[...]
bag of the family treasure, which later they tipped i[...]
muddle and smeared with oddments they found here[...]
invented.

The basic complaint which drove them from their v[...]
was a profound discontent with the world. Creation, s[...]
soul of man was concerned, was in their opinion a mess[...]
of bungling which should never have been attributed t[...]
Father. The world was bad, under wicked control or plain[...]
There was an absolute rift between men and the world. T[...]
of the unsatisfactory system was some subordinate, perha[...]
ous personage, not the Supreme God. Bertrand Russell seem[...]
put the Gnostic view in a swift witty sentence when he s[...]
a matter of fact, the world as we know it was made by t[...]
at a moment when God was not looking."

To garnish this basic theory they used, as it comes down[...]
in some of their literature, a jumble of adaptations and cari[...]
from other religions. They mauled the Bible. They advance[...]
assortment of novel alternate Creators. They sneaked Jesu[...]
Redeemer away from the New Testament, altered His backgr[...]
and thrust long speeches into His mouth. They snatched charac[...]
out of the Old Testament and stood them on their heads, mak[...]
good people bad and vice versa. And they made a topsy-turvy

me historically, putting many a Biblical cart before its horse. They introduced pagan elements and classical terms and characters from Greek mythology and from Eastern religions. And they combined his cast of religious personages with heroes, heroines and villains of their own invention. The scenes of their dramas sometimes rushed through space, encountered brilliant lights, dealt with planets and vile hells and monstrous animals.

And continuously their personages made discourses, talked and talked. Pistis Sophia (Faith-Knowledge) is quoted in thirteen discourses averaging two printed pages each, called her "Repentances," which are interspersed with long speeches by others, including Jesus.

It is fair to keep in mind that much of our information about them comes to us at second hand via the hostile reports of their Christian rivals and that along with their wild mythology we have in their surviving writings passages less weird and more or less related to normal Christian thinking, as for example the lately rediscovered Gospel of Thomas and Gospel of Truth. But there is no denying that the Gnostics splashed about.

A sect which especially fascinated the shocked interest of outsiders was the Ophites or Naassenes (names derived from the Greek or Hebrew words for snake). Although they are said to have incorporated sometimes a live snake in their religious ceremonies and even to have attempted to break bread with the snake in a sort of communion, I infer that their serpent worship was more symbolic than actual. It was an expression of their criticism of the Old Testament story which their doctrine turned upside down so that the God of the Old Testament became the villain and the serpent who offered wisdom became the hero.

All this merely riles the modern or makes him laugh. But in those days when Christianity was beginning Gnosticism was dangerous. Christianity possessed little historical proof. The faith was based on the claim of revelation. (Many Christians believe it was the Holy Ghost who by inspiration wrote the New Testament books.) Distortions and inventions threatened to knock the props from under young Christianity's beliefs, made Christians ask themselves disturbing questions.

But the Gnostics gave Africa a new sort of wisdom, taught the

courage of the question, opened the way to independent individual thinking. It was a lesson in mental athleticism which early came to Mediterranean Africa and crude counterparts of which I have seemed to note in the pagan hinterland. Africans gained vigor, for it took keen wits to appreciate or to repudiate the Gnostic philosophy and an active imagination to grasp and accept or discard the Gnostic myths and allegories.

In the soul gymnasium which was Christian Africa the struggle with Gnosticism was weakening and harmful.

More harmful yet in a tangible way was the Donatist revolt in what we now call Algeria and Tunisia. This was one of the most important religious-political upsets of all history, for it cracked the Roman hold on northern Africa and eased the way for Islam's entry into the West, into Europe and into deeper Africa.

It was a combination of exaggerated, almost inconceivable religious hysteria with something like a Communist revolution. In the frenzy of some of its manifestations Donatism came very close to madness. The excitation went on for a century.

It happened in this fashion. When Christianity suddenly emerged into safety and honor, Christians looked back with tight-lipped disdain at those self-styled Christians who had tricked and dodged away from the lions and the other torments of the persecutions, and maintained that prelates of this ignoble sort were unfit to administer sacraments. The orthodox regarded this as a potentially dangerous attack on the Church's authority, seeming to class the priest as a dismissable servant rather than as a representative of the Almighty. The value of the priestly function did not depend on the priest's behavior but upon his having been consecrated.

But this quarrel which split northern Africa's Christians in two was only partially, almost incidentally doctrinal. The pious indignation was an expression of an unrest much more human and earthy which squirted out through a religious gap as water might pierce the weak place in a dyke. Africa was under foreign control and was restless. For some of the Donatists the religious schism developed into an outburst of the perennial antagonism of the laborer against the man who need not work and the irritation of prolonged foreign presence in their land—an irritation felt since the days of Dido, the Carthaginian. Into the struggle rushed the poor, the workers, the slave laborers, the Berbers crushed by Roman colonists and Berbers disappointed that Christianity had not given them the equality of their hopes. In bands they fell upon farms and villages, killed the prosperous, slaughtered their cattle, burned their orchards and fields and razed their houses. These furious gangs got the name of Circumcelliones (Those Who Prowl Around Farms).

With their savagery they mingled something of the mystical. Under a cry "Praise God!" they would ravage the country. In the name of Christ they would drag a rich man out of his chariot, establish his slave in his place and oblige the rich man to trot along on foot. Thus, so they said, they put the promises of Christianity into execution. Some among them craved martyrdom and, fearing the wrongdoing of suicide, would force some stranger to kill them or be himself killed.

The Donatist schism was about fifty years old when a Roman emperor who had reverted to paganism desired to re-paganize Africa. A part of the program was to insult the orthodox church by extending favor to the Donatists. It may have been these cantankerous Africans whom Julian had in mind when he stated that experience had taught him that most Christians behave more savagely to one another than wild beasts. The so-called Apostate Julian died and the Donatist fortunes sank again. At last, after a century of bickering by the intelligentsia and bloodshed by the lowly, the Donatist heresy was officially classed as a crime.

But if the heresy went underground the rebellious mood lasted. It is said that secret Donatists served as guides for the Vandal invaders who overthrew Roman control. The Berbers, the peasant population and the workers had tasted barbarism's freedom. The glamour and prestige of the Roman Empire, the colonial master, were smeared and in their eyes Christianity had been degraded. As Dr. Greenslade, viewing the result of the Donatist revolt from Europe's aspect, puts it in his *Schism in the Early Church,* it was the "loss of North Africa to Christendom."

Arianism, part of the equipment of the Vandals, which overran most of northern Africa, got there by a strange route. It traveled around in almost a complete geographical circle from the place of origin of Arius, who launched the doctrine, to where Arianism finally arrested its sweep of African conquest.

Arius was an exceptionally vigorous man from Libya. His theory was a prolongation of a puzzle as old as Christianity itself. It was an effort—one of the efforts—made to deal with the uncertainty about the origin and position of Jesus, which uncertainty in its simplest and crudest form had once prompted the hostile to the vulgar taunt, "Son of the Panther," referring to birth out of wedlock.

By the time Arius sponsored his theory (fourth century) the Church had emerged from the bewilderment of primitive Christianity and the problem which tormented theologians was not one of divine genealogy but of what one might describe as divine protocol. Did Jesus stand beside the throne of God? Or did he sit there by God's side? There were pathos and grandeur in the mental struggles of embryonic Christians in their hunt for some formula where their factual, written language was so slight and confusing.

The Arian approach to the puzzle was based on reverence and love of Christ, but it threatened to rip Christianity apart. To put it very simply, Arians could not believe that Jesus was the equal of Almighty God. God was unique. Jesus was a younger member of the Firm. Jesus was a demi-God.

It was an attempt to explain their faith by some variation of human parenthood, to imagine with reverence what might be the divine father-son relationship.

Africa was the center of the controversy. St. Antony is said to have quit his precious solitude to come to Alexandria and preach against the heresy. Eusebius was an Arian for a while, but changed sides. The Emperor Constantine, who had hoped Christianity would consolidate his people, was worried and summoned high clerics—Africans and others—to talk things over.

The council was held close to the site chosen for Constantine's brand-new capital of Constantinople and gave the place where it was conducted (Nice or Nicaea, now Iznik in Turkey) lasting fame because its name was applied to the Nicene Creed, there formulated. Arianism lost the fight. The conference was a very imposing affair, with several hundred bishops in attendance and the emperor himself, "like some heavenly messenger of God, clothed in raiment that glittered, as it were, with rays of light, reflecting the glowing radiance of a purple robe." Despite such gorgeousness Constantine sat not upon a throne but on a little stool and conducted himself "with patience and modesty."

Arius was re-excommunicated. (It had happened to him before.) But the battling over his theory continued. At a subsequent conference the meeting became so rough that it finally broke up in disorder. One episode had been the appearance before the members of a woman who gave evidence of fornication and the scandalous discovery of a prostitute in a bishop's chamber, not at the bishop's desire, so his party insisted, but because she had been placed there spitefully by the opposition. Constantine is supposed to have made the generous remark that if he found a bishop in the act of adultery he would cast his imperial mantle over the episcopal sinner.

When Arius fell down suddenly dead in the street it undoubtedly gave another argument to his opponents. But Arianism lived on. It still lives. And it was to go back toward its African birthplace in force. It traveled widely in Europe. The Goths lapped it up. The founding bishop of Gothic Christianity bequeathed Arianism to the people along with the Bible, which he not only labored to translate into Gothic but for which he had obligatorily invented a Gothic alphabet. An example of the Gothic version of the Bible of Ulfilas (the four Gospels) done in gold and silver letters upon parchment was, at last accounts, the chief treasure of the University of Upsala in Sweden.

Arianism swept back into Africa. The Vandals, after a looping journey around Europe to Spain, crossed the Strait of Gibraltar. They seized North Africa from Tangier to Tripoli and even threatened Alexandria. With them came a wide Arianization of the local population, which bred a receptivity to Islam when in turn the Arabs came. For between the Arian attitude toward the unique Father-God and less important Son-God and Islam's One-God Allah with respectful references to Jesus there was a certain resemblance. Indeed some Christians viewed Islam at the start of its activity as a sort of Arianism, and even maintained that the Koran had been composed by Mohammed's ghost writer, who was an ex-Arian monk.

The Vandals had dealt with the religious sentiments of the people, both orthodox and pagans, with startling ferocity. Their "missionary" methods are largely communicated to us through Catholic sources, naturally embittered and probably exaggerated. The miraculous item about the band of obstinate orthodox at Tipasa (near modern Algiers) who, having been martyrized by the Arian Vandals who cut out their tongues, were still able to praise God according to their convictions, speaking "clearly and perfectly," does not inspire our confidence.

North Africa's bishops were a natural target for Vandal persecution. Here are the statistics of their lot, as offered by Gibbon: 466 bishops were summoned to Carthage for a so-called religious conference. Eighty-six of them prudently decided to recant and turn Arian; twenty-eight managed to escape by flight; two were slaughtered; forty-six were shipped to Corsica to fell trees for the Vandal navy, and the rest—302 bishops—were banished under wretched and humiliating conditions to the wild back country of Africa.

The most important of the multitudinous North African bishops —astonishingly numerous, especially for a region only partially Christian, where there were many pagans and some Jews—did not share the misery of the 466. St. Augustine, Bishop of Hippo (long known as Bône, renamed after Algerian independence), died at the age of seventy-six, while the Vandals were besieging the city, and long before the purge of the bishops.

St. Augustine, the mighty hunter of heresies, is probably the most famous of all Africans, for who—even Cleopatra—is more continuously remembered and discussed? (*The Times* of London stated recently that during the decade 1950–60 "a book or article on Augustine or one or more of his writings was published on a rough average every day.") He was a tireless heresiologist, classifying with indignation eighty-eight various heresies, which is a tribute to his fighting loyalty to a faith which he believed must be just so, and a proof of the great number of the pious whose beliefs were different. The creed of his own convictions included a sternness about infant baptism about which there has been much argument.

His own family shows an example of the mixed-up religious situation in North Africa: his mother was a Christian, St. Monica; his father was a pagan and St. Augustine until well into adult years was a Manichee. His own experience—paganism in his childhood home, himself an ex-Gnostic—could have made eventually for ultra-rigid Christianity.

The Manichaean influence may have been strong. In his *Confessions* he wrote that during "the space of those whole nine years like a vagabond in mind I gave heed to the teachings of Manichaeus." Some, like Wilhelm Bousset, think that they recognize traces of these teachings in Augustine's Christian writings, as if, having cut his young religious teeth on a Gnostic faith, he could never get the taste out of his mouth.

It was a religion of vigor and appeal named after Mani, who was crucified about A.D. 275 by the Persians. It lasted longer in force and traveled farther than any other Gnostic system, inspiring the "Albigensian heresy" in southern France that was put down in blood and destruction by the Albigensian Crusade (1209), and spreading as well from the Atlantic to the Indian Ocean and into Central Asia. Manichaeism attracted many North Africans as it did Augustine; in Egypt it was the same, and in 1930 there was discovered there a fourth-century library of seven volumes, estimated thirty-five hundred pages, of Manichaean literature. Its code of behavior was strange and included abstinence from meat and wine, permitting vegetables only and such to be of the bright colored sort, and a super sex-asceticism. But this severity was the ruling for the higher-ups, the "Elect," whose intense austerity is said to have inspired Christian monasticism, and to whose influence Byzantine theologists imputed the celibacy of the clergy. The rest of the Manichees might live more normally.

One oddity has been mentioned with regard to the Manichees. It has been suggested that they invented that action which is our most common social ceremony—the handshake. Manichees would meet one another and grasp right hands, the gesture having sacred significance. It is true that the clasping of hands to seal an agreement or on making a promise was a custom in antiquity and among early Christians, but it was not a routine salutation. A fourth-century Christian source quoted by Jonas in his treatment of Manichaeism notes it as a Manichaean peculiarity. It would be for the Manichees a manifestation of the mystic importance of the right hand over the left, which in its various primitive forms and their possible physical results in the way of dexterity is an anthropologist's puzzle.

If the Manichees did introduce to Europe and elsewhere the hand-shaking custom which they practiced from religious motives and which we have so far divested of the spiritual that we teach it to our pet dogs, it does not seem to have penetrated into inner Africa. Pagan Africans regarded it with amazement when Europeans came and in some regions not only imitated the habit but embellished it. After the hands had met in the usual way each person before letting go completely snaps his first two fingers against the same two fingers of his friend—a lively extra to the Manichees' sober ritual.

For Manichees the clasping of right hands had a profound senti-ment. It associated with their own value in the Creation scheme, about which in the Gnostic manner they held views very different from those of Christianity and to which views Augustine had lis-tened in his youth when he, too, was a Manichee.

Augustine, an ardent Christian for forty-four years, "made his way to Christ," as an early medieval historian puts it, in time to be spared contact with Arianism. He was also saved involvement in a new doctrinal dispute then gaining force. He died before he could obey summons to attend the Council of Ephesus, which was to argue about the nature of Christ and the standing of His mother. This and ensuing similar discussions introduced many doctrines with puzzling and pretentious names which set forth theories and specu-lations about the divine personality, as if mankind were attempt-ing to psychoanalyze God.

From it all Egypt chose Monophysitism and resented bitterly at-tempted direction from the home authorities to believe otherwise. There were violent quarrels and persecutions.

This belief that Jesus possessed one single nature which united the human and the divine appealed to Egypt, Nubia and Ethiopia. Mono-physitism went to the Egyptians' heart. They dressed their vision of Jesus in fanciful tales of His babyhood which showed how even in infancy He was both divine and human. His babyhood was par-ticularly dear to them. It was their unique and exclusive proud heritage, for Jesus, who did not go to other foreign lands, had, so the New Testament stated, visited their country.

And the doctrine's special reverence and interest in Mary, the mother, suited them and reawakened sweet memories, an almost atavistic attachment, and matched the new lady of their worship to an ancient affection. Isis, the kind, opened the door to the sacred Mary.

Better than a theologian's definition to convey an idea of what their creed meant to simple people, the Copts of Egypt, are the local legends about the Holy Family's sojourn in their country, wherein we see portrayed the single nature of Christ, the almost simultaneous manifestations of the little boy and of God. Let us take the narrative of Theophilus, Patriarch of Alexandria, just before and just after the year 400. The narrative is in the first person, just as it is supposed to have been told to Theophilus "when Mary appeared to him."

"I carried my Child sometimes on my shoulders and sometimes on my back." Mary was very tired, but when she set Him on the ground, "He would walk along a little way at a time, holding onto the hem of my skirt, and then, like all children who cry out to their mother to carry them, He expected me to carry Him."

Suddenly the tone changes. It is a demonstration of the Coptic creed, the combination of human and God in one person. The whimpering Child became the divine performer of miracles.

In the Egyptian pagan city which had snubbed the refugees the Infant Jesus, riding still on Mary's tired back, caused the heathen temples to fall down and the idols to be dashed to pieces. Wild beasts and mountains "came and worshipped my Son, and when we journeyed onwards they also journeyed with us" till Jesus "turned towards them and, placing His right hand upon the mountain that was towards the East and His left hand upon the mountain that was towards the West, said unto them, 'Stand ye still!' " The mountains obeyed.

In another legend Mary is quoted as she supposedly recounts what happened after Jesus performed another miracle. "I found Him," said she, "sucking my breasts, and the Child said, 'Whilst I am clasping thy breast with My hand I am also grasping the ends of the world.' "

The simple legends of Coptic Egypt show what has been called "the curious results of the attempt to graft the Christian religion upon the old pagan religion of the country." The reverse may also have been true. The grafting may have been reciprocal. Some of the pagan religion of Egypt may have been grafted onto Christianity.

The thought that African paganism influenced Christianity in the matter of the Virgin story and in the matter of the Trinity is startling, but is nothing new. Egyptologists, historians, theologians and anthropologists have ventured to discuss it. Who first advanced it we do not know. There must have been in the mind of Arius a feeling that some of his opponents carried along memories of ancient Egypt, and during the centuries since the days of Arius others have felt the same.

For Arianism, though it gradually disappeared as an open form of belief, did not die but hibernated. It was a long winter, lasting until the very end of the Middle Ages, when Arianism came out to look at its shadow and was revived in Unitarian thought.

Isis, who allegedly laid an egg in the Christian nest, was a pagan goddess of the highest standing, no voluptuous Venus but the perfect divine lady of paganism. She was the personification of feminine creative power, the loving wife and tender mother. The worship of Isis was very old. In the Dynasty I a Pharaoh called himself by the honorary title "Son of Isis," and her worship traveled far and lasted long. The Roman Empire some thousands of years later was putting up monuments to Isis.

The superhuman circumstance of the conception of her child— she "drew seed unto herself" after the death of the beloved Osiris —and her maternal courage—she brought forth the child Horus in danger and in hiding—touched the heart of Egypt. She became the ideal figure, a divinity so loved that many images of her seated on a throne, suckling her child, have been found in ancient tombs. It was a representation "so like that of the Madonna," says the author of *The Golden Bough*, "that it sometimes received the adoration of ignorant Christians."

Isis is related to the maternal type found under other names and sometimes in less gracious guise in many ancient religions, and she is the heritress of something far older than her rise to divine standing in Egypt. Isis slipped across the threshold from prehistory. Her ancestress was that exaggerated, sometimes monstrous maternity which survives in prehistoric fecundity art.

Christianity in Africa was dying. Islam was coming closer to push not into a going spiritual state but into a vacuum, for Christianity, which had been so strong in Africa when much of Europe beyond the Mediterranean was scarcely aware, or was quite unaware of its existence, had with few exceptions run its course. African Christianity had poisoned itself by tempestuous efforts, doctrinal disputes. Monophysitism was its last African battle. It was all, as Harnack says, "a gruesome story."

Very suitable, dignified and congenial was it for multitudinous bishops to discuss and monks to ponder on abstract doctrinal distinctions, for the intellectual to spread his tail like a peacock as he displayed his brilliant theology, attacking or sponsoring Gnosticism or Donatism or Arianism or Monophysitism or some other of the almost uncountable contenders within the disputative family. Inevitable was that "disastrous fact in Christian history, the interference of the state." Inevitable that politics and government decrees continuously ordered alterations in believing so that one who believed in Jesus in an out-of-style way was regarded as more wicked than one who did not believe in Jesus at all.

But what was the effect on the ordinary simple-minded man in the street in Africa's cities, in Alexandria and Carthage, on the laborer in the fields and vineyards and orchards of all this bickering about something near to his heart? The common man felt brown and dry and lonely. Where was Christ's warm comfort in all this blather—all this government interference? The common man, who has to bear the burden of defense when a country is attacked, was dispirited and let down.

It is no wonder that when the Arabs came with another bone in their teeth, a succulent bone and one less spiny for the chewing, Africa accepted the offering.

Islam rode, almost slid across from the Nile to the Atlantic. In the west there was some opposition, Berbers fighting to protect their land rather than their religion, which was then various, some still pagans, some Christians, some ex-Christians who in discouragement had reverted to paganism and some Jews like the Jewess general who led them. Egypt's opposition, directed by "Makawkis" (Arabic rendering of Cyrus) of ill repute, who, the Egyptian historian Ibn-Abd-el Hakam, writing a century later, says, instructed the Copts to give no resistance to the Arabs, was so small it seemed almost a perfunctory gesture.

So Islam came and Christianity in Africa—almost all of Africa—slipped away.

There is an Algerian legend that the Christians, "once masters of the country," literally went underground, that underneath the sands of the Sahara they possess and still inhabit a Christian city pleasant with the rivers and brooks which they took with them upon their supernatural migration.

POCKETS · Christianity wilted but did not die after Islam came to Africa. North of the desert and beside and beyond the Nile it lived, and rumors would have it that it lived or flickered in hidden spots—in the Sahara, in the African forests. The tenacious Christians were heroic people clinging to their beliefs, sometimes under danger and humiliation and always under difficulty. The rumored Christians, even where they turned out to be non-existent fancies, show the continent's continuing interest in a religion vaguely heard of, a thing strange and reputedly potent, show a readiness to declare, when explorers inquired, that there were indeed people of this odd faith somewhere—somewhere in the far beyond—or that foreigners, identifiable in wishful thinking as Christians, had been their neighbors or rulers in the long ago.

As to the survival and experiences of Christians in Egypt there is no mystery. The Egyptians greeted the invasion of Islam with nonchalance, even satisfaction and collaboration. They were not at first unkindly used by the Arab conquerors and they were no longer plagued and depressed by foreign dictates as to their doctrine, as in Byzantine days. They were inured to conquerors. The native Egyptian population had not been the masters of Egypt for many centuries.

The Arabs dealt in a practical way with the Copts. (The word is a variant of "Egyptian"—"Gupt," "Gypt"—but has come to be applied exclusively to the Coptic Church.) The Arabs were not numerous, and that great conquest of theirs, which made history like Alexander's and lasted far longer, was of a vast sweep. Egypt was but a section in ambition's map. Let the Copts worship to suit their notions, paying for it of course, as a luxury item, and use the Copts as functionaries to handle local affairs under a series of Moslem governors—ninety-eight of them in the first two centuries.

There was at first no intense hostility toward Christians. Moslems had come early to some comprehension of comparative religion and respected Christianity, although very sure that Islam was better, an opinion borne out by the facts of battle—the Moslems were winning.

In contrast was the virulent anti-religious reaction of Europe's Christianity, surprised by a new sort of enemy, attributing the enemy's success to special malevolence and applying to the popped-up new system a fantasy of invective. To medieval Europe the enemy was "that diabolic and absurd sect" whose founder, a madman, claimed to be God, or alternately was a Catholic cardinal turned heretic and pretending to be a prophet, who when he fell down drunk, or perhaps in an epileptic fit, had been devoured by hogs, as a finale to his disgusting sex life.

Islamic tolerance in Egypt did not last indefinitely. Long before the Crusades the Copts, those tributaries and second-class persons in a Moslem world, met an increase in obloquy. Their position had its ups and downs. A special color of clothing was obligatory; nasty emblems of a dog or ape or a devil were to be put over their house doors. In relatively modern times things were yet worse. In the streets of Cairo "a brutal Turk struck the explorer Belzoni so fiercely on the leg with his staff that it tore away a large piece of flesh"; Belzoni was thirty days helpless, with no redress. Burton believed that shortly before his time in Egypt a Christian "passing before a mosque on foot was liable to be seized and circumcised."

The situation of the Copts must have been precarious and soul-troubling when the Crusade menace came close and Egyptian soil was invaded, when Moslem hostility toward the Christian part of their population justifiably boiled to hatred and when the Copts' own hearts were torn between religion and patriotism, between secret sympathy for the Christian invaders and hope of seeing Christianity restored and a natural fear that these foreigners might conquer and ruin their homeland.

It would seem a most unsuitable time for a European Christian saint to choose for a missionary visit to Egypt, but that is just what St. Francis of Assisi did. He contrived to see Kamil, nephew of Saladin, and tried to lead the sultan to an appreciation of the Gospel. The sultan treated the brave saintly visitor with courtesy.

Through the centuries the Coptic community survived, still survives. But with the years it shrank. This Christian pocket became smaller and smaller. When Islam came to Egypt the people of the country were largely Christian. Now they are said to make up less than 8 percent of the population.

The experience of the Nubian Christians contrasts with that of the Copts. They resisted the Moslem attack, geography aiding. Amr tried, Saladin tried and the Mamluks. When vanquished at last in war they recognized also defeat in religion. A few remembered. A report came to Father Alvares that there were still churches standing "with crucifixes and figures of Our Lady painted on the walls." A Madonna and Child a thousand years old was discovered on a church wall in Nubia (now the Republic of Sudan) in 1963 and was brought to the New York World's Fair. While Alvares was in Ethiopia—it was in the sixteenth century—a message was received begging that "priests and monks be sent to teach them . . . for they had lost all their clergy and their Christianity."

There are no indications that Christianity survived in a practical way west of the Nile: "African Christianity with all its 560 dioceses disappeared from the face of the earth." Carthage, once a pivot of the faith, was only a memory. Pope Leo IX in the eleventh century, looking backward, wistfully declared, "The chief archbishop of all Africa is the Bishop of Carthage. He cannot be laid aside . . . even if Carthage is abandoned." But a few years later even as a mere name "the Bishop of Carthage" was a dead title, for the prelate who never saw his see was no more. St. Louis made use of the almost ruined city in his Tunisian Crusade. Charles V found a few Christians near Tunis, descendants, Marmol says, of captives a sultan had put there in a sort of concentration camp. A few other traces: an abandoned monastery in the hinterland of Libya inspected by Barth, a church at Tlemcen, Algeria, which Christians still frequented in the days of El-Bekri (eleventh century) and was still standing three hundred years later, and the surprising mention of a "Bishop of Fez" in the thirteenth century.

It is sometimes difficult to assess such traces, to know whether the people involved were descendants of original early Christians who declined to go over to Islam or whether they were newcomers or descendants of newcomers—war prisoners, prey of raiders and pirates or pirates themselves (renegades who reverted to their old faith), converts of some sort, ex-soldiers from points which Europe seized at times along the coast, traders from Europe, etc.

Take for instance the mention of a "Bishop of Fez" in Morocco in the thirteenth century, which might be regarded as indicating that six hundred years after the Moslem invasion the city still sheltered an important congregation of surviving faithful. Aside from the fact that there was no city of Fez to shelter anybody until a Moslem ruler founded it, the fact is that the "Bishop" in question is like the "Bishop of Carthage," a nominal office in a nominal bishopric. The Fez bishopric was created in name only because some courageous Franciscan missionaries, presumably inspired by the efforts of St. Francis of Assisi in Egypt, reported conversions. This new Christianity in Africa, including whatever may have been accomplished through the work of Ramon Lull, who preached and was killed in Algeria, appeared in the thirteenth and start of the fourteenth centuries.

Sometimes one seems to see in folklore and fables evidence that

Christianity lived on. Out of these fantasies I pick two—a magic tale and a fabulous explanation of a still existent object of modern tourist interest which both give, I think, a better idea of the strength and mystery of Christianity as conserved in Africa's memory than do the sparse mentions of little groups, edifices and of Rome's attempt to keep alive a flicker of faith by the appointment of non-functioning bishops, or by unprovable historical suggestions. Among the last, for example, are such legends as that a very early king in the Lake Chad region (Mandara) was a foreign Christian or that the people of the ancient Empire of Ghana had been Christians before Islam came. (I have already mentioned the unproven legend that they were Jews.)

Here are the two bits of fantasy. One of the wonders of what is now Algeria is a very ancient edifice which the local population has for many centuries been certain was the "Tomb of the Christian Woman" (Kbor er Roumia) and which so figures on modern maps. This edifice is over two hundred feet across, and if it was thought to be proportionate to the size of the defunct it indicated a belief that the Christians of antiquity were a giant supernatural race. Why did imagination fix upon a woman for the fancied occupant of this enormous tomb? What woman? Was it a distorted memory of the prestige of Mary, mother of the Christian's Christ? As a matter of fact, the tomb cannot have contained the remains of any Christian. It dates from before our era. The name long ago given to it by the population is an absurdity, but is impressive as showing a strange undying reverence for the religion which disappeared.

A folk tale of a mountainous region on the present Algerian-Tunisian border surpasses yet parallels some modern European beliefs. It is told with insistence twice over with variations by the renowned Arabic geographer El-Bekri. It concerns, he was assured, "one of the disciples of Jesus" who was murdered there and whose body has hung suspended in a crevasse through the centuries. Blood still drips from his slashed throat, wild animals have not touched it, "all the parts of the body, big and little, have resisted decomposition—one would say that he had been killed that very day, yet he was discovered there before the conquest of Africa by the Moslems."

El-Bekri interjects first a query, "Can it be true?" and then adds the comment, "God can very well do whatever He wishes!"

There has been a lot of learned discussion as to whether the Tuareg of the Sahara, a Berber white Moslem group, are ex-Christians. The main basis for this supposition is their display of the cross. A cross frequently appears in their ornaments. There was a cross upon their leather defense shields, the hilt of swords and daggers was in the form of a cross. This armament of theirs was observed in action not so very long ago for the Tuareg fought till recently. The decisive battle was in 1902 against Europe's effort to penetrate the great desert and shortly before they had very competently and ruthlessly destroyed a French mission seeking to study a trans-Saharan railway project.

They are one of the oddest groups in the modern world and have been the subject of much literature, some of it very careful, and respectful as well—for they are not primitive folk but a tribe, practically a nation of social and cultural curios, small in numbers but vast in interest. As the Sahara's wise man, Gautier, said, "It is strange that so small a fraction of humanity bears a name of world-wide notoriety." Two facts about the Tuareg have puzzled us: that their men, for a reason nobody yet has been able to explain, wear dark veils completely covering their faces up to the eyes while their women go barefaced and that the desert-wandering Tuareg, whose facilities for cultural effort is minimum, should possess the only present-day African writing system. (One excepts a few systems invented imitatively since colonization and the Ethiopian script, which is of Arabic derivation.)

In the transformed Sahara of oil projects and airplanes they are, from the picturesque and romantic point of view, a dying race, though by no means dead in other respects. At the first meeting of the Assembly of independent Algeria two Tuareg deputies from the mid-Sahara appeared in their customary face veils—to leave off his veil would be to a Tuareg male indecent—and the Tuareg of the Sahara's southern rim have gravely embarrassed the Republic of Mali —this was nothing new for the Tuareg in old times blockaded Timbuctoo at times and made the city their tributary and were sand pirates of the desert, roaming caravan pillagers.

However, in the pre-colonial days, when they were the kings of the Sahara, they abstained from pillaging caravans in the month of Ramadan, when pious Moslems from sunrise to sunset fast and refrain from love-making. This was their own quaint tribute to Islam, for they were Moslems, more or less—probably less, it is said. They acquired Islam along with the rest of the western Saharan tribes in the eleventh-century revival movement of the Almoravids, their fellow tribesmen and fellow veil wearers, whose rush to power originated in a religious upsurge.

Whether they were once Christians is an open question. They now observe Mohammedanism nonchalantly and have conserved or adopted aspects of paganism including food taboo. Duveyrier, who lived among the Tuareg for a long time, wrote in his *Journal* that men of standing thought it wrong to eat plumed animals. Rennell Rodd in *People of the Veil* records something similar. Also they declined to eat the flesh of the big lizard, not from natural repugnance but from what Gautier describes as "a taboo that smells like totemism, because, as they have said, 'It is our maternal uncle.' "

They took a sinister interest in demons, jinn and also in witches. A witch would milk the teats of the moon and make poison thereof, with the addition of scorpion venom and other vile things.

Imagination could also find a gentler outlet. Père de Foucauld, who lived and was murdered among them, said, "Everybody here is a poet!" I offer just a line from a love poem which is charming because it so sincerely and sweetly reflects the author's thoughts and way of life. Of his sweetheart he says, "She is more beautiful than a white camel who has rested for six months." And I find a rather noble imagination in one of the Tuareg riddles which Père de Foucauld collected:

"They are above us, and if God did not hold them back they would kill us."
Answer: "The stars."

It is the instinctive thinking of people of the tent, living their lives open to the sky and reacting to the fearsome grandeur of the stars.

Sometimes the names of unknown personages, presumably minor

deities unknown to Islam, come into their talk. And there might be a survival of paganism in the delight they take in having their women fat. This would be a heritage from the very ancient adoration of fecundity. In the tomb of their legendary ancestress, Queen Tin' Hinan, excavated in 1925–33, there was found along with the lady's skeleton and jewelry a fecundity charm, a pendant representing an exaggeratedly obese female.

The fact that the Tuareg alone among Africans possess a writing system seems to bear out the opinion of one of their very early European admirers. He was Frederick Horneman, who in 1799 reported upon the Tuareg to his employers, The Association for Promoting the Discovery of the Inner Parts of Africa (one of whose original members, by the way, was Edward Gibbon). Horneman said that they were "the most interesting nation of Africa," and that "if cultivated and enlightened their natural abilities would render them perhaps one of the greatest nations upon earth." Horneman's prophecy has not yet been fulfilled, but it may be one of Africa's future surprises.

The letters of the Tuareg alphabet are mostly represented by straight lines and dots, some curves—nothing of the spidery grace of the Arabic. A peculiarity is that the words can be written starting either from the left or the right, or running either upward or downward, which makes for hard reading. Often each word is encircled. I saw Tifinagh (Tuareg writing) cut into a flat rock in the Sahara in which each word was put inside what seemed like a graven footprint.

Tifinagh is a heritage or adaptation of a very ancient script which also was used by the Libyans (Berbers) and which the Tuareg alone kept alive—or are now letting die, though once they could all read and write and their women were especially literate. There is even a tradition which is repeated with reserve that the Koran was put into Tifinagh, probably untrue.

It is striking that these people who lived in little tents no bigger than beach umbrellas and liked to say that a family's complete possessions could be loaded upon one camel were the sole hyphen which carried into modern Africa antique African literacy and that they have prominently and vigorously carried along the emblem of

Christianity, whether or not they ever practiced its faith and whether or not the cross they display actually derives from Christianity. For the cross is not exclusively the perquisite and mark of that faith. I have read that all of the several varieties of the cross which carry the names of St. George, St. Andrew, the Maltese, the Greek and the Latin can be traced to antiquity long before our era. There survive relics to show that Egypt in Dynasties VII and VIII admired that form of the cross design known as the swastika, which was to become an early Christian emblem and later went to work for the Nazis, and which oddly enough appears carved all over the stomach of a Loango (Congo) woman in an illustration based on a photograph in Baumann's work on primitive African civilizations.

Crosses have been noted almost everywhere in Africa, across the top of the continent, in spots from the Red Sea to the Atlantic and in places deep in the sub-Sahara and in the desert —crosses tattooed on faces and hands, crosses on sword hilts, crosses as a jewelry design and as a design for charms, crosses on house and hut doors, crosses as a magic mark on the chests of sick people, crosses to frighten lightning away. Some pagans would emphasize an oath by wetting their finger, making a sign of a cross on the earth and touching the earth-covered finger to their tongue. The "handa," the Katanga copper cross shaped almost like a capital H, was widely distributed as coinage.

Astonished explorers noted all this in localities where no Europeans had been before and there could be no notion of their having been adopted in imitation. Sometimes an inquiry would bring the answer, "Our fathers did the same."

Leo Africanus, the famed African traveler, discovered a cross manifestation that had been carried along for a thousand years without reason or question by some of the Berbers of the Mediterranean. "Each has the habit," he wrote, "of painting a black cross upon his cheek and another on the palm of his hand." This, explained Leo, dated from the time "when the Vandals seized the country, because of which great numbers of the people were driven to the Christian faith, which people the king of the Vandals ordered his officers not to oblige to pay tribute. Some claimed to be Christians without it was known whether they were or not and it was ordered

that the Christians should be signed and recognized by the cross."
The Vandals left, "but this habit has lived on without their knowing
why."

Some of these various African crosses were merely a favored geometric design or were an element in superstitions quite apart from
any Christian association. Some were relics of Christian contacts or rumors of the past, a crude reaching toward the forgotten
and the intangible. What effect have the vestiges, the vague perfume
of a forgotten, probably a barely experienced faith had upon African peoples? It is one of Africa's unanswered questions.

The clue of the cross badly fooled Europeans in the early days of
exploration. The wish to discover a hidden Christian empire inspired
credulous eagerness, observing which, the native narrator may have
added fancy touches in a desire to please. The story centered around
a copper cross.

Here is a passage from de Barros, composed in 1553, about a cross
which beckoned to Portuguese explorers and of whose potency they
had been told by the people of Benin (western Nigeria): "Toward
the East at twenty moons' march from Benin there was a king, the
most powerful of all the region whom they called Ogane and who
amongst the sovereigns of these countries was held in so great veneration as is the Pope of Rome by Christian kings. When a new king of
Benin mounted on the throne he would send an embassy to Ogane
asking him to confirm his rights. In confirmation Ogane . . . sent
him a cross in copper which he should wear around his neck. Without this insignia the people considered their king was not consecrated
and was not fit to govern."

The de Barros passage goes on to say that the ambassador never
saw Ogane, he being behind a curtain. To the Portuguese, just as
to the ambassador, Ogane remained invisible. They never found
him, and there is no historical confirmation of the yarn about Ogane
the great Christian pontiff and the copper cross he bestowed on
worthy kings. Perhaps the story grew from the Portuguese delight
and curiosity when they were shown a coin which was or which
resembled a Katanga cross. This is possible, although Benin was a
long way from Katanga.

Copper was a great traveler, for Africans loved it. In much of

Africa it ranked as a precious metal. The famed Kankan Musa of Mali on the Sahara's southern rim told an interviewer who passed it along to al-Omari that the copper mine in his territory was his greatest source of revenue: the copper was sold to Negroes in the gold countries for two thirds its weight in gold. In many African places copper was the money standard. The coins were sometimes bars or wires about ten inches long, sometimes flat cakes or rings. The Katanga cross was an elegant presentation which undoubtedly went to far places if only as a native numismatist's trophy, and may have been seen in Benin by the Portuguese.

The mysterious Ogane may have been a fancy picture of the Oni (Ruler) of Ife, an elder and pagan brother state of Benin. Similar names for places and people were common in the region: Ogan, Ogun, Ogiso (meaning "King"), etc.

There were rumors that Ogane was the royal title of the King of Mossi, an important pagan nation a considerable distance from Benin to the northwest. The Portuguese home government interpreted this as "Moses," may have discerned a Biblical-Christian relationship and sought to enter into relationship with the Mossi.

Portugal's intensive investigation of Africa predates that of the rest of us and was upheld by the papal Bull of Pope Alexander VI at the end of the fifteenth century, which split the possession of the non-Christian newly discovered worlds down the middle, giving the western side (the Americas) to Spain and the eastern side (Africa) to Portugal, the basic idea being that pagan inhabitants had no right to own any part of the earth.

To Portugal a fellow Christian in Africa was more desirable than the nominal possession of a continent, and Ogane fitted into and further confirmed and enthused a search for the Christian master of kings in some far land which had excited Europe for three hundred years.

The search had been inspired by the great Prester John fake. It was a hoax—a sort of holy hoax that once it got going could not stop, bred sincere conviction and identification of a fancy figure who never existed and, because people had faith in it and believed it true, a sort of universal self-hypnotism. It had gorgeous and strange details. Unhampered by geographical precisions, it slipped across Asia and then into Africa.

The announcement was a stunning document, the so-called "forged letter" of the mid-twelfth century: "John, Priest of the Almighty power of God and the strength of Our Lord Jesus Christ, King of Kings and Lord of Lords to his friend Emmanuel [Manuel I, Comnenus of Byzantium], Prince of Constantinople, wishing him health and the continuous enjoyment of Divine Favors." The letter continued with details about John the Priest's empire (Prester John, as we call him), some of which are reminders of Eldad the Danite, some of the mythical story of Alexander the Great and some are novelties. "When we go to war," he stated, "we have carried before us fourteen golden crosses ornamented with precious stones in the place of banners and each of these is followed by 10,000 mounted troops and 100,000 infantry."

Before the palace was a marvelous mirror erected upon a many-storied pedestal. In this Prester John could discern everything that went on throughout his dominions and detect conspiracies. Courtiers —thirty thousand of them every day—were his guests, eating off tables that were some of them of gold and some of amethyst. There were also tables of the most precious emeralds supported on pillars of amethyst, "by virtue of which no person sitting at the table can become inebriated."

Prester John himself was served by seven kings in rotation each month, for he was emperor over many kings—the most powerful and glorious of all mortals—"if you can number the stars of heaven and sands of the sea, then you can calculate the extent of our dominion."

If we agree to assess fiction writers by the effect their works have had upon people and events we cannot deny that the author of the "Prester John Letter" was the greatest novelist the world has ever known. All Christendom was impressed and much of the rest of the world was affected. Europe's thoughts and actions were impelled by what he wrote. By the standards of the day his was a "best seller." It was launched on the world long before printing and when literature had to be copied by hand for distribution. "The criterion of popularity of medieval books is the number of manu-

scripts that have survived or are known to have existed . . .
Chaucer's *Canterbury Tales,* with more than sixty manuscripts,
ranks among the favorites," says S. H. Steinberg in *Five Hundred
Years of Printing.* Copies of Chaucer's work had to survive the
vicissitudes of Europe for only six hundred years, the "Prester John
Letter" for about eight hundred. Nearly one hundred copies of
"Prester John" have survived.

The author is presumed to have been the Bishop of Mainz. Manuel
I passed it on to Frederick Barbarossa. The Pope saw it. Even Iceland
heard about it. England conferred upon it the supreme compliment
of using its hero's name for children. In 1219 a man called Prester
John appears on the record of Lincolnshire, "his parents evidently
having named him after the great priest-king" (from Stenton's
English Society in the Middle Ages). The Pope indited a reply to be
delivered by hand, his effort being hampered by the fact that
neither he nor anybody else knew Prester John's address.

The story had everything, a three-way appeal. It appealed as
a new religious announcement—and speculation about religion was
the leading intellectual activity of those times. It had a very practical
interest: Prester John's million and a half soldiery would be a priceless
aid in combating the great Moslem danger. And it had that appeal
which is timeless. With its picture of gold and jewels and luxury
it beckoned to greed.

Marco Polo traced him in Asia as Unc Khan, "the same we call
Prester John," the liege lord of the Tatars, to whom they paid
tribute until Ghenghis Khan. Joinville tells of the interest St. Louis
took in the struggle of Prester John with the Tatars, and his defeat.

The mythical priest-king shifted to another continent. The search
moved toward Africa. To Europe's idea "Prester John" had become
almost the hereditary title of the Emperor of Ethiopia, not his
personal name, for the Prester John of the romantic yarn would
be by then some three hundred years old. Ethiopia was hidden and
mysterious and impenetrable, cut off to Christians by Moslem Egypt
and so completely isolated that Ramon Lull and others tried to
formulate a plan to blockade Egypt with the idea of improving
Prester John's situation.

A series of explorers sailed farther and farther down the West

Coast of the continent, whose shape and size and width from west to east were unknown. They discovered a continent and along the way collected rumors like the tale about Ogane, the Christian emperor of the interior. They went to the tip of Africa, and despite Ptolemy's long-respected theory that the continent had no southern end but curled up and joined onto Asia, they discovered that they had come to Africa's end, that the coast, till then to their east, had shifted to their north. Finally da Gama, first to make his way right around the Cape of Good Hope to India, was told when he reached Mozambique that "Prester John resided not far from this place . . . in the interior, and could be reached on the backs of camels." Geographically the information was not correct, but it "rendered us so happy that we cried with joy." So states *A Journal of the First Voyage of Vasco da Gama,* which became the theme of Camoens' *The Lusiads.*

So Africa below the Sahara met Europeans who came hunting for one of Africa's own. These Europeans, the Portuguese, marked the coast of Africa with their signs. In the beginning, at the time of Henry the Navigator, these signs were simple and unpretentious— wooden crosses and the motto of Henry, "Talent for doing good," carved by sailors upon a nearby tree. Later as their expeditions went farther along the coast they carried with them impressive stone columns "as tall as two men" called *pedrão,* which bore the Portuguese emblem, a column to be set up at spots which seemed significant.

The first pillar went up at the mouth of the Congo River, "known thereafter as the River of the Pedrão . . . thus taking possession in the name of the King of all the territory so far discovered," de Barros says. Down the coast the pillars were planted, staking out a claim to a continent. One went up on an islet near the point where to their amazement they came to Africa's end, and columns were set along Africa's East Coast. If these signs had been able to give real and lasting possession rights Portugal would have been, as the Papal Bull stated, the master of all the sub-Sahara.

As Europe's ships, which astonished Africans thought might be huge fish or giant birds, sailed along their shores and visited their beaches Africans had contacts, some good, some profitable, some tragic and some very funny with the strangers. Comical was the attempt to get in touch with Prester John by sending some specially chosen Negresses who had fallen into Portuguese hands to hunt for his headquarters and sing the praises of Portugal's piety and greatness or, failing direct contact with Prester John himself, to talk in such fashion that the news would spread and reach his ears. The Negresses went ashore one by one, arrayed in handsome dress and supplied with "gold, silver and spices" as proof of Portugal's wealth, generosity and goodwill. The places where the several Negresses were set ashore—the first at a place where a *pedrão* was erected— are difficult to identify on the modern map, but would seem to be along the Angola coast and beyond.

The plan that a solitary Negress, foreign to the locality and tribal languages, landing on an Angola beach could get in touch with or convey a message to Prester John, residing in Ethiopia—something like twenty-five hundred miles off by crow travel, seems ultra-optimistic. But the King of Portugal, who designed the idea, had been misled by the Ogane tale, and he did not know how wide was Africa.

I wonder what these ambassadresses thought of their quaint mission.

Well intended, but sometimes disfigured according to modern ideas by being mixed up with the slave trade, were the early attempts to convert the population to Christianity.

At Benin conversion efforts were abortive. The slave trade endured. The King of Benin, Esigie, was intrigued and even ordered a son to become a Christian, but the new religion had only a brief success. According to a contemporary Portuguese report, the king himself declined to be baptized and also declined to discharge his faithful old idols. If the Christian deity would bring him success in war he would add Him to Benin's staff of divinities, but he refused to give Him his exclusive patronage. He did not favor monotheism any more than he did monogamy. Benin's peculiar psychology, which combined a delicate art expression with profligate human sacrifice, did not adapt itself to conversion. The foreign slave trade, however, began and prospered.

Into the region at the lower lip of the Congo's mouth Christianity

entered with the slave trade trotting at its side and gave Negro
Africa its first taste of colonialism, a tentative brief glimpse of
what would be the sweeping movement of the nineteenth century.

The region affected was the old Congo kingdom of which the
Portuguese had heard when they set up their pillar and renamed
the great river—then locally known as the Zaire—the River Pedrão.
The Congo River now carries the name of the ancient kingdom—
Zaire and the nickname Pedrão are forgotten—and spreads across lands
the kingdom of old never knew. The name has been hard-worked on
modern maps. It figures as one section of Portuguese Angola. There
is ex-French Congo with the capital Brazzaville. And there is the
vast ex-Belgian Congo. All these keep alive the memory of an ancient
land where colonization of a sort tried and failed and Christianity
stepped in and soon stepped out again. The word *congo*, so long
remembered, meant in the Bantu languages of the locality "hunter."
Another local word, *ngola*, meaning "king," was mispronounced
and gave its name to Angola.

The pagan king of the Congo kingdom when the Portuguese arrived was master of a considerable territory. He was overlord, a sort
of little emperor who dominated many Bantu tribes and several
minor kings. He was fascinated by his first contact with Europeans
and by their religion. "The Holy Spirit manifested itself in his pagan
soul," wrote a contemporary Portuguese, and he sent a message to
Portugal, requesting that priests be supplied to baptize every one
of his subjects. Portugal also was fascinated, responded with Christian encouragement and in due course expressed the wish to trade,
ivory and slaves being suggested.

It was colonialism's fairy story. Portugal sent priests. The King of
Congo assumed a Christian name. His capital town was retitled
São Salvador. His new name was João. It had been Nzinga-a-Coum
and his capital had been Mbanza. A church was erected with miraculous speed, less than eight weeks from foundation to dedication.
More churches went up. São Salvador's ruins show that it had twelve
—ruins, yes, for the fairy story did not last. Priests and teachers
and skilled workers came from Europe, even two German printers.
The aristocracy assumed a Portuguese style of dress. Men wore capes

and cloaks, women veils and jeweled black caps. This seems unbelievable but is of record.

Evidently the Portuguese fashions in costuming did not spread to the lower orders. A group of Capuchin missionaries were abashed when asked to baptize "a handsome young woman, stark-naked." They caused her to "cover herself with a few leaves."

There are several missionary narratives of the times. We read that there was very encouraging eagerness for baptism but that the priests learned to their chagrin that the Congo kingdom's commoners called the ceremony "to eat salt," the region being saltless and salt a rare delicacy, so that the Catholic ritual of baptism, which included putting salt in the convert's mouth, had an appeal quite aside from its sacred import. But the Capuchins worked hard. Idols and fetishes were destroyed. Polygamy was forbidden, but was said to have survived by the simple process of calling all but one of the female companions "concubines" rather than "wives."

It was for a while a Christian country. But it was also a slave traders' playground, an inexhaustible mine for human victims. A generation after conversion and imitative civilization began slave exploitation was so heinous that the Congo King Affonso complained bitterly to Portugal that the country was being depopulated and corrupted. Traders tempted the people and seized "our subjects, even the sons of our noblemen and our own relatives." From the Congo kingdom and nearby Angola (a part only of modern Angola), which had been under the domination of the Congo kingdom and where the Portuguese presently established themselves, slave exportation has been estimated at ghastly figures. It was not the sort of slavery Africa had known and accepted as normal, but a wholesale exploitation and exile. "It is strange to remember," says Kingsnorth in his *Africa South of the Sahara,* "that as the slaves were exported the Portuguese arranged that a bishop should bless them from a marble seat, which was specially built for the purpose on the harbor side."

The weakened and demoralized Congo kingdom was attacked by pagan ultra-savage and cannibalistic invaders. São Salvador was wrecked. Christianity writhed and died.

There survived little traces, images without meaning, once solemn objects turned into toys or trinkets or lucky charms, crucifixes that had become fetishes without special significance, tales about local gods that were suggestive of Christ and the Virgin Mary.

Christianity at the Congo's mouth had lasted about a century. It was one of the resultant aspects of the search for the fabulous Prester John.

Ethiopia claims to be the oldest of the Christian nations. Certainly no other nation has carried along continuously as an intimate part of its national life so many and such old Christian associations. Ethiopia is convinced of having actually participated in the events of the Old Testament and of having mingled its own personalities with Old Testament figures. Moses married one of its women. As I have said, from Solomon's romance with their queen was born their King Menelik. They believe that some of the Biblical mentions of "Ethiopia"—that indefinite and confusing name—refer to their nation. In their early literature a fourteenth-century history about their King Amda Syon is quoted with joy a passage from Psalms which they interpret as a promise that their nation will survive till the Second Coming of the Son of God: "Ethiopia shall stretch out her hands unto God."

A second chapter of the Solomon romance with their queen tells how the companions of Menelik, their son, indecorously smuggled the Ark of the Covenant out of Jerusalem and brought it to Ethiopia.

Coming to New Testament associations, we find that Ethiopia assumed proprietorship of the eunuch of Candace, who was converted by St. Philip and carried Christianity back to his homeland, which incident, as already mentioned, actually applied to a quite different queen, one of the Candaces of another land—Nubia.

Ethiopia appropriated Candace and built a tradition around this non-authentic national queen, convinced that it was she who erected at her capital, Axum, "a very noble church, the first there was in Ethiopia, and named it St. Mary of Syon." I quote from Father Alvares, who describes it in what is said to be the earliest European book about Ethiopia, first published in 1540 and entitled *Truthful Information about the Countries of Prester John of the Indies.*

The Virgin Mary and the Child Jesus themselves visited Ethiopia and lived there for three and a half years, according to a legend, the rest of which is ultra-fantastic, with items such as how the Virgin later restored to life nine hundred thousand men and nine hundred thousand women in a cemetery somewhere in the Near East. (Legends charmed us all in the Middle Ages, and Ethiopia's Middle Ages had a prolonged Middle.) Mary has held an exalted place in Ethiopian ritual and in its creed. She has been revered as "the Mother of the Creator of the Universe." Some picturesque instances of the influence of the country's Mariolatry will be cited in a later part of this book, where I will try to tell something of Africa's art and Africa's literature.

About the theft of the Ark we have a detailed account in Ethiopia's famous book of ancient history and legend, *Kebra Nagast*. Some young Jews who had been designated to accompany Menelik to Ethiopia conceived the idea of stealing the Ark of the Covenant, containing the Decalogue, which the Jews of old believed had been inscribed by the finger of God upon tablets of stone, and carrying it along with them into their exile.

They kept the plan a secret from Menelik. On the journey from Jerusalem to Ethiopia their piece of sacred luggage gave them miraculous speed and facilities. Their horses seemed to fly, never touching the ground, the riders floating half a yard above their backs. A cloud by day and a pillar of flame by night showed them the way, and the Red Sea opened a dry path before them. Solomon, who ordered out an army and started after them, gave up the chase. Menelik, still ignorant of the precious treasure they transported, must have been amazed. They had delayed telling him lest he turn back and make restitution. But when finally he was told he "danced and clapped his hands."

In Christian Ethiopia there is the still surviving souvenir of this dream that the Ark came to their country. The Tabot, meaning "Ark" or "Chest," a miniature reproduction of the ancient object, is the most supremely sacred of things in their churches, never to be touched by others than priests, kept at the altar except on special occasions when it is carried abroad under a great umbrella, borne upon a priest's head and wrapped in a silk cover. The Tabot has gained a wide symbolism, and the term is sometimes applied not only to the object itself but to the altar or even the church where it is kept.

Two Tabots accompanied their emperor, Prester John, when he traveled. They were carried by priests and in front went a cross and a bell ringer. Also went four lions, going before the king and bound with strong chains. Father Alvares tells this and how he saw and spoke with the African Christian monarch whom he regarded as Prester John and who in Ethiopia possessed several names—as often happened with their royalty—being called David, and by a name translatable as "Illuminated-by-the-Virgin" and another "Feared-by-Lions" and also Lebna Dengel, meaning "Incense-of-the-Virgin," by which history usually knows him. This I mention both as a curious circumstance and as proof of the potent Christian tone of the land and its intense preoccupation with the Virgin Mary.

Lebna Dengel was not the impressive figure of the Prester John myths and hopes, nor was Ethiopia itself, so Alvares found, a great empire but rather a country on the verge of having to scrap for its existence. Its Moslem neighbors were attacking. Finally Lebna Dengel, whose other name was Feared-by-Lions, ran before the Moslem general whose name figures in history by his nickname, Gran, "The Left-Hander," and the country was ruined and plundered. One object looted was "a calf with four legs which is called in their language, *Tabot*, made of gold," according to the invading Moslems, as quoted in an editor's footnote to Alvares's description of the church in question, mentioned earlier, a sort of Ethiopian Westminster Abbey, burial place of kings.

Battered Ethiopia was saved as Christianity's pocket in Africa by the help of Portuguese soldiers led by Christopher da Gama, son of the great Vasco. Christopher, before whose ardor, says *The Lusiads*, "The Red Sea was jaundiced with fear," perished and the Moslems paid him the tribute of hatred toward a dangerous antagonist, insulting him when he could no longer fight back. They buried his head alongside the body of a dead dog.

This gruesome relic was dug up afterward by Portuguese Jesuits who had come to Ethiopia on a religious mission. One of the Jesuits tells how he gathered up the teeth and the lower jaw, and adds,

"No words can express the ecstasies I was transported with at seeing the relics of so great a man."

This was Father Jeronimo Lobo, whose account of Abyssinia was put into English by young Samuel Johnson a century later. It was in Father Lobo's narrative that Samuel Johnson picked up a passing mention of a name which stayed in his head and which long afterward he bestowed upon the hero of his novel *Rasselas*, which though rather dull to those of us who read it as students is said to have been the most popular of Johnson's writings. It has interest in that it was a very early English attempt to deal with African thought and psychology. Letting his fancy roam, Johnson told of the philosophizing of the imaginary Ethiopian Prince Rasselas.

Father Lobo's visit to Ethiopia was a part of the prolonged effort to induce the country to become Catholic, an effort which failed. To Ethiopians there was only one form of Christianity—their own. Their faith and ritual had stiffened under so many attacks: pagans all about them, Jews who by the force of Judith had seized power and driven the Christian dynasty into hiding and who through the years were a menace, Moslem neighbors who were and remain a chronic threat, plus sectarian discords.

In the time of that great ruler Zara Yaqob, a close predecessor of Alvares's Prester John—to take an example of the country's religious problems about which we have detailed information in the chronicle of Zara Yaqob's reign—there occurred "the insurrection of 'the children of Estifa' [a sect] who would not bow down before the Virgin Mary nor before the cross of her Son." Zara Yaqob dealt firmly with heretics. In this case he ordered their noses cut off, their tongues also and that they be stoned to death. He gained the name of "exterminator of the Jews" who were proselytizing. He met the threat of idolatry, of serpent worship, of the worship of strange gods even by his own sons and daughters and publicly flagellated all suspects, even royalty. And in protection against sorcerers he caused the interior of his palace to be continuously sprinkled with holy water.

The religion of the Ethiopians was not a cushioned comfort for the soul but a battle, and Christianity was their war cry. To them religion was not, as with many peoples, a philosophy and a discipline. It was the very vertebrae of the nation. It was their form of patriotism.

Theirs was an unusual situation. The country was doubly isolated —by its neighbors and by geography. It was so situated that it was impossible to get into or out of their territory without traversing lands that were geographically difficult and usually hostile. The long and complicated search before the outside world could get in touch with Prester John proves how hard was the approach. To get out of the country and meet the outside world was so hard that during all the Middle Ages there are few records of Ethiopian travelers to Europe.

One class of Ethiopians did leave home in numbers, not for Europe but for the Holy Land. Every year a band of pilgrims went via Nubia and Egypt to Jerusalem. With them would go traveling churches in the form of tents and Tabots carried by priests in turn, so that replicas of the Ark allegedly filched in the long ago went back to the city that had been Solomon's.

They journeyed usually in safety, under special paid Moslem guard, but Alvares tells of a pilgrimage that ended in tragedy. He witnessed its departure, even traveling with the pilgrims for a couple of days. They were 336 travelers, among them fifteen nuns. They were attacked. The Moslem guard could not protect them. The old men pilgrims were killed. The young and presumably the nuns were sold as slaves.

Ethiopia's Monophysite Church depended on the authority of the Copts of Egypt. The head of their church was until modern times sent to them from Egypt. Sometimes the Ethiopian nation was on strained terms with the Egyptian nation, and the procurement of their religious leader from a foreign second-class group in a hostile Moslem country was awkward and was offensive to national pride. The title of the religious leader was *abuna*. Sometimes Ethiopia dispensed with an *abuna* altogether. Zara Yaqob is quoted as saying that he would sooner die than receive a dignitary from a country of heretics. Eventually and rather recently Ethiopia's church became self-governing.

Trouble made Ethiopia strong. Its religious intensity was awesome. Its piety was extreme, even eccentric in its multitude of fasts, its self-inflicted deprivations and sufferings, its ritual dancing. In it all Ethiopia found the self-confidence to be for a time the only independent country in Africa except the Liberian Republic.

There was something real in the Prester John myth when it shifted to Africa, something more real than actuality, for it was a myth born of desire. Prester John of Ethiopia was not the gorgeous emperor of the romance—"the most powerful and glorious of all mortals," eating off a table of gold with amethyst legs. He had another power, the strength to carry along the essence of Christianity for more than a thousand years.

Ethiopia crouched on her mountaintops and growled at the world, a world still pagan or turned Moslem. She was the sole vigorous survivor of a faith that had been at its strongest in Africa and there had died young when Islam came.

ISLAM IN AFRICA

ISLAM CAME ·
THE DARKER MOSLEMS

ISLAM CAME · Islam, which was eventually to isolate the continent, at first exhilarated and united Africa. It was accepted from the Nile to the Atlantic and by the veiled men of the desert and by many of the Negroes beyond the Sahara.

The Berbers of North Africa, once the shock of the Arab invasion had passed, were proud to be connected with a triumphant movement. Islam was a success. Islam was born grown-up; it was without the timid maltreated babyhood of early Christianity. A religion and a conquering nation had been twin-born. Nor was Islam brought to them by a defeated people like the Jews, who had come to Africa in exile, sometimes in slavery.

The founder of this new religion was set before them as a self-made man of wisdom and victories, and they saw his followers as world conquerors in whose forward march they were glad to join. For them Islam had the prospect of gain and it offered the added glamour of mystery and intrigue.

Like a drawing string Islam pulled Africa together. Most of the population within the reach of Moslem influence gradually joined the new religion. Missionaries who were traders and traders who were missionaries introduced Islam to Negroland. The clam of inner Africa opened its shell.

Negroes liked Islam. The prostrations pleased them, as well they might, being not only picturesque but an excellent health measure, as were the ceremonial ablutions. Like other Moslems, they found that the act of performing rites in company, as was often the case since they were at fixed times, was good for social goodwill, democratic sentiment—even for business. The dramatic privations of Ramadan, the month of starving by day and stuffing by night, excited them. Those few who could tackled the adventures of the pilgrimage—a tough adventure it was indeed to make the round trip from inner Africa to Mecca, but what prestige crowned the returning hadj. To him and to those he told of far lands it was education incomparable. Education—Islam also brought to the Negro a written language and a Book!

Mediterranean white Africa also liked Islam. In many ways as it was displayed in the early days of the invasion Islam suited their fashion of thinking and their emotions. Emphasis fell on men and mysteries instead of on theological theorizing. When later doctrinal arguments came they were offered with a human handle, so to speak, not as abstract ideas but as the vehicle for living individuals of powerful appeal.

The mysterious Mahdi fascinated the African mentality. In its exalted sense the term "Mahdi" meant that unique personage who would establish an ideal world—the "Expected Mahdi," a counterpart of the Messiah. He would, it was believed by some, first appear in the Far West. A profound local hope sprang up that he might first declare himself on the Moroccan Atlantic coast at the now dead city of Massa. The place became a resort for pilgrims, each hoping to be on hand to meet and greet him and join his blessed band. Some even worked out the date when he would arrive—1310, the seventh century by the Islamic dating system. But the "Expected Mahdi" never came to Massa. It was "delusion and stupidity," says Ibn Khaldun in the *Muqaddimah*.

But there were many Mahdis, men claiming direct descent from the Prophet Mohammed and the possession of mystic power, who did appear. A series of self-declared Mahdis have inflamed Africa since the early days of Islam.

Mahdis have made news in relatively modern times, some very powerful, some rather ridiculous. A noticeably upsetting Mahdi was the remarkable Sudanese who launched a conflict that killed Gordon and who was eventually crushed by Kitchener. Among the laughable Mahdi pretenders are a dozen different Mahdis who are said to have declared themselves simultaneously in Nigeria at the start of this century. In West Africa in comparatively recent times the redoubtable El Hadj Omar carried his mystic claims to the extreme by letting himself be regarded as the reincarnation of Jesus—"Omar Jesus" (meaning the Prophet Jesus of the Mohammedans).

In Moslem North Africa the religious element has almost always entered into politics and very often a movement big in history has been started by an alleged descendant of the Prophet. These descendants, the Sherifs, are the bluebloods of Moslem Africa and the founders of many dynasties. A dynasty which claims Sherifian origin now reigns in Morocco.

Africa's drama and discord, the greater part of all North Africa's history for centuries proceeded from the innocent career of an Arab girl who died at the age of twenty-three. Fatima, the Prophet's daughter, was Mohammed's treasure. Mohammed dreamed of perfume on the night she was conceived. She was listed by him as one of the four perfect women of all time. She was Mohammed's sole surviving child, his other children having died young. Thus her two sons were the ancestors of all the Sherifs, were the mystic basis for all the self-declared Mahdis—or so all the Sherifs and all the Mahdis have asserted.

Fatima became a saintly almost deified personage to a large section of the Moslems, symbol of womanly comfort to the oppressed and sacred as the unique perpetuator of the blessed blood of the Prophet.

She has been the subject of hyperdulia, almost a counterpart of the adoration of the Virgin in the Cult of Mary.

Fatima was the wife of Ali, the boy cousin of Mohammed who had been one of his very first converts, and since Mohammed had left no instructions as to a successor Fatima's husband thought that the position should be his. His claim was set aside. The disappointment seems to have hurried Fatima to the grave; she died following the premature birth of a third son.

Later Ali did become caliph, only soon to die assassinated. The almost cult of Ali was one of those branches which grow upon religions. Ali became to a large section of Moslems a figure which was nearly a deity. William James in *The Varieties of Religious Experience* tells of a modern Ali adorer who for thirty years never said a word except "Ali—Ali—Ali." Ali was, certain Moslem theologians have said, the same Biblical figure, the Suffering Servant whom early Christianity associated with Jesus. The Suffering Servant or God-man is older than the Bible, appearing in the mythology of Babylon. Those who made Ali a sacred hero plucked the idea from the air of the Near East. And from the air—the air sprayed with Gnostic imaginings—again they plucked the idea that Ali was infinitely superhuman, that he, along with Fatima and their two sons and the Prophet, had been created before the time of Adam. Some even maintained that it was Ali who rightfully should have been Allah's Prophet and the founder of Islam.

Ali, who inspired all this, does not seem to have been in actual life a very impressive individual, and he is said to have resented the effort to sanctify him and to have caused to be burned to death certain who broadcasted the theory that he was God.

The Shiites, the Ali party, were and are still one of the two great Moslem sects, though their prominence in Africa is no more. They split apart from the other great Moslem party, the Sunnites (orthodox). A further protestant group important in the early days was the Kharijites, or "Those Who Went Out," their slogan being something like "We hate Ali!", well proved by the fact that it was a Kharijite who murdered him. Their antagonism was not merely against Ali as an individual but against the tenet of the Ali party that in perpetuity Islam must accept a descendant of Ali and Fatima as the sole man worthy to be master of all the Moslems, b ally and temporally. This dogma of the heritage of a my divine spark was disgusting to the protestant and democ jites.

In the Middle Ages, Kharijitism was strong in Africa and at time the Kharijites nearly wrecked the power of the ruling Shiites. Now their African importance is trifling. Their main holding is a peculiar group of oases in the northern Sahara called the Mzab, so self-isolated for about a thousand years—their women have never been allowed to leave home—that this Berber community through inbreeding has developed or conserved something like a special physical character. They themselves say that they are the sole survivors of the unadulterated Berber race. Thus their hatred of Ali has actually led them to a unique racial situation.

To the African temperament there seems to have been something fascinating in the intrigue, the whispered talks and the rumors of plots and poisonings in which were involved the secret and surreptitious arrivals among them of the ambitious, mysterious, romantic almost sacred individuals who claimed to carry in their veins the blood of the Prophet via Fatima's mating with the revered Ali.

First come of these noblemen of Islam was Idris, whose son Idris II, the famous Moulay Idris, was the traditional founder of the city of Fez and via his corpse launched in spirit the Moroccan kingdom's modern government.

The first Idris was the great-great-great grandson of Mohammed and an opponent of the orthodox government of Islam, the Abbasids. By perilous and secret ways he fled to the western corner of Mediterranean Africa and at the end of the eighth century established a dynasty which lasted for about two hundred years.

To the Caliph Harun ER-Rashid he was dangerous, and the caliph sent a man to destroy him who was "daring, audacious, crafty and wicked, strong in argument, eloquent and deceitful." (I quote from *Roudh el-Kartas*.) This competent villain easily wormed his way into the confidence of Idris I and found means to poison him. How this was accomplished excited the African imagination for generations. Some say he bestowed upon Idris I a flacon of the poisoned perfume of the civet cat, at which he sniffed, fell unconscious and died (from El-Bekri, who described the poisoner as "a demon in human form"). Others attribute Idris' death to poisoned fish or eels. Other suggestions are too unpleasant to repeat. As the author of *Roudh el-Kartas* sagely remarks, "God knows the truth!"

His concubine, a brainy Berber woman named Kinza, was then pregnant. Idris II was born. By the time the boy was eight years old he knew the whole Koran by heart, or so we are told. I remind the reader that the Koran in English editions makes about four hundred printed pages. He assumed government when still a child and is credited with having founded the city of Fez when he was less than seventeen.

Now we come to the curious influence this man was to have on Africa in the centuries to come, even today. Moulay Idris was an immortal. Six hundred and nine years after he had died in mysterious circumstances—he choked to death on a grape, poison suspected —a remarkable discovery was made during the repairing of an old mosque. This was a human body in a perfect state of preservation which was pronounced to be that of Idris II. As a miracle this may seem to us dubious, but it was for Morocco an occurrence of great and lasting national import. It roused religious fervor and played into the hands of the ultra-religious element on the then confused political scene. To the credulous it showed that the *baraka* of Idris was a living thing in his body, undimmed after six centuries. (*Baraka* was a blessed spiritual atmosphere possessed by some and possessed to the highest degree by Mohammed, who transmitted it via Fatima to his descendants.) Thus the way was opened for a new dynasty which eventually took over, a Sherifian dynasty claiming, like the Idrisids, to descend from Mohammed through Fatima and Ali.

Sherifian sultans came to power. Certain are familiar to most of us: Ahmed el-Mansur (the Victorious), who sent soldiers on a seemingly impossible military expedition across the Sahara and conquered Timbuctoo, and Moulay Ismail, who startled Europe by asking France in the time of Louis XIV to send him a princess for his already overcrowded harem.

The belief in the mystic value of the *baraka* was unshakable. A ruler having it was a protection to the country. Westermarck tells of the confidence of the population. A ruler—he is speaking about Morocco—whose *baraka* was strong and pure caused crops to prosper, women to bear well-formed children and fishermen to catch abundant fish.

Some of the powers attributed to the *baraka* of those they revered seem fantastic, some rather touching. The *Rawdat en-Nisrin* (Garden of Wild Roses), a late fourteenth-century historic work about Fez, tells how the cap and pantaloons of a certain possessor of the blessing when shown to a woman in difficult labor would reduce her pains. The *Roudh el-Kartas,* composed a little earlier, recounts a miracle which befell a bearer of the *baraka*: he saw himself in a dream having a sexual ejaculation, "a jet of fire which rose in the air and shone upon the four cardinal points and then concentrated over Morocco." This was regarded as a joyous omen. (It requires mental agility to sympathize with the myths and superstitions of a religion other than our own.)

The strongest mystic blessing dwelt, of course, with members of Mohammed's family, and this family's genealogy grew vast and complex. The family tree of the Sherifian rulers of Morocco became as tall as a giant oak. A Spanish traveler who called himself "Ali Bey" was allowed in the first part of the nineteenth century to examine the genealogy of the then sultan (the same with whom the United States and England negotiated in the Barbary pirate days), and tells that it contained a series of thirty-odd names between Hassan, son of Ali and Fatima, and the Sultan Soliman. For comparison, the editor of Debrett's Peerage is quoted as saying that only fourteen English families trace titles back to the War of the Roses—in the fifteenth century. The Sherifian genealogy starts in the sixth.

Though the influence of Mohammed-Fatima-Ali line, which Idris brought to Africa, has survived till modern times it was another similar line which made a far deeper impression in early days, not alone in Africa but across Islam as a whole.

This family line founded Cairo—a memorial indeed to the little Arab mother who was "always a virgin," for the dynasty of Cairo's founder is called the Fatimids. Their power lasted for nearly three centuries, and for a time they were the strongest force in all Islam, overshadowing the Caliph of Baghdad.

The Mahdi who was the dynasty's founder shrewdly chose to declare himself in Mediterranean Africa, far from the enmity of his homeland. The Fatimid moral and military grab of northern Africa and later of Egypt was competently stage-managed at the start and eventually carried to its ultimate grandeur at Cairo by two men of genius.

The first was the "Dai," as Arabic historians call him, usually rendered into English as "Missionary," though he was a far different person from the missionary we know. He was the advance agent of the Fatimid claimant, or pretender. The pair, the Dai and the claimant to Mahdism, were respectively a man of single-minded devotion preparing the way for his revered master and the man who truly believed that he was the "Hidden Mahdi," or else they were a couple of slick adventurers. This was a question bitterly disputed at the time and of an oddly deathless interest to researchers. As recently as 1958 a study on the subject was published in Cairo by Dr. Husayn F. al-Hamdani. Ibn Khaldun, who is regarded as a prime source on the history of the Fatimids, took a generous view. A modern French historian calls the founder of the Fatimid dynasty "a prince of impostors."

In all events the advance agent succeeded in convincing the people of Mediterranean Africa. He enthused a simple, imaginative, sentimental people, naturally prone to adore a mysterious personage, prone to hero worship and brave in the fight for a ruler who combined sacred and temporal power. Those whom the Dai could not enthuse he tried to exterminate, though not with complete success, as shown by a later uprising. He launched the dynasty.

The second man of genius who took the Fatimids to greater glory was the ex-Christian and ex-slave General Jawhar—his name meant "Gem"—who consolidated the top of Africa for the Fatimids from the Atlantic to the Nile and had the new city of Cairo started and waiting when his master, fourth of the Fatimids, came to assume the proud rulership of Egypt.

After the Fatimids had been for two generations rulers in Egypt a religious maniac came to power who was so greatly intoxicated by the sacred heritage of his family that he went a step beyond the claims of Mahdism. A very big step it was: he announced that he was the Incarnation of God. This must have shocked his subjects, but perhaps less violently than one might suppose for Egypt was then deeply inclined to the mystic and the magical and the occult. And there may, too, have lingered still in the air of Egypt a memory of the old days when their rulers—Pharaohs, Ptolemies and even Romans—were self-deified. But the pretensions of this Fatimid eccentric were different. The God with whom he identified himself was the unique Allah, for whose name he caused his own—which was Hakim—to be substituted in mosque services.

Eventually he disappeared without trace. Probably he was assassinated for his public and personal cruelties, which had been monstrous, rather than for his religious idiosyncracies. However, he inspired a new Moslem sect, the Druses, who believed, still believe that as God's Incarnation he was immortal and that he has gone into some mystic concealment and will someday return. A renowned offshoot from one of the variations of such mystical thinking was that organization called the Assassins.

Another souvenir of the so-called "Mad Caliph" is a very important piece of history. Hakim ordered the destruction of the Church of the Holy Sepulchre at Jerusalem. The "profane labor" of destroying even the cave in the rock, which was revered as the actual Sepulchre, especially shocked Christianity. Though the church's reconstruction was permitted later Hakim's act was one of the big contributary causes of the Crusades.

Mad Hakim was the son of a Christian mother, said to have been a Russian, and the vizier who had to sign the decree for the demolition of the church was a Christian Copt. It is strange that a half-Christian ruler in Africa obliged a Christian hand to an action which largely provoked the Crusades that shook Europe and the East for centuries.

Cairo, which had been Fatima's gift to Africa, increased in grandeur as Baghdad diminished. Presently it became the intellectual center of Islam, and its University of Azhar, like the Karaouine of Fez (which celebrated its eleven hundredth anniversary in 1960), was earlier than any university of Europe.

Islam's men of letters came to Cairo and wrote its praises. European visitors were too often either enslaved women in harems or sad and silent prisoners from the Crusades. One of these prisoners was St. Louis of France, who saw Cairo's walls decorated with Christian heads and was himself saved by the payment of so enormous a sum that, as Joinville says, "they began to count the money for the ransom on Saturday in the morning, and they took for the counting the whole of Saturday and Sunday until night."

Those were the days of Africa's victories and opulence. The gold from inner Africa supplied money to waste. When the Fatimid general set out to capture Egypt he carried with him "one thousand loads of money," in the grandiloquent phrase of Ibn Khaldun. One can read in medieval Arabic history lush descriptions of the sumptuous costumes in which the rulers of the Fatimid and subsequent dynasties appeared at ceremonies, or of the royal umbrellas garnished with golden ornaments under which they sheltered from the African sun. But the whole picture is summed up in the simple statement that one of the Fatimid princesses possessed twelve thousand dresses.

White Africans from the western Mediterranean region and black African Moslems from beyond the desert marveled at buildings five stories high. Another outsized part of the Cairo scene which puzzled all visitors in the Middle Ages was the Pyramids. The medieval European notion was that they were "Joseph's Barns" from Pharaoh's day, in which grain was conserved, it being poured in through a hole at the top into the vast cavities at the Pyramids' base. Several questions, such as how it got out again, arise.

Edrisi mentions the possibility that it was Alexander the Great who erected the Pyramids as a companion effort to the building of the Alexandria lighthouse.

An interesting suggestion was advanced by a Spanish Moslem traveler and author named Ibn Jubayr, who saw Egypt in the days of Saladin, shortly after Saladin had ousted the Fatimids. Presumably the suggestion was a theory told him by local residents, and it explains only one of the Pyramids, which he himself inspected and measured. He thinks it was the tomb of Ad and his sons. Ad appears in the Koran and in Islamic traditions. He was the great-great-grandson of Noah and he fathered a tribe which turned out badly, being idolaters. They were gigantic people, from sixty to one hundred cubits tall. That was the reason for the enormous tomb.

Alexandria was still Alexandria the Great, but it was an altered sort of greatness. The lighthouse lit the way no longer to an intellectual center but to an international trade center. And with age the lighthouse itself was fading. Ibn Jubayr enthused about it in the year 1183, attributing its existence to "Great and Glorious God" and pronouncing it to be in a good state of preservation and visible for seventy miles. A century and a half later Ibn Battuta reported that one of the faces of the lighthouse was crumbling, and on returning to Alexandria some years later found the lighthouse was decaying into ruins. Soon afterward it was pulled down.

It had lasted for over sixteen centuries and was a symbol of that passage in Africa's life when the continent was in the middle of the world, a world center with many contacts—a passage which when the lighthouse fell was coming near to its end. Africa would presently shut her doors, or destiny would slam the doors, and her isolation would begin.

The lighthouse had shone upon a mixture of races and cultures and illuminated many different faiths. Alexandria was unique. Probably no city ever received so assorted a lot of people. The Copts of the country—the Egyptians—had mingled with Greeks and Jews, with Romans and all the various peoples and beliefs which accompanied them, with early Christian fathers, local-born and from the Near East, with Arabs and Moslems, with Berbers and Negroes—some pagan slaves, some Moslem converts. And now came jostling crowds of traders—European Christians and men from the Orient. Merchants from twenty-eight different Christian states, including England, were listed by a Jewish traveler who was in Alexandria in Fatimid times—some of these countries are no longer named on the map of Europe—plus a considerable number of Moslem localities. Alexandria had become "The Market of the Two Worlds."

Egypt was trade's bull's eye. She received goods from the East and exchanged them for the goods of Europe. There was as yet no route around the tip of Africa; Marco Polo's adventures suggest how difficult was the overland way to the Orient. The Crusades and local disorders impeded the route via Arabia and Syria. Egypt had practically a monopoly of the trade with India and even handled trade with China. Goods were landed at Red Sea ports, carried across country to the Nile and downriver to Alexandria. Marco Polo, who outlines the route with care, describes it as "the least difficult and shortest."

Egypt took 10 percent of the value of goods when imported and when exported. The ships incoming to Alexandria brought her much needed wood and iron and sometimes things more beautiful, such as those "rich and noble stuffs which were made in Italy," which Leo Africanus noted in the shops of Cairo—"cloths of gold, damask, satin," made for exportation, Leo thought, "for I can affirm I never saw them in Italy."

The exports were exotic. The choice was unlimited. A medieval Jewish traveler said, "There is nothing in the world you cannot find in the traders' warehouses of Egypt." He had the chance to examine a "list of the goods which came into Egypt and which the Gentiles take to Christian countries—3300 different kinds, mostly spices and medicines."

Ibn Jubayr, on pilgrimage and making from the Nile to the Red Sea to cross to Mecca, tried to count the caravans he saw along the road that were carrying Oriental goods toward the river, "but could not because of their number, especially those bearing the merchandise of India. The greater part of it was pepper. It seemed to our fancy to equal in quantity the dust." More pleasing to the nose were other Oriental things—cinnamon, incense, cloves, musk.

"There are 36,000 vessels which sail upstream to Upper Egypt and downstream to Alexandria laden with goods of all kinds," said Ibn Battuta, "and a continuous series of bazaars from the city of Alexandria to Aswan."

At Alexandria there were separate trading establishments and hostels for each nationality of foreign traders. At Cairo there was luxurious hostelry for commercial travelers from Europe. I wonder if these hotels had the same amenities as that Cairo hotel which is described by a visitor in Saladin's time, named Abd El-Latif. He reported that he lodged in a hotel possessing modern conveniences— bathrooms with faucets giving cold and hot water, an apparatus to distill and purify drinking water and a sewage system. This bit of

Africana is in humiliating contrast to conditions in contemporary European inns. The source is not a boastful Cairene but a Baghdad doctor whose observations historians take seriously.

This highly organized, blandly hospitable and very profitable trading system seems to have had a life of its own and, except for certain brief passages when Europe's Crusaders actually tackled Egypt itself, to have ignored the friction and the hatreds of opposed governments. The general battling and broiling of the Crusades rarely arrested the arrival of the wood and iron or the dispatch of the pepper and the spices. Yet meanwhile continued the ups and downs of the struggle between Moslem and Christian navies for the supremacy of the Mediterranean.

At the start of the Moslem invasion of Africa sea fighting or any sea travel or the mere aspect of the sea was new and alarming to Arabs of the Prophet's country, who were desert people. They had a cat's sentiment about great waters. The analysis of sea travel offered by the Arab leader who conquered Egypt has often been quoted: "The sea is like a great creature upon which weak creatures ride like worms upon a piece of wood."

But soon the Arabs became naval experts. They learned about the sea from the peoples they conquered and converted. To the new Moslems of the Mediterranean the sea and ships were no mystery.

The Berbers of antiquity worshipped the sea. Herodotus would have it that the Greeks got their knowledge of Neptune from the Libyans, and Westermarck believes that the Berbers of the far western corner of Africa were adorers of the ocean. Without doubt they were used to boats, and the Phoenicians of Carthage taught them new skills. Those were accomplished seamen who ferried Hannibal's elephants from Africa to Europe.

With Islam there came to the Berbers a certain change of attitude. The sea was no longer adorable. Some even dramatized the simple statement in the Koran that Allah "hath subjected the sea" into a myth: Allah had been obliged to discipline and humiliate the sea for its insolence by sending a magical little creature smaller than a mosquito who drank up all of the sea's water, then spat it out again— salt water now, which before had been sweet. That took the sea down a peg!

As for the Egyptians, the Nile, which split their country in two, had made them boat-conscious from primitive days. Some say that the earliest boats of which we have knowledge were theirs. There were large Nile boats in Dynasty I and at the end of the Dynasty III they ventured into the Mediterranean. Breasted mentions a surviving representation of Dynasty V ships that went to Phoenicia. Presently they were sailing down the Red Sea and on to Somaliland. One of the most romantic and well-recorded expeditions in ancient history is that of the incense seekers of Queen Hatshepsut, and later an Egyptian ruler sponsored a sea journey by Phoenicians which may have gone around the tip of Africa.

After Moslem power became strong the Inner Sea saw many Moslem naval victories. There was a time when their ships crisscrossed the Mediterranean in every direction and "the Christians could not put to sea even a plank." This was perhaps more boastful than true. There came a time when Europe attacked Africa brilliantly. Barbary pirates proved that Africa had not forgotten seamanship by carrying their raids even as far as Ireland.

But notwithstanding battles at sea and on land there was in those fine days no isolation of the African continent. To remote Negroland went rumors about Christian Europeans seen in the trading places, at Alexandria and lesser ports. At the port of Tripoli in Libya, to mention one among other points, business was such, says an early fourteenth-century observer, that ships were at anchor side by side "like horses in a stable." The Fatimids at one time employed five thousand sea captains.

The Fatimids were magnificent with the Cairo they created and their Alexandria, the world's most brilliant market, and the Idrisids very romantic, but the founders of these two lines were by no means the sole spectacular descendants or *soi-disant* descendants of Mohammed to make history in Africa.

The sacred aura had wide appeal. Several royal lines claimed such lofty lineage. Sometimes the claims were questioned: Were the Sherifian dynasties of Morocco truly Sherifian? The subject was discussed at length by El-Oufrani in *Nozhet-Elhadi*. The same sort of argument in the case of the Merinids, who reigned in Fez is set forth in *Rawdat en Nisrin*, where Ibn el Ahmar repudiates their claim. Similar querying exists about the Sherifian non-royal claimants, who were multitudinous. As Ibn Khaldun remarked with his usual cold wisdom, "The claim to Mohammedan descent is a great title to nobility . . . Therefore it is subject to suspicion."

In fairness we must mention that the vast number of those who claimed to descend from Mohammed was not in itself a cause for suspicion—one of his two grandsons, according to tradition, married more than two hundred women.

Far more solemn, though also subjected to query, were the claims of those mysterious and revered individuals who emerged from time to time as Mahdis. To Africans, who by nature loved the marvelous, the appeal of the Mahdi was irresistible. To the Mahdi claimant himself it was a risky adventure, often with a fatal finish.

Almost always the Mahdi emerged inimical to local authority. The credulous acceptance of the sacred claimant, his swift rise and almost inevitably swift fall are an indication of the temper of Mediterranean Africans of those days—keen and courageous hero worshippers, ultra-ardent in religion, inflammable but given to quick changes. Those were the years—the medieval years—when with Moslems, as well as Christians, religion was everybody's great emotional preoccupation, and in Mediterranean Africa it took also the place to some extent of nationalism, something which northern Africa could not really possess since Mediterranean Africa was geographically incoherent, an immensely prolonged strip between sea and desert or between sea and mountains.

Mahdis would come, gain a following and support, and would be forgotten. And then another would come. Here are a few as recorded by Africa's own historians:

There was Ibn Abi-Omara who in the late thirteenth century declared himself to be "The Long-Awaited." Incidentally, he gave out that he could transform any metal into gold. He took Kairwan, Sfax, Sousse and announced he was sultan. He went on in triumph and captured Tunis. Then disaster came. He was "put to all the tortures which men without pity are capable of inflicting," says the narrator, Ibn Khaldun, with bitter emphasis, justly indignant for his own great grandfather, finance minister at Tunis, had been arrested and strangled by the pretended Mahdi.

Less successful, though perhaps comprehensible, were the pretensions to Mahdihood advanced earlier in the thirteenth century by a member of the Fatimid family after the dynasty had been deposed by Saladin. He sneaked into Morocco and attempted to start a movement, was betrayed by one of his own band and killed.

Mahdi hopes glowed on in Africa's mind. Four centuries later there was uttered in Morocco the prediction that the True Mahdi would come soon, some reasons being—the list seems confusing—the successful expedition across the Sahara and conquest of Timbuctoo, the plague then raging, government uneasiness and the increasing cost of living.

Abou Mahalli gave out that he was the awaited one and had come to lead a holy war. He had his moment of power, marched on Marrakesh and was killed in battle. They cut off his head and hung it from the ramparts of the city, where, El-Oufrani tells us, it remained for twelve years. Notwithstanding this visible proof, his disciples believed their Mahdi was not dead but had disappeared and would one day return.

Two Mahdi curios among the many were the unfortunate innocent, a child whom certain Berbers inimical to the first Fatimid exalted as a rival, giving him the title of "Mahdi" and whom the Fatimids killed, and that strange figure who assumed the name of "Saleh" ("The Saint").

Saleh was a very early starter in the Mahdi series (eighth century) and a very bold one. He even announced as a sort of side line that he would oust Jesus as the chief of the Christians. He constructed a competitive Koran of his own, yet oddly hedged by stating as a sort of personal recommendation that his name, "Saleh," appeared in the Koran of Mohammed. Saleh made a great impression on Africa's imagination. Her historians record his pretensions at great length.

Another local prophet also wrote a Koran of his own, composing it in the Berber language. He was a man of magic powers, by name Hamim, who came of a family of magicians, and his claims went beyond Mahdism, for in his supposed sacred book he called upon his followers to say, "I believe in Hamim," also to say, "I believe in his Aunt Tanguit and in his sister," which seemed to be putting the

Hamims on the level with Allah. The two women were sorceresses, and the sister, El-Bekri assures us, was "one of the most beautiful women in the universe."

Hamim abolished the pilgrimage and said that—contrary to the prohibition of Islam—it was all right to eat pork, but specified that only the flesh of the sow was permitted food, for, he said, "Mohammed used the term for the male pig in his ruling but said nothing about the female pig." Another of his dietary rules was to forbid eating eggs—as indeed did the other prophet, Saleh—which oddly coincides with or was inspired by or in some fashion was the inspiration of that violent distaste for eggs as food often observed in Negroland.

But of all the Mahdis one stands out a giant, dubious in his Mahdi claim, perhaps deliberately tricky, perhaps self-fooled, but a man of power who cleverly used the Mahdi glamour to fascinate and consolidate his followers. Since he came from Berber mountain people the establishment of lineage from the Arab Prophet, a requisite to Mahdihood, presented obvious difficulties. At least three differing genealogies were invented and respectfully advanced, the matter being discussed with prudent reserve because of the vast prestige of the man, and carefully mentioned by various Moslem historians with pens that walk on tiptoe.

The empire he founded survived in itself, split among its heritors, and was the great force in Morocco, Algeria and Tunisia (I use the familiar names of modern geography) till the end of the Middle Ages, so strong at one time that it frightened the Egypt of the great Saladin with the menace of another conquest from the west as in Fatimid days. Its fleet was mistress of the western Mediterranean, and Saladin sent pleading letters to beg for its help against an anticipated Christian attack.

This mightiest of the Mahdis was Ibn Tumert (died 1130), the founder of the Almohads.

Africa's reactions to Islam are clues to her character. We have considered one of her reactions, her sensibility to the mysterious hero.

Another quite different aspect of Islam's effect was the resultant mingling of the two-colored Moslems—the white ones and the black ones—into a single Islamic mass. Islam was able to weave the black and white strands together, perhaps not into a fabric, but into a lacy web. Of this there are many indications.

Up from the Sudan, the central Sudan beside the Niger, came a mulatto, son of a Berber from northern Africa who crossed the Sahara as a trader, and a Sudanese Negro mother. This mulatto became a great leader of the whites of the north. He instigated a revolt against the Fatimids. His armies captured Kairwan and Tunis and drove the then Fatimid ruler to take refuge in Mahdiya, which the first Fatimid had built as a "protection for the Fatimids at a time of danger" and had named after his sacred title. (Later this was called "The City Africa" by Europeans.) The power of the Fatimids —this was in their earlier period, before they conquered Egypt and founded Cairo—was nearly wiped out.

The importance of this bit of history lies in the fact that a half-black African could and did become the leader of white Mediterranean Africans both as military chief and preacher.

No Mahdi, he, Makhled Ibn-Keidad of the two nicknames, Abu Yezid and "The Man on the Donkey," was on the other side of the Islamic theological fence, the Kharijite side, which scorned and murdered Ali. On his gray donkey he traveled and talked, preaching Kharijitism of a particularly extreme sort. Berbers listened. He opposed Fatimid control and again they listened. They had emerged from their first enthusiasm about the Mahdi and were getting tired of Fatimid pretensions and taxation. They returned to the Kharijite doctrine, which had been popular before the mystic Mahdi came. Kharijitism was a people's creed. Perhaps the extreme form which The Man on the Donkey preached, the name of which has been translated as "The Levelers," catered to the same craving for equality which made rebellious Berbers in the days of the Donatist schism drag the master from his chariot and make him run panting behind while the slave rode in his place.

Kharijites had indicated their democracy and their disregard for lofty lineage when the founders of the sect said, "Why, we would accept and revere as master and spiritual leader even a Negro slave if he were recognized as a man of great piety!"

The Man on the Donkey came halfway to proving the sincerity

of this statement, for he was half a Negro and was born of a slave mother. He was born at Gao on the Niger. His mother was presumably a pagan, for Gao had not yet been converted to Islam. Her name, Sebika, comes down to us. She was quite unconsciously a Negress of great importance, for she, the mere concubine of a trader, gave birth to a son who very nearly destroyed the Fatimids and so very nearly deprived the world of Cairo.

It was so close that in their last refuge, Mahdiya, the starving people were eating corpses. But The Man on the Donkey collapsed, failed, was captured and killed. A gruesome proof of Fatimid fears and the need they felt to make this enemy a ridiculous memory was that they caused his corpse to be skinned—perhaps the ghastly business started while he was still alive—and had the skin "filled with straw and placed in a cage for a plaything for two monkeys who had been trained for the job." (From Ibn Khaldun.)

The downfall of The Man on the Donkey, like his rise, was unaffected by race prejudice. He was merely another of Africa's heroes who came up quickly and slid down even more quickly from his pinnacle. It was his enemies who emphasized his black blood in the legends told of him after his fall. He was "a black and furious savage." Further details told of his hideous cruelties and of his lust, how he allegedly deflowered four virgins every night.

Again Islam showed how it could meld the continent together when, although the Sahara split Africa into two pieces, pious people of the Sahara itself hyphenated the two pieces together. This happened when a group of Berbers of the desert pushed with religious fervor into the land of the Negroes to the south and almost simultaneously into Mediterranean Africa. Having established power in Spain and Portugal, these Middle-of-Africa people eventually held dominion over one of the largest empires of those or any other pre-colonial times.

These Saharan conquerors were veiled white men, like the Tuareg of today, whose tribal brothers they were as members of the Berber Zenaga tribe. The Zenaga spread from the Atlantic to Libya. In Arabic history their name is rendered as Senhadja, early European travelers called them Azanaghas, Azounas, etc., all variations of the name of the same great tribe which was said to possess seventy branches. The Zenagas were known to Ptolemy the geographer. They gave their name to the Senegal River and to a modern nation—a Negro nation, although the Zenagas were white—the Senegal Republic.

The Zenagas of the desert were people of dash and daring, the Vikings of the Sahara and Barbary Pirates of the sands, preying upon caravans, taking their profit from the continent's trade in the days when, the Nile excepted, there was no way to get from the north to the south and back again except by the camel route across the sands.

The branch of the Zenaga to which belonged the conquerors whose feats of religion and arms sewed Africa together were the Lamtuna, known during their days of triumph as the Almoravids. Theirs was a conquering shuttle back and forth across the Sahara and beyond, and must have startled and enlightened both the Negroes and the whites.

Men who seemed white pushed into Negroland. Men who seemed to the stay-at-home North Africans to be nearly black, colored anyway, pushed into Mediterranean Africa, for the Almoravids were white men with dark skins, and among them were probably some with a fraction of Negro blood, possibly some full-bred Negroes.

The Almoravids were rather recent converts to Islam. What had been their religious status before is uncertain. Ibn Khaldun says they were idolaters. Others suggest that they may have been Christians. On the ground of simple probability one inclines toward Ibn Khaldun's belief. At any rate they were slack in their Mohammedanism. A certain chief, having himself experienced a religious awakening, imported a holy man to read the Koran to them and teach them Islam's moral code.

They rebuffed the moral code, and the holy man, pained and indignant, retired to a hermitage upon an island presumably in the Senegal River. Remorse and curiosity led many to follow him, and his community grew into what Islam called a *ribat*.

A *ribat* was a fortified holy place. Starting from the days of the Arabic invasion, *ribats* were established across the top of Africa for defense and as centers for the Holy War. Interesting claims were made about these *ribats*: that they made it possible to communicate in a single night by a system of signals from Ceuta at Gibraltar to Alexandria in Egypt and that there was a series of *ribats* stretching across Islam from the Atlantic to China.

Of them all the most famous was the island warrior hermitage founded by the Lamtuna's holy man. This group was called "the men of the ribat," from which came eventually the rather clumsy European rendering Almoravids.

The Lamtuna of the island started a Holy War to compel the rest of their tribe to piety and the mending of their morals. This developed into a campaign of general conversion hither and yon, across and up and down the great spaces. With a mingling of fervor and ambition they captured Ghana, the gold market and took possession of the secret "Mountain of Gold." They drove far into the land of the Negroes. They drove into Morocco and Algeria. They drove across to Spain and Portugal. They founded a capital, a new city, Marrakesh, "The Baghdad of Africa," so called, from whose name comes that of the whole country of Morocco. Traditionally the city's name meant something like "Hurry! Step lively!" in the Berber language, it having been located in a dangerous place where brigands used to wait for caravans.

The Almoravid king won the title of "Ruler of Both Shores"— Africa and Europe. The Veiled Men, as Arabic history calls them, had conquered from deep in Negroland to Porto and Lisbon and the Pyrenees. In Spain they took over from a quantity of minor princes who were each, in the words of a poet of the times, "like a cat that blows itself up to imitate a lion." Christians, too, they vanquished. It was during their conquests that the romanticized hero, the Cid, played his part and died and that was fought the battle of Zalaca, so awesomely described in Arabic history, where Alphonso VI is said to have escaped with only a hundred of his people while eighty thousand of his cavaliers and two hundred thousand of his foot soldiers were killed, their heads being sent as gruesome souvenirs to various spots in Africa "so that men might thank Allah."

Propelled and amalgamated by Islam, men of the Sahara had founded an empire that encompassed a great slice across the continent from the Atlantic to Tunisia, some fifteen hundred miles, while from south to north its outermost points were nearly two thousand miles apart from the Niger to the Pyrenees.

Did the Almoravids, one wonders, rule all this from behind the veils which had made them notorious at the start? The name "Veiled Men" stuck to them in history. Speaking about Saharans in general, El-Bekri said, "The veil is a thing they do not quit any more than their skins." But it is significant that the face of Yusuf ibn-Tashfin, the second of their dynasty, is described in *Roudh el-Kartas* as having a brown complexion, aquiline nose, small beard, which indicates that he, at any rate, lifted his veil. Incidentally, and suggestive of a Negro strain, he had kinky hair. His son and successor, Ali ibn-Yusuf, whose mother was a Christian captive surnamed "The Perfection of Loveliness," is described as having a white complexion, proof that he, too, went veil-less.

Empires are fragile. The Almoravid empire collapsed. The rising Almohades killed their last ruler. Ibn Khaldun says that these people of a hard desert breed were ruined by the luxury of town life. They had leaped too suddenly into the bed of ease. To this add an element more mental than physical.

The Mahdi of the Almohades preached the Almoravids off their throne. Islam, the great mixer of Africa, had brought the Veiled Men of the Sahara to the Mediterranean and beyond and taken them down deep into the land of the Negroes, and Islam—a quarrel about Islamic dogma—destroyed them. Heresy, the old-time disturber of Africa in its Christian days, again raised its destructive head. The Almoravids, who had fought and died for Islam—and their own ends, were accused of the theological crime of anthropomorphism.

The Almoravids were infidels, the Mahdi cried, more fit to be attacked in a Holy War than the Christians or the idolaters.

It seems strange that an empire some two thousand by fifteen hundred miles square should have changed hands for a question of dogma. The losers in the dispute, the Almoravids, understood sacred texts literally, gave a naïvely realistic interpretation to what the Koran said about Allah, so that to them God took on bodily attributes and became in a way manlike. They took their point of view so seriously and vigorously that in public and with ceremony and by royal Almoravid orders they burned the great book of Islam's famous philosopher and mystic, *Ihya Ulum al-Din,* a verification of the knowledge of Islam, by Ghazali and in all the wide Almoravid Empire any existing copies of Ghazali's works were condemned to destruction. (Africa was by then becoming book-conscious. The great mosque at Marrakesh was known as the Mosque of the Book-sellers, in front of which were one hundred book stalls to either side.)

Perhaps the Almoravid way of thinking proceeded from a craving on the part of these recently pagan Saharans for the religious companionship of their ancestors, who could depend upon the visible image or the sanctified animal or place, or upon some touchable, caressable fetish. Perhaps the Almoravids felt lonesome in Islam's very spiritual atmosphere with only the remote comfort of the immaterial, intangible and impersonal Allah of the Moslem ultra-pure monotheism. "Allah is One, the Eternal One. He begot not, nor was He begotten. None is equal to Him," says the Koran. And when telling about the Creation in six days the Koran says specifically, "no weariness touched Us." Islam opposed the idea that Allah "rested" on the Sabbath; repose for Allah was an anthropomorphism.

There have been many cravings similar to those of the Almoravids, witnessed by an insistence upon or a curiosity about the Almighty's physical attributes. I read that St. Augustine after his conversion to Christianity looked back with disgust at the Manichaeism from which he had emerged and its notion of "God with corporal form . . . whether he hath hair and nails." (From his *Confessions.*) I read that Philo insisted that God was "without feet . . . without hands . . . without eyes," that Maximus of Tyre cited Plato that God had no color or size. I read that Maimonides expressed anger at an early Jewish treatise which purported to give the bodily dimensions of God, that Eusebius deplored "the anthropomorphism of the Old Testament." Such repudiations of anthropomorphism show by their very emphasis that there was a considerable general longing to ascribe human characteristics to the Divinity.

Oddly Islam, whose longing for contact with the Divinity was indirectly gratified by the human Mohammed, who was Allah's public relations man, and in Africa frequently re-gratified by political leaders who traced descent to the Prophet, accused Christianity of being a wickedly anthropomorphic faith, and also of committing the grave sin of attributing associates to God. They frequently referred to Christians as "the polytheists" or "believers in a partnership." The Trinity, which sometimes also confuses Christians, was non-comprehensible to Moslems in any other sense. To them Christianity was tritheism. Some Moslems got the notion—Mohammed himself had it—that the Trinity consisted of God the Father, the Virgin Mother and their Child Jesus.

To Moslems who disapproved of any art form which represented living things (Mohammed is said to have objected to chess because of the little figures of the chessmen) the Christian habit of showing the Divinity in human form in paintings and the like was regarded as idolatrous. Indeed the adoration of such forms of art was violently deplored by a great body of medieval Christians, as Byzantine history shows in the prolonged and ferocious disputes and warring between the Iconophiles, called Iconodules, and the Iconoclasts.

Islam as it moved into pagan Africa was to meet and sometimes almost to domesticate graver embarrassments than the theological impropriety of anthropomorphism.

THE DARKER MOSLEMS · Islam worked its way among the pagans of darker Africa by various methods and routes, slowly and with confused results.

Despite Islam's horror of idolatry—a mania almost—the meetings of Islam and paganism were not in Africa a bloody process on the whole. The Koran incited true believers to harshness toward infidels.

To idolaters there was to be only the choice between conversion or death. Says the Koran, "Therefore strike off their heads and strike off the ends of their fingers . . . and they shall also suffer the torment of hell fire," and, a few lines further on, praises those pious Moslems who "have fled their country and employed their substance and their persons in fighting for the religion of God." Elsewhere we read that Moslems "promised to fight men of all colors" for Islam's sake.

It seems significant or suggestive that sura number eight of the Koran, which I have quoted and which was the favored inspirational literature used by the Mohammedan promoters of Holy Wars, has the title "The Spoils," meaning "Booty." (Each sura has its title, some are rather puzzling, such as "The Cow," "Iron," "The Ant," "The Blood Clots," etc.) This title hints at a motive which would have practical appeal, at a tangible reward for an aggressive religious campaign.

But geography was stronger than the Koran. It was geography which dictated and determined Islam's conversion methods in Africa. Islam sailed southward along the East Coast. There is a picturesque tradition that Persian Moslems arrived at a region nearly 10 degrees below the Equator before the end of the tenth century and established at Kilwa an Islamic state. Their leader was son of the Sultan of Shiraz, who supposedly had left home in pique because the fact that his mother was an Ethiopian slave was humiliating. Alternate reason for the Shiraz expedition was the evil dream of the sultan himself about a rat with an iron snout, presage of danger to Shiraz. The traditions may be over-fanciful, but there is no doubt that Islam came early to Kilwa, as well as to other places down Africa's East Coast, including Zanzibar.

Islam's influence sailed far but seems to have penetrated very slowly inland. Ibn Battuta, the mighty traveler, was in this part of the world in the early fourteenth century and found the people of Mombasa "pious and possessed of well-built mosques," then continued south-ward to Kilwa, whose people were "jet black." Their ruler was "vir-tuous" and observed the rules of the Koran. But right beside their town were "heathens." So it remained. It was not until relatively modern times that Islam pushed deep into East Africa.

On the other side of the continent Islam's efforts were impeded but not permanently blocked. On the West Coast sea travel did not yet exist. There was the sand wall of the Sahara. Cross-Sahara military ventures leading to conversion by force were almost impossible. We have mentioned that of the Almoravids their point of departure was in the Sahara itself.

I know of two lightning jabs into the desert in the very early years of the Arab invasion, neither of which advanced the cause of Islam's religion. They were made respectively by Sidi Okba and his grandson and are recounted by Ibn Abd-el-Hakem, the ninth-century historian whose account of the Arab conquests in Africa is the oldest document we possess.

Sidi Okba, the same Mohammedan enthusiast who rode into the Atlantic and rebuked the waves for curtailing the further spread of Islam, went something like two thirds of the way across the central Sahara. His missionary work was more ferocious than effective. He followed the sura "The Spoils" literally and cut off fingers and ears along the way and demanded heavy tribute in the form of slaves.

His grandson tackled the western desert and reached the Sudan and Ghana, performing an expedition that was short and profitable and returning with "enormous booty" but with conversions null.

It was not practicable to convert the pagans of inner Africa by the method recommended in "The Spoils," though the prospect of spoils was dazzling—that gold with which people believed mid-Africa was stuffed like a cushion.

By a compromise method Islam entered inner Africa on tiptoes and gently by way of the trader-cum-missionary. It was difficult and dangerous and slow.

The trade part was very enticing. That gold of Africa, whose location was kept secret, was a trader's dream, everybody's dream, the foundation of Africa's fame and fortunes and misfortunes and wide-flung business—one could draw a check in Baghdad and cash it in Morocco. To golden bait was added the prospect of slave buying for the Eastern market. Profits were startling. Articles that were trashy and cheap like beads and bright cloth were eagerly bought on the desert's lower rim. But most in demand was salt.

Salt they lacked in Negroland and salt they craved and the salt from the Saharan mines, of which traders' caravans could add a supply on their route southward, was supposed to be the best, a veritable life-saver. "At the season of the year of the great heats their blood corrupts and putrefies," wrote Ca'da Mosto, telling of the Saharan salt trade, "and if it were not for salt they would die. They take a little piece of salt and dissolve it in water and drink this every day." A surprising case of primitive medical instinct.

Tradition says that there were localites in the gold-producing lands where salt could be exchanged "measure for measure" for gold. Right up to modern times salt values were astronomical. The Frenchman Binger, when exploring in the 1880's the country of which he became the first colonial governor, now the Ivory Coast Republic, found salt selling at ten francs the kilogram. This was the old gold franc, so salt cost nearly one gold dollar per pound. I have seen merchants at small trading points south of the Niger chopping blocks of Saharan salt into little pieces as carefully as if they were precious metal. Salt money was the currency used in some regions. Alvares remarked it in Ethiopia in the sixteenth century and Raffray in the late nineteenth observed the same, the salt coins about nine inches long and very thin; a historian of Marchand's disappointing race toward Fashoda tells that in the lower Congo salt was "the only money." (Hadn't it supposedly won converts to Christianity?) The British consul in Liberia from 1913 to 1920, R. C. F. Maugham, told about "salt sticks about as thick as a man's forearm which were currency in the hinterland."

These trans-Saharan traders, if they got back alive, earned high profits. But many perished. Crossing the Sahara until recently—the first automobile crossing was accomplished by the Citroën expedition in 1922–23—was one of the very dangerous adventures: thirst death, death by sandstorm, death by brigands' attack. But so it was by such courageous and greedy messengers that Islam penetrated into Africa's depths.

Every Moslem was an involuntary missionary by the mere fact of his behavior. His very actions, especially the prostrations, roused pagan curiosity. His book, the Koran, when a learned man was in the traders' company, was an amazing thing and fascinating to people who till then were unaware of writing. That marks upon paper communicated words from eye to eye was a sort of magic. Paper itself became and continued to be magical, something alarming, to be treated with reverence and fear. Binger tells how gifts wrapped in paper or with a label on them would be refused as dangerous. Pagan Africa's first sight of the Koran must have been a startling experience.

There is pathos in the legend which tells how Islam came along with the book to a region in what is now the Chad Republic. In the long ago a local ruler found a copy of the Koran under a tree. He had never seen a book and did not know what it was, but suspected it was a magical object. So he slaughtered a black goat and respectfully wrapped the mysterious thing in the animal's skin. As the years passed succeeding rulers imitated his act, sacrificing more black goats and adding more skin covers to the bundle. Finally arrived a young stranger who unwrapped the Koran, explained its meaning and all the people were promptly converted to Islam.

Many pagans resented Islam. And these were not always the less intelligent members of the Negro public, as Maurice Delafosse found from his wide study of Africans. His opinion carries authority. Delafosse was a twenty-year resident in Africa, part of the time as colonial governor, was co-translator from the Arabic of the famous Sudanese work *Tarikh el-Fettach,* wrote a book about more than sixty of the languages of West Africa and composed the three-volume, over 1100-page book entitled *Haut-Sénégal-Niger*—and no valuable book ever had a poorer title. Its title is meaningless, was meaningless before it was published, being the name adopted and almost immediately discarded for a big section of French colonial West Africa.

So this important piece of writing became a pathetic lost creature—a book in search of its subject! This is regrettable, for in its presentation of the peoples, languages, history and civilizations of a wide tract of the continent, homeland of some of the most interesting of all the world's Negroes, it is a book which though half a century old would be a treasure in these days when we are trying to understand the African background and psychology—if only it could summon the reader and the student with a comprehensible title.

Africa's geography is slippery. Many corresponding losses of name significance can be expected along with corresponding confusion in book titles. Some time ago "Mali" and "Ghana" took the place of "Sudan" (French) and "Gold Coast," and "Malawi," etc., and others follow. How long will cumbersome and uncouth inherited colonial names like "Upper Volta Republic" be acceptable national handles to their peoples?

Sometimes there were ugly incidents between old pagans—and how old was paganism? As old as Africa's thought—and the Moslem neophytes in the world's religions which had popped up only a few centuries before. Revered idols were ill used. Mosques were rudely located in sacred groves. Angry pagans defiled the mosques. Something of this sort happened when missionaries from pious Mali came to convert Kano in what is now known as Nigeria.

Mali, whose name is revived by the Mali Republic, had been a fairly early convert to Mohammedanism insofar as its rulers were concerned, though there were many pagans in its vast empire—Maqrizi said it would have taken a man three years to walk across it. It had copper, it controlled the gold mines, the salt mines and the rich trade near the Senegal and Niger rivers, plus a lot of jungle country. The people of Mali and their successors, the Songhai, dominated such big empires as had Rome in her successful colonial days, and such as some modern nations have lately liquidated.

It was Mali's Moslem emperor who appeared on Europe's medieval maps—a black man with a gold ball in his hands—and who made a spectacular pilgrimage, five hundred slaves marching before him, each carrying a staff of gold. When he passed through Cairo on his way to Mecca the Sultan of Egypt, the renowned Nasir, welcomed him with enthusiasm, and instead of insisting upon the customary prostration before his throne invited the Mali Moslem emperor to sit alongside him.

But Islam in Negroland was then and always distributed in a spotty fashion. Sometimes, but rarely, groups of relatively recent Islamization undertook Holy Wars against their neighbors. The first great Askia of the Songhai Empire on the Niger conducted such a sacred slaughter against the Mossi, important pagans in what is now called the Republic of Upper Volta. Askia Mohammed first sent an emissary to the Sultan of the Mossi, calling upon him to join the Moslem faith. The sultan said he would have to consult his ancestors, for the Mossi held their forebears in intense reverence. He permitted the emissary to be present at the consultation at which an aged man appeared and said, "No!"

Afterward the emissary had the chance to speak privately with the aged man. "Who are you really?" demanded the emissary. "I am Iblis [one of the devil's Islamic pseudonyms]," said the pseudo ancestor. "I led the Mossi astray intentionally, so that they may die as unbelievers."

The anecdote is from a Moslem pen—it is told in the *Tarikh es-Soudan,* and it is colored with the anti-pagan prejudice of much of the early written history of Negro Africa since Arabic writing which was the by-product of Islam was all that was available.

Askia Mohammed, the story goes on, attacked, killed many and took captives who turned to the faith of their captors. The Mossi country as a whole remained firmly pagan. This, says the *Tarikh es-Soudan* was the only Holy War in the region. The Sudanese historian wrote of what he knew. Later events altered the picture.

Long after the *Tarikh es-Soudan* was written inner Africa experienced violent holy warring within herself, into which entered in some cases the element suggested by the sura's title "The Spoils," or which combined religion with the search for power and was sometimes a reaction against Christian intrusion.

There was the Holy War—the jihad—and Nigerian conquest of Osman dan Fodio, the Fula. How much of this brilliant effort was of religious inspiration and how much was motivated by lust for conquest has been the subject of much argument. There was Fula religious fighting also in the Guinea and Sierra Leone region. And along the upper Niger, Amadou made Holy War against the pagan Bambara, built himself an ephemeral empire, was a self-styled prophet, a claimant of descent from Mohammed and called himself "Prince of True Believers." There was El-Hadj Omar, already mentioned, who, some said, was the reincarnation of Jesus (the Koranic Jesus) and some called Mahdi. And Samory, whose religious sentiments were probably much diluted by ambition. There was the Sudanese Mahdi and the so-called "Mad Mullah" of Somaliland, who runs us into the start of this century.

So Holy Wars or wars that were more or less holy washed a bloody wave across the continent from the Atlantic to the Red Sea for more than a century.

The result of Islam's drives both gentle and bellicose is that almost one third of Africa's total population was Moslem when colonialism gasped and African independence drew its first deep breath. At that time one half of Africa was pagan (described as "primitive or religion unknown, or none"). Figures on the religious position of Africans are of necessity non-exact and are startlingly variable, but it seems indisputable that when Africa began to emerge from colonization pagans were the big majority and the reality behind the estimated figures might give paganism an even stronger lead. There is said to be a present-day increase of Moslems.

When de-colonization began there were an estimated thirty-four million Christians in Africa, a post-colonization crop with a few exceptions, such as the Copts of Egypt, the Ethiopians and the early white South Africans, and a crop whose future now seems uncertain. Continued loyalty to a faith and a code of behavior taught by the colonial master who has moved away is unsure. Conversions were not always authentic. And there is the impression in local minds that the foreign missionary, along with his earnest desire to convert pagans, had a conviction of racial superiority and his own patriotic ideas. We have noted that groups of foreign missionaries have been expelled from new nations—Sudan, Chad, Congo. Paganism is very old and very strong. Islam predates colonialism by many centuries (with the exceptions noted above) and to some extent has melded with the primitive sentiments and attitude.

As Islam moved in it often seemed that paganism and Islam lived together in Negroland in a way that would be impossible to parallel in a medieval European setting. In Africa there was no St. Bartholomew's Night, no Albigensian Crusade. It was a manifestation of African tolerance and suppleness, that characteristic which made Africa accept Europe's colonization with elasticity.

The capital city of Ghana was really two cities, six miles distant from each other. One was Moslem, one pagan, where the king lived and where was the sacred grove which sheltered the idols. But in this pagan city there was a mosque where, so El-Bekri says, "Moslems who came to do business with the monarch could go to say their prayers." Timbuctoo, despite its important mosques and its university, which was a renowned center of Moslem learning, and despite the pompous statement in the *Tarikh es-Soudan* that the city "was never soiled by the cult of idols," was in a varying and dubious religious position. Under the alleged "roofs of gold" slept many pagans.

The very early European explorers noted the uncertain and muddled situation as they pushed into the continent. The narratives of Mungo Park and René Caillié, each of whom traveled deep into the interior—between them they investigated and in some cases were the first Europeans ever to tell about sections whose modern names are Mauritania, Senegal, Mali, Sierra Leone, Gambia, Guinea, Ivory Coast, Park telling of the Niger, Caillié about Timbuctoo—give a picture of religious confusion.

It seems as if just a single day's march could bring contacts with Moslems and pagans and people who straddled the two. Lander, who was later to settle the great "Where does the Niger go?" question, in his account of an earlier adventure in the Hausa country which he shared with Clapperton and which he alone survived, continuously speaks of "idolatry and Islamism so blended into each other that it would be difficult to draw a line." Laing, who first of European explorers saw Timbuctoo but was murdered before he could write an account of the place, explored the back blocks of Sierra Leone and wrote a careful book. Of one important tribal section he said, "The king being a Mohammedan whilst his subjects are principally Pagans, a system of toleration is established."

Islam was more important to Africa as a drawing string that pulled the continent and the two races together than as a purely religious influence. In Negroland a lot of paganism survived, even in supposedly Moslem regions, and mixed in with Islam, and its Islam, even when undiluted, was usually of an elementary, rudimentary sort.

It was hard for the converted pagans to put away the beliefs which had been their comfort through the ages, hard to forget old fears, hard to discard the peculiar and to us sometimes disgusting trappings of idolatry and to forego the potent value of human sacrifice.

They clung to their magic. They decked themselves in amulets, and many of them insistently retained that pagan totemism with taboo attachments which is variously named in Africa and often known as *tana*. The dogma of Islam opposed this, and sometimes Negro Moslems would seek to discover or would invent Islamic legends which would explain and justify their sentiment toward the revered animal which was the spiritual ancestor of their tribe or group.

This mystic association of themselves with some animal or other was both a religious sentiment and a sort of social background which probably marked a very early system of political get-together, the beginnings of tribalism. Freud expounds this idea in *Totem and Taboo,* and I find a delightful suggestion in Huizinga's remark, "To the men of the Middle Ages the coat of arms was undoubtedly more than a matter of vanity or of genealogical interest. Heraldic figures in their minds acquired a value almost like that of the totem."

In Africa the totem animal was treated with veneration, to kill or hurt it was a crime, to eat its flesh was as wicked, detestable and disgusting as cannibalism is to ourselves—even worse, for one who ate the totem animal by mistake and unaware is said, when he learned what he had done, even years afterward, to have died in self-horror. The eating of the totem animal was like the eating of the beloved and revered. Africa showed our own cannibal prejudice, the loathing we have toward eating one of the group to which we belong.

The totem animals covered almost all of Africa's zoology, one being that romantic creature, the manatee, supposed inspiration of the mermaid myth. There were manatees in the Niger, and its choice as a mythical ancestor is rather easy to understand, for the manatee has an almost human face, female breasts and carries its infant under its arm like a human mother. It is said that the manatee was acknowledged to be sacred even into modern times by a group near the Niger who were long-time Moslems and even claimed to be Sherifian, that is, descendants of Mohammed! The hippopotamus has been a widely accepted patron. It was the totem of the distinguished Keita family; the Mali emperor whose representation adorns the medieval map with a gold ball in his hand was of the Keita family; the last of the Mali dynasty, a relatively humble chief, was a Keita; the name of the first President of the Mali Republic was Keita.

The original choice of this or that animal by various groups was often attributed by local legend to the kindness one such animal had shown to their people in the long ago because the animal was conscious that there was some tie between itself and the group in question. A Fulani clan in Senegal migrated across dry country, and when they were near death by thirst a hidden water supply was intentionally and carefully revealed to them by a large edible lizard. A widely distributed family in Guinea, now Moslems, conserve the memory as sacred of the snake of goodwill of their pagan days. A mother had left her baby alone and crying in the hut. His crying ceased suddenly. Surprised, she returned and to her horror saw that a viper was alongside her child. Then she saw that the child was sucking the viper's tail contentedly, as if it were the mother's teat, and presently the viper quietly slipped away. One can say that this family in their choice of a totem animal forbidden as food shrewdly picked a non-appetizing creature that would not be missed on their menu.

Totemism was hard to relinquish at the behest of Islam. It was a manifestation of Africa's feeling of closeness between animals and mankind.

An interesting part of Islam's adventures in inner Africa was the editing and transformations of the careers of some of the Koranic personages who also figure in the Old Testament. Eve received imaginative treatment in a Sudanese (now Mali) version: Eve, called merely "Adam's wife" in the Koran and Awa in the Sudanese legend, saw to her innocent bewilderment a face—her own—reflected in a puddle made by the devil's urine and took the face for another woman, and was told by the scheming devil that it was her rival, whom Adam loved. Thus Awa yielded to temptation.

Africa's Moslems were especially fascinated and moved to revise the story of the Flood, and I submit that one of its versions contains some of the oddest details and adornments to be found on the subject. This is perhaps a big claim for the Deluge has a wide literature. Its anthology would be immense, starting probably with Manu of Sanskrit memories, whose benevolent fish piloted him to the top of the Himalayas, and running through Utnapishtim in the Epic of Gilgamesh and the Sumerian Ziusudra, and the Old Testament tale and that of the Koran, and "the greatest Deluge of them all," which Plato says wiped out the continent of Atlantis, and picking up a

Chinese Noah who "had a large head and red eyes, disheveled hair and a mournful appearance," and pausing to consider with respect the old theory of which Mircea Eliade reminds us, that the Flood is a symbol which was realized in "Christ, the new Noah, rising victorious from the Waters to become the head of a new race."

Negro Africa's story of Noah is unique in Deluge literature, insofar as I know, because it is the first told by a jinnee. His name was Chambarouch and his story is given in the sixteenth-century *Tarikh el-Fettach*, written in Timbuctoo by a Negro. It tells how the origin of the peoples of the western Sudan was involved with Noah.

Before the Deluge, Noah had befriended a certain giant named Oudj, who was "the biggest man on earth." (Noah himself was believed to be gigantic; his tomb near Damascus was reported by Ibn Jubayr to be thirty *ba'* in length. A *ba'* was the measure of two arms extended.) It was Oudj whom Noah told to collect wood to build the Ark. Noah then gave Oudj some magic bread, so that for the first time in his life the giant's appetite was satisfied. The Deluge came. Oudj climbed to a mountaintop, the water coming up to his chest, and cooked himself meals of fish in the sun.

When the Flood was over, Oudj, who did things in a big way, slept for a year and in his sleep had an amorous dream whose torrent swept over five of Noah's slave women and resulted in the birth of twin babies—a boy and a girl—to each of them. Oudj lived long thereafter but came at last to a tragic end, being killed by Moses because on the side of Pharaoh he had tried to crush the people of Israel with a great rock.

When the children Oudj had fathered grew up Noah gave them permission to live beside the Niger as fishermen on the condition they should carry part of their catch to Noah. This, fish being perishable, would seem to locate Noah's post-Deluge residence in nearby Inner Africa, which conforms with other local legends, such as that causing Nigeria to have been Noah's birthplace and Bornu to mean the "Country of Noah" (Ber-Noh) and another which makes a town in what is now the Republic of Chad the site where the Ark finished its voyage, bringing as passengers the tribal ancestors.

Chambarouch's story and the rest remind us of the many legends of ancient Jewish presence in the sub-Sahara—the "seven princes descended from the King of the Jews," and others.

The high importance and in this case prestige attached to jinn is indicated by the care and respect with which Chambarouch is mentioned and his story is reported in *Tarikh el-Fettach*. Like all jinn, he was usually invisible, and his story was communicated via one of his followers. He was the chief of a jinn tribe, an erudite historian and a pious Moslem.

To us the jinnee seems a vague creature encountered in Oriental wonder tales.

To Moslems the jinnee was a superman on whom Allah had practiced creating before he undertook to make men and on whom he had used superior material. Says the Koran of this pre-Adamic effort, "we created man of dried clay . . . and jinn we had before created of subtle fire." Certain jinn became Moslems, influenced by Mohammed in person. A sura in the Koran entitled "Jinn" tells about this, and at the place where the sura was allegedly revealed to Mohammed, Richard Burton says that he visited a commemorative mosque.

Some jinn, like some of mankind, were good, and some were naughty. Chambarouch was one of the very good jinn. He made ten pilgrimages to Mecca. He had talked with Mohammed and he was at the time *Tarikh el-Fettach* tells about adviser to Sudanese royalty.

As a group the jinn of Africa came to assume in the popular fancy the place of what we call "luck"—those happenings which harm or help us without reason. It might be an invisible jinnee who made a brick fall from a roof and knock out a man's brains, or it might be a jinnee who in secret brought a poor woman an unexplained gift of gold pieces. It was a jinnee who caused some sudden deadly sickness. Jinn seem especially to have excited the imagination of Negro Moslems, for jinn recalled the magic elements of the paganism it was so hard to forget.

It was natural that in places where Islam and idolatry came close together some of the obstinate pagans showed antagonism or exuberant contempt toward the nearby Moslems. Sometimes they would openly and scornfully mimic Mohammedan prostrations in a sort of comic dance.

Then sometimes pagans would good-naturedly adopt some bit of Islam while still retaining their paganism. Perhaps, having heard of the mysterious importance of Mecca, they would boast that their fetishes and magic charms were originally imported from there, or that from Mecca had come the inspiration for their powerful local secret society. It is said that a personage called Allah or a similar name was sometimes added to their caste of gods, showing a similar receptivity to that which Christian missionaries in Africa have noted in modern days in the pagan readiness to give a non-exclusive niche to "the white man's god."

Those who welcomed conversion would often try to approximate Islam to their inherited notions, to find some synthesis between their tribal religion and the new faith, a desire carried along into modern times and sometimes manifested in the pagan manner of absorbing Christianity.

This last is a post-colonization effort and outside the scope of this book, but it has a psychological affinity with my subject. As a general view of the pagan mind meeting and seeking to domesticate a new religion it is interesting to read of the improvizations, supposed improvements and remolding of missionary teachings in such studies as Sundkler's on the South African Bantu prophets or Baeta on prophetism in Ghana. As Malinowski said in an inquiry on Africa, *The Dynamics of Culture Change,* "Under the stress of emotional crisis the indigenous belief becomes stronger than the alien creed."

A quaint case of the remaking of a new faith to bring it nearer to local ideas and preferences was the fashion which a group in Southeastern Nigeria installed Christianity, as told by Messenger, one of the contributors to *Continuity and Change in African Cultures.* They syncretized their own god Abasi with the Christian God and assigned a home in the local church to the Holy Ghost, whom they particularly revered. Even I have noted what seem like primitive combinations with Christianity in West Africa.

This semi-receptivity of new things while still retaining a grip upon the old is typical of the continent's non-changeable nature. She keeps her feet squarely planted on the ancestral soil and has survived almost unaltered through repeated colonial intrusions—from Phoenicians to Belgians and Italians (who were her last European arrivals).

Some Negro Moslems showed intense orthodox devotion. Many poor men tackled the awesomely difficult pilgrimage to Mecca alone and without funds. The adventure of the pilgrimage and its prestige and pious value, and also the chance to travel, which roused atavistic longing, the memory of those migrations which are the fabric of African history and prehistory—these reconciled them to hardship and danger.

They brought back—if they survived and got back—startling stories about one of the world's much legend-bedecked places—perhaps the most bedecked of all.

They could tell that they had visited as a part of the pilgrimage ceremonies Arafat, where Adam and Eve, driven from Paradise, met again after 120 years of separation—a second honeymoon of giants. A splendid couple. The proof of Eve's magnificent proportions was offered to the pilgrim at Jidda, the Red Sea port for Mecca, where her grave was displayed, it being 420 feet long. On the grave is a place for devotions, a chapel, marking the supposed location of Eve's nombril and ornamented with a stone "fancifully carved to represent the omphalic region of the human frame," to use Burton's phrase. The stature of Adam himself is variously given in legends as from the height of a high palm tree to so great that his forehead scraped against the sky.

This represents the ultimate in Islamic myths about gigantic humans, though a Moslem mystic "spoke of enormous legions of angels, certain of whom are so big that to go from their foot to their ankle would take 500 years," adding, "There are worlds in the invisible world into which thy geometric measuring has never penetrated." This passage (quoted from a lecture of Professor Hellmut Ritter of Frankfurt at the 1957 Symposium on the History of Moslem Civilizations) is not only an indication of the fascination giants had for the Moslem mind, but seems a prevision of our present passion for the immensity of figures and the vast measurements of space.

The Kaaba, Mecca's jewel, was older than mankind, some legends said, being originally an edifice angelically built in Paradise before the Creation, shipped to the earth for the benefit of Adam and set up on an emplacement which had been chosen and prepared before the rest of the world was created, Allah extending the earth's sweep in circles around it. The picture of the giant Adam in his days of early innocence residing in a house with a roof made of a ruby (the present Kaaba was reconstructed with more modest materials by Abraham after the Deluge) and cherishing the famous and revered Black Stone, which is about six inches across, with his gigantic hands is a strain on our imagination.

But probably African pilgrims did not look legends in the teeth. They had contemplated "an awful sight which distracts the senses in amazement and ravishes the heart and mind," as Ibn Jubayr said when he saw the Kaaba. They had touched with their hands that nail which was driven into the middle of the Kaaba's floor and marked the center of the world, "The World's Navel," according to Islam. The earth in old times was punctured with navels. Jerusalem possessed one, and a seventh-century Christian reported seeing the column which stood at Jerusalem's umbilical spot. There was a world's navel at Delphi and the much discussed mythical navel city of Axim on the Equator, or perhaps to be identified with a still existent Indian city, and so on. The multitudinous world navels lost value when the world ceased to seem flat, but the search was a proper and patriotic expression—people seeking to have the honor Creation's debut for their own country: "Here the world began!"

For the Moslems from Negroland the world's center was a long way from their home. But by the right of Islam they had proprietorship. Thus Islam united Negro Africans with the great outside world. The pilgrimage was a deep experience to Africa.

But it demanded almost superhuman devotion to carry out the journey, hard on all and especially hard and very dangerous to any humble lone pilgrim. There was for most of them the Sahara to cross. Many then took the trans-Red Sea route, where they were thrown into frail ships on top of one another like bundles. The round trip took several years. Even when a great king like Askia Mohammed, who went weighed with gold—three hundred thousand gold pieces— and retainers and a big military escort to ease his way, it meant an absence of two years. The pilgrimage of the spectacular ruler of Mali probably took three years. Both rulers narrowly escaped death en route. Two other Negro kings were murdered. A lone and poor pilgrim, obliged to work his way, to attach himself to groups and to linger along, would sacrifice a big portion of his life to his mission.

To make the pilgrimage was optional, urged on Moslems but not obligatory. Another part of Islam's program fell upon every Moslem every year of his life—childhood excepted. This was the month-long, all-day-long fast of Ramadan—no food, no drink even from sunrise to sunset and no consoling amorous episode allowed till the night came. It is said that these rules were in some localities sternly applied. During Ramadan a very early European explorer, Major Denham, was in the Chad region. (He and his companions had discovered the lake and patriotically named it "Lake Waterloo," which did not stick, else we would have a new nation called the Republic of Waterloo.) Denham's narrative tells how anyone surprised quenching thirst or visiting a woman during Ramadan in the daytime was condemned to five hundred blows with a hippo-hide whip.

A recent instance of Ramadan's potency is touching. In 1960 an earthquake in Agadir in southern Morocco killed an estimated twelve thousand. From under the ruins of a house on the second day following rescuers dug out two teen-age boys and pressed drink and food upon them. The boys refused. "It is forbidden. It is Ramadan!"

It was in the same region as this that Sidi Okba supposedly upbraided the Atlantic for holding back Islam's drive almost thirteen hundred years before. The impeded Moslem drive swung back into Africa and in its own supple strength melded with the impalpable strength of paganism and kneaded together half a continent and races of two colors.

Now millions of Moslem Africans are not merely members of some tribe, perhaps remote and insignificant, but members of a continent.

THE RACE RELATIONS IN A TWO-COLORED CONTINENT

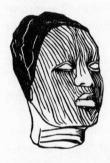

CAMELS AND ISLAM DREW AFRICA TOGETHER. The camel came first. Camels for general transport moved westward into Mediterranean Africa a few centuries before the Moslem Arabs arrived.

As the camels carried Islam southward there resulted a new sort of contact between the two color groups which ran in separate stripes across Africa. The two groups had in general met in social inequality since the upper stripe met dark folk who had been brought northward in slavery and to the lower stripe white people were usually intruders who came to invade or bamboozle them. Thus the white attitude had been uppish and that of the blacks resentful. During the centuries Islam penetrated into Negroland there came, theoretically at least, a brotherly sentiment on the part of the whites toward such of the black people as accepted their faith and a comradely confidence on the part of Negro Moslem converts.

But, putting aside the mutual tolerance bred of a religious amalgamation, it would be interesting to consider how in a general way did Africa's white folk and its black folk react upon one another. Africa presented a unique puzzle to its people, the puzzle of two indigenous colors. The continent had possessed from prehistoric times what the other continents acquired recently—a mixed true Negro and a white population. Africa had two races. It was the birthplace of the race problem.

With camels and the Koran the pale and the dark met in a large way. Incidentally, the white Africans who came into the country of the Negroes, though of the white race, were not of the same light complexion as those Europeans who arrived later by sea. They were usually Mediterranean Africans and Egyptians, what some anthropologists have called "dark whites" or "light browns." Nor were all the colored Africans whom these met "true Negroes"—a term which is sometimes used scientifically and is confusing. Ethiopians repudiate the suggestion that they are Negroes; some modern people of color maintain that Egyptians are of Negro origin. But when the first members of the two color groups came face to face the shocking spectacle of another human so startlingly different was not softened by definitions.

Let me make it clear that what I am trying to look into is not the present racial problem of the world in general, nor the racial situation as met in Africa after European colonization started, but the purely on-the-spot interracial instinctive reactions to the color split as met inside the Africans' own continent.

There is considerable Arabic literature to indicate how the "dark whites" felt. Naturally we have no written record of the mass reaction of the blacks. But when we pluck a few curious bits from the narratives of very early European explorers who happened to encounter native groups that had never before seen a white man, we can be sure that the reaction was one of sheer horror.

White people were presumed to be lepers. And that, strangely, was not the worst of the notions. More disturbing was the thought that whites were the returned spirits of the dead. At Benin in the early days of European trading a local woman venturesome enough to accept a white man sexually was punished with death. An early nineteenth-century explorer, Major Gray, thrust out his hand in a friendly manner to an old half-blind woman. When she saw that his hand was white, "shrieking, she fell to the ground." Another old-time English traveler, Rankin, when in the back country of what is now Sierra Leone, lay resting under a tree. A child came with her mother to examine him and, "discovering the monster, sprang upon her mother's back in an agony of fear and would not cease screaming." A medieval Moslem from Almería, Spain, was shipwrecked on the African coast. The black people were astounded and "convinced that we had our bodies dyed white they scrubbed us with palm oil."

The ultimate expression of black racial prejudice against whites was reported by Ibn Battuta: cannibals declined to eat white people —they were "not ripe." The not-ripe theory was of long survival. Some six centuries later a modern Moslem traveler was informed that there were in the former French Sudan many who believed white people had been prematurely born babies who, had they stayed the normal time in their mothers' wombs, would have been Negroes.

The first feeling of alarm and shrinking later merged often into a sort of pathetic admiration.

An offshoot of the primitive Negro color sentiment was that mixture of reverence and squeamishness they felt toward the albinos, who seem to occur rather often among them. Negro reactions to the freakish white was varied: "valued though their color was not admired," says Speke, the albinos held an almost sacred position in some localities. An albino had only to indicate some man or woman as undesirable "and an immediate immolation of the victim ensued," wrote Major Ellis in his study of the Tshi-speaking people of the Gold Coast. Especially contradictory was the position of albinos near the Congo mouth. At Loango they were "court fools." Another report puts them on a pedestal as divine beings whose divinity was recognized in that they could take anything they wanted from the markets without paying for it.

In the Gambia-Senegal region the French explorer Mollien, who identified the sources of both rivers in 1818 and wrote about his accomplishment, says that he was confronted deliberately with an albino girl "to see what effect she would have on me." Mollien describes with distaste her chalk-white face, her Negro features and her feebleness of manner and tells how he shuddered visibly, at which one of the bystanders said, "If you too feel disgust at seeing people of your race you should not be astonished that your color displeases us!"

To the white Africans the racial shock was not so great. It had come gradually. Dark races had been familiar since antiquity, since the days before history began. Gsell cites a report from the fourth century B.C., passed along by Diodorus of Sicily, about a black tribe —migrant or indigenous—living in coastal Tunisia. The Sudan, in which were dark people and in the long ago true Negroes, was at Egypt's southern door.

All white Africa from Egypt to Morocco and from ancient to almost modern times was accustomed to the spectacle of great armies of black soldiers. The extensive use of foreigners in the army is no oddity. A big foreign army of a different race—Negroes fighting for whites—and of slaves fighting for their owners is rather more surprising. But so it was in Africa. Back in the Dynasty VI, Negro troops by the thousands were part of Egypt's army, and we hear of black soldiers by the Nile on into the Middle Ages—thirty thousand Negro swordsmen in the eleventh century. It was black troops who at the "Mad Caliph's" command burned Fostat. In Tunisia the Fatimids used Negro soldiers against "The Man on the Donkey." A medieval account of the parade of an Almohade sultan's black guard, his "Guinea Troops," so called, is picturesque—lances in hand, sword at belt, dressed in white robes, with silk flags flying. Even to Spain went Negro troops. At that famous battle of Las Navas de Tolosa, which was fatal to Moslem power in Spain, they say that ten thousand Negroes perished.

In Morocco the sultan's Black Guard was renowned into modern days, the soldiers bred with care in a process which seems to resemble cattle raising. In the time of the Sultan Ismail the herd of black fighters numbered as many as 150,000 men.

Such large-scale aspects of the Negro—romantic, picturesque, sometimes heroic—plus the workaday contacts with slave labor and the attractions of pretty dark girls in the harem accustomed white Africans to their black co-continentals.

As to what white Africans thought on the color question, we can assume that, since most of the Negroes they met were slaves in the army or the harem or the field, and of pagan origin and savage antecedents, they viewed them as inferiors. But I think that their color was not held against Negroes or mulattoes in high places. Nor were slaves or ex-slaves, whether black or white, ill regarded when they scrambled or officially emerged out of slavery and attained importance, which a surprising number of slaves succeeded in doing all over the continent.

Africa's slaves of position and power and how they got there form a curious study. Some—I shall mention a few of these—even became rulers and conquerors.

Many slaves rose to good government situations. As an observer noted when traveling into West Africa nearly a century ago (Paul Soleillet), a superior slave group formed a sort of aristocracy, "like those who in our society belong to the administration and the army." The reason was that local kings and chiefs preferred to entrust power to a tested slave rather than to a relative who might be envious or dangerous. European travelers insist that Bornu was the land of opportunity for slaves. Nor was this the case just in Negroland. "There are those," wrote Ibn Khaldun, "who by accepting slavery hope to attain high rank or get money or power. This was the case with the Turks in the East." Slavery was hard, sometimes tragic for the average, but a possible opening to a career for the few.

Many slaves became historic figures. I mention certain of these elsewhere—Kafur, the black master of Egypt; Jawher, who conquered Egypt for the Fatimids; a slave who became a reigning queen in her own right in the days of St. Louis, and I shall presently list a few others.

But strangest of all Africa's slaves of importance was Lokman, the author—a non-writing author, of course—and I shall put him at the top of my list of the continent's great slaves.

Lokman of Nubia was the Father of Fables, about whom the Greeks heard mention as an "Aethiopian" (Ethiopian or Negro) and, using his racial origin as a name, invented an imaginary Aesop.

Such, at any rate, is a very generally held theory. By some he has been regarded as the prototype of Balaam, who was a seer, although his ass's remarks put the wisdom of his master in the shade. And it has even been suggested that the legendary Ahikar, who supposedly worked for King Sennacherib of Nineveh, was but a reintroduction of the wisdom of our Nubian first fabulist.

The cornerstone of a special narrative form, allegedly attributed to shadowy figures of whose actuality there is some doubt, was Lokman. Lokman was a Nubian slave who gained freedom because he ate a melon which had gone bad and which his master had given him unaware. "Why did you eat the nasty thing?" his master asked. Lokman, the slave, said that he accepted uncomplainingly a bitter fruit from the hand from which he had received many favors. The master set him free, and Lokman's career and his travels began.

He knew King David well. For a year he watched King David working with iron and making iron rings. Finally King David made a coat of mail and tried it on. Lokman surveyed the king without envy and said, "I have a solid coat of mail of my own that protects me. It is to hold my tongue and shut my mouth."

Lokman was so widely famed in the Orient that Mohammed gave value to the Koran by dedicating a sura to him, the thirty-first. One much quoted bit of wisdom attributed to Lokman is the saying, "Moving mountains from their places would be easier to me than to influence people's psychology."

Ugly, deformed and a Negro slave, Lokman has been esteemed as the source of a certain imaginative expression of common sensical wisdom—the fable. He attained a unique standing, one of the oldest names in literary history. And the fact of his slave origin did not stand in the way of his recognition.

In the life story of Ngolo, the slave emperor (1750–87) we meet all the essence of Africa's slavery—its opportunities, its cruelties and the absence of obloquy its victim could enjoy, the ready welcome to greatness which a slave might expect were he an exceptional individual.

Ngolo the Bambaran was exceptional. He was a brilliant soldier and administrator, and from his center at Ségou on the Niger he spread his empire as far as Timbuctoo. His fame traveled across the

Sahara. Moroccans heard that the region which they had conquered and had dominated so profitably and which had now slipped out of their grasp was under the efficient black thumb of an ex-slave.

An Englishman, Jackson, who was for a long time in Morocco and who was an avid collector of African gossip, tells in his *Account of the Empire of Marocco* about the sovereign of Bambara who possessed three palaces at Timbuctoo containing "an immense quantity of gold" and bossed the place competently—"the police is extolled"; he appointed the local governing board, and everyone enjoyed religious liberty—Jews excepted—for Timbuctoo as a trade center attracted both Moslems and assorted pagans. Jackson gives his name as "Woolo," which was another way of reproducing the sound of "Ngolo."

Ngolo's dynasty survived for a century and a half, and it was his son and successor who is picturesquely named "Mansong" in Mungo Park's narrative. Mansong suspected that Park had been friendly with an enemy king whom Park also picturesquely named, calling him "Daisy," (modern historians have adopted a soberer rendering of the two names; I like Park's way best) and forbade Park to enter Ségou, but sent him a consolation hospitality gift of five thousand cowries, then the equivalent of one pound, this being enough to feed Mungo Park and his horse for fifty days! When Park returned on his second expedition Mansong was more affable and authorized Park to build at one of his Niger ports that boat which took Park to his doom.

Ngolo was a member of a hereditary slave group called the Ton-Dion, or "Slaves of the Law," an invention of the local king, who conceived the cunning idea of paying from the treasury the fines or tax debts for criminals or delinquents in exchange for which the criminal or debtor became royal property and obligatorily joined a sort of royal guard. Debtors too old for military service gave a son as substitute. Ngolo became a "slave of the law" when a boy of eight.

When Ngolo was about fifty, one of the successors of the Ton-Dion system's inventor doubly infuriated the slave group. He became a convert to Mohammedanism, which was detestable to them as pagans, merry drinkers and worshippers of supernatural spirits, and he was of a vicious cruelty. He came down in legend as having mixed the blood of sixty thousand slaves into the walls of his city. Early European history carries along this dubious legend at which common sense rebels, considering the immense force of laborers it would have been required to carry out so horrid a building enterprise and the crippling financial loss involved, for slaves were money. A slave would be quoted like currency in bargaining when no actual slave changed hands. We hear that even after colonial rule was suppressed slavery prices were still quoted in slaves—even such a gruesome price as "a slave and a half" would be mentioned.

The Ton-Dion rose in a mass, a big powerful mass by then, and massacred the king and all his family, two girls excepted. Ngolo protected the girls.

A series of several Ton-Dions tried to rule in vain. Ngolo took charge and built up an empire of real importance, which he, the ex-slave, ruled till he was ninety years old, and founded a dynasty over which the "Ngolessi" (Ngolo's Posterity) carried on until dislodged by French colonial ambitions.

Two brilliant dark fighters who simultaneously but separately impeded colonial ambitions elsewhere were of slave associations—one was a former slave, the other the son of an enslaved mother. They were Rabah, who hacked his way to becoming sultan in Central Africa and died fighting Europeans in 1900, and Samory, who mastered a wide sweep of West Africa and after fifteen years was defeated and sent into exile on an island in Gabon.

Slavery came into Samory's boyhood when his mother was captured and dragged away. Samory set out to gain her freedom and— so the story goes—was in the service of her master for "seven years, seven months and seven days." This was not the malicious gossip of his European enemies, who indeed discredited its truth, but a part of Samory's official biography, told at his own court when he had risen to power, and was reported by a French army officer who was sent to try to negotiate with him. If it was merely a fancy touch invented by his public relations men it is all the more significant, for it would prove that slavery was not viewed with contempt, that a legend about slavery in the family and a devoted effort to rescue a slave were calculated to increase the leader's glamour and prestige.

Both Rabah and Samory were, of course, reviled by Europeans of the day and, like many other conquerors, they deserved reviling. These two were especially hateful because they hampered other conquerors of a more benign sort—the Europeans—and augmented ill will between colonial groups who suspected one another of flirtations with each of the African leaders, and of supplying arms. Rabah had siezed one of colonialism's indispensable regions, a piece of dark cake which London, Paris and Berlin were planning to slice. Samory impeded the taking of Timbuctoo and the push into Africa along the Niger. There were none but vile words applied to Rabah, and Samory was described as a pagan fiend who wore Islam as a pretense and impudently called himself "Commander of the True Believers," who forbade the mention of his prename, ordering that he be addressed by the semi-religious title of "Almamy." ("Almamy" was the Negro variant of the Arabic "Imam," He Who Stands in Front, applied to the prayer leader, but eventually given among Negroes an augmented value as meaning also the big political chief.) His full name was Samory Touré. The popular name of Touré reappears as that of the first President of Guinea, Sekou Touré, and had figured in history when Mohammed Touré founded the great dynasty of the Askias in the fifteenth century. It was even popular enough to be attributed in a Senegalese legend to one of the Pharaohs of Egypt!

The violent efforts of the two men—competent generals both of them—held back what then seemed Africa's only proper destiny, to be a continent of colonies. With decolonization we look at the two through another window—very cruel, yes, but a part of Africa's passionate clinging to her own crude and muddled form of independence. Both hated Europe's intrusion, and so did those Africans whom they did not kill or enslave and who joined their ruthless armies.

It is noticeable that slavery association was no deterrent to leadership in either case. This is why I mentioned two figures who, coming after colonialism had cut its sharp teeth and was starting to bite deep into the continent, are beyond the boundary of this book.

Most of the slaves whom northern Africa observed were Negroes, and this caused Africa's whites to assess the Negro as a lowly race. But northern Africa also saw slaves who were white people, Europeans and Christians or ex-Christians, many thousands of them, the victims of the Barbary corsairs. In addition there were the enslaved survivors from shipwrecks on Africa's Atlantic beaches and captives siezed in shore raids. The result was to give Africa a poor idea of Europe, to emphasize Islamic dislike for the Christian religion and to feel contempt for the many Christian captives who gained liberty by switching to Mohammedanism—the so-called renegades.

Cities saw Europeans of all nations. An English mission seeking to ransom British captives reported that in 1721 there were in the city of Meknes alone three hundred English, four hundred Spaniards, a hundred and fifty Portuguese, a hundred and fifty-two French, fifty-seven Dutch and twenty-five Genoese. Nineteen of the Englishmen in despair had "turned Moors," that is, abandoned Christianity. Africa saw such pitiful gangs driven half naked to the slave markets and whatever might have been the proud station or value of these Europeans in their homeland—among them were Cervantes, captured when coming home a hero from Lepanto, St. Vincent de Paul in his youth and the later immortalized original hero of *Robinson Crusoe*—they made a shabby appearance in Africa. The young creatures, boys and girls, would obligatorily be put to poor uses. Most of the adults became common laborers. "The streets resounded with the noise of their chains, especially in early morning, when these unfortunates, weighed down with irons and wearing iron collars, were driven out to work." This is from a pitying North African, Ibn Khaldun.

Several of the ex-Christians played a part in African history. Not only were very many pirate ships captained by renegades, but ex-Christians even became repeatedly governors of North African localities during the early period of Turkish occupation. And one of the most remarkable military expeditions of all time, the successful crossing of the Sahara to conquer the Askias' empire and grab the riches of Timbuctoo, was commanded by a renegade.

A couple of shipwrecked captives who escaped from slavery supply us with entertaining but not very reliable travel books which fired the fancy of the early nineteenth century and whose reminiscences were pubished in the impressive style of the day. Captain Riley's *Loss of the American Brig Commerce, wrecked on the western coast of Africa, in the month of August, 1815, with an account of Tom-*

buctoo, on deckle-edged paper eleven inches high, weight nearly five pounds, cover of cloth and green leather with gold trimmings, appears to have gone into sixteen editions and communicates information collected by Riley about the Sahara then unknown to Europe, one item being that it was the frequent custom to feed camels in the desert on coal. Robert Adams, born in New York State, a captive seaman, claimed actually to have gone to Timbuctoo, where he saw the king wearing gold epaulettes.

An earlier traveling Christian slave who truly saw Timbuctoo though he wrote no book was the Frenchman Imbert, a sailor who guided by compass a newly appointed Governor of Timbuctoo across the empty spaces of the Sahara in the winter of 1618, and so accidentally preceded the explorers, Laing, Caillié, etc., of two centuries later.

During the big days of piracy and Christian enslavement Turkey supervised northern Africa west of Egypt in a vague and variegated way. Turkey's control there was insecure, administered often by independent persons in the occupation forces or others, though it was sometimes very stern. Morocco avoided Turkish conquest. Tripoli in later days was almost a prison state. On the whole it was a very wide but not very insistent empire which, as empires do, died a lingering and agonizing death. It was in 1830 that France successfully invaded Algeria, a great blow which Turkey quaintly tried to camouflage. "Would you believe it," wrote the Frenchman Mathuisieul, who in 1901 managed to visit Tripoli, then completely shut off to Europe, "our occupation of Tunisia [which had occurred in 1881] has not yet been accepted diplomatically by Turkey and even the situation in Algeria has not been recognized by the Sublime Porte?"

The Turkish conquest of the Barbary States was of great military and nuisance value. It did not result in the establishment of colonies either for exploitation or habitation, and one seems to look in vain for any indications that Turkish presence influenced northern African thoughts and sentiments as had the coming of the Arabs.

The Turks were not fellow nationals of the Prophet. With them there was no lofty glamour; in fact they were more recently lifted from paganism than the North Africans themselves. No Turk could claim to be of Sherifian descent, and I have never heard that native northern Africans pretended to be of Turkish ancestry for the sake of prestige, as some are said to have pretended with regard to Arab genealogy. The Turk was a strong and burly conqueror, but almost a dowdy one. And his methods were harsh.

It was not a happy period for the people. As to their reactions I have almost no African information. The great age of northern Africa's Arabic historians was over. Available are several early eighteenth-century accounts by European observers who tell about the hard times of the "Moors," as they called the native population. These writers—such as Dr. Shaw, consular chaplain at Algiers (published 1738), Laugier de Tassy, marine commissioner (1725) and Morgan (1731), writing about "a country and a people among whom I have passed so many years"—had to watch their compatriots and co-religionists clanking through the streets in chains, which would have subdued any sympathy for the local people, so we can be sure that their accounts of the local discomforts and humiliations of the "Moors" are not exaggerated.

Both the law and social regulations discriminated against the "Moor." No matter what his crime a Turk was not publicly tried and punished. A "Moor" was judged sternly and publicly executed atrociously—perhaps tossed down to agonize for days on the infamous Hook or buried alive. In social contacts the "Moor" was the inferior, obligatorily treating the Turkish military men as "high and powerful seigneurs." No Turkish women came with the occupation. Marriage of a Turkish soldier to a Moorish female met with official opposition; he was deprived of his food and lodging allowance and lost standing. The children of the marriage were ill regarded. They formed a class called scornfully *koulouglis*.

The Turkish attitude in all this was self-protective. The Turkish occupation force was a tiny minority. Laugier de Tassy says that there was in the country (Algeria) but one Turk to every two hundred of the native population. With fraternizing and intermarriage the Turks would have lost control.

For the people of the Barbary States it was a rehearsal of the more definite colonization and protectorate systems which were to come later with the conquests by European nations. It was a sort of colonization before colonization.

For North Africa it was in general super isolation. The European holdings in Barbary were largely abandoned; one of the last, Oran, which had been the door of hope toward which runaway Christian slaves struggled, lasted till the end of the eighteenth century. Pirates brought booty and slaves. European governments paid blackmail tribute.

Turkish soldiers presently discarded the governors shipped from Turkey and took to choosing their own rulers. In Algiers the ruler liked to be called "Sultan." In Tunisia the system developed into a hereditary dynasty. Tripoli went through conflicting phases. For a time it was open house to Europeans, and it was from Tripoli that a series of the early explorers of inner Africa was launched across the desert. At Tripoli the English consul Warrington, in office for some thirty-odd years from 1814, was, like Prince Henry the Navigator, a godfather of African exploration, and by marrying him to his daughter gave to Laing a doubly cordial send-off on his Timbuctoo adventure. Later Tripoli slammed the door. This Libyan door was pried open by Italy, and now its hinges are greased with oil.

The effect of the Turkish centuries on the people of that wide stretch of North Africa seem shadowy, the two races non-mingling. Linguists state that the Turkish language did not have surviving local influence and the study of certain manuscripts of the period show that the ordinary Turk of Algiers adopted few terms of Algerian Arabic. It seems significant of the meager intellectual baggage brought to the Barbary States by the Turkish invaders that a collection of Turkish popular verses, soldiers' songs, etc.—in a late eighteenth-century collection of manuscripts which have been considered with painstaking care—were inscribed by an Algerian Turk in Turkish words but *in Arabic script.* (*Chansons des Janissaires Turcs d' Alger,* edited by J. Deny in *Mélanges René Basset.*)

Egypt had known Turks in power far earlier than the Barbary States. From the opening centuries of Islam, Turks had come to the lands of Islam from the East. They were slaves turned masters, and through the years they and their kinsmen kept coming and getting more masterful—Seljuks, Mongols, Tatars, Ottoman Turks. They picked up the Moslem faith and swallowed it with enthusiasm. They were splendid warriors and they wanted to fight everybody, and as time passed they almost did do this, and piled up bloody victories. They were the "never tired Turks," of whose vigor and endurance al-Jahiz, the ninth-century Arabic writer, told so romantically in the days when Turks were a benign and protective element as the Sherif's guards.

A brilliant Turk came to Egypt in the ninth century originally in modest guise. He was a slave sent as governor, as was Baghdad's odd habit, about which I have already quoted Ibn Khaldun's comment. It would seem almost as if slavery to bright young aliens had the advantage of a sort of scholarship, was an opening to betterment for persons without family influence.

This slave was by name Ibn-Talun. He soon tossed off Baghdad and founded an independent dynasty. One of the Talunids even attempted unsuccessfully to conquer Tripoli. Ibn-Talun, though not African-born, was one of Africa's slaves of consequence. Egypt was no longer Baghdad's colony. He and his successor built a place of fairy tale glamour, and they themselves were gossip's tidbits—the blue-eyed lion who crouched beside the royal master while he ate, the quicksilver lake on which the sovereign slept upon an inflated floating mattress. The mosque built by the first Talunid, who died in 883, was described by Stanley Lane-Poole just one thousand years afterward as Moslem Egypt's earliest surviving monument which preserves its original design and ornament. The luxurious capital city, El-Katai, which he built—there was no Cairo then—we know only by gorgeous medieval words.

Another short dynasty, also Turkish, was founded presently in Egypt by Ibn-Tughj, on whom had been conferred the noble title of Ikhshid. He was an Egyptologist, causing old tombs to be dug up and discovering ancient and marvelous treasures—the figures of old and young men and women and children having eyes of precious stones and faces of gold and silver. But the most striking feature of the Ikhshid dynasty was its end. The Ikhshids went into a unique sort of decline, during which the royal persons were gently replaced by a Negro ex-slave.

The two weak-kneed sons who followed Ibn-Tughj lolled back

in luxurious idleness as figureheads while Kafur, a Negro slave whom Ibn-Tughj had bought at a bargain, ran the country. For nineteen years he was virtual and for three years titular ruler, listed as the fourth Ikhshid in the dynastic list.

That this should happen is surprising, and that it could happen indicates as clearly as any episode in all of Africa's history the continent's fraternity of race, the ready acceptance of the blacks by the whites.

Turkish influence lapsed after Kafour but came back with the Ayyubid dynasty, which Saladin founded, with the succeeding Mamluk sultans, the beys, the pashas and the khedives. In the eastern Sudan the term "Turk" came to mean a frightening and detested authority.

Africa beyond the Sahara must have heard with amazement of the Mamluks—the word meant "Owned"—the white slave sultans who ruled over Egypt from the middle of the thirteenth century and wore their slave origin unashamed.

The Mamluk attitude shows in the fact that one of the early Mamluks, Sultan Kalaun, permitted the surname of "The Thousand Man," meaning that he had been bought for a thousand dinars, a high price, remembered proudly. (Kafour's price was only eighteen dinars.) A later Mamluk sultan, Barkuk, on the eve of battle made a stirring speech to his slave soldiers, assuring them of his confidence and esteem, telling them he had paid a high price for them and saying he, too, had been sold in his time, "as you were sold to me." These two items are respectively from Ibn Battuta, who was in Egypt shortly after Kalaun's reign, and from a contemporary Latin biography of the other sultan by an Italian who knew Barkuk, which has been translated and edited by Fischel.

White Africa came to know many whites who were slaves and who held high places, and this tended to another appreciation of slavery as a social and a racial standard, and meant that slavery was not necessarily and exclusively a black man's degradation and indeed that it was not always a degradation at all and could not be used to their discredit as a general estimate against the Negro race.

Slavery had its own prestige. During more than half of the period between Talun the slave, who founded a dynasty, and the predecessor of Nasser, who founded a republic—not quite eleven hundred years —Egypt's heads of government were people of slave origin or from slave groups.

The picture of the continent's slavery is wide. It sweeps from the slave who rose to be king to the slave who was butchered for a cannibal repast or killed as a sacrifice—the last an adaptation to pagan religious ceremonial of an old-time arena entertainment.

A slave might be a creature for foreign export—perhaps the hardships of the Sahara. (Richardson says child slaves of four or five years old walked from Kano to Tripoli.) Perhaps the misery of the Middle Passage to the Americas. Perhaps from eastern Africa to the Near and Middle East. This last was the oldest trade of them all, which drew away Africans during the centuries from before the Christian era in total numbers comparable with the estimates suggested for the shorter and more intense trans-Atlantic human exportation.

But the great mass of Africa's slaves were domestic workers, secured by kidnapping or in tribal wars. They were the victims and often the motive of the wars that were facilitated by the multitude of African tribal divisions. Slave hunting was on a small scale, not as in Europe's early days, when, according to one of the studies in *Slavery in Classical Antiquity*, "Caesar is said to have captured a million prisoners in Gaul."

Africa's domestic slaves were fairly treated. Here are some comparisons with labor conditions at home and of their own day made by early European observers who traveled in Negro Africa. "Their fate would be preferable to that of some of our own [French] peasants if anything could compensate for the loss of liberty," was René Caillié's reflection at Jenné near the Niger. The slave's position is "better than that of the agricultural laborer in England," wrote Major Ellis, speaking of the Gold Coast, but modified his good words by mention of the liability to sacrifice at the master's death.

In Morocco, Jackson noted that some owners would liberate the domestic slave and some freed slaves would decline freedom. Far up the Nile traveler Petherick said, "As everywhere in the interior of Africa within my knowledge, slaves are treated affectionately, both master and slave proud of each other." But Petherick added that the

Niam-Niam were stern with the slave who tried to run away. If they caught him they ate him.

Docile slaves in Negro Africa might get to be like family members, might be adopted into the tribe which had captured them, might intermarry with the owner's family, they might work part time on their own behalf, get rich and possess slaves of their own, might become themselves chiefs.

In the literate parts of the continent the position and rights of slaves were laid down with formality. Ethiopia's ancient book of law, *Fetha Nagast,* went into the subject in detail. A few items: A slave must not be set free if he has no means of subsistence. (That is, a sick or old slave may not be thrown out to starve.) If a slave commits murder by his master's orders not he but his master is responsible. The master is advised to set slaves free for a variety of reasons, including the slave's conversion to Christianity and expressed desire to become a priest or monk. A slave's liberation to be rescinded if he is insolent or of rough conduct toward his master.

Islam went carefully into the slave situation. In a book about the Sahara and North Africa which is over a century old General Daumas brought together what he says the doctors of Moslem law thought on the subject—eighteen chapters, totaling twenty-four fine-printed pages, with sources given (which I have not attempted to check). The reader of these complex opinions appreciates how intense and careful an interest was taken in the slave's status.

All this was slavery, African style, before she turned temporarily maniacal under the lure of foreign slave demands and before she later fell under the control of the outside world and was obliged to abolish slavery altogether. The latter must have puzzled Africans who knew their legends. First white foreigners bought slaves with heartless avidity. Then they moved in as colonial masters and—having learned that lesson Christianity had portrayed a thousand years earlier, the slave dealer with a torn purse, which meant that the slave trade does not pay (image in an ancient Coptic church described by El-Bekri)— told bewildered Africa that slavery was wicked and outlawed Africa's comparatively mild and gentle system.

The continent's old-time and vague understanding about what slavery meant was a concept without boundaries. It was a social map that stretched from the slave as king to a slave as a suitable object for human sacrifice with a wide space between where domestic slaves existed in relative comfort, and where here and there a slave was a cannibal's dinner.

This vague uncertain attitude was Africa's misfortune. Slavery lost its meaning. And so also and necessarily did liberty. The easygoing irresponsibility and tolerance had its aspects of cruelty and of broadmindedness, but as a whole it weakened the continent's fiber and made Africa's spine wobble. It can have been a determining element, *the* determining element in her isolation. It held back the "African Clock." It degraded Africa abroad and it can have produced that feebleness of spirit which welcomed the nasty business of the big slave trade and which facilitated, or at any rate did not in general oppose forcefully, the continent's colonization.

In its attitude on the color question white Africa respected theoretically the lofty ideal attributed to Mohammed. I do not possess any clear statement of his about Negroes in the purely racial sense, his favorable mention being restricted to such as accepted Islam. As I have said, there is a tradition that Mohammed said a white man is not superior to a black man "except by reason of his piety."

One of the chapters of the Koran in which there is much vigorous warning to idolaters states that the divers colors of mankind are according to Allah's plan, and a Moslem tradition on the Creation tells how Allah made the first man out of seven different colored handfuls of earth according to the different complexions of mankind.

Another tradition is that Mohammed was asked by a black man who wished to become a Moslem whether in Paradise he would have a place alongside white Arabs. Mohammed's answer was an emphatic "Yes!" and he added, "The black skin of the Negro will spread splendor at a distance of a thousand years."

Some of us who read this cannot help thinking with mixed sentiments of the Black Muslims of the United States, whose activities and ambitions were certainly not in the Prophet's mind when he uttered the prophecy of which Goldziher, the great Islamologist, tells, his words passed along to us by van Grunebaum. A wide Negro future rather than an isolated group movement is presumably what

Mohammed foresaw, but it is imprudent to try to interpret the words of a prophet. Anyway, his prophecy is interesting.

The Arab Prophet's reassurance to the Negro Moslem contrasts with the situation at Heaven's Gate as forecast by some of the Zulu prophets: at the gate the Black Christ turns away the white and admits only his faithful Negro followers.

A very early convert to Mohammed's religion was a certain Negro slave named Bilal, who became the first *muezzin,* caller of the faithful to worship. In the hard days of Islam's struggle Bilal, tradition says, suffered cruel torturing. He is famous among Africans of color as a brave and steadfast Negro who served Islam in the days of the Prophet, and Mohammed is supposed to have called Bilal of the stentorian voice "the first fruit of Abyssinia."

But gentle religious sentiment did not altogether mold opinions. Whites preferred their own complexions, and a noble action attributed to a grandson of Mohammed's is significant. He miraculously changed a Negro who had done him a service into a white man. This color prejudice was a manifestation of ethnocentrism, a term which psychology defines as "an exaggerated tendency to think one's own group or race is superior to others." It was not alone the Negroes who then met the disapprobation of white Moslems.

Let us consider the reflections of Masudi about Europeans. Masudi has been called "The Herodotus of the Arabs." He was a native of Baghdad, a great traveler who knew Africa both white and black, and he wrote part of his encyclopedia, invitingly entitled *Meadows of Gold and Mines of Gems,* in Egypt. It can be assumed that in the judgments he offers he spoke for the intelligentsia of white Africa of the day, that is the tenth century. So far as Europeans, the people of the north, were concerned, he proclaimed that they lived in a cold climate, had gross natures, harsh manners, dull understandings and shaky religious beliefs.

His comments upon the Negro race has in comparison a certain exotic charm and note of respect. He attributes their color and character to the magic influence of the stars. After he has described the Negroes' physical characteristics as produced by the heavenly bodies and after he has mentioned the effect of the Negroes' physique upon the working of their brains—"the nicety of distinctions and the action of understanding being confused"—Masudi goes on to say that astrology ascribes the character of the Negroes to Saturn, and quotes some lines of verse:

> . . . Saturn is an old man and a powerful king.
> His complexion is black and this is the color of his dress
>   and of his sulky mind.
> He exercises his influence upon the Zanj . . .

("Zanj" in this case is used as a general name for black Africans. The name was also applied to specific regions or to all the East African coast and is carried along in the name of Zanzibar.)

It seems a glum picture of the Negro racial atmosphere. But to learned Africans and others of Masudi's time Saturn, as the proprietor of a planet and an instrument of destiny, had high standing. He had a potent place in the revered science of astrology, which had been resurrected from Greek literature by the Arabs and then re-translated into Latin for Europe's delight. There survives—in fact it was reissued only the other day in a German translation—a manual of its magic composed in Arabic in Masudi's century which became widely popular in Christian Europe. Its title was *Picatrix*, and Jean Seznac in *The Survival of the Pagan Gods*, a study of mythological tradition and its place in the Renaissance, gives the formula of a prayer to Saturn: "O Master of sublime name and power, O Master Saturn . . ." So Masudi really did hitch black Africans to a noble star.

A white African of importance, Ibn Khaldun, took a more practical view. Ibn Khaldun, who was born and who died in Africa (Tunisia and Egypt), looked at the African Negro not from the stars but from the earthly eye, both critical—very, sometimes—and historically appreciative. He gave us in his history of the Berbers the only detailed account we possess of the rise and fall of the great black Empire of Mali, which came to its peak of importance within his lifetime. The passage of Negro history is told with respectful care and is based upon data he procured from four different individuals who had lived in Mali territory and whom he cites by name.

I think that with the rise of the Mali Empire and the arrival in Egypt of black royal pilgrims—Mali and Askia—with their sumptuous retinues white Africans revised their views about Negroes. They met black kings of wealth and wide-sweeping empires. Such did not fit the statement that Negroes "have attributes that are quite similar to those of dumb animals," which, oddly enough, comes from Ibn Khaldun. But he is telling here of peoples of "the first zone," the savages of Equatorial Africa, of whom he had heard reports, and he concludes his comments on the Negro by saying, "The same applies to the Slavs." He was strongly of the opinion that climate makes the man.

Color, Ibn Khaldun asserts, is determined and swiftly altered by climate. Color does not result because of "descent from a black human being, be it Ham or anyone else. Negroes who settle in the Temperate Zone . . . are found to produce descendants whose color gradually turns white in the course of time. Vice versa, inhabitants from the north who settle in the south produce descendants whose color turns black. This shows that color is determined by the composition of the air." Ibn Khaldun then quotes from Avicenna:

> Where the Zanj live is a heat that changes their bodies
> Until their skins are covered all over with black.

Ibn Khaldun's association of complexion with climate might be in a large sense acceptable to modern anthropologists, although they seem to show a prudent reserve in making statements about racial differences—in declaring baldly just why Negroes are Negroes. "The fact is that we simply do not know the racial history of the Negro," says Sir Mortimer Wheeler. But certainly modern anthropology would not back Ibn Khaldun's assertion that persons who move to a new climate automatically produce descendants of a new color. Climatic influence was surely confounded with the results of local mating.

But contemporary European anthropology was even more imaginative, and until Henry the Navigator's seamen returned with the same complexions they had worn when they left home there had been a strong uneasiness in Portugal lest any white man who went beyond Cape Nun in southern Morocco would instantly turn black.

A contribution to the speculation about white and black Africans comes to us from a very ancient piece of fiction, *Ethiopian Story,* in which the third-century Phoenician novelist Heliodorus tells how black parents, the King and Queen of Ethiopia, had a dazzling white daughter because the mother while receiving the father's embraces gazed upon representations of white Greek demi-gods which decorated their bedroom.

I mentioned how Mohammed's grandson allegedly turned a Negro into a white man. Gold did the same. A European report included in Valentim Fernandes' description of the West African coast composed in 1506–07 says that Negroes who worked in the gold mines were found to have turned white if ever they emerged from the mines —they were obliged to live underground with their women, who there bred children in earth's gold bowels. Such was the bewilderment of Europeans when first brought in contact with Negroes that it was soberly recorded in a French medieval document which survives today that the marriage between a Negress and a certain white man had produced a striped child with odd ornaments. She was black with a white band on her forehead and had a white thumb and white ring finger on her left hand.

In Africa the unfamiliar complexion was a puzzling and disturbing thing, and it was not made simpler by the variation of terms applied by one color group to the other. The darker tinted men of the white race might be called "green." Negroes might be called "blue." Mulattoes or light colored "red."

To white Africans it was those dark faces which they never saw which roused dismay. Ibn Khaldun wrote that beyond the river to the south of the Negro empires (the Niger) was that territory whence came the slaves. "Beyond to the further south there is no civilization. It has been reported that they dwell in caves and thickets, eat herbs, live in savage isolation and eat each other."

Those Negroes lurking in the forests, those mysterious cannibals, appalled white Africa. Travelers' tales, which were the basis of medieval geography, emphasized them. The menace of the man-eater was a barrier to direct trade. In the depths of Negroland was Africa's wealth—the gold, the ivory, the pepper and the slaves. Was the cannibal danger intentionally exaggerated by the intermediaries, the people on the borderland of that supposedly infamous region in the reports they gave to traders from the north with the motive of discouraging northerners from penetrating into their rich preserves? Was cannibalism Africa's secret weapon?

The threat of poisoned arrows and wild beasts might not have stopped the greedy and the brave. The fear of being eaten did. It was frightening in a way that had a teeth-grinding nastiness. It grated against a prejudice which existed in antiquity but was non-existent in prehistory, a flickering prejudice, very strong with some, non-existent—even honorable and sacred—with others. The legends of Alexander the Great tell of his disgust and alarm when he found peoples who ate the flesh of human beings and how in a letter to his mother he told of his fear that they would teach "their vile depravity and would pollute the world," hence he built the impassable wall against Gog and Magog.

In Africa the cannibal scare was a trade wall built in part on actuality, largely on rumors. Cannibals were there, but it is likely that they did not "devour all strangers," as El-Bekri's informant had been told and as El-Bekri repeated. Maybe, having observed the traders' shudder, the borderland intermediaries made "Beware of Cannibals" their slogan.

The slogan, if such it was, was early adopted. Back in the ninth century the inventive Eldad the Danite had already met rumors of the cannibal hazard and inserted in his East African adventures an account of his capture by the Rom-Roms, who after a shipwreck ate his plump companion but thought Eldad was skinny and "put me in chains till I should grow fat." Eldad foiled them by banting. He hid the food given him and remained scrawny until escape came.

Another and more reliable author, Ibn Battuta, passed along a story told him when he was in Mali about a party of cannibals who had come to visit the Sultan of Mali, who was then reigning. They were a stylish lot, dressed in silk mantles, and they had a gold mine in their home country. "The sultan received them with honor and gave them as his 'hospitality gift' a young Negress to be their servitor or concubine. They killed and ate her and, having smeared their faces and hands with her blood, came to the sultan to thank him."

A variety of fanciful names were locally assigned to cannibal peoples and reported by Arabic authors—names of only vague geographical or tribal significance. An unbroken belt of reputed cannibalism stretched across Central Africa: Niam-Niam (or Gnam-Gnam), Yem-Yem, Dem-Dem, Rem-Rem, Lem-Lem. Perhaps the rhyming names were suggestive of the champing of the cannibal jaw. Schweinfurth says Niam-Niam meant "eaters." This name was applied especially, though not exclusively, to the Zande land in Central Africa, which lured old-time explorers—Petherick, Schweinfurth, the Italian Piaggia, and the only important old-time woman African explorer, Miss Tinne—and has intrigued modern anthropologists, notably Evans-Pritchard.

Word of a renowned center of anthropophagy was passed along by Mungo Park. It was in the Maniana region and its people were ferocious fighters and ate their defeated enemies; "the term man-eater (*madummulo*) was applied exclusively to them." Mungo Park's cannibals were not the only local gourmets who liked "the meat that talks," both as a luxury food item and for its psychological values, and a particularly horrifying punishment in the old days of Negro empires by the Niger was to exile an offender into "the country of the cannibals."

The most notorious and influential of all Africa's cannibals were the Jaga in Angola. It was an English explorer—an involuntary explorer—who observed them and told about them almost two centuries before Mungo Park. He was Andrew Battell, a sailor who after a complexity of mishaps fell into their hands and became their captive and associate in the last decade of the sixteenth century. He got away, and the story of his African experiences was printed in 1625. He tells of the violent life of his cannibal masters and also gives the first account of Pygmies and gorillas.

The Jaga made history. Their competent savagery was largely responsible for the final de-Christianization of Angola and the old Kingdom of Congo. Cannibalism with them and with other fighting groups farther east was not only a pleasure and an expression of triumph after victory but an element in their fear-inspiring tactics.

Even now and despite Europe's stern prohibition during the colonial period and the subsequent striving of the new nations there are sometimes dubious reports of man-eating. In 1964 a Paris court rejected a defamation suit brought against a French newspaper which had accused a Congo notable of "eating six people, including two ministers." A curious aspect of the cannibal scandal in reverse is that in old days black Africans often sincerely believed that the Europeans were man-eaters. When the first whites from Europe arrived on the Atlantic coasts the natives promptly attributed cannibalistic motives to them. Ca'da Mosto (1455–57) was told by the inhabitants of the Gambia region that they knew he "lived on nothing but human flesh and bought slaves only to devour them." Nor did the suspicion die so long as the slave trade lasted.

Cannibalism, which so invigorated some Africans in old days and which still at rare intervals is said to reappear even today, was a worldwide and very ancient magic and mystic act, appearing in a sublimated form in the Eucharist, deduced to have been ritually performed by Chinese prehistoric humans five hundred thousand years ago and manifested when an African king would eat parts of a defeated king so as to destroy the danger of his surviving inimical spirit. In those aspects anthropophagy was neither horrid nor wicked.

By an odd quirk we today while viewing it with a shudder are moved to regard cannibalism as a joke, publishing frequently comic drawings of cannibals and their victims or even—as recently appeared in an important American weekly—showing a savage shaking into his kettle from a box marked "Instant Man."

Man-eating in African forests and the talk thereof served quite a practical purpose in medieval days, when the riches of inner Africa beckoned to the traders from the north. The Negro intermediary was a slick fellow. He exaggerated the cannibal dangers. Also he recounted myths about the lands where the gold was which created a weird atmosphere likely to scare off intruders. He built a wall of magic, sometimes sinister, sometimes rather charming, like a fairy tale.

One quaint story was told and believed by the outside world through the centuries: that gold grew up out of the ground like a plant every year at a special season in a certain unrevealed region and that those who lived there went out and gathered it—the men and the women and the children all plucking bits of gold from its roots. This was told in the tenth century and again about the year 1000 in *The Book of Marvels,* and by many others, including Edrisi, and was told all over again by the Sultan of Mali when he visited Cairo in the fourteenth century. The Mali ruler added something significant. He said that it had been found that if conquest of the gold country was attempted the gold plants would not grow. The Negroes of the gold land had not lost their cunning. They would pay tribute to mighty Mali, yes. But there would be no intrusion—or rather the intruder would get no reward. The gold was their secret.

Other twists to the magic of the gold regions told how any man smothered by falling earth while digging was himself transformed into solid gold, how gold was the spit from magic crocodiles, how a serpent god whose severed head shot miles through space created a field of gold where the head fell to earth, and how a jinnee underground controlled the golden treasure and sometimes captured diggers and dragged them down to work for him.

The people who actually plucked, or picked up, or dug up the gold were an exclusive lot from the days of secret "dumb trading," which Herodotus described, to the modern days when Europeans arrived. One of the earliest British explorers, Lyon, who never got beyond northern Africa, repeated what had been told him and called them "the invisible nation." In Fernandes' description of the West Coast one reads a typical story such as was communicated to gold-hungry strangers. None but people of one tribe, it was said, was allowed to approach the gold mines. This tribe was composed of heathen blacks "of terrible aspect whose lips were so thick that they constantly put salt upon them being assured that, if they did not put on salt, their lips would fall off." They also suffered from internal maladies which they cured with the salt for which they exchanged their gold—the precious salt of the Sahara.

Once, the story goes on, the Sultan of Mali had caused one of these oddities to be kidnapped so that he might look at him and learn about the secret gold land. The captured man refused food and drink, would not speak and died. For three years after his death (this part of the story is from Ca'da Mosto, who heard the same tale) the indignant Thick Lips refused to trade. Then their lips began to putrefy for lack of salt, so they were forced to recommence.

While the shrewd Negro proprietors of the gold land hedged themselves in by myths the also shrewd seekers from the north did some inventing. They tempted the Negroes of the gold land with a return myth, a medical myth, that the salt from the Saharan mines which they offered had unique curative power not possessed by any other salt and was justly worth its price in gold. A variant of this was the swapping by an early European trader of bilge water from his ship as a cure for toothache!

Aside from an attempt to understand and speculate about old-time opinions and legends as to how the whites and the blacks of Africa reacted to one another in the days before colonization we meet one fact which is certain—that white Africans accepted Negroes socially. Since then the racial attitude has probably been altered by colonialism's prejudices, and was again altered at colonialism's end and Africa's spirit of get-togetherness.

White Africa, Egypt and Mediterranean Africa, looked with respect at some prominent people with colored faces. Some colored faces even wore crowns. One of the dark royalties may have been Queen Nefertari, whom Egypt adored and venerated for centuries, putting her memory upon a pedestal almost unequaled in Egypt's history, and who is "depicted for some unaccountable reason with a black countenance." (I quote Sir Alan Gardiner's words in *Egypt of the Pharaohs*, 1961.) The reason may have been that the great queen was black. Such was the opinion of Sir Flinders Petrie and some others. And, whatever was her actual complexion, the fact that she was shown as black (or sometimes blue) in contemporary official portraiture seems to indicate there was much racial tolerance and to presuppose that Negroes were socially acceptable.

This queen of the dark portraits was the almost unique great-grandmother of the famous Queen Hatshepsut, the "Queen Victoria of Antiquity," for the incestuous marriages of Egypt's royalty made their family tree into a nearly branchless pole. Surprisingly to our usual ideas, this did not produce odd or degenerate offspring, bearing out what Freud wrote in *Moses and Monotheism*: "It is not even certain that there lies any danger in inbreeding." Egyptian incest, based on a wish to keep pure the sacred royal blood, but, so Breasted says, imitated by the rest of Egypt, contrasts with those punctilious, complicated and probably very long-established rules of black Africans as to who should not marry whom which are often noted by anthropologists, though black royalty in certain localities sometimes mated incestuously. Islam sternly forbade incest. Dido, the legendary Phoenician foundress of Carthage, is said to have married her uncle.

Later Egypt had an indubitably dark ruler, Pianki the Ethiopian, and later yet another, Karfur, whom I have just mentioned. And the notable Mustansir the Fat of Cairo, who played a major part in the history of all North Africa, for it was he who was responsible for the disastrous second Arab invasion across the top of the continent and into the Sahara, had a black Sudanese mother. The rule of this half Negro was the longest in Moslem annals, Hitti says.

Several sultans in Morocco were mulattoes. The history of the Merinid dynasty, which reigned for about two centuries, notes the skin color of each sultan—which is in itself significant. Many are carefully designated as "white of skin," several are "tawny," one is "swarthy" and at least three are bluntly called "black" (from *Rawdat en-Nisrin*). In the Merinid period the sultan customarily picked his successor from among his usually many sons, and the fact that a son might have inherited the dark complexion of his mother evidently did not blot out his chances.

The mating of white royal fathers with black women was not only frequent but was probably regarded as a luxurious privilege. Colored women were white men's prizes. The sexual appeal of the dark woman was celebrated, a sort of byword. As a symbol of the passion rouser in men "the Ethiopian woman" (meaning in this case the Nubian) figures in the records of the fourth-century Egyptian Christian monks in the translation of Anân Ishô, where the monks are represented as making pitiful struggles against tormenting visions of "the Ethiopians" in the so-called "War against Fornication."

The Negro spouse was viewed seriously, not just as a bedtime playmate, and the mulatto child was not disdained. What Edrisi wrote shows the indifference white Africans felt toward color. After telling in lusciously and embarrassingly detailed terms of the sexual charms of Nubian women he says, "Because of the delights of their embraces the princes of Egypt desire to possess them and make them the mothers of their children." The Islamic sentiment was that "the mothers are but vessels . . . the fathers account for nobility." The darker skins within which the "nobility" was enclosed seemingly was not a handicap. In his study of medieval Islam, Dr. von Grunebaum says that in Moslem society "the offspring of a Negro mother and a white father was admitted to full equality."

One especially interesting African, a king in Algeria long before Islam's day, may have had Negro blood. His appearance on coins has suggested this. He was King Juba II, whose father was the defeated enemy of Julius Caesar, who as a child was the show piece of a Roman triumph, whom Rome set up as king with a capital near the modern city of Algiers, who wrote voluminously—his writings were lost but cited extensively in Pliny's *Natural History*—and who married into two remarkable families of the time when B.C. was just merging into A.D. One of his wives was a member of the family of Herod the Great. Another of his wives was the daughter of Antony and Cleopatra.

All in all, the two-colored continent seems to have handled its race relations with mutual adaptability and considerable common sense.

AFRICANS WITHOUT A BOOK

BOOKLESS FREETHINKING ·
BIG GOD AND LITTLE GODS ·
THE AFRICAN AND HIS
ANCESTORS

BOOKLESS FREETHINKING · That great block of
Negroes with whom white Africa never came into close relations,
the unconverted to Islam, were, still are the essence of Africa. They
carried along Africa's real self, which contacts with the outside world
affect but will not soon destory, a heritage which will shape Africa's
future and in part our own, for Africa has become very important
to us both in its behavior and in its thoughts. Those bookless people
who shrank from the "religion of a book"—the Koran in their case—
and disliked the smell of civilization are well worth consideration.

We begin to suspect that the dark African of pre-colonial days was
not the mere "child of eight" of an early traveler (Richard Burton).
We begin to discern in his thinking and in his ways, which we used

to lump as unmixed savagery, a disconcerting glimmer which has a startling value. I read in the words of wise and sensitive Professor Mircea Eliade a suggestive reference to a new appreciation of Africans and others: "Ethnic groups which until now had no place in world history except for glimpses and passing allusions are preparing in their turn to enter into the great currents of contemporary history," and later in the same passage in his Foreword to *Images and Symbols* he adds that our culture "unless it shuts itself off into a sterilising provincialism will be obliged to reckon with other ways of knowing and other scales of values than our own."

We can venture to study what dark Africans thought and did with a certain respect, even deference, for we are beginning to suspect that their self-isolation from civilization, partly geographically caused and partly from instinctive repugnance, may have been prophetic. The civilization of the outside world, the white world, so absolutely sure of itself when it started to compare itself with Africa at the debut of colonization—those were our days of smug delight—has suffered of late a jarring shock. We can no longer feel the bland certainty of those early colonists that our way is the only right way, inevitably and indisputably the right way, and that we are marching steadily toward bliss and perfection.

Sometimes one of us in a mood of mingled gloom and whimsicality wonders to himself whether, despite tangible deprivations—like books and boots and bathtubs—the dark African waiting in his pristine backwardness and watching civilization stub its toe was not instinctively a shrewd fellow. We ourselves keep speaking about "the good old times." This is a regret that pagan Africans need not feel; they have carried "the good old times" along with them.

Primitive Africans in their queer quaint fashion have threaded their way in comfort through considerable thinking and have recognized, accepted and retained in good standing certain things which we hide in the dark closet of the spirit, but of which we are aware in shame-faced secrecy, and they have domesticated into their social code, which merged with religion, ideas we know and ourselves follow.

The big section of dark Africa which had declined or never been approached by Islam and which knew Christianity not at all was spiritually in a floating, free position. Its people could make up their philosophy and religion as they went along. Their booklessness—in Negro Africa in pre-colonial days the book would have been the Koran—made for a state of thinking which was free-flowing and flexible. They really did find their books in the running brooks. They enjoyed the freedom of non-literate thinking, not bound down by written words that were fixed and oft repeated and destructive of experience and imagining.

Mohammed had deep reverence for religions with a book and thus put a high moral value on literacy and shoved the pagans out into the cold. But paganism did at any rate give dark Africa a less bickering form of piety. Their religious behavior was sometimes ugly, sometimes cruel and we have often called it silly, but we are not aware that people suffered from religious wars and religious persecutions among themselves, though contempt for another tribe's religious behavior may have been used as a general war incentive, especially in the period of the big foreign slave demand.

But there are things quite as interesting and more significant about these bookless people than their religion—ways of handling their lives, some of which might be worth our study for an understanding of Africa and some, I venture to say without hesitation, because they can give us hints of simple wisdom or even trouble us by suggesting some human understanding we have lost. Primitive people, as compared to ourselves, "have perhaps an even truer sense of reality," says anthropologist Radin, and Leakey, in his lecture printed as *The Progress and Evolution of Man in Africa,* listed enthusiastically some "tragedies" unknown to many African tribes which afflict our society, such as destitute widows and orphans, unloved lonely spinsters and uncared-for elderly people.

Other aspects of their social behavior shock and startle and disgust us.

It is often hard to sift the religious elements apart from magic and from things which are a matter of social habit, the sort of behavior that has to their ideas seemed best suited to their conditions of life. Where there is no book to record the moral code it is difficult to distinguish between the sacred and the profane. Indeed with a book this is sometimes difficult.

Religion is a hard term to define. Once we "people of a book" used to declare that the bookless African pagans "have no religion at all," an idea which is implied in the dictionary definition, the simplest being that a pagan is one who is not a Christian, a Jew or a Moslem, thus defining paganism not as a belief but as a negation of religion. Later many students came to the opinion that the African pagans had nothing else! That they were stuffed with religious sentiment to the eyeballs and that everything in their behavior except the most rudimentary acts had a religious explanation and motive. Maybe the truth lies between the two opinions.

We were inclined to think that for people who lived in isolation and did not read religion was the sole intellectual expression, that religion must be their big mental It. I think African pagans did considerable mental work that was non-religious and that perhaps we have overused the term "religion" as an elastic coverall for what has been noted in the behavior of Africa's bookless.

We can only guess what was their way of thinking before Europe pushed in. Our sole source is the accounts of certain early travelers who noted native ways and the manifestations of what they supposed to be native religion and jumbled the lot together. Frequently the pictures they give us are darkly colored by the strict intolerance of the day and by their own personal discomforts and dangers, and are often marked by a grin or a shudder. Most were scandalized. Some were sympathetic. Obviously none could know what the native thought or what was behind his actions.

The earliest account I know of about the paganism of Inner Africa from the European Christian standpoint is that written by the Catalan Ramon Lull, not an explorer but a missionary.

Ramon Lull, St. Mark and Dr. Schweitzer are the three best-known Christian missionaries to Africa; Livingstone is more familiar as an explorer. Lull, as I have said, when nearly eighty was finally stoned to death at Bougie in Algeria, where he had unwisely and insistently intruded with his preaching—a dangerous nuisance to the exasperated Moslem population; to Christians, an imprudent but noble martyr. This was in the year 1315. Four hundred years afterward the English chaplian at Algiers, Thomas Shaw, told in his book of travels about Lull's cavern of meditation on the rocky coast near Bougie.

Lull's conversion efforts concentrated, so far as we know, in the Mediterranean region, but he ventured to write a book about the paganism of the land of the Negroes entitled *Blanquerna,* title from an imaginary Pope, which is a fictional work but which introduced some interesting if doubtful details. *Blanquerna* tells of blacks who "adored idols and likewise adored the sun and the stars and the birds and beasts," and in a later passage mentions "a dragon who was adored as a god."

It is most unlikely that Lull collected this information and misinformation personally. But we can assume he set it down with sincere conviction. He was not attempting to write a religious thriller. One is curious as to what were his sources. He knew Arabic and traveled from Egypt to Morocco. He was an early and profound student of Islam, and presumably he reflected the Moslem attitude that all who were not "people of a book," such as Africa's pagans, were idolaters, although as a matter of fact idolatry in the way we usually understand the term—as the offering of worship to some image or object as to a god—does not seem to have been on dark Africa's religious program.

The great Arabic geographer, El-Bekri, who did not himself go into Africa, passed along a tale which may have come to Lull's attention about the Dem-Dem cannibal country, where there was "an enormous fortress upon which is placed an idol in the form of a woman which they worship as their god, going to the place as pilgrims." Delafosse, with his bloodhound's scent for Africana, has traced what he thinks is the source for this queer El-Bekri item, so outside the pattern of African paganism, in a tradition which has a patriotic rather than religious basis.

The tradition deals with ancient times in what is now the Republic of Upper Volta, in which ruled for many centuries one of the longest continued royal families in world's history—thirty-four rulers in direct line. Their traditions tell of a remarkable princess called Yennenga, a woman warrior who repudiated men because she feared that motherhood would keep her from marching at the head of her troops. But a runaway horse carried her to romance and she forgot war, became a mother and named her son by the tribal equivalent of the word "Stallion," in memory of the adventure which changed her life.

Yennenga became the heroine of the Mossi people of Volta. Her tomb was venerated and a place of pilgrimage till recent times—that is, for over about a thousand years. At the death of a Mossi king one of his horses and one of his wives were there sacrificed in Yennenga's memory. Delafosse suggests this might have been the basis of El-Bekri's item. And it may well also have inspired Ramon Lull.

Word of "the dragon who was adored as a god" might have been brought to Lull's ears by stories told by trans-Saharan traders about the reptilian elite in the legends of Negroland—reptilian royalty sometimes—or about the snake worship which long afterward was to make the lower African West Coast famous—or infamous.

Or perhaps he heard some confused echo about that dragon which tyrannized over a part of Africa and was exterminated by the timeless legendary figure Alexander the Great under his pseudonym of Doul Karnein. The pseudonym meant "Man with Two Horns," and resembles the reference to Alexander by the Prophet Daniel, whose vision of a mysterious goat with several horns has been interpreted as an allusion to Alexander (Daniel 8).

Alexander's mythical African adventures ignored time. Before history began he cut the Strait of Gibraltar, setting Africa free from Europe—a prevision of de-colonization! He appears in Ethiopian literature as a pious Christian who believed in the Trinity. And his exploit with the dragon is undated. In the twelfth century Edrisi tells how Doul Karnein destroyed the monster. He put out two poisoned bulls stuffed with a mixture of resin, sulphur, chalk and arsenic, also fishhooks, so that the dragon could not vomit when he took sick. It was without doubt an oft told and garbled story and might have been the foundation for the statement that Africa knew a dragon god.

The myths and rumors I have told may seem rather fanciful as sources for the devout Christian missionary Ramon Lull's sober effort to present in a plea for saving Africans from paganism, but Lull was a figure in the Middle Ages, when imagination and pious credulity danced a pretty dance hand in hand and often their favorite parlor was Africa.

Direct on-the-spot observation came with exploration. Long before the science of anthropology in the modern sense was born certain explorers of Africa did some anthropological investigation in their own untrained and rough-and-ready fashion and sized up local paganism. They were Portuguese. From their reported observations that natives possessed and treated certain objects with devoted respect derived the idea of calling African paganism "fetishism," the term being derived from a Portuguese word applied to images and relics regarded as possessing magical virtues.

The term "fetishism" as applied to African religion appears to be little used scientifically these days, though common with older anthropology and still a favorite in popular talk and literature. But the word has definitely moved into intellectual white society in a quite different sense. It is one of our African imports. In addition to the usual dictionary meaning "fetishism" is used in psychology, thus defined, "sensual gratification derived from touching a part of the body of a person or a piece of wearing apparel belonging to it." This seems a long way from the religion of black Africa.

In the original African sense the fetish was usually understood to mean an object prepared or collected and cherished by human hands. Odd were the substances used in its confection, according to the seventeenth-century record of the Dominican missionary Father Godefroy Loyer, who studied the subject on the spot and with a certain comprehension—"the exactitude of their respect for their fetish would make a slack Christian blush," he wrote. He mentions as fetish materials scraps of wood, teeth of a dog, a lion or a civet cat or bits of ivory, an egg or bird bones, or a fowl's head or bones of an ox or a goat, or fish bones or a ram's horn or a thorny branch or some piece of tree bark. Such stuff, chosen and cherished according to the fancy of the individual Negro, was not, Father Loyer emphasizes, regarded by him as a god.

The fetish was a comforter, a magic toy, a charm, and its function, like that of charms the world around, was to protect or gratify wishes or even to harm the enemy. The name spontaneously given to it by the early explorers shows that there appeared to them to be an analogy between the fetish and the sacred objects of power which were revered in their homeland. But fetishism, we are assured, was not a religion in itself, nor was the fetish an idol. It was some bit of junk, not adored for itself but only because it was considered to be the temporary home of supernatural power, and like as not, it would be discarded when its supposed usefulness was finished—a triumph of pure imagination. It was without enduring value as a sacred thing, not like the holy images which figured in the iconoclast war of Byzantium, not like that crucifix over the door of the imperial palace, which was believed to have used human speech.

On the puzzle of the fetish let me tell two of the multitude of instances seriously recorded. One is pretty and imaginative, the other so strange as to make one tremble a little.

The pretty one: it concerns the Bambara of West Africa. A man wishes to win friends, to be liked by all the world. Let the maker of the fetish find two trees of different species which grow very close together. Let him chip off a bit of the bark from each tree, crush the two bits together in a mortar, carefully collect the resulting powder and put it in a little leather bag. This the man will wear around his neck and his social problem is solved.

The other instance deals with the self-inflicted martyrdom of a patriot when his tribal group, certain Bantu people living near the Congo mouth, felt the need of protection by a fetish of great potency. A youth of high spirit or a famed and daring hunter would be chosen for the terrible honor. The members of the tribe go into the bush and call his name. A sacred tree is cut down from which the fetish will be made, and as it falls it bleeds blood. To them and to the chosen hero there is a mingling of his life with the power of the fetish. Quietly and as he knew he would he slips into death within ten days, his life a sacrifice to what he believes is his people's welfare.

This, as Dennett tells the story in *At the Back of the Black Man's Mind,* was spiritual suicide, not self-destruction by poison or weapon or hunger strike. Nor did it correspond to the extraordinary tragedy of the "Kaffirs" in South Africa, who in 1857 deliberately committed mass euthanasia—thousands of them, twenty-five thousand of them, some said—misled by the prophecy of a lovely new world of delight for their people. The fetish hero's death, expected and unavoidable and unassisted, was a psychological thing, a case similar to but on a

174 · AFRICA BEFORE THEY CAME

bigger scale than the stigmata sometimes recorded about Christian *exaltées*.

Another instance of fetishism lacks the spiritual pathos of the youth's self-sacrifice though it also deals with a fetish of public utility. Tauxier records it in his book about the Bambara and says it was told him by a native who stated he had witnessed the grisly performance when a boy in the region of Ségou on the Niger. It was evidently a long-established custom. The fetishes in question, called Makonghoba, were family treasures and were ceremoniously bathed in the blood of the defeated chief after a tribal victory. After this the chief's corpse plus the body of an ox were stewed together and consumed in a sort of ritual meal.

Animism, a democratic acceptance of all the world's equality, a complete denial of the inanimate and the attribution of a soul like his own—or shall we say a personality—to every bush and rock and pumpkin (calabash) and to the animal world, and to the rivers and brooks and puddles—this was bookless Africa's point of view. It was amplified sometimes by ascribing special dignity and power to some specific piece of nature—a mountain, tree or a stone. The term "animism," though applied to primitives elsewhere, became an especially convenient blanket covering for Africa's form of paganism—perhaps too convenient, or too sweeping.

UNESCO has used it, saying of today's African pagans "most of the people are animists." This is perhaps an oversimplification. It seems almost to transform a general attitude into a religious formula; one might almost think animism was a dogma and a ritual, that it was as definitely a religious belief as, say, Methodism. Sir Edward Burnett Tylor, who, though he did not invent the term, launched animism upon the public, declared almost a century ago that it was "the groundwork of the Philosophy of Religion from that of the savages to that of civilized man," and gave seven long chapters to the subject in *Primitive Culture*.

But whether animism is indeed the basis of all religion and the backbone of the religion of pagan Africa or whether it is not a religion at all is a point about which anthropologists have disagreed, as indeed anthropologists often do when discussing the delicate and intangible cobweb of Africa's paganism, Tylor's diagnosis covered, rightly or wrongly, the thinking of millions in Africa—outstandingly the great primitive pagan center of the world. It was bequeathed to later anthropologists for them to adopt, criticize, bicker about or disagree with. One student who maintains that animism is "not a religion at all" wrote informally, "Sir Edward Tylor tied a can to the tail of a continent."

At any rate it would seem that in those pre-colonial days before we of the outside world came and gradually beclouded their image there was in bookless Africa no such thing as "a thing." Nothing was inanimate. Perhaps it was Africa's expression of an understanding of the wide world and all therein, a simplified and sympathetic approach to all of nature's elements, which were so very close to her people's outdoor lives—their sort of science, their understanding of industry.

The Greeks, whom we always like to cite, sensed that "all things that move have been invested with personality. The stars and the rivers are persons." (From Hatch in *The Influence of Greek Ideas on Christianity*.) Christianity in this respect was influenced and had to meet and fight nature worship. "The religion of nature was a mighty foe," says Harnack, "it still avails to beguile our souls." Certain of the Gnostics for their part believed stones were animate beings. The Gospel of Thomas hints at the subject, and a piece of medieval Ethiopian literature, also recently brought to our notice (English translation in Wolf Leslau's *Falasha Anthology*), handles the same idea with ungloved fury. This is *The Book of Abba Elijah*, in which the Falasha Jews of Ethiopia repudiated an aspect of animism as idolatry and repeated God's own very words of disgust. God reprimands and designates punishments to the various elements of nature—the sea, the trees, the stones, the wells, the mountains, the sun and the moon —because they have seduced man to idolatry. Yet God's reprimand would in itself imply that the elements have the capacity deliberately to plan man's seduction and so seems to suggest that Abba Elijah attributed animistic sentiment to the mind of God Himself!

BIG GOD AND LITTLE GODS · Granting the immense gap between God and gods, between Almighty God and polytheism, it was a startling discovery to early Christian visitors to the Africa of the pagans to find splashed right across the continent a sort of monotheism, a belief in a big boss god, a god in chief who was often believed to have been their creator.

It was not Christianity's sort of monotheism, which itself Moslem felt varied from the absolute divine exclusivity of Islam. But to discover any faith of this sort in a supposedly muddled and fetish-ridden land caused amazement and roused questions.

Very many dark Africans spoke of a boss god. But they also revered or felt fear mixed with detestation for a bunch of other gods, a staff of other gods who were executive specialists in different fields of either protection and kindness or attack and danger. And they crowded their world with a large cast of regionally varying and very troublesome demons and spirits. The gods in chief who were scattered across bookless Africa had differing names and differing personalities and characteristics. Their usual residence seems to have been in the sky.

I shall not fatigue the reader by offering an attempt at a Who's Who listing of such of these "Supreme Beings" and their associates as I have been able to identify. It is enough to say that in a recent missionary symposium entitled *African Ideas of God* the "Index of God-Names" as used by various tribes in pagan Africa runs over three double-column pages.

This profusion of different divine names is not surprising in a continent of so many languages. How many languages is an unsettled question. The estimate keeps growing. A few years back Westermann set the probable total at about six hundred. In 1961 two papers presented at the Leverhulme Conference gave the total as one thousand and as between one thousand and two thousand. Greenberg is more conservative and more exact, listing 730 languages by name. Obviously many of the different tongues are exclusive little languages, having only a small clientele.

Many of these languages are Bantu. Westermann, who estimated the total at about six hundred, lists at almost two hundred of what he calls "the better-known Bantu languages" and gives another list of what are sometimes called "the semi-Bantu languages," which runs to almost as many more. Bantu, as shown on his language map except for a few spots, slices off the whole lower part of the continent from ocean to ocean. "Bantu" was an arbitrary appellation invented by an early student of languages because of a linguistic similarity among a large group of tribal tongues. This must not be misunderstood. If one each of the several hundred Bantu and semi-Bantu people were to meet would they converse with ease? No! It would be Babel.

Naturally the term "Bantu" is sometimes loosely used, giving the impression that it refers to some special single tribe or political group or geographical locality. The members of "The Bantu Club," if I may so dub them, are not held together by any human values. They differ widely in physique and culture and do not share mutual history or traditions, and "The Club" was not of their organization, but a tag of Europe's invention, just as were certain place names like Nigeria, gracefully invented by Lady Lugard, and Sierra Leone, which Portugal inspired.

Where and when and how in the long ago there emerged the underlying web which attaches all the Bantu languages together and reaches a thread into the semi-Bantu languages is a problem about which specialists are puzzled and constantly speculate. Their uncertainty and avid curiosity are shown in the fact that two learned publications, *The Journal of African History* and *Journal of African Languages,* recently carried almost simultaneously articles on the question and that at the 1961 Conference on African History and Archaeology there was earnest discussion regarding two differing theories: one (of the American professor Greenberg) that the Bantu languages sprang from West Africa, the other (of the English professor Guthrie) that they spread from a nucleus in Central Africa.

All this is a subject for specialists, and I would not go into it except that the term "Bantu" has become puzzling since the publicizing of the race difficulties in South Africa, being often used in news items in an exclusively South African sense, as if Bantu were a regional tribe or piece of geography. Many of us may regret that the "Bantu" theory which Bleek advanced a century ago took so firm a hold, for Bantu has become a very confusing word. Perhaps after a time "Bantu" will either drift into disuse or into some specific usage that has a practical and definite and easily understood meaning.

The varieties of Bantu religions were many. These people who have been whimsically lumped together for linguistic reasons were presumably non-associated in their own minds in pre-colonial days, and they evolved their own religions in their separate local fashions. Bantu speakers in Uganda and Kenya, in Tanganyika and Nyasaland, Zulu and Xhosa and Swahili, and tribes in Angola and in the ex-Belgian Congo and in the Cameroons, and so on, philosophized in their own varying fashions and circumstances and conditions, mostly monotheistically—sometimes the god in chief makes the sun shine or the rain fall; sometimes he is a nebulous creature. It was part of the vast sweep of monotheism of one sort or another across bookless Africa.

The overall picture is very imaginative, a mixture of the human that is almost childish, with a complexity of intergod family relationships and disputes which reminds us of the classics or of ancient Egypt.

Simple and rather touching was the monotheism of the Pygmies, who have been in the world's news longer than any other people of Inner Africa, for the dancing Pygmy, "a Deng of the god's dances from the land of the Horizon-dwellers," of the Pharaoh Piopi II of the Dynasty VI was mentioned when news was recorded on stone, and the Pygmies of 1964 got onto paper pages as world's news when they astonished us by routing five companies of the Congolese army and put white residents into near panic. I find a quaint item in Baumann's encyclopedic work on the civilization of African peoples: that after the death of a forest Pygmy his life force would be carried up to the sky to the chief god, Tore, by a fly—a suitably tiny symbol chosen by a miniature race.

Here are a few examples from legends and folklore about the big gods of Africa:

We find that the overgod, Oyisa, was asked to come down to Benin to discuss life prospects with the king, who did not want ever to die, and that upon landing at another place Oyisa, like any humble traveler, lost his way and had to inquire for directions. But on reaching his destination he authoritatively informed the king that his death was inevitable. A curious combination of simple ignorance and infinite power.

The Obassi of the Ekoi, who straddled the Nigeria-Cameroons frontier, were duplicate gods—one was kind, the other, more powerful, was harsh. The harsh chief god had five wives. Four did the housework, the other was his pet. The favorite became infatuated with seven handsome young men all at once and shut herself away with them in her quarters. Obassi, warned by one of the working wives, listened outside and ordered the pet and her seven sweethearts to be killed.

A Supreme Being of great power held sway over a region which formed a part of what is now the Ivory Coast and Ghana. He had created all the little gods and mankind and the animals. According to local usages, he went by various names, often hyphenated, in which something like Nyamia was always featured. A learned African, Amon d'Aby, who was for many years the official archivist of the Ivory Coast, lists Nyamia's titles as they were used by the Fanti and other groups, including the Apollonians, romantically so named by early Europeans because of their beautiful bodies. The Apollonians called him Nana-Nyamale, meaning "Grandfather-god."

Yet the family life of this widely revered super god, as represented in regional folklore, was far from secure. For example, a son was born to Nyamia and his wife. He had to go away on business and, taking his wife, he left the baby in his fine house in the sky with its six doors. A wicked giant managed to climb up to the sky, broke all the doors, seized the child and carried it down to earth in a bag, the giant nonchalantly passing the unsuspecting god along a forest road. But presently Nyamia's slave, who had loafed along behind his master, met the bad giant, demanded to know what was in the bag, fought the giant for its possession, won the combat and carried the bag, unopened, up to heaven to his master, who had just discovered the broken doors and the loss of his son.

"Any reward you desire!" said the god to his slave. "Just anything you like to give me," said the slave.

This and other similar stories which Tauxier includes in the passage on folklore in a work largely dealing with Nyamia show a familiar attitude toward the god in chief which might seem absurd did we not recall that quaint and human items sometimes occur in the myths of the wise and even in the pages of those religions which possess a book.

Let us consider in contrast that people of splendiferous polytheism whose family of gods, operating in a pattern and mingling directly with royalty, have reminded many of us of ancient Egypt. I mean the Yoruba, a group who lived in the southwestern inland part of Nigeria and who were the Oxford and Harvard, the Athens and Alexandria of intellectual paganism.

Of gods and goddesses it is said that they had 401. No other form of African paganism in Negroland has become so familiar to the outside world. I find that over twenty of Yoruba's deities rate a separate biography under his or her name in the last edition of Everyman's *Dictionary of Non-Classical Mythology.* Many writers have dilated on the Yoruba gods, often with confusing and conflicting data. A Yoruba scholar, the Reverend Dr. Idowu, has lately published a book on the divinities of his native land called *Olodumare God in Yoruba Belief,* which though interesting makes the situation yet more complex. The partial cast of Yoruba's gods which follows is my attempt at a sifting simplification.

It began with Olorun (alternately called Olodumare), a contracted form of the Yoruba words for "The Owner of the Heavens," who sent his son down to create the world, then just a big wide ocean. Odudua, the son, performed the task—and there was Yoruba with the city Ife as its spiritual center and Odudua its first divine king, despite being sometimes revered as a he- and sometimes as a she-god. In his male personality I find him appearing as the shrewd personage in a bit of African history by an African writer, Egharevba, who, when he wrote his *Short History of Benin,* was curator of the Benin Museum. Benin is Ife's neighbor. Odudua, the king-god, was asked by the Benin to give them one of his sons as a ruler. As a test he sent them seven lice with instructions to take care of them and return them after three years. The lice duly came home healthy and bigger. Odudua then said, "People who can take care of such minute pests as lice can undoubtedly take care of my son," and dispatched his son to Benin. Such is the story told by Egharevba.

Odudua's wife is the presumed subject of an often reproduced and very beautiful piece of Ife brasswork.

Among the many other members of Yoruba's divine royal family were the god of iron, the god of fire, two gods of childbirth, the god of prophecy, the god of trade and a goddess of the River Niger. The god of lightning was an especially picturesque figure and a favorite subject in the oral traditions as recorded by the Reverend Samuel Johnson, valued as the best source on Yoruba's early history.

The lightning god's name was Shango. He was a magician. He blew smoke and fire out of his mouth, and he invented a method to summon lightning which, alas, was so potent it got beyond his control. His palace and many of his wives and children were destroyed. Shango in fury and remorse murdered a lot of his subjects and then plunged off alone into the countryside and hanged himself on a shea butter tree. To Yoruba he became the god of thunder and lightning and remains so into our own times, so that it is still the custom to exclaim when there is a clap of thunder, "Welcome to your Majesty!"

In Yoruba, Africans have met a conflict between religion and national pride. Two irreconcilable and flattering theories about their own origin clashed.

One was that they—first of all mankind—had been created here on the spot when the son of "The Owner of the Heavens" was let down on a chain—quite possible to their creation myth, since the sky in those days hung so low that a man could almost touch the heavens with his hand. With him he carried a symbolic basin of sand and a symbolic scratching chicken to transform the sea into habitable land.

The other theory which was their proud tradition was that their forebears had come to their present homeland by migration from a noble setting in the East.

Their problem paralleled and predated the conflict of Genesis and Darwin which disturbed our own public. Bookless Yoruba may not have appreciated the gravity of the contradiction, the chasm between the two backgrounds they attributed to themselves. They appear to have handled the matter with aplomb and to have driven the two theories in double harness, as the two following items will indicate.

A very early European traveler who was in their midst in the 1820's, having gone that way en route to his solving of the Niger mystery, heard in the market place of their capital city, Katunga (no relation to Katanga), about the sacred locality "called Iffie [Ife], which is stated to be four moons' journey from Katunga, where their first parents were created and whence all Africa has been peopled." (From Richard and John Lander's *Journal of an Expedition to Explore the Course and Termination of the Niger.*)

Almost simultaneously that famous character, the Sultan Bello, son of the Fula conqueror Osman dan Fodio, and himself an interesting historian and a covetous and undoubtedly well-informed neighbor of Yoruba, wrote in his African history, of which Lander's former employer carried away a copy to England, "It is believed that the inhabitants of Yoruba descend from the sons of Chanaan of the tribe of Nemrod. It is thought that they established in western Africa after having been chased out of Arabia. Pushed back from the coast between Egypt and Abyssinia, they drove into the African interior as far as Yoruba, where they settled." (Translation from an Arabic ms. brought away by Captain Clapperton.)

Many of the Yoruba people still maintain their old religion and at the same time boast of their eastern origin, and some thoughtful folk of our own think that the second part of their belief—the part about the eastern origin—is a possibility. Johnson, whose early history of them is taken very seriously, said, "That the Yoruba came originally from the East there cannot be the slightest doubt." A long journey, but Africa's traditions are full of such long journeys. Migration runs like a thread through her past. There is scarcely a place whose inhabitants do not think they came from somewhere else, and often anthropology supports their traditions. The Masai proverb runs, "Nobody can say he is settled anywhere forever; it is only the mountains that do not move from their places."

The theory of Yoruba's eastern origin—Egypt preferred—was strengthened because of the resemblance in their religious layout, especially in the matter of a divine monarchy, to the ideas of the ancient Egyptians, and it associates with the old-fashioned opinion that thought was born and exported the world around from Egypt. To this add the more generally held notion that simple bookless Africans could not have devised a religion so complex on their own initiative.

It was the latter sentiment, the denial to Africans of the capacity to do their own thinking or imagining, that caused Europeans in the early days of exploration and colonization to deduce that the rude forms of monotheism observed in pagan Africa must necessarily have derived from some Christian influence, some vague rumor, some second- or thirdhand account of God which had drifted to their ears. It seemed almost a miracle and gave Europeans great satisfaction.

Indeed it was doubly acceptable because the sole alternative was so distasteful. It was abhorrent to think that God would have placed in the minds of these savages the instinctive realization of Himself as Creator and Supreme Being—albeit in a one-syllable sort of fashion—which it had required explanation, revelation and argument to convey to our own ancestors. It contradicted the basic belief that "The One God . . . used the figure of Yahweh, the God of Sinai, as a means of revealing Himself to a particular nation," a phrase which Stanley Cook attributes to a former Archbishop of Canterbury.

Later anthropology tackled the question and, after studying the general subject of primitive religion, concluded on the whole that a sort of monotheism was instinctive in mankind. Perhaps it corresponded to the instinctive desire for an individual human ruler, a king—"the idea of society is the soul of a religion," as I understand Durkheim said. Thus Africa's "Supreme God" was not a distorted reflection of the God of the Old Testament. But it is not a question that can be comfortably settled by scientific discussion. Certain people are pained to the heart at the suggestion that embryonic, undignified and miscellaneous forms of monotheism predated, or operated independently of, their own. Many missionaries in Africa have dodged the dilemma and "with few exceptions have adopted African names for God," not using the name "God" but giving whatever was the local supreme god's name as a synonym and employing "personal names like Nyama, Leza, Myambe." I quote and cite this from the Reverend Edwin W. Smith, a missionary and a learned author on Africa and the editor of *African Ideas of God.*

It is regrettable to one who attempts to study pre-colonial Africa that anthropology's investigations came only after colonization had begun to affect Africa's thought more or less. For this there are two reasons. One is that there was practically no peaceable penetration to the interior and absolutely no possibility for that safe and prolonged easygoing contact which in his Introduction to *Anthropology of Folk Religions* Leslie says is necessary for successful field work. No chance to "eat and work, gossip and worship with them."

The other reason was that there were not any anthropologists anyway in those pre-colonial days. Darwin has been called "the father of anthropology." Tylor was its midwife and Frazer in *The Golden Bough* then sang a confusing but charming song of widely shared myths to which Africa was allowed to contribute vague whispers and whimpers, which later on-the-spot observations have not always confirmed. For in those days, insofar as Africa was concerned, the new science of modern anthropology had to make a small dab of the butter of on-the-spot information spread over a very large slice of theorizing. There were mostly armchair anthropologists, "content to let laymen collect the facts on which they based their theories," as Evans-Pritchard says.

Sometimes the African examples cited by famous early anthropologists are disfigured by a poor grasp of geography and what we know of local history. Sometimes their sweeping statements are laughably generalized, as if they had no vision of the vast size and variations of the "Africa" they mention. Professor Leslie says, "It is an impressive fact that none of the more influential theorists"—he lists half a dozen of the leading authorities, including Tylor and Frazer—"had a direct knowledge of primitive societies."

It is natural that such indirect research did not tell us much about

Africa's paganism, on which firsthand knowledge is hard to come by even to the modern trained searcher—"information rarely given willingly," says Radin. For, as Delafosse after his many years in Africa found out, "they hide from strangers the dogma of their beliefs and what is fundamental in their religion."

Recently there have been some brilliant and courageous field anthropological studies in Africa, where climate and political circumstances have made it hard. And modern missionaries have made contributions often inspired by a new tolerance and broad-mindedness. These things are interesting but very varied, for "about no subject in social anthropology is there more conflict of opinion than about primitive theology." I quote again Evans-Pritchard. He goes on to say that the diversity is not wholly due to respective religious convictions of the searcher, but "must be attributed to the amorphous, indefinite character of the facts themselves."

To those who wince and repudiate anthropology's theory that Africa's monotheism was indigenous, not acquired, the problem of how she divined that there was a Supreme Being in the sky is further complicated by several suggestions other than some grapevine story about Christianity. Africa might have borrowed her monotheism from Islam, echoes of which might have been heard deep in the lands of paganism. Or even some memory of Jewish teachings might have survived. Some legends have it that the Jews traveled far into black Africa.

And, of course, Akhnaton of Egypt comes to mind, he who used to be credited with being monotheism's inventor, in fact still figures in a very widely read book, *The World Almanac* (1962), which lists his introduction of monotheism in its section "Memorable Dates" —and whatever may have been the previous fumbling primitive reachings toward an only god, it is certain that monotheism was first presented by Akhnaton (mid-fourteenth century B.C.) in a sumptuous, grandiose and government-sponsored fashion, with the king and the new capital named after the new sole god.

We wonder whether Aten, who had the most spectacular and the shortest career of any major god in history—he did not outlive his sponsor, whose reign was short and who did not officially advance Aten's claim till he had been Pharaoh for six years, could have had lasting influence in remote parts of Negro Africa. Even in Egypt itself monotheism found few enthusiasts and was immediately forgotten, and we are told that the Pharaoh made little effort at missionary work on Aten's behalf outside Egypt. There was a town officially named Gem-Aten in Nubia; at another Nubian town archaeologists have found a little Aten shrine joined to the orthodox—i.e., polytheistic—temple.

That an ephemeral dogma unpopular at home and little known in the adjacent up-Nile country should have traveled triumphantly under various guises across all Africa and lived for over three thousand years seems an ultra-improbability.

It is natural that many of Africa's own thinkers who have now become men of a book—of many books—and who look back upon the bookless should claim the faith of their ancestors as something purely African. An interesting collection of writings by African scholars, *Présence Africaine,* contains an essay on indigenous African religions by William Leo Hansberry, winner in 1964 of the first Haile Selassie prize for work benefiting Africa, which concludes with a statement that Negro Africa originated its own fundamental religion. *Muntu* (a book title which is the singular of *bantu* and means "Human Being") terminates a sensitive discussion of "God" by an essentially African definition of the Supreme Being, saying, "God is . . . the 'Great Mantu,' First Creator and First Begetter in one."

The literary expressions of Africans' thoughts today are like the statements of our own anthropologists in that they give an image of Africa after years of colonial influence. Both offer us a mixed drink, the pure essence of Africa as it was pre-colonially, diluted by a dash of Europe.

However, it was not the super gods in the various tribal skies but the swarms of tribally assorted little gods and spirits and demons who came into the daily life of the bookless Africans and were to them so real that they seemed to be constantly underfoot, constantly giving them shudders and shivers, and less often comfort.

The demon and little-god population which activated the imagination must have been very large and much variegated in its supposed powers and functions. I think they were not revered as deities, but were regarded as a dangerous or a potentially protective element to whom tribute was paid as blackmail. I think that just as the African bookless imputed "souls" to inanimate things by a system of thought called animism they also personified circumstance and envisioned a band of spirits who were responsible for the happenings of their lives—good happenings and bad ones, big ones and little ones. I think that their lives were more *alive* than our own.

Underlying the little gods and spirits and demons there was often an inherited ancient wisdom. Their attacks were punishments, their protection reward for prudence or energy. Their interference was a warning. Many of them were associated with physical misfortunes, health disasters or were manifestations under fancy guise of their own deserts for negligence, laziness or carelessness. Some, of course, seem to have been just comical or dramatic—storybook fancies—which brought something bright or scaresome to exhilarate the lively minds of the bookless, who lived without the nerve relief and the escape that fiction and its cousins—the cinema, the newspaper, the radio, television and all the rest—give to us.

The origin or the wisdom behind the invention and the subsequent belief in some of these creatures seems easy to guess at. Take the dwarf demons whose feet are put on back to front and who skulk around and into the little homes at night, stealing food which is not covered, poisoning what they leave and licking out dirty dishes. Here is a warning to housewives of the danger of negligence, given Africa's multitudinous noxious insects and Africa's torrid climate. This is a Mandingo and Bambara notion, the demon dwarfs being called Wokolo.

The Wokolo were irritable. Sometimes they would attack people and scratch them with their nails, which were so long that "they were like goats' horns." This caused lumps and bad sores. A person might even catch some horrid skin disorder by merely walking about in the woods where the Wokolo hid themselves, and so, of course, did those women who were induced to have intercourse with the dwarf demons. To such unions were ascribed deformed and witless children. Here charity met warning. An excuse was offered for the virulent skin troubles—yaws, kraw-kraw, perhaps even leprosy. There was some consolation for a bad birth, and with this a warning against marriage to a disfigured mate.

The Megboula also had, along with other powers and activities, influence upon the sex life of tribes folk. They were water men, descendants of a mating between a local girl and an aquatic monster of Lake Chad. They were curios of high degree—in form like humans, having long red hair, hoofs like a horse and gold rings on their fingers. Sometimes one of these spectacular creatures would seduce a girl and put her with child. We wonder whether in the long ago these fabulous personages may not have been the dream or subterfuge of a wayward pregnant girl, or a convenient excuse if she did not wish to name her lover. It is interesting to speculate how a myth was born.

Africa's demons came in all sizes. There were the Tise, tree dwellers, like humans but much bigger, who walked with their feet at the top and heads on the ground, to match, I suppose, the outline of a tree. By night they invaded homes, and it was prudent to leave a drink ready for them for, if offended, Tise could cause a person to break out in pimples and boils all over the body. In the same tribal region, the land of Mossi, were the smallest demons of all, the Kikirsi, some black, some red, who were about an inch tall, who loved sweets and were the protectors of pregnant women and of children, but capable of wicked tricks if anyone offered them pepper.

The Zulus had a furry dwarf named Thikololoshi and numerous water spirits. The Niger had a resident family of water spirits. Its chief was Faro, who lived with his wives and children in a handsome house at the bottom of the river. Sometimes to their alarm fishermen glimpsed one of his wives. In the liberal days of big sacrifices—I mean human sacrifices—it was the custom to make this offering to Faro to insure a full rising of the Niger. In more economical and disciplined times Faro got chickens or tomatoes, of which latter he was very fond. In the puzzling Zimbabwe ruins archaeologists have found birds cut out of soapstone, which, it has been suggested, were "lightning birds" like those which some Bantus mount upon poles to keep lightning away. If so we have a very old belief which splits the difference between the manufactured contrivance and the supernatural spirit.

Similarly the demons called Boudas are a very old superstition, and although their headquarters have been in Ethiopia, which is neither bookless nor pagan, they properly fit with our subject, being either a pagan heritage or having invaded Ethiopia from a neighboring pagan land. At one time when Ethiopian Christians were violently disputing with the Jews they asserted that the demons who afflicted them were Jewish. The Boudas and another demon group, called Zar, possessed psychological power. By their sinister gaze they could produce hysterical crises in their victims, particularly in unmarried women. People suspected of being Boudas were being exterminated up to the middle of the last century.

A gruesome specialist in Africa's array of spirits was Sapatan, god of smallpox, reported from Dahomey, and under a slightly different name functioning in Yoruba.

Asom of the Ivory Coast was even more shocking. He was the god of syphilis, established upon a little island whence "he sent syphilis to mankind." Asom seems to have been a late-comer to Negroland. Leo Africanus, who traveled widely in Africa in the early sixteenth century, declares that syphilis though common in Barbary was unknown among the blacks, and adds the startling statement that anyone so afflicted would be immediately cured if he went to the Negro country. "No sooner breathe the air of that region than he would return suddenly to his former health as if he had never been sick." Leo further asserts, "I have seen with my own eyes more than one hundred persons who without other remedies have been entirely cured by this mere change of air."

So as not to stop this swift survey of Africa's demons on a sour note I will tell about the useful and intemperate demon farm workers of Nubia, about whom I read in Burckhardt's *Travels in Nubia*, he having read about them in Maqrizi, who himself read about them in the writings of Ibn Selim of Aswan, the tenth-century historian. Across a stretch of country "two moons travelling in length and breadth" all of the heavy farm work—clearing the ground, sowing, reaping, threshing and winnowing—was performed secretly at night by spirits who received as reward a quantity of *bouza* (fermented liquor) which was left ready for them.

THE AFRICAN AND HIS ANCESTORS · There
was another and yet vaster group of spirits over Africa who were
not evil but highly esteemed—the spirits of their ancestors. Bookless
Africa pretty generally practiced what is sometimes called ancestor
worship.

The revering of ancestors has been a habit across the world and
recorded from antiquity, and it is a phase of a noble first chapter
in the lesson of life which teaches animals to breed and to carry
along their racial patterns of behavior. To bookless Africans it gratified as well an appetite for self-perpetuation in history from which
their inability to write debarred them. Field workers in anthropology
tell us of tribes who remember exactly their lineage for ten and twelve
generations, going back to an unforgotten individual ancestor. Hom-
age to the ancestor is part of life.

The fear of death's nothingness, a refusal to accept death as final
and the conviction of survival—a happy survival, a bossy survival
where the dead enjoyed as great or greater influence than when alive
and where they, potent in the affairs of their descendants, were revered and petted by the living—it was a belief comforting to a
man as the years of his life passed by.

It was not a religion. It was a social obligation. It expressed their
family feeling, exceptionally strong in these people. And it expressed
their intense loyalty to the health of the family tree, the desire to
keep the tree alive and productive, which was their philosophy of
life. To fail to show ancestor reverence would have been a civic
crime. Ancestor reverence was the conformation to an established
social pattern: parents should breed many children; the children

they bred should carry along the honored memory of the parents—an endless chain of procreation.

Thus a family survived as an integral organization, family pride was augmented, tribal confidence invigorated. The past held the future in its mouth. The past must be treated with honor.

Ancestor reverence was by intention a kindly thing, but it was sometimes expressed and celebrated with shocking cruelty. It involved always the sacrifice of something of value—food, drink, fowls and other animals, and sometimes the sacrifice of the highest currency of all—the lives of human beings, their slaves.

The last was beyond the ambitions and the financial means of the ordinary, was the splurging luxury of royalty and the very high-up, of which I shall speak later.

As a tribute to the ancestor a sacrifice of some sort, small or large, was a needful gesture, mark of esteem and the price of the ancestor's goodwill, the expenditure by the living of something of value to himself, for "in any sacrifice there is abnegation since the sacrificer deprives himself and gives." I quote from *Sacrifice: Its Nature and Function*, by Henri Hubert and Marcel Mauss, an important work almost seventy years old and lately translated into English.

Among the humble and workaday the deprivation was real but modest. With the pretentious it took on prestige value also, and the honor to the departed was sometimes hideous, being said with flowers of blood.

But whatever the style of celebration the ancestor was not deified. He was the same human as when in their company, but he was now viewed as their messenger or intermediary with the powers of destiny. Therefore the ancestor's goodwill was vitally important to the family's welfare. Self-interest dictated that their ancestor be kept in a cozy and contented mood so as to be continuously their benevolent and protective representative and in some cases their adviser.

Ancestral goodwill would be courted by offerings of food and drink. Occasional snacks, draughts of the local beverage, such as palm wine, bouza or dolo, would be placed at the ancestor's grave or at a memorial altar set up in his honor, or sometimes inside the house or before a statuette of the dead. These statuettes were not worshipped as idols but corresponded to the treasured family portrait or enlarged photograph of the deceased in some of our homes, aside from the fact that they received token feeding.

In a far part of Africa and in early Christian times the very Christian St. Monica used to carry to the shrines of the saintly dead "provisions of cakes, bread and wine, according to the custom in Africa," (Algeria was her homeland) St. Augustine, her son, tells in his *Confessions*. Sintra, the fifteenth-century Portuguese explorer, was the first to report the same custom from Negroland: "They adore statues of wood in the form of men, to which when it is mealtime they offer meat." One pities the doubly charged native housewife who cooked for both the living and the dead.

These repasts for the departed were token offerings. But I find an odd item in Labouret's study of the Mandingos about the supposed actual craving for food of the newly dead and how in the first few days his hunger was like that of the living. Food would be left at his disposal. It would be found in appearance untouched, but "the food had lost its essence." When the family ate it they discovered that it no longer had any vital element.

Sometimes celebrations would be held in the ancestor's memory with singing and dancing. It might seem odd that dancing should have been a big part in a ceremony of such solemnity, for we picture the dancing Africans as riotous gay Negroes kicking up their heels in the moonlight. One Xavier de Golberry said, "When the sun sets all Africa dances!" It was a brash assertion since his knowledge about "*all* Africa" was based upon a sojourn on the coast at Senegal in 1785–86 and to him, as to the rest of contemporary Europeans, the continent was just a mysterious vacuum inside a coastal *passe partout*. His imaginative phrase caught popular fancy and has been often repeated like a proverb. And it was often proved true. Laing told about a dance at Sierra Leone which "kept up without intermission for two days and three nights." Dancing was not exclusively a gay entertainment. It had official and even melancholy usages. "Every event, either in the life of the family or that of the community," was marked by dancing, wrote Talbot. Caillié describes ritual dancing he watched at the funeral of a local old woman in what is now the Ivory Coast Republic. First a group of little children, then a group of men, then a group of women danced in turn with dignified athleticism, singing a sad tune. Modern Ethiopian Christians dance at religious services, and it is said that the earliest of the Christians elsewhere ritually danced. It was reported that during the discussions about Catholic liturgy in Rome in 1962 African missionary priests to Negro countries expressed the desire to include native dances as part of the religious rites with the idea of making Catholicism more homelike in its appeal to Negro converts.

At ancestor dancing festivals the spirit of the ancestor might, so the participants believed, participate unseen. He might even take possession of a dancer, might inspire him to speak for him to the family.

Communication with the ancestor via what we would call a system of spiritualism was a widespread practice. The messages received from the ancestor were not the usual expressions of affection and reports of a comfortable situation in the afterworld. They were advice on family and community matters, reprimands, even prophecies based upon the ancestor's position as intermediary with the great powers of destiny, or so many Africans believed.

A very detailed account of the method of spirit communication is given in a short book sponsored by the Belgian Royal Colonial Institute under the title which, translated, runs, *The Communications of the Natives of Kasai with the Souls of the Dead*. Kasai is one of the major sections of the Republic of the Congo, adjoining Katanga, so much publicized of late. It possessed a highly developed system of spirit communication, which was presumably handed down from the remote past of the region and which the Belgian investigators say closely resembled our own spiritualistic séances, though certainly some of the magic equipment and proceedings were outside the scope and tastes of our sect.

The Kasai séance system included the training of the medium from youth, his equipment with a weird collection of magic paraphernalia—little bits off the bodies of wild animals, scraps of special plants, a fragment of the flesh of a man who had been killed by lightning, and so on, packed into little bags made of the skin of giant lizards or of ring-spotted or striped fur. It also included his severe mental and moral preparation for the role. In the séances both complex magic and hypnotism were employed.

In another part of Africa a fiasco in the matter of ancestor consulting resulted in the "Kaffir" suicides which I have already mentioned as a case of mass euthanasia. The self-victimized "Kaffirs" in question were of the Xhosa group, whom South African Europeans had tagged, along with other colored peoples, with this nickname borrowed from the Arabs and used as if it were the name of a tribal group, which of course it was not. The Arab word *kafir* meant anyone who refused Islam.

To this special "Kaffir" group the spirits of their dead were supposed to have given orders to the people at large and to have prophesied a miracle. The orders were to clean out the food supply, to kill and eat all the cattle and consume all the crops. The miracle to be awaited was promised for a specific day in the near future. Two suns would rise on that day, a hurricane would blow all the white invaders into the sea and there would appear beautiful ripe grain and herds of fine cattle.

The "Kaffirs" carried out the orders but waited in vain for the miracle of duplicate suns and hurricane and plenty, and they died of starvation, perhaps twenty-five thousand of them—a pitiful tragedy bred from credulity, like so many in history.

It seems as if the great body of Negro Africans who formally revered their ancestors had attained an absolute and almost tangible realization of immortality. Theirs was "a true community of the living and the dead," but it was not a system of thought which opened the doors to new ideas. This may have been one of the reasons why pagan Africans lagged in the march of progress. The question "Would father, grandfather, great-grandfather approve?" would have but one answer, "No!" Mentally they were the moss of the ancestral tree.

Yet their attitude toward their dead has for us the interest of contrast. Pagan Africans pampered the ancestral spirit, who was supposed to have the power to protect the descendants. They revered their ancestors as still important—death had not been a misfortune but a promotion. They were highly placed personages, the confidants and influencers of Destiny.

Pagan Africans' point of view differed from the attitude of a great body of Christians who believe the ancestor spirit to be in danger and needing the help of the living, and who seek by intercession and prayer to obtain the soul's repose in the afterworld.

The pagan put his forefathers on a pedestal. It might seem touching respect and devotion except that the method of petting the deceased and keeping him a well-disposed influence was sometimes so horrid. Benevolent in intent but hideous in performance was the sacrifice of human beings for the honor and comfort of dead notables, the explanation for which was that the departed ought to enjoy in the spirit world prestige and status corresponding to his standing on earth, that if he was the possessor of women and slaves while alive a similar retinue should surround him in the hereafter. Otherwise he would be angry and vengeful and their interests would suffer.

The world has been disgusted at pagan Africa's sacrificing of men and women, of which those sacrifices performed in the ritual of ancestrolatry are but one manifestation; I shall mention others. "For mankind to sacrifice his fellow man is inhuman," we have said. On the contrary, it is exclusively human. Animals, so far as I know, do not kill members of their own kind in the hope of influencing destiny. This was man's invention—a very ancient invention and very widespread around the world, including Punic North Africa's notorious child sacrifices. It seems a built-in part of man's psychology to try to buy Destiny's goodwill, to attempt to trade with Fate—that is, with whatever were his Supreme Beings—by the irrevocable gift, by the destruction of something of value to himself. This might be some animal, from a picayune chicken to a rare racing camel, or a human possession, a slave who was worth money, or even a child of his own flesh or a woman beloved.

Pagan Africa's thinking walked along the same path, not a pretty one but one which was well trodden. One can see similarity with items in our own religion—Abraham in Genesis, the mystic association of sacrifice with the Crucifixion, plus much in prehistory. But that such things should happen in the actual modern world seemed a shocking anachronism. We saw pagan Africa living in our own yesterday.

But Time is our teacher and tomorrow's anthropology may look back with a frown upon our present civilization and say, "Just human sacrifice all over again!" when they consider our performances in genocide, or even our routine risk and destruction of humans in struggles for national prestige.

Africa's pagans kept alive an ancient and disreputable piece of psychology for various uses, one being to send the deceased father of a family to another world in style. Other motives for human sacrifice were supposedly utilitarian and considered to promote the public welfare. Some of these were regular observances, part of the local seasonal life, what might almost be called civic formalities.

Among these was the habit of throwing boys or girls into the great rivers to encourage the waters to flow generously. An Egyptian medieval tradition is that it was customary to toss a gaily dressed young virgin into the Nile to be the river's "bride." When Islam took over Egypt this shocked Moslem sensibilities, Islam being deeply opposed to human sacrifice, which in this case seems to have been tolerated hitherto by the Christian authorities of the country! (We must bear in mind that the tradition comes to us from Arabic sources.) The victorious Arab general substituted for the virgin a written missive, thrown into the river, which solemnly invited the Nile to do its duty.

On the other side of the continent corresponding sacrifices of young people were offered to the Niger. In the Lagos region was "the horrid custom of impaling a young female" every year to secure good rains for the crops. The late eighteenth- and early nineteenth-century traveler who tells this made a peculiar note about these "females about to be destroyed . . . their minds have previously been so wrought on by the fetish men that they proceed to the place of execution with cheerfulness." If true (it is quoted from Captain John Adams' *Remarks on the Country from Cape Palmas to the river Congo*, in the anthology *Nigerian Perspectives*) it is another curious and rather touching case of the ready acceptance of death in the supposed public interest.

Human sacrificial contributions were also offered intentionally to the river crocodiles in addition to the many victims the crocodiles secured by their own energy and tricks. The city of Bamako, capital of the Republic of Mali, may have got its name from two words meaning "Crocodile Business" because its site was the place where the offering of a virgin girl was made every year to the Niger.

A variant on the theme of sacrifice for the public good was the immuring of living people in city walls with the idea that it would make the city strong and prosperous. This was done at the great medieval city of Jenne in the ex-French Sudan. A young girl was entombed alive in its walls. Part of this legend is almost unbelievably gruesome. The voice of the girl, nearly smothered in clay, was heard assuring the wall builders that they would remember her tribe in the days of the new city's prosperity.

Her double prophecy was realized. Her family still boasts the grim but proud name, "Corpse of Jenne," and the city itself, having turned to Islam, became not only a sort of holy city, despite its pagan start in life, but "a city great and flourishing and prosperous," according to the *Tarikh es-Soudan,* and was "one of the great markets of the Moslem world." It was called "the place of gold," says René Caillié, the first European to see and tell about it, and the fame of its glittering trade is proved by the fact that, in medieval opinion, it disputed with Ghana the claim to be the name from which the word "Guinea," gold's synonym, was derived.

The town within those walls, magically strengthened by the girl's sacrifice, was long regarded as impregnable and allegedly withstood ninety-nine sieges. The mosque was one of the wonders of Negroland, a unique example of ancient African architecture. (It was reconstructed under colonial rule.) We may read a striking item about Jenne in an early journalistic account: some of the city's houses had possessed for centuries indoor water closets with sewage. Incidentally, a similar report comes from Kumasi, where in 1817 Bowdich found that "every house had its cloacae, frequently upstairs, within a small closet into which boiling water was daily poured down."

In the Lake Chad region live children were built into the defending walls of towns. This horrid and to our ideas nonsensical fashion of ensuring municipal protection and prosperity was not exclusive to pagan Africa. Among its counterparts elsewhere is an instance that was far away and very ancient—the bodies of children discovered in the foundations of buildings in Palestine "leave no room for doubt," says Professor E. O. James in *Sacrifice and Sacrament,* "that oblations of this character were a common occurrence among the Canaanites to strengthen the walls of houses and cities."

It was a vegetable which caused many human sacrifices in a part of Africa sometimes called by botanists "The Yam Belt." The yam, a true cosmopolite in vegetable society, which appears to have been both an import to Africa and an indigenous plant which Africa already possessed and cultivated, was a plain food item whose name is now applied in the United States to a variety of the sweet potato. The yam was no semi-magical luxury growth like the silphium, which made Cyrene in Libya so rich and famous in antiquity that its representation was graven on its coinage, a plant which could cure almost all illnesses, also the stings and bites of dangerous animals and, when steeped, supplied a drink which produced abortions. Nor did the yam offer the almost hypnotic charm of the lotus, presumably silphium's neighbor in Libya or Tunisia, Homer's "divine mysterious fruit," which, once tasted, caused a man to "quit his house, his country and his friends," and which so fascinated Odysseus' sailors that they tried to desert the ship and stay always in Lotus land. The yam was just a plain practical food. All that it could do was to feed people—and kill people, hundreds of them.

The yam attained a mystic importance in its sub-Saharan homeland, located in parts of what are now the Republics of Mali, Ivory Coast, Ghana, Dahomey and Nigeria, where the year's yam festival was as important to the people as Christmas, let us say, is to us. One big and tragic difference was that at the yam festival humans were sacrificed, their blood used as a libation to the yams at their maturity. The festivals in question were sometimes spoken of by Europeans as the Yam Customs, the word "Customs" in this case not meaning a habit or way of life, but having a special significance associated with sacrifices.

The reason behind the yam sacrifices is not clear. It was not to give sporting excitement to a festival of rejoicing when the yams were ripe, like the arena cruelties of classic days. The slave was to the farming community a valuable property and would not be destroyed merely as an amusement. One may read and consider in this connection the words of Mircea Eliade ". . . the essential theme [is] that creation cannot take place except from a living being who is immolated"—this is true even of the vegetable species—for "the edible plants sprang from the body of an immolated divine being." Certainly the bookless of "The Yam Belt" did not explain themselves in such words as these, but they may have conceived in instinctive simplicity the idea that they ought to give back to the earth which fed them some return gift of value.

With colonialism's control sacrifices at the yam festival were officially prohibited. Amaury Talbot, who was a British Nigerian official, tells of a yam festival he saw in the early part of this century and how an old slave had been placed in a crouching position within a little fence, presumably representing symbolically the forbidden human sacrifice which had been offered in pre-colonial days. One is struck by the macabre yet comic pathos of the scene: the old slave well aware of what had befallen the slaves of old in behalf of yams and rejoicing in the obligatory change, the crowd debarred from a mystic ceremony deeply imbedded in their beliefs and trying to find the old time mystic comfort in a shabby imitation, suspecting perhaps that a resentful yam crop might take its revenge.

When Europeans gained control in pagan Africa they tried and to a large extent succeeded in stopping human sacrifices, although this was difficult. I remind the reader that the picture I am giving refers to pagan Africa in pre-colonial days. Regions which were converted to Islam became in principle non-human-sacrificial, but sometimes we find mention of Moslem localities yielding to the atavistic urge.

It is possible that the stories of sacrifice which in pre-colonial days shocked and disgusted the European public were exaggerated at the source and grew worse and worse as they passed from ear to ear and pen to pen. There has been an avid appetite since classic times for tall tales from Africa, and appetites breed their own food. There is a further possibility that Africans, seeing in the European observers the first step to a dreaded European grab, deliberately emphasized and enlarged as a deterrent the sacrifice performances which they had noted were disgusting and frightening to the white folk and deliberately made it impossible for foreigners to dodge witnessing these spectacles. It may have been their form of cold war against the intruder.

One may read and—even if one discounts them somewhat—one will shudder at Bowdich's story of Ashanti killings (1817 mission) at Ellis about the Tshi-speaking peoples of the Gold Coast in an account published in 1887, at Burton, on the "Customs" in Dahomey (1863 mission). I mention familiar writers in English whose accounts are readily consultable and in which one will read of human sacrifice wholesale.

At royal funerals and at later ceremonies in memory of royal dead the human destruction was sometimes as sweeping as in some catastrophe of nature. Earthquakes and hurricanes would do no worse. At the obsequies of a sixteen-year-old prince at Kumasi 150 were sacrificed, and every regional chief was expected to contribute a slave, a hideous comparison to the sending of floral tribute. At the funeral of a queen three thousand died, towns each supplying one hundred, small communities ten. At yam time in Ashanti about one hundred were sacrificed in different quarters of a big town. Burton quotes a letter from a native Christian missionary reporting the killing of more than two thousand at Abomey, Dahomey.

One royal funeral sacrifice occurred as recently as 1899, the pampered personage being a queen in what is now the Republic of the Ivory Coast, a woman of great local importance who had been in her time an enthusiastic sacrificer to ancestry. When she died she was covered with powdered gold and hung with necklaces and belts of the local treasure, aggry beads. French colonial authority sought to keep her funeral unsmirched by the death of victims, but learned afterward of the suspicious disappearance of a certain slave girl.

The most nauseating yet dramatic instances of astronomically multiplied human sacrifices occur in the literature that concerns certain parts of the West Coast. From elsewhere come reports of restricted sacrifices. Sometimes the wives of princes were buried alive with their dead husbands in Zandeland. Near the Congo mouth marriage rites practiced by some caused the wife to swear to die with her husband. We hear of other individual sacrifices more personal, more emotional, such as the sacrifice by a chief of his first-born son to bring an end to a ruinously prolonged tribal war, the sacrifice by a pagan queen of her only son to save her army from disaster, the killing of his first wife and eldest son by one seeking the rank of big chief, as proof that he was ready to pay the greatest of prices and to give his whole self to his people's service.

The last matches in a way the Chaka myth by the African novelist

Mofolo about the mighty Zulu. Chaka was the military genius whom historians like to call "The Black Napoleon." In Mofolo's story he murdered his pregnant beloved to prove himself fit for the role of great conqueror.

Again there was the scapegoat sacrifice, whom the crowd would jostle to touch as he was led to his execution so that they might transfer to him their sin or trouble or death. Such actions as these belonged to another school from the multiple displays at some West African places, of which the most shocking was Benin.

Benin, just before the British took over, indulged in a frenzy of sacrifice gone mad. What the members of the punitive expedition saw and told when they entered Benin City after the annihilation of a British mission in 1897 is one of the nastiest pieces of reading one can find anywhere, created great stir then, and is still often quoted: mutilated slaves dying on the ground, the royal domain framed in dying men, headless bodies propped up here and there, decomposition and blood and death stench everywhere. Benin was hysterical with fear. It saw a dingy future—or dingy it looked to them, who for seven hundred years had lived as they liked, seeking Destiny's protection in the only way they recognized, by sacrificing people.

About twenty-five years later came a rather simple, almost comical incident which shows how quickly Benin lost its baleful and awesome glamour. The British colonial rules had sternly forbidden the old-time "inhuman mourning law," as the modern Bini calls it, wherein the honored sacrificial regime was formally scheduled: medium-class persons, one cow each for the funeral of a father or a mother; for high-class personages, a human; for small fry, a fowl. The Benin figurehead king under British supervision was accused of the ritual killing of one of his wives, who had disappeared. After a long search she was found in hiding. She had run away "with a Sobo man." The writer of the libelous letter which had accused the king was fined fifty pounds.

A CONTINENT WITH ARTS OF ITS OWN

CREATIVE ARTS · ARTS IN BODILY AND MENTAL RE-CREATION

CREATIVE ARTS · Africa's art startled us when first it was transported from Africa or shown to us in photographs. It was frightening. It dragged strange feelings out of the back of the mind of the beholder. Also, as art, it amazed certain of the great figures in our own art world.

Africa—that is the Africa that was uninfluenced from without, the bookless and the pagan—has given to us in its art the clearest image of itself, of its thinking and of its feeling and of its daring curiosity and creative impulse. Africa's arts as a whole were many and, as I see and shall attempt to describe art's manifestations on the continent, some of its ways of expression were not in our sense arts at all, but rather the expression of a state of mind and sentiment, of certain fears and a profound and often cruel craving for experiment and re-creation.

Let us take a quick view like tourists at an art museum, across and up and down the continent and across the centuries, picking up some of the most characteristic and revealing items. Then we will consider the yet more intimate art, where human beings themselves were the artists' material, the art of rearranging, altering, sometimes deforming and mutilating the bodies of men and women to accomplish their own ideas of pulchritude or from social and religious conformism.

The impulse to produce art is very old. Leakey says of Adam's ancestors that they must have made rough drawings in the sand with their fingertips. Sir Herbert Read goes further: "I believe art is primarily, even historically prior to language as a system of communication. I cannot prove that. Nobody can prove it."

Africa can show, though few of us can go where they are and see them, stone engravings and colored pictures of vast venerability. Just how vast is not certain, but ancient Egypt's famous and familiar displays are, in comparison with some of them, relatively modern. Items of Africa's art have been found on the faces of rocks all over the continent—north, south, east and west—less noticed in the west—and in the middle, the Sahara. Some of them are pronounced to be very old, variously and tentatively dated. It has been suggested that some were made as early as 10,000 B.C. Some are, though prehistoric, of relatively recent production. Prehistoric, yes, but in much of Africa prehistory has no meaning and is a term of dateless duration which runs up alongside us and snaps at our heels.

A racial group where prehistory has lived on both as a way of life and in a form of art is that of the Bushmen. Some Bushmen still use stone implements; their Stone Age lasted into recent decades, and they were continuing to make rock paintings until a few years ago. Since these small yellow people are called "a vanishing race" one can almost say that they did not effectively climb out of prehistory. Their stone art will live after they are gone, the record of a very old people, a vision of something the world seems about to push off its dish.

Their rock pictures are widely distributed. Laurens Van der Post says he has "followed his [Bushman's] progress as a painter for about 1500 miles," northward from the Cape of Good Hope and for another fifteen hundred miles westward toward the Atlantic. Thus it is clear that the Bushmen were enthusiastic artists and catered to an enthusiastic public of art lovers. One tries to imagine the thrill of it all in primitive conditions when first a man made a picture, made marks upon a rock that reincarnated the image of an animal or a human being. It must have been a strange, almost frightening sensation.

The Bushmen clung to their art on the rocks. We even know the name of one of their nineteenth-century artists, which was Gau-wa; he used to carry his colored paint pots on a belt around his waist, and was reported on by Stow, an important authority on South African natives cited in Desmond Clark's *Prehistory of Southern Africa*. The rocks show the whole life of the Bushmen's ancient and almost changeless race, its interests, its actions, its culture and its etiquette: animals insistently shown for the Bushmen were a hunting people, men and women of their own special sort, or of their fancy, their style of men's apparel—for Africa had many different forms of decorating and safeguarding the penis—their females with nature's flesh-made fig leaf, the "apron" about which a French traveler brought the titillating news to European readers in 1790, and with super-hefty thighs, and the shelf protuberances which we call steatopygous and which Bushmen called one of woman's greatest charms.

The Sahara gained much publicity as a rock picture setting and must have puzzled many who visualized the great desert as an endless stretch of sand. Best known are the careful observations of scientific investigators, including Lhote, Gautier and Reygasse. But the startling rock pictures have been attracting an assortment of international studies almost since Europeans dared venture to explore the desert.

The first to be startled by art in so unlikely a setting was, so far as I can discover, a pair of officers in a military mission under a French general named Gavignac in 1847, that is, shortly after the French undertook the conquest of Algeria. One of the officers, Dr. Jacquot, wrote a book. The place which so surprised the officers is just over the brink of the Sahara south of Oran and is one of few rock art displays reasonably convenient for the interested traveler, being near what was in the period of French colonial control "a fortified railway station." Now the place is owned by the Republic of Algeria. But the rocks are the same! And they record ancient times, for the drawings include elephants.

Three years later Barth, the brilliant and infinitely careful German explorer who was a member and eventually the leader of an English mission, reported a rock art discovery in the Fezzan region far south of Tripoli which is painstakingly described in his important five-volume work, *Travels and Discoveries in North and Central Africa*, so that for many the credit is given to Barth of first finding pictures on Saharan rocks. Barth offers a drawing of what he found, the principal piece of sculpture showing some human figures, one with the head of a horned bovine, the other with the head of a sharp-nosed birdlike creature, facing each other and armed, while between them is a small horned animal.

A Moroccan Jew, Rabbi Mordokhai Abi Serour, a great Sahara adventurer and trader, searched for and sent news of rock art in the Oued Draa neighborhood in the Moroccan, the western part of the desert. Oskar Lenz, an Austrian who was the next after Barth to push into then secret Timbuctoo, confirmed the rabbi's story. An Egyptian explorer, Hassanein-Bey, found rock drawings in the oasis of Ouenat on the borders of what was then Italian Libya and Egypt (1923).

This partial list of Saharan searching by men of many nations has interest as showing the variegated world curiosity about this puzzling subject. Rock pictures and engravings which have been found recently in the desert are familiar, especially the beautifully reproduced representations of the Lhote discoveries in the Tassili. The native term *tassili* means a big plateau cut by rock gorges. There are numerous *tassilis* in the desert, but on the modern Saharan map Tassili is specifically applied to a region which adjoins and partially embraces the Hoggar and which, Lhote says, is as big as France.

All of Africa's rock art is curiosity-rousing stuff. We wonder about the artists. We wonder about the half-told tale in the pictures with many clews but no solutions. We wonder why in hard primitive conditions art was produced, often in very awkward spots. Perhaps to the bookless people the making of pictures was a way—the only available way—of telling about themselves, and to tell about oneself is a fundamental impulse. Animals manifest it when they roar or twitter in off moments of loving and fighting.

The art on rocks told the story of Africa's lives and thoughts and something of Africa's history. Among those long-legged humans springing across space and those chariots with galloping horses, sometimes three abreast, so exactly abreast that only one body shows—with, however, six forelegs and six hind legs—are animals far from their present habitat—elephants, hippopotami, rhinoceroses in the desert and in North Africa—and there are many humans that are half animal: human bodies and animal heads.

These fanciful hybrids appear across the continent, in Negroland, the Sahara and the Mediterranean region, in Egypt, of course, and in the art of Carthage, where was a particularly odd creature (reproduced as a plate in *L'Art de Carthage,* by Fouchet). This is a lady, demure and dignified in a classically draped gown that sweeps the ground, conventional as an old-fashioned schoolmarm to the neck, upon which rises a lion's jowl and face.

The mixed human and animal figures so widely distributed in Africa's art have produced much speculation but no conclusions.

Was this mixture an expression of Africa's feeling of the closeness between men and animals? Or did the semi-disguise of the humans show what one might call a news item, a representation of the ruse of the hunter? Did it represent some relationship with Egypt of the animal-headed gods—an influence from Egypt or even an idea which went *to* Egypt in the very long ago?

Was the planting of animals' heads on men's bodies a magic-inspired notion which survives today in the veiled Tuareg and to a certain extent in the masks noted in sub-Saharan Africa? Was this disguising based on a profound dislike, a superstitious fear of showing a man's face?

Or was it experimenting? Was the putting of a beast's head on a human body a symptom of the craving for physical self-experiment which has been and still is so widely practiced?

As for the now exotic animals which rock art shows so far from their present homeland—the hippopotami, rhinoceroses and the many, many elephants—here we read a dramatic chapter in earth's history, presented in simple clear lines and not needing to be told in the cautious words of science. Sahara was not then *sahra* (the word means "uncultivated," and was eventually applied in our geography to the whole great desert), but a region where the river horse was comfortable and the great feet of the elephant moved over springy green ground.

Then a desert was born; the big animals of the rock pictures were there no more. When in the autumn of 1593 an elephant which had with infinite difficulty been brought across the Sahara from tropic Africa as a gift to the Sultan El Mansour was led into Marrakesh in Morocco it caused a riot.

But in older days elephants were a part of the practical life and of folklore. Elephants were featured in war and peace. The elephants of Hannibal that climbed over the Alps are among the most famous animals of history. Ivory was so plentiful that Pliny passes along a piece of gossip that elephant tusks were used in northern Africa to make fences, doorposts and palings around houses and stables. The folklore of classical Africa dealt with elephants in an almost affectionate manner. Elephants were deeply religious, worshipping the full moon by lifting aloft tree branches and saluting the rising sun with their uplifted "hands" (trunks). A quantity of folklore at about the time when they were a part of North Africa's normal animal population was collected and written down by King Juba II.

To Mediterranean Africa there came an abrupt change in the etiquette of art. As in all the continent, its people had found satisfaction in their own portraits and those of their animal associates on rocks and later observed the statue representations of the human and animal world which were displayed during the colonial period by Greeks, Romans and Carthaginians, of which last we have few indications, both because Punic tastes were practical rather than artistic and because the destruction by the Roman conqueror was extensive. They had become familiar with certain local personages, such as the goddess Africa on coins in the days of Juba, a woman with an elephant's skin hanging over her head, and Gurzil, the bull deity. Then Islam came with a sudden embargo. The Islamic code forbade the representation of living things (as indeed did also the Old Testament; see Exodus 20:4).

There was, when Islam came and imposed its art rules, considerable statuary of men, women and animals in North Africa, illustrating pagan mythology, Christianity and actual persons of note. Roman Carthage possessed in its ruins many items which Moslems regarded as improper curiosities. El-Bekri and Edrisi comment on the Carthage arena whose walls showed "images of all the animals and of all kinds of artisans" with the tolerant detail of an archaeologist reporting something queer found at a prehistoric site.

The ordinary North African public assimilated the idea that representation of men and animals was a nasty piece of pagan idolatry. Barth in the wild country south of Tripoli, then a part of Turkey's immense African holdings, found a forty-eight-foot monument which, he says, was then (1850) sixteen centuries old and which was ornamented with representations of panthers, young women, centaurs, chickens, a man and a woman and the bust of an old lady, which the sparse regional populations pronounced to be alarming and idolatrous.

Morgan, the historian who passed many years in Algeria in the eighteenth century, writes, "They cannot bear the mention of them [statues] without visible horror; the sight of them sets them to shuddering . . . Many times I have been riding with Moors. They would dismount at the sight of some mangled figure and with curses and execrations against the Christian Dog, Jew, Infidel who had presumed to take the Creator's work out of His hands [would attack the statue], sometimes spoiling a good lance or dagger in order to pick out the eyes or deform it as much as possible."

The most striking indication of Moslem hatred for statuary is reported by Leo Africanus from the ancient city of Constantine in Algeria, where there still stood a marble edifice on which were graven human figures. The locals believed the building had been a school whose masters and pupils "because of their vices and damnable wickedness had been turned into stone."

The Turks, though Moslems, were sometimes less prejudiced and lax, and from Talun through the Mamluks, Islam's rule was on occasions ignored, but I do not think that the human figure was used in the religious connection as in Christian art. One of the Talun dynasty went so far as to adorn his palace with painted images of himself and his wives and singers. Under the Fatimids we are told that one of the viziers "pitted the painters against each other to paint dancing girls."

In general, however, Moslem Africa repudiated the sort of art which Islam considered to be idolatry's twin.

So art in Moslem Africa was not an expression but a repression. Beautiful things were made, some mosques, some palaces, many beautifully decorated little objects, but these things were displays of skill or the satisfaction of local pride rather than an outlet for peoples' imaginations and sentiments—or of themselves.

But up the Nile and swinging eastward it was different. Ethiopia stood apart and had an art which was quite its own. Here the portrayal of people, human and sacred, was the artists' delight and the public's satisfaction. In the matter of its very individual and different art, as in other ways, Ethiopia seemed almost like a visitor which had landed upon Africa's soil than an actual and true part of the continent. Ethiopia was isolated among hostile neighbors and in a form of irritating servitude to Egypt because it was from the Coptic Church there that it was obliged to accept its official religious master.

Compensating for this irksome and humiliating situation was the belief that Ethiopia held the survival of Egypt's people in its hands, for Ethiopia had, it was thought, the power to arrest the Nile's flow and turn Egypt into a desert.

It was a cat's cradle of a diplomatic mix-up, an international situation of unequaled awkwardness. Neither, though hostile, could do without the other. Ethiopia would lose its contact with God, Egypt could lose the sole source of its food—or so each party thought— if they quarreled drastically. The fear of damnation or of starvation respectively threatened them.

Sometimes Ethiopia tried a bit of blackmail, made threats about control of the Nile. Sometimes Egypt, taking advantage of a gullibly pious neighbor of another faith, would offer quaint bribes of dubious authenticity: the alleged sponge given to Jesus when He was crucified or some pieces of the True Cross as price of an undisturbed Nile. For Egypt was not only "The Gift of the Nile" but the Nile's trembling slave. Famine came with a rush if the Nile chanced to flow lazily.

The Egyptian Maqrizi in his *Treatise on Famine* gives a long and tragic story, starting with the days of Egypt's "King Afrawus, who was on the throne in the time of the Deluge of Noah," presumably the same as the I Dynasty Uenephus, in whose reign "a great famine seized Egypt" (from Manetho via Africanus), continuing to Makrizi's own time, the start of the fifteenth century, in which he recounts a series of miseries caused by thin harvests. Sometimes the harvests were so thin that Egyptians turned to cannibalism and even ate their own children—"the father would devour his son roasted or boiled"—the crime so widespread that magistrates had to let it go unpunished. Always, word for word, the famine is because in the year whose misery he records "the Nile flowed feebly." Even the first famine of all, in the reign of "King Afrawus," just before the Flood, was "for the failure of the Nile."

Egypt's nerves centered in its river's welfare. This did not make for amity or good contact with the neighbor which supposedly could tamper with the Nile—though what Ethiopia might have done is indeed questionable. Ethiopia beside Laka Tana, source of the Blue and far more productive branch of the Nile, was distrusted and lonely while its religious life was upset by dependence upon an unfriendly country. There by the Nile were the fluctuating temperatures of a long-lasting cold war.

Ethiopian art was true to Ethiopia, a character study in itself, typical of an isolated introvert, a violently, rabidly, pathetically and intensely Christian place hemmed in by hostile non-Christians and gaining only temporary comfort from Christians when they came. Portugal and Spain were helpful but disturbingly wishful to turn the land to Catholicism. England and Italy came as intruders.

One can be sure of one thing with regard to Ethiopian paintings. That is that anybody who has looked at one of them or at a reproduction will not easily forget it. There is no need to go to Ethiopia to prove this, for much of Ethiopia's art left home against Ethiopia's will and may be seen in museums, university libraries and in collections and reproduced in books. There was extensive looting as an addenda to the British expedition motivated by the desire to rescue European captives. Explorer Stanley in his apprentice African days witnessed this as correspondent for the *New York Herald*. Part of the spoil was illustrated manuscripts from the Ethiopian royal library.

A big proportion of the country's art dealt with religion, being the work of monks and priests for the illustration of manuscripts about Biblical and miraculous things and for the decoration of churches. Ethiopia possessed plenty of churches to decorate. Gondar, its onetime capital, is reported by a traveler in the late nineteenth century, Achille Raffray, to have had forty-three, the population being then estimated at six thousand, split between Moslems and Christians. Lalibela, which was also once its capital, had eleven churches hewn out of rock. Alvares, in the sixteenth century, looked at them in amazement and said, "The like of them and so many cannot be found in the world," and they are still described today as "among the world's great marvels." They were constructed, one can hardly say erected since they were cut down from ground level into a solid block of stone, even the altar being a piece of the monolith. The building of religious edifices out of proportion to the needs of the local population, which has been a common form of piety in many lands, inspired Ethiopia to an almost fanatical degree. Eleven solid stone churches so closely packed that sometimes they were even superimposed was Ethiopia's tribute to God.

A favorite subject, as I have said, semi-religious, semi-patriotic, is the love life of their ancient heroine whom we call the Queen of Sheba with Solomon. It is Ethiopia's national pride, and the story is told in various series of realistic pictures similar to the method of the comic strip, some going back to the destruction of the wicked snake oppressor by the father of the heroine, and all showing as a high point the warm scene wherein Solomon with his big eyes rolling in lust is leaning out of his bed to clutch the Ethiopian queen, bejeweled but with outthrust naked breasts.

A puzzling item in Ethiopian pictures is that the good characters are represented full face and the bad people—enemies or non-Christians—are shown in profile. This system causes an odd effect in group scenes, especially in battle scenes, where, for instance, the Ethiopian attacking army, lances poised, is shown in profile but with every soldier turned straight toward us, round faces and big eyes meeting our own. It would be interesting to know what was the moral, religious or magical explanation, the psychological reasoning behind the insistence upon a full-face representation of the persons they respected and the one-eyed showing of others. Professor Ullendorff says that insofar as he knows the custom is exclusively an Ethiopian peculiarity.

But it is pictures of the Virgin Mary which have been the backbone of Ethiopian art. Such pictures are countless and represent her in many miraculous situations. A large number of these are reproduced in Sir E. A. Wallis Budge's *Legends of Our Lady Mary the Perpetual Virgin and Her Mother Hanna* and *One Hundred and Ten Miracles of Our Lady Mary*.

To an unprejudiced eye, whatever may be the religious sentiments of the eye's owner, there is something not only quaint but touchingly simple in these pictures. Both those who share the "Cult of Mary," though not to the extent of the Ethiopians, whose reverence for the Virgin has been dubbed "Mariolatry run mad," and those whose religious thoughts take another form must appreciate the benevolence pictorially attributed to their sacred heroine, though some must smile at the primitive, almost earthy fashion in which her good works were sometimes conceived and performed.

We see the Virgin nourishing a certain local saint. She is seated on a throne and holds in her arms two figures to which she is giving suck, the Baby Jesus at one exaggeratedly large breast, at the other breast the saint who by his projecting feet and what seems to be the suggestion of a beard is an adult (Plate XXXII of the *Legends of Our Lady Mary*).

Again we see the Virgin in a small tentlike shelter, one breast exposed and holding a presumably milk-moistened finger toward a figure cross-armed and smiling in ecstasy. She has restored his sight "by anointing his eyes with milk from her breast" (Plate XXVI from the same title).

The oddest and also the most interesting in another connection is the set of pictures showing how the Virgin saved the soul of a sinner. The miracle these pictures illustrate is strictly and exclusively Ethiopian. (Some of Ethiopia's miracles of Mary are influenced by medieval non-Ethiopian sources.) The story told in the pictures (Plates LIV, LV, LVI) and the translated accompanying text (from *One Hundred and Ten Miracles*) concern a cannibal.

The cannibal was "by name" a Christian but a maniac in anthropophagy. He "devoured eight and seventy people, friends, acquaintances and kinsfolk," and when reduced to friendlessness by his own appetites he tackled and ate his wife and his two children. The first picture in the series shows the cannibal handsomely dressed, dagger in hand and two beheaded and dismembered humans at his feet. Another picture shows him seated at his ease, a headless female beside him, a morsel held toward his lips; evidently he ate his humans raw— as indeed used to be the Ethiopian fashion with regard to four-legged meats, behavior indignantly reported by some early travelers.

Another scene shows the cannibal giving drink from a water skin to a beggar who had pleaded with him "in the name of Mary." The climax shows three episodes: the cannibal's soul is a sort of portable furnace en route to hell; Mary is telling an angel to weigh the drink of water against the cannibal's profligate destruction of humanity to satisfy his cravings—result, the water drops outweigh the victims! —and finally the cannibal's soul is saved by Mary's intervention and sheltered in the folds of her robe.

In these last scenes the cannibal, hitherto in profile disgrace, appears for the first time full face.

Aside from the curious drama and what seems to us the remarkably broad-minded sympathy of the Virgin, the story has interest by the inference of a surprising tolerance toward cannibalism.

The bookless Africans had a different attitude toward art. They had no Moslem inhibitions about human portraiture and they had no sacred stories to tell, as had Ethiopia. Their artists, using wood, stone, fired clay (terra cotta), iron, and bronze and brass formed by the lost wax method, working across the sub-Sahara and across twenty or thirty centuries, produced an original art of vibrant vitality and queer searching images which has been of world importance.

Involuntarily bookless Africa made two contributions to the world, one very grave, one gay.

Africa, against her will, gave us the makings of the present race problem.

Africa, the same bookless, savage Africa, gave us her art, which has inspired, we are told, some of our own greatest and directly or indirectly many others, altered modern painting and sculpture and had much to do with the newly exhilarated public interest in art.

Today's ordinary people have been intrigued and enticed by art's new look. A lively interest in pictures and statuary, partly curiosity and amazement, partly a groping consciousness of some new view of things and thoughts and emotions, replaces their somewhat machine-like and imitative pseudo delight in the classicism and naturalism of a few decades back.

Great names like Picasso, Matisse, Braque, Epstein, Henry Moore, Modigliani are mentioned as having received deep impressions from Negro African art, from Africa's carvings and her masks.

It is strange that self-trained primitive peoples had in their fingers and their eyes something to teach us, the heritors of the Greeks and the Renaissance. It is strange that they communicated to us from their isolated simplicity an individual and new look at the world and humanity, an aspect that was unfettered by the actuality of photo-graphic accuracy, an aspect that offered tentatively some vision of the wished-for, the frightening, the fantastic, the magical, as if possess-ing the power to fish some unthought thought out of the back of the mind. The influence which the art of pagan Africa has had is one of the oddest of the many odd episodes in her contact with the world.

The suggestion that African Negroes had any art at all sprang upon us suddenly when artists, including Gauguin and Van Gogh, took notice of some primitive stuff at a colonial exhibition in Paris in 1888. Till then the usual reaction to masks and carvings had been disdain or disgust—and the same reaction is still felt by some—based on the contemptuous idea that these queer concepts were the fum-blings of savages trying to portray reality. Later discoveries, such as the Benin-Ife-Nok objects, showed that this was not true (hundreds of pieces were brought to Europe from Benin alone), that when they so desired, actual portrait making was well within their grasp, that they could produce work "to rank with the world's masterpieces," that (I now quote from Frank Willett's article about the Ife heads) "these objects would stand comparison with anything which ancient Egypt, classical Greece and Rome or Renaissance Europe has to offer."

Early travelers, explorers, colonial planners and missionaries, if they noticed the art of native people at all, considered what they saw com-ical or hideous or heathenish. With colonialism great quantities of native productions were brought to Europe and displayed as objects of anthropological rather than aesthetic interest.

Nowadays Africa's art has swaggered into art museums and special shows, is reproduced in handsome books, so that the figurines of Nok and the sculptures of the Benin region and even some of the rock paintings are almost as familiar to us as art created by the paler hands of our own masters. Africans in their homeland have discovered, like native peoples the world over, that art is profitable and salable, and the old things are being imitated for the market, though there is perhaps in the masks and "idols" and quaint animals of the modern artist not the same driving search to express the inexpressible, to portray the invisible that there used to be. In older days a Congo sculptor when a European plagued him to define what he had carved answered, "Do you never look at the clouds?"

Across Africa art was produced in metals—less often in iron, though sometimes, for instance in Dahomey and near Lake Chad—prolifically in bronze or brass by the lost wax method. A clear and simple explanation of this process is given in *The Art of Ife,* a booklet published at Lagos by the Nigerian Museum. I quote: "A model is made in wax, usually over a mud core. It is then covered with layers of mud, after the drying of which the wax is melted out, to be replaced by molten metal. The baked mud is finally broken away to expose the cast within."

In earlier days we suspected that the natives must have been taught this complex and delicate operation by the Portuguese, with whom they were in contact in the fifteenth century. This suspicion did not survive. The process was something which Africans taught to Africans. It was an accomplishment that was far older than the fifteenth century and that was used in regions the Portuguese did not penetrate, such as the Lake Chad locality. It was communicated with ceremony and decorum, according to legend told by Egharevba. The King of Benin who reigned about 1280 had seen works of art so made at Ife. He formally made request of the King of Ife that an expert be sent to Benin to display and teach his technique. One whose name was Igue-igba was sent as a royal gift from king to king. Igue-igba was highly competent and left many designs to his successors and—here is a case of remarkable art recognition—was deified.

He is to this day, says Mr. Egharevba, worshipped by Benin brass-smiths.

But there was the group of African metalworkers whose members were more feared than loved and were sometimes despised. These were the ironworkers. There was, it is true, a god of iron in Yoruba among their large band of divinities, but on the whole the individual blacksmith was in a dubious social position.

His was not like other occupations. He transformed a lump of something like rock into implements that could cut and kill. He worked in a dark and dangerous place, amid shooting sparks and clanging noise, keeping the secrets of his trade close hidden, forbidding intruders and especially women to approach. He made the tools of war and death, the knife that frightened the young at circumcision and excision time—indeed in some regions it was he who cut the boys and his wife who operated on the girls.

Actually it was he who made the money, the actual money itself, the iron money which was currency in some localities, the stick-shaped money which was recently used in some parts of the West Coast and which was probably used in older times in much of interior Africa, the ring-shaped pieces which explorers Denham and Clapperton observed in Bornu, and also in places outside Negroland; South Morocco's little iron money weighing about an ounce, mentioned by Leo Africanus, and the iron *hakuna,* like a long needle, listed in Omari's account of Ethiopia.

When Europeans came as coastal traders another form of iron money, called "bar," was introduced, rather as a unit of comparative values for trading between whites and blacks than as an actuality. A bar, originally fifteen pounds of imported iron, became an imaginary denomination. Thus a prime slave would be priced at say thirty bars; two and a half bottles of rum at one bar; twenty leaves or more of tobacco at one bar; a coral bead at one bar; and so on.

The blacksmith was a mysterious and magical worker, almost super-human. His was almost a race apart. Those around him were very conscious of him and could not take him in their stride. He was feared, was often regarded as a pariah, yet he had special honors and powers and privileges. A French traveler along the Niger just at the verge of colonialism observed that the blacksmith was always a free man, could never be enslaved, also—perhaps this was an insult—any article of clothing which he or his family touched was immediately given to him.

The peculiar position of the ironworker was largely of his own contriving. The secrets of his trade passed from father to son. One of Africa's modern students of native ways quotes a saying among the Akan of Ghana that one does not teach the son of the smith to forge, God (meaning the supreme god of the Akan) does. Paul Soleillet describes the establishment of the ironworkers at Ségou on the Niger, who "though they passed as impure and having dealings with demons" were thought to have King David as their patron. They maintained in front of the smithy two hired singers (*griots*) who chanted the smiths' powers, masters of iron and fire, makers of swords and lances and bullets.

Iron was a mystery. Explorer Lander, not far from Kano, heard the pathetic confidence of an old chief who kept two pieces of the metal in a down-lined box, believing they were a male and a female and that they would produce young ones. Quite recently Dr. Harley recounts in his additions to *Tribes of the Liberian Hinterland,* by George Schwab, the daylong ceremony which was performed at the installation of a new smithy near his mission. Evidently the special conviction of a magic destiny survives by intention. If the blacksmith has had to pay a price, if he was one of those whom the Mandingos called "a scrap of dung," it was in part of his own doing, or that of his ancestors.

It was in Ethiopia that the blacksmith's condition sank to its lowest and grimmest. He was classed as a bouda, a demon, because he practiced a magic avocation. So definitely was the bouda obloquy fastened to the blacksmith that Tylor, anthropology's early student, thought it was a tribal name—"the tribe of Budas of Abyssinia," he says. When some of the Falashas, the Jewish group, became blacksmiths it made the ironworker a "bouda" double distilled, since the demon accusation had already been hitched to the Jews of the land. Father D'Almeida's history says that the fifteenth-century emperor Zara Yaqob killed all the blacksmiths he could lay hands upon, which takes believing, except that Zara Yaqob had the record of being an enthusiastic executioner as well as a fanatical Jew-hater (in his writings he asserted, presumably with sincere conviction, that they ate babies) and that he had a quivering fear of magic.

It was on moral grounds that the Masai of East Africa are said to have distrusted and despised the blacksmith. The ironworker made the weapons which tempted man to fight, so it was a mean job, fit only for slaves—a case of double standard.

Probably there was behind the many cases of shrinking from the blacksmith an instinctive fear of iron's immense potentialities and dangers. Africans are imaginative. Imagination is in the African air.

There is a fable of the Basutos of South Africa which seems to reach into those fears which inspired the shrinking of the primitives and which inspire the pacifism of today. It was recorded over a century ago, and tells how in the days of old a prodigious monster snapped up and swallowed all mankind. So big he was that "the most piercing eyes could hardly take in his whole length." One pregnant woman escaped and hid and gave birth to a son who in the instant while she turned her back became a full-grown man and tackled the monster. The monster opened his great mouth and swallowed him whole. Within his immense belly was all humanity, still alive, and the hero hacked a hole in the monster's side, "through which the nations of the world" escaped.

Were they grateful to the rescuer? Not at all. He was to them a dangerous prodigy, and he saved his life only by flight.

ARTS IN BODILY AND MENTAL RE-CREA-TION · There was a form of African art in which another material was used—not rock, or wood, or metal, but their own skins and bones.

A hyphen bridging the gap between creative art and this form of re-creation was the mask whereby the appearance of the human face was temporarily altered, sometimes retaining a human aspect of varying oddity, sometimes immensely enlarged and sometimes made in the shape of an animal's muzzle.

Africa's masks, when brought to our notice, are sometimes lumped loosely and confusingly as "dance masks," which gives the impression that they were an adornment for some native version of the masked ball. Part of a dancer's gear they may have been, but often the dance was not a gay festivity but a ceremonial, even a fearsome exercise. In the latter case the purpose was not to embellish the wearer, probably not to deceive the public as to his identity, but to impart high self-confidence and to envelop with anonymity and a dignity, almost superhuman at times, one lately seen in some workaday capacity. We hear of masks for ceremonies of initiation, circumcision and excision, for religious or magical performances, sometimes for trials and executions, and at the solemn official appearances of chiefs.

We know that African masks have attracted and influenced some of our modern artists. To many of us they are displeasing. But whatever their look or their usage they satisfied and catered to a desire to alter the appearance and in a way the personality of the wearer. This desire associates with that form of art mentioned above, the impulse to tinker with, to improve—according to the Africans' notion—their

own bodies. Africans' efforts at self-embellishment, personal alterations and sexual operations are disturbing.

There were some interferences with their own skins and bones
which were not motivated by a desire for personal re-creation, such
as those springing from simple coquetry or from superstition, like
the tattooing of good luck emblems, or those based upon piety, or
those which were degradations inflicted during religious persecutions.
For example Berber girls often wore a tattoo sign on the face to
avert the evil eye, and among many systems of hair adornment this
one is reported from seventeenth-century Benin: the hair was "curled
round their heads like garlands, one half colored black, the other
red."

Sometimes there were compulsory markings forced upon minority
religious groups in the Islamic part of Africa, for instance those
imposed on occasions on the Copts of Egypt or the Jews of North
Africa. Once when Christian Ethiopia faced heresy and a reversion to
paganism people were ordered to wear on their persons slogans of
piety: on the forehead an inscription recognizing the Trinity, on one
hand the motto, "I deny the Devil in the name of Christ," and on
the other an expression of adoration of "Mary, mother of the Creator of the Universe."

Again there were self-disfigurements or torments undertaken for
religico-magical reasons, such as the amputation of a finger in some
southern African localities as a sacrifice calculated to protect the
lives of one's children, or even the cutting off of a finger of the
baby itself when he was only a day old, or the self-castration of
early Christians in Egypt, or that search for extreme sanctity which
Alvares observed in Ethiopia, where in Lent not only monks, priests
and nuns, but many of the lay people passed the night every Wednes-
day and Friday in cold water outdoors up to their necks—and cold
it was, being, Alvares said, "the season of hard frosts."

Tribal markings, scarifications on the face, had a practical motive.
They were tribal discipline and control, and were the identity papers
of a people who had no paper and did not write. One may note the
small and carefully planned differentiations between some seventy-
five tribal markings in the exact diagrams given by Captain Binger,
an explorer who studied a relatively small section in the 1880's.

A fancy touch is soberly offered by the African author of the history of Benin. A fifteenth-century king named Ewuare lost two sons in especially tragic circumstances and ordered as an official state mourning that no one was to wash or to have sexual intercourse for three years. People began to run away, and to prevent a complete depopulation Ewuare ordered the tattooing of his subjects in a special manner and sent word to neighboring rulers that persons so marked should be denied refuge. "This," the historian concludes, "was the origin of the tribal mark."

But there have been noted many widespread and differing instances of mutilation, cutting and hacking and pricking and manipulation which seemed motivated solely by the Africans' wish to change their own bodies. These varied practices in their re-creative art, uncouth and often ugly, these efforts of African beauticians and surgeons make us wince. Women's faces and bodies—sometimes their whole bodies —ornamented with patterns or prickings or cuts or burns. Holes cut in male and female ear lobes and distended so as to take and retain heavy lumps of wood or metal. Big nose disks. The hideous female "platter mouths," not common but noted in tribes as far apart as the Volta region and the neighborhood of the Zambezi and the upper Nile.

The knocking out of certain teeth or the sharpening of them to points and the pain which must have been endured by the young person at the hands of the amateur dentist working with make-shift instruments makes us shudder. And the result made travelers into the regions where such was the practice shudder too, for those sharpened teeth, they believed, were the cannibal's emblem. Masudi announced this in the tenth century.

A particularly unwholesome form of ornamentation was the system of encircling the throats and ankles of women with rings upon rings of metal wire. Naturally such corseting had its result. We are told that among the Masai when the calf of the leg was so bound it checked normal development, and since the custom persisted it is evident that such leg alteration was desired.

It would seem that primitive Africa was very leg-conscious. Re-verting for a moment to art as presented pictorially and in carvings and bronze, we note many indications of this. There was a widespread preference to portray humans with stumpy short legs, with a disproportion of head and trunk size to the underpinnings. One can observe this in reproductions of figures from Benin, Congo and Chad in the remarkable art of the Sao. One can often discern suggestions of the same in Ethiopian pictures.

This contrasts with rock art portrayals where in some cases we see a lithe-limbed individual with thin legs of great length seeming to slice the air like the wings of a bird, and where with the rock art of the Bushmen a woman's trunk rests on the great fundament of steatopygia and her billowy thighs have the ultra size called steatomeria. Representations of those lithe legs may have resulted from wishful-seeing. The rock art display of voluminous supports was true to actuality. Professor Tobias has mentioned the theory that, such being the female form sweetest to Bushman male eye, it increased and generalized through sexual selection. This, if true, would make steatopygia a variant of Africa's longing to reconstruct itself, another manifestation of Africa's re-creative art.

An important such manifestation was the sexual operations on both boys and girls. On circumcision there is a large literature ranging from prehistoric, anthropological and religious discussions to Freudian speculations. In Africa the custom was very ancient. It was far older than Islam, which itself had adopted it from the pagan Arabs it converted. It is said that the practice is not even mentioned in the Koran. Egyptians were observing the custom at least a thousand years before Islam's invasion, for Herodotus noted it.

In pagan Africa the custom has been common but not universal. Some corresponding operation upon the girls has been even more common and very ancient if we are to accept the evidence of legend, which would have it that the first sexual mutilation of one of Eve's dark sisters was the invention of a wife of Abraham who became jealous of a Negress, his concubine, and by force performed the excision operation upon her. (From Professor Monteil's collection of legends of the western Sudan.)

A combination of the desire to produce bodily improvements in female humanity with a strict morality and a catering to the slave market was the custom of safeguarding virginity by the sewing of a girl's private parts when she was very young. This was noted for example in East Africa and the Ethiopian region. Elsewhere was a system called infibulation, whereby rings or clasps or clamps were used.

These habits excited shocked amazement and were reported in detail—sometimes very horrid detail—by some of the early travelers, such as Burckhardt, W. G. Browne and Portuguese laymen and clergy. It helps to take away the grim taste, our vision of pain and discomfort, to read explorer Sintra's roguish decorum in the account of the de luxe and seemingly chic chastity guards proudly worn by certain noble females of a West Coast locality which he, first of the Europeans, visited. I quote: "The wives of kings and noblemen and of people of high station all have the extremities of their nature pierced with some holes, like the ears, and in these for dignity and to denote their importance they wear rings of gold which they can remove or put back as it seems good to them."

The various operations were inventive experiments which were parts of a general social pattern. Very different was the making of eunuchs, a commercial and cruel business undertaken for profit by the slave trade. Burckhardt, reporting from "the great manufactory" in Upper Egypt, says the price of a slave boy was increased threefold by this mutilation. The "manufactory" was run by "two Coptic monks"! They were not the only such operators, but theirs was a place of particularly sinister fame, where the Moslem slave trader was able to earn a big profit yet dodged the actual commission of a crime—it being in his religious code a grave sin to castrate man or beast. Browne says that such "manufacturing" was the hereditary business of certain families. Northeast Africa, being near the transit facilities of the Nile and Red Sea, had been a recognized center for the business from as early as the tenth century.

Among non-Islamized Africans or those converts who were slack there was eunuch making, though not to a wholesale extent. Sometimes criminals were thus punished, or sometimes foolhardy males who interfered with the wives of notables. Eunuchs were sometimes part of the native royal entourage, or might be sent as choice offerings to fellow kings.

There is poetic justice in the fact that sometimes these doubly ill-used men—for they were presumably slaves as well as eunuchs—

gained privileges and posts of high authority. There was black Kafur, who practically ruled Egypt for many years. The list of eunuch generals and admirals in African history is a long one.

The successful careers of the castrated impressed early European travelers, who record items like the black eunuch whom Windus in 1721 found acting as the emperor's treasurer in Morocco, who kept a seraglio "purely out of ostentation." In Bornu the explorer Lieutenant Colonel Monteil knew the sheik's "first eunuch and man of confidence," whose duty and privilege it was to transmit the royal powers to a chosen successor. This the eunuch in question did three times—in 1881, and three years later, and again after one year—proving himself thus to be a sort of "king-maker." Laugier de Tassy, who was there two centuries after he became a local hero, tells of the tradition about a Negro eunuch who gained the name of "The Liberator of Algiers" during one of the city's crises (1541)—Algiers has seen so many! The eunuch prophesied and, some said, even brought about that astonishing great storm which ruined Charles V's attempt with more than five hundred ships and an army of about twenty-four thousand to conquer North Africa.

We find that some of the bodily rearrangements which went to the production of Africa's re-creative art on human canvas were associated with, sometimes performed simultaneously with the ritual initiation observances which celebrated youth's emerging out of childhood into adult society.

For the boys and often for the girls it was an educational period, sometimes quite lengthy, apart from their families and wherein bodily ordeals and magic scarring combined with physical exercises and practical instruction. The elders taught and tormented the young folk, partly from a wish to share with them a part of their knowledge, wisdom and courage and partly, we suspect, because with age, which comes so quickly in primitive life, there also comes a fear of the beauty and grace and strength of youth, its vigor and fecundity, a fear which roused the impulse to scare the dangerous young thing by mysteries and pains, by vague sexual warnings and magic whisperings, and to band the young into groups by ages which would be easier to control and discipline. It was perhaps the primitive way of coping with or preventing juvenile delinquency.

As an educational system it seems gloomy and peculiar. But at any rate bookless Africa to a large extent did have a school system, probably possessed it long before our world adopted a general system of education for everybody. And the African way was democratic. It was not restricted to the children of high degree or to the specially gifted.

It was strictly non-coeducational. In the girls' schools there were also pain and scarring, also lessons in woman's work and a wife's special abilities. Sometimes the girls were taught tricks of poisoning.

Sex matters were insistently emphasized in both schools. There was a strange procedure in some of the institutions which is disgusting to us but which to them had some magic and mystic value—nor was it a value special to the bookless Negro; a similar procedure is mentioned in the Gnostic literature of the Copts in the early years of our own era along with an indignant comment supposedly made by Jesus.

About the Negro schools I quote Marie-André, a White Sister missionary, a lawyer and a social anthropologist of some standing, who tells how after the girls had submitted to excision as a part of their initiation "the residue of the operations, dried and pounded, was carefully put aside to be used when the boys were initiated . . . to season the sauce of a repast." George Harley, doctor and missionary and anthropologist, confirms and amplifies this in his *Native African Medicine,* speaking about "a soup" containing a similar ingredient which was eaten by the boys and saying that the girls consumed a corresponding "soup" made from the discarded flesh of the boys after circumcision.

The Gnostic reference is in *Pistis Sophia,* in which work, in the Gnostic fashion, are mentioned persons familiar to us in the Bible, including Jesus Himself. Thomas is represented as asking whether "it is seemly or not [when] some take the male seed and the female monthly blood and make it into a lentil porridge and eat it," at which Jesus was wroth and outlined the awful punishment such would receive in a region where "there is neither pity nor light but howling and grinding of teeth."

Closely involved with the educational system of bookless Africa was often the regional secret society—in fact the ghastly "soup" mentioned above was part of the curriculum of a Poro school, the Poro being one of the most important of those groups which early Europeans discovered on the West Coast and dubbed "secret societies" and whose name of Poro, or Purrah or the like, they would tell about, usually in a context of anger mixed with something like awe: "the terrific Purrah" or "the Purrah whose deeds of secrecy and darkness are as little called in question as those of the Inquisition in former times." It and the other secret societies, of which there were many, impeded colonial discipline and were as far as possible discouraged.

There is an impression that the secret society idea is a very old one, that it was a part of the sex war of the primitives, based upon the male desire to get the upper hand over women with their mysterious ability to eject a small human from inside their bodies and upon the hope of attaining this upper hand by the use of group magical threats and taboos.

The original purpose of the secret getting together—if such was its original purpose—expanded. Some societies even had female branches. Some took on an atmosphere of pagan religion. Many assumed the initiation ordeals and instruction of the young. Some were governments in themselves, trying and punishing offenders, and sometimes holding the titular chief or king in check if he was despotic. Others became evil, oppressive and blackmailing gangs or worse, such as the ferocious Leopard Men and Heart Men.

Whatever and whenever may have been their primitive start, the secret societies are believed to be very old. Some have suggested that certain of them came to Negro Africa from Egypt. Egypt seems to have been well aware of this element in Negroland. Ptolemy the geographer evidently knew about the Poro. Many have professed and some still profess the opinion that certain of the Negro African societies are closely related to our own Freemasonry, which in itself some have claimed as African in origin, having allegedly started in Egypt.

Secret societies, the acquiring of tribal markings, the initiation operations that went with youth's passage to adult life, sexual ceremonies, plus other acts, of whose motives we are not certain—all these included bodily mutilations and were associated with a great pattern which showed itself clumsily but surely. It was a striving to make themselves look different and so to make themselves feel different and be different. If it was art it was art of a cruel sort, but it seemed to give them satisfaction, and it was a long-continued practice.

Leakey says that skulls of great antiquity found in Africa, including a skull found near Timbuctoo, "show evidence that the upper central incisors were deliberately extracted early in life." They were wearing masks in the days of rock art. When Ibn Battuta visited East Africa in the fourteenth century he noted tattoo marks on jet black faces; the women of Sao by Lake Chad wore deforming labrets, and some of their old portrait heads suggest a practice like "platter mouths"; the antique art of Ife in certain cases shows heavy facial scarification. All of which proves that Negro Africa early invented and faithfully and widely pursued this form of self-inflicted art— or magic.

"The human body has been treated like a simple piece of wood which each has cut or trimmed to suit himself . . . sometimes with great imagination," wrote Arnold van Gennep more than fifty years ago in that book of his, *The Rites of Passage,* a classic lately put into English. Van Gennep was speaking not alone of primitive Africa, for this search for self-losing has not been hers exclusively.

In Africa it has been and still is strong, uncouth but strong. It seems like the bookless counterpart of the Gnostic intellectual strivings in northern Africa and elsewhere in the early days of our era. The Gnostics deplored the work of Creation and tried to alter it by philosophy and fantasy. The bookless Africans tackled it in a tangible—and painful—fashion, changing details in their own bodies, expressing their longing for something different in themselves as created. The Gnostics used words, contriving counter-Creation myths to those advanced by the other religions which disheartened them, presumably thus finding comfort. In both cases—in the intellectual and imaginative Gnostics and in the crude surgery of the bookless Africans—one may see a form of magic.

There was magic indeed in another method of improving on the original design, at least temporarily, by producing a change of mind. and this method Africa, like the rest of us, discovered and employed.

There was escape in the potency of strong drink and of certain drugs, even of coffee and tobacco. These, while the effect lasted, caused a new sort of mentality, a psychological re-creation.

When Islam came Africa split, in theory at any rate, between the converts and the rest on the drink question. Repeatedly the Koran condemned it. "Wine . . . is a great sin and advantage also to men, but the sin is greater than the advantage," says the sura "The Cow." The phrase coupled with sin—"advantage also"—is interesting, perhaps significant of an appreciation on Mohammed's part of drink's capacity to alter and relieve the mind and for a while to remake the individual. Granting that this was Mohammed's way of thinking, we see an explanation for what has seemed a puzzle, the contradiction between the prohibition of wine drinking and the glowing promise as one of Paradise's big attractions that there would be "rivers of wine delicious to those who quaff it." The wine of Paradise was traditionally reputed to be non-intoxicating. It pleased the palate but did not alter the brain.

Islam's rule must have been hard to accept. The absorbing of strong drink was a very ancient habit and a part of Africa's traditions. The bibulous weakness of Noah and the resulting disgrace of Ham, his son, were traditionally associated with Africa's racial origin, a people born because of wine—the Hamites. Egypt's Osiris taught mankind how to brew beer, which became the common drink of ancient Egypt. Wine was imported for the wealthy from Greece and Phoenicia, and perhaps they even got nectar, that sweet wine mixed with honey and perfumed with flowers.

Did Africa obey the prohibition? The answer is, not always. About two centuries after Mohammed's time and long after the Moslem conversion of North Africa a Tunisian ruler who died in 841 found it necessary to pass a law forbidding the use of wine at Kairwan. The raisin wine at Cairo was "a thousand times stronger than malmsey," reported a rabbi who was there in the fifteenth century. When Lane wrote about the Egyptians as he observed them more than a hundred years ago, he said that many were drinking in secret and that some "did not scruple to do so openly." Many, many goblets of wine went down Moslem African throats.

Their historians incline to deplore wine drinking vigorously, taking the tone that such was a form of debauchery sometimes combined with unnatural vice. But the poets of Islam—as Omar Khayyám would lead us to expect—told of wine drinking in joyous phrases.

We even find the wine argument involved with a very early investigation into food preservation. The physician of Harun ar-Rashid, the eminent Dr. Jabril ibn Bukhtishu (the name meaning "Saved by Jesus"), who was a non-Moslem and a non-abstainer, proved to Harun ar-Rashid the wholesome efficacy of wine when he poured undiluted wine over a dish of fish, simultaneously poured cold water over another dish of similar fish and left still another serving of fish in its spiced sauce, and then after a lapse of time displayed the result proudly to Harun ar-Rashid, the abstainer. Dishes numbers two and three had gone bad, but the wine-bedewed fish was still edible. But the caliph remained a teetotaler. The incident is told by Ibn Khaldun.

The experimenting doctor was brilliantly successful in his profession. Harun ar-Rashid paid him an extravagant fee for bleeding him twice a year and giving him a weeky purgative drink, and from the nobles of Baghdad he received additional high rewards. In his thirty-six years of practice he earned, according to Professor Edward G. Brown in *Arabian Medicine,* enough dirhems to equal three and a half million pounds sterling.

In Africa as well as elsewhere in Islam a compromise was found by the aid of what the Moslems regarded as man's best friend, the date. A date beverage was made either by an infusion of dry dates (*nabidh*) or by tapping the date tree for sap (*lagmi*). The beverage was a sweet syrup, at first non-intoxicating and approved by the most pious. Ar-Rashid drank it, and Mohammed himself would drink it at its innocuous stage, when it was not more than two days old. Date wine gained unjustified acceptance by many of the devout as an alleged non-intoxicant, which was true only in its kitten stage. Presently it became progressively tigerish, and *lagmi* had also the quality of breeding flocks of small red insects. But some African Moslems, hankering for a change of mood, would, we are told, tolerate the red visitors and would pretend to be unaware of the fermentation and would drink with easy conscience and an enjoyable exhilaration. A

French visitor in Tripoli (Libya) in the days of Turkish control compares their quibbling with that of the Catholic who slightly changed the name of the capon he ate on Friday to "carp."

Negro Moslems were franker, or so some of the very early European visitors to inner Africa tell us. The Europeans who visited the coast, the West Coast, soon brought with them the drinks of civilization— rum, gin and brandy, which altered the situation. This sophisticated and powerful sort of drink greatly pleased the Africans, and was sometimes bought in human coinage. Many Negroes live today in North and South America because of a chief's appreciation of and longing for the strong drink of the Christian white man.

As for the days before the arrival of this costly novelty in inner Africa, here are two pictures of the drink situation in Moslem Negro-land. In eastern Africa at Darfur in the Sudan, drunken rowdiness caused the Moslem sultan to order that all the houses in the country be searched for the utensils used in making the local drink *merissa,* that the women who made it should have their heads shaved and that drunks should be beheaded. Some of the population were ex-pagans who loved their old ways and the mental reanimation and relief of drink. The sultan's prohibition efforts failed. This was in the 1790's.

At about the same time far away from Darfur in Sansanding (now in the Mali Republic), Mungo Park sojourned while he contrived from a pair of battered native canoes to build a single vessel, His Majesty's Schooner Joliba (another name for Niger), on which he made his last and fatal journey. It was a Moslem town whose only public buildings were Islam's mosques. The outdoor market contained a subdivision where beer was sold—"eighty to a hundred calabashes of beer, each containing about two gallons." Strong stuff it was; English ale was "as nothing" compared to it, declared one of Mungo Park's party.

The downfall of Timbuctoo, which Morocco conquered (1591) by an almost impossibly difficult trans-Saharan expedition, was characteristically attributed by the pious Islamic *Tarikh es Soudan* to moral decadence, the first item in the list being the drinking of wine; other items, sodomy and incest.

Of drink and the Negro temperament a non-Negro African has something to say. He compares their inherent "joy and gladness,' caused by a climate where "heat dominates the temperament," to "the inexpressible joy and gladness" which a drunken person experiences because of the heat which wine generates in his spirit. Such was the theory of Ibn Khaldun: that the climate of Africa was wine in itself. Nonetheless the Negro craved the extra brain warmth of alcohol and, Koran or no, was often strongly tempted to get it.

"They drink a wine made from barley," wrote Herodotus in his account of the customs of Egypt, and this "wine" was produced almost all over Africa from various grains and called by various names, most familiar to us being *bouza,* a word common in Africa and elsewhere and possibly the same as our own word "booze." Sir Richard Burton asserts this; dictionary confirmation seems uncertain. A prettier name for one of the African local beers was *Om Belbel,* meaning "Mother of Nightingales" because it made the happy inebriate sing.

It was the women of Negro Africa who were the beermakers. Sometimes they were very inventive in concocting drinks. We hear about one made from dates and cheese which reminds us of Circe's brew before she maliciously and magically tinkered with it—that "posset of cheese and meal and pale honey mixt with wine" which Homer describes. There was discovered the trick of making sweet liquor from wild fruits, little plums and the like, of making effervescent intoxicant from certain roots—*jin-jin* or *sin-jin*—even of making drinks from various sorts of grasses or weeds. And, of course, there was the renowned palm wine.

The discovery of palm wine was not made by a woman but by a dog, or that is how the story ran. A hunter with his dog came upon a palm tree which an elephant had knocked down, boring a hole in the tree trunk with his tusk from which sap was running. The hunter thought it might be poison and gave some to his dog. The dog survived. So the next day the hunter tried the liquid, liked it very much, but fell down dead-drunk. When he recovered he collected some of the liquid in an earthen pot and carried it to the king. The king tried it and fell down dead-drunk. The bewildered people fell on the hunter and killed him. When the king came to he was very indignant and slew those well-meaners who were responsible. A sad episode, but palm wine became very popular.

There were African dream-makers and temporary personality transformers that were not liquid. Of these tobacco was the most widely used and also rather puzzling, and I will speak about it in some detail after a little note about another. The other is the kola nut. I am not including any mention of the kif of Africa, for the use of kif or hashish has been the habit of specialists, not the general practice of people seeking to reconstruct for a time their individuality.

The kola (or cola or *goro,* etc.) seems to have been exclusively an African item on the world's psychological menu. Its curative, invigorating and stimulating value—it reputedly could make dull men clever, tired men strong, old men ardent and could keep a native army in fighting trim—was partly real and partly imagination-fostered, and even partly magical—a big accomplishment and mystic influence for an unimpressive-looking smallish nut of not very pleasant taste.

When the powers of kola were first discovered I cannot ascertain. It was already a leading article of commerce across the continent in the days of Leo Africanus; he calls the kola *goro.* Jobson was the first to tell England about the strange nut. In *The Golden Trade* (1623) he calls it *gola.* After one eats it the river water, he says, tastes "like white wine, carrying that sweetness as if it were mixt with sugar." It is said that early in the fourteenth century kolas were being imported into Morocco, and it must have been a peculiarly hard job of trans-Saharan importing, for the kolas' homeland was in moist country inward from the West Coast and the kola did not tolerate drying, but required to be kept semi-humid. Many a trader must have gone thirsty in the desert to keep his precious kolas moist.

Just where were those forests in which the kolas grew was in old days a trade secret like the location of the gold mines. Thus there was infinite difficulty about procuring the nuts and vast difficulty in carrying them to far markets. It is no wonder that such of the exotic luxuries as ever reached these far markets fetched fantastic prices from the rich, who hoped that the eating of the famed kola nut would work for them and in them some miracle.

The maximum recorded seems to have been the trading of one

kola nut for one slave—a high price for a nut some inch and a half long and a low price for a human being.

Africans loved tobacco. Some used it discreetly to give the reality of their lives a short rest, to veil the harsh outlines of anxiety, to cast around them an undulating mist which slightly blurred consciousness and made the personality purr gently, as if it massaged the tired muscles of the mind. Others used it with a violence that produced stupor, even frenzy, as happened in the case of that Prester John with whom Europeans first came into contact.

When and how Africans discovered tobacco's charms and powers is, as with kola, uncertain. There can be no doubt that the coming of imported tobacco from the Western Hemisphere, which we usually credit as being tobacco's sole parent, boosted tobacco and gave it the prestige of a luxury item whose "bar" value on the coast was high. But it seems sure that Africa possessed and used tobacco of its own before the arrival of the foreign kind.

One after another of the early explorers speak of "indigenous tobacco" in various regions, mentioning in some cases that the people had for a long time been aware of the use of the plant, that it was "very strong" and that the natives preferred it to the cultivated tobacco of the American variety. Among these early explorers were Barth, commenting on the eastern and central sub-Saharan region; Schweinfurth, upper Nile; Binger, interior south of the Niger; Lenz, Morocco and Mali; Meniaud, in a detailed study of tobacco in Niger-western Sudan region; Browne, at Darfur in eastern Sudan. I understand that pipes of great age—supposedly tenth century—have been found in the Chad region, but whether it was tobacco that was smoked in them we naturally do not know.

There are historic references and recorded traditions which suggest —prove, if we take them without question—that Africa must have had tobacco of her own, for some deal with dates before America and the American natives who "indulged in fumigation" were simultaneously discovered by Columbus, and some deal with times which seem too near to 1492 for us to believe that the tobacco they refer to was foreign or grown from plants of foreign importation.

Tobacco was a leisurely traveler. It did not reach Europe till almost seventy years after the discovery of America; shortly afterward Nicot carried some to France from Portugal and became tobacco's godfather. In Africa it was an enticing import in coastal trading, according to Mungo Park and others, presumably appealing as a novel delight in localities where the indigenous sort did not occur. Since we know that it remained for so long an exotic rarity at West Coast ports it seems improbable that it can have penetrated swiftly inland or across the desert to North Africa.

The tobacco that features in this incident, for example, can be assumed to have been Africa's own breed. El Oufrani tells it in his history. It seems that the guardians of the elephant whose arrival in Morocco in 1592 caused a riot brought with them also another novelty—tobacco. It would be most unlikely that the elephant's companions brought any but the aboriginal variety. It was at least two years later that tobacco made its first appearance in the inland part of Africa south of the Sahara, in the Timbuctoo neighborhood, much closer than Morocco to the West Coast ports, the distribution points for the imported variety. The *Tarikh es-Soudan* tells how soon thereafter a caid, wounded by a poisoned arrow, smoked tobacco, which caused him to vomit and thus saved him—suggesting that "fumigation" was a novelty to him.

In contrast Ethiopia's first meeting with tobacco was a disastrous scandal. Labna Dengel, the same who later was accepted by the Portuguese as the mysterious hidden Christian emperor, and his soldiers used tobacco at a festival in imitation of their neighbors, the Galla, who evidently were hardened and long-time tobacco users in their pagan rites and in their medical practices. The soldiers became crazed, fell to fighting among themselves and finally destroyed the king's castle, while the king himself, excited with narcotic dreams like a ferment within him, cried out, "If Pharaoh and Nebuchadrezzar were to join their armies to attack me I would win! O Lord, I implore You to send me an enemy to fight!" His prayer was presently answered with dire results when Ethiopia was invaded and sacked by "The Left-Hander" (Gran). Tobacco became hateful, so the legend goes, its use was punished by facial mutilations—lips or noses cut off. (This legend is from the text, translated from the Amharic, of Guébré Sellassié's account of Ethiopian history given as a prelude to the Chronicle of Menelik II, and from the editor Maurice de Coppet's remarkable notes.)

Tobacco's adventures with its users were sometimes queer and sometimes indecent in the period before colonization gradually brought our genteel smoking habits into African life. Noted by travelers, for instance, were a king in the Guinea region who smoked a pipe five feet long, the bowl of which held a quarter pound of tobacco, a sheik in southern Morocco who rolled his tobacco in butter and smokers in Mali who put butter into the pipe bowl before putting in the tobacco.

El-Tounsy, who traveled in the Sudan at the very beginning of the nineteenth century, tells how tobacco was actually used as money. It had a quality which is novel in coins, having "an odor so strong that often one who sniffed it was afflicted with vertigo." The method of tobacco minting was to pound green leaves in a mortar into a sort of dough and to form this substance into hollow cones which were dried and put into circulation.

That very careful observer of Saharan manners and morals, Duveyrier, tells that certain desert women, "married at eleven, mothers at twelve and old at twenty," felt the need of an aphrodisiac and were in the habit of applying tobacco—the *doukhkhan*, very strong and piquant, to their private parts.

A frank interest in various other aphrodisiacs was characteristic of the continent. Its authors deal with the subject without reserve and sometimes give quaint details, as in two curious accounts from two of the most familiar of geographers, Leo Africanus and El-Bekri, describing respectively the amazing powers of *surnag* and of a nameless water-growing plant.

Surnag grew wild in the Atlas Mountains of North Africa and was an aphrodisiac so potent that a man whose nights of loving were but a regretted memory would, if he chanced to urinate upon a *surnag*, recapture all his old vitality. But unhappy the peasant girl or shepherdess who so relieved herself. *Surnag's* power robbed her, all innocent as she was, of her virginity, might even cause pregnancy. Leo Africanus records these "facts." El-Bekri in his hearsay account of

"The Land of the Negroes" tells how the king of a country which he names but which I cannot identify on today's map had exclusive control over an aphrodisiac "of the highest degree," growing in a marsh. It was his and his alone. He had "an immense number of wives; when he wished to see them he notified them a day in advance, took the dose and visited each and all of them in succession without the least fatigue."

So it is surprising that Africa approved of *cat* (also written *qat, tshat*) for which one of the claims was that it was an *anti*-aphrodisiac. *Cat* was described as a substance which "excited, gave joy and permitted a person to deprive himself to an extent from having sex relations." *Cat* was African. It grew in Ethiopia and was renowned from early times. The words quoted above are from the *Masalik,* written in the first half of the fourteenth century, whose author tells slyly that when a king of Yemen was offered a *cat* tree as an exotic contribution to his park he declined emphatically with a harsh "No!", adding, "Why should I make use of a thing that would deprive me of my joy?"

However, Yemen promptly adopted the *cat* habit, attracted by the promised excitement and overlooking the detriment. Indeed almost simultaneously with the incident in the *Masalik*'s joking comment one of the many Moslem enemies of Ethiopia declared that among his main motives for trying to conquer the country was the desire to raise on a large scale "*tshat,* of which the Moslems are fond." (From the Ethiopian narrative about their fourteenth century King Amda Syon.)

The African attitude toward tobacco (which had at the start its ups and downs in Europe—the downs sometimes running to cruel punishments of the smokers) was on the whole liberal. Islam, of course, had something to say, but was hampered by the fact that tobacco was not prohibited in the Koran, though there is a traditional saying of Mohammed's on the subject, which presumably was invented after the use of tobacco became general and which Sale, who gives it in his Preliminary Discourse to the Koran, declares would, if Mohammed really said it, "prove him to be a prophet indeed!" The prophecy ran that in days to come "there would be men who would bear the name of Moslem but should not be really such, and that they would smoke a certain weed which would be called tobacco."

Surveying the situation up and down and back and forth across the continent, we find that many smoked freely and freely drank strong drink. These included the non-Moslem sub-Saharans plus slackers everywhere. Others smoked but did not drink—many Moslems, and oddly enough, the Bushmen. Some drank but did not smoke. These were the Ethiopians, Christians outside the Koranic prohibition, and they produced "very good grape wine," as appreciated by Father Alvares, who went there to visit "Prester John," also *talla* (beer), mead, a grass beverage and others. Not only produced, but copiously consumed, so that by some they were reported to drink to excess, and Bruce is quoted as saying that some of the poor pretty well lived on bread and beer. But Ethiopians had a fierce objection to tobacco, and in their hatred cherished the legend that tobacco grew from earth polluted by the Christian so-called heretic Arius, whom they classed in villainy along with Judas.

And finally there were some localities which forbade both the liquid and the nicotine aids toward remaking the world and their own selves for a brief moment. Timbuctoo went into this era of double prohibition during a period of ultra-pious control and so continuously did the people of the seven oases of the Mzab, whose religion was a cluster of "Don'ts," so that even an outsider caught smoking in their community was in danger. In the code of the Sudanese Mahdi, who caused the British so much trouble, tobacco was classed as even viler than wine.

"When the Devil was driven out of Paradise," runs a Mzabite saying, "he stopped at the door and urinated there and at that spot was born the tobacco plant," a variant of the legend about Arius. Ethiopia in its antagonism to tobacco went yet further, saying that at the death of Jesus all plants in sorrow faded and dried up—except the villain, the tobacco plant.

These are mean legends to invent and attach to the origin of a plant which has had so much to do with making the world's—and Africa's own—business go around and has played only a modest part in the sometimes strange and savage efforts at that personal re-creation for which Africa has instinctively hankered.

To re-create themselves, to alter and—to their ideas—improve upon their own bodies and to change for at least the moment the workings of their own minds, has been the Africans' daring and dangerous adventure, the expression of the striving imagination of peoples often isolated, and in some sections bookless.

AFRICA'S LITERATURE

IN ARABIC AND OTHER SCRIPTS ·
THE DARKER WRITERS,
MOSLEM AND CHRISTIAN ·
THE AUTHORS WHO TALKED

IN ARABIC AND OTHER SCRIPTS · Writing

was in Africa's blood, her heritage. "Written language was by no means in its infancy even at the beginning of the 1st Dynasty," says Professor Emery in *Archaic Egypt*. There must be today many an African either in Egypt or in other regions where Egypt penetrated whose direct ancestor was able to write and did write with the implements of the day at least five thousand years ago, at which time my ancestors, and maybe yours, were able only to snare wild animals and catch fish. This African may today be one of the bookless or may be one of the modern post-colonization and post-decolonization authors, such as have inevitably been influenced by Europe and America and so are outside the scope of this book.

In the interim between antiquity and colonization Africa used imported or rearranged writing systems. (The Tuareg and the Ethiopians derived special systems from non-African sources; in post-colonial days Vai and some pictorial systems developed in Negro Africa.) As Punic, Greek and Latin waned Arabic spread wide. Largely it appeared in complete guise—Arabic words in Arabic script—sometimes in mongrelized form. Sub-Saharans would write their native words in Arabic letters; on occasion a Jewish author would put Arabic words into Hebrew characters, and a sort of bastard semi-Arabic script was invented to make the Arabic alphabet fit the pronunciation of a native language.

The greater part of Africa's authorship since Islam came has naturally been composed in Arabic by Arabic speakers. Of the work of Negro Moslem writers and that of Ethiopians in their own script something will be told in the next chapter, "The Darker Writers."

Few of us are familiar even by its title with any book written by an African in pre-colonial times, excepting perhaps *Confessions* of St. Augustine or *The Golden Ass* of Apuleius, although the names of certain African authors of antiquity are known to us: Ptolemy, some of the early Christians and perhaps that of the picturesque sixteenth-century travel writer, Leo Africanus. Yet what Africa wrote was a display of herself. Her literature, written or at first orally transmitted, is the basis—except for her art the only basis—we have for an understanding of her thoughts during the centuries of her isolation.

In the passage which follows or elsewhere in this book as various subjects have come up about which they had something to say there are mentions of a mixed lot of authors who were of African birth or were in close contact with Africa.

The earliest writings of all, those of ancient Egypt excepted, we shall never read, for Rome contemptuously tossed them into near oblivion. These are the national library, the so-called "Books of Carthage," which after the destruction of her enemy, Rome, indifferent as conquerors of the records of thoughts and acts of the Asians in Africa, slung into the hands of the native petty royalty, the Numidians. Juba II used some of this material in his own books, now lost. The sole survivor of the national library of Carthage was a treatise on agriculture. As source material for history the loss is regrettable. As information about Africa's thought at the time less so, for Carthage seems never to have melded into Africa, but to have retained throughout its African centuries a colonial aloofness.

There have been some writers whom Africa could not claim as her own yet cannot ignore. Take for high examples Maimonides and Masudi, the first a very great Jewish philosopher, born in Moslem Spain, the other that "Herodotus of the Arabs" already cited several times in this book, who was born in Baghdad. Both died in Egypt.

Maimonides spent most of his adult life in Africa, fleeing from Spain to Morocco to escape persecution, fleeing again from Morocco to Egypt for the same reason. In Egypt he wrote his famous *The Guide for the Perplexed*, which is still, eight centuries afterward, so important that it was recently advertised in a de luxe three-volume edition translated from the original Arabic into French, price the equivalent of thirty dollars, in a paperback edition at $1.85, and is appearing in the United States at fifteen dollars, in a complete English version. Maimonides is one of literature's unforgettables.

Like many Jews in medieval Africa, he became a doctor. As we know, he was personal physician to Saladin, and so efficient and reputed that Richard Coeur de Lion tried to seduce him away to become his own doctor.

In Morocco, his earlier place of refuge, "a curious old house in Fez is pointed out as the residence of Maimonides . . . There are thirteen windows in the house to symbolize, it is said, the thirteen dogmas of Maimonides" (meaning the thirteen articles of the Jewish creed, as he enumerated them). This I quote from Nahum Slouschz, who was a devoted and sometimes credulous investigator of Jewish conditions and traditions in northern Africa and was associated in the first decade of this century with the Israel Zangwill scheme "to create a Jewish colony in Cyrenaica with the consent of the Turkish government." Already this seems like very remote ancient history: the Jews have attained dignified national status; the Turks are ousted from Cyrenaica, also the Italians, who succeeded them, and Cyrenaica is a part of the United Kingdom of Libya, where oil fountains sprinkle sudden wealth upon the land.

Masudi, like the great Jewish philosopher, traveled far, but his traveling was for the joy of it, not from fear. He went from the Atlantic to the China Sea and down the east side of Africa to beyond the Equator and gave an account of what he saw and heard and imagined at great length (thirty volumes), of which an abridgment in French translation is in itself nine volumes long and has the gay title *Meadows of Gold and Mines of Gems.*

His writing has charm, is so often informative and wise, so often fanciful, even absurd to our ideas—a mixture of encyclopedia and fairy tale. When he chose he was a thoughtful geographer. He was shrewd enough to question some of the theories of Ptolemy to which Christian Europe gave respectful credence almost into modern times— for example the notion that Africa swirled around to hook onto Asia.

He had confidence in the earth's grandeur. The dimensions of the globe, he said, for Masudi was a sphere believer, equaled a five-hundred-year journey. This estimate, astronomical as it sounds, can be reinterpreted as unintentionally prophetic in a way differing from Masudi's idea. It was indeed to be a journey into the future of more than five hundred years from Masudi's time, mid-tenth century, to the first earth circumnavigation, the Magellan expedition of the early sixteenth.

Like many Moslems of the day who inherited Greek theories, Masudi thought the world was round although the orange he envisioned was overample. An earlier African, Eratosthenes of Alexandria, born in Cyrene, was more modest as earth's *corsetier* and, estimating the size of the world's belt by a method of his own invention, came amazingly near to the figure of modern geography—insofar as we are able to approximate the standard measurement length he used to our own. He "flourished," as classical biographers say, in the third century B.C. Even before him a Sicilian Greek, Dicaearchus, composed a work called *Journey Round the Earth*, thus preceding Jules Verne by about twenty-two hundred years, though probably his was more a description of the world as then known than an account of circumnavigation.

Masudi, though fanciful, gave a more reliable account of the earth than did that other African, Cosmas, a sixth-century Egyptian who thought that the suggestion of a spherical earth was a blasphemy, though the Scriptural passages on which he founded his conviction of flatness (I have read most of these in Psalms, Isaiah, Job, Ezekiel, etc., also in the Koranic sura called "Lokman," which is equally vague) seem more poesy than statement of fact.

Cosmas' discourse is available in English translation. His flat world is picturesque and rather pleasing, and medieval European Christians and probably the Christian remnants in Africa continued to like it very much: an oblong with waters all around the inhabited earth, a cover on top whereupon was Heaven, and Paradise was located in the outlying suburbs, apparently within reach of the daring sailor, for, said Cosmas, "If there are men who in order to procure silk for miserable trading do not mind a journey to the limits of the earth [China], how would they hesitate to go where they would enjoy the sight of Paradise itself?" (This from George Coedès' translation of Greek and Latin texts about the extreme Orient.)

There stands out one whose name is the very name of the continent: Africanus—Sextus Julius Africanus. Yet he may not have been an African after all. The learned Eleventh edition of the Encyclopaedia Britannica says he was; erudite Professor Cross says he was not. With Africa he had and still has, whether or not he was born in Libya, a very close connection, emphasized in the history of Egypt. The high priest Manetho invented, or at any rate recorded, a list of Egypt's dynasties, the frame on which we hang Egypt's ancient history, and it was Africanus who incorporated the Manetho list (now lost) in his chronology. Josephus did the same. And Eusebius imitated and altered Africanus' job argumentatively. The Africanus version would seem to be historians' preference.

Africanus' *Chronographiai* dealt with the world since Creation, which he calculated to have been in the year 5500 B.C., considerably earlier than Archbishop Usher's familiar theory of 4004 B.C. Such systems seemed more flattering than the scientific estimates of today. A person could feel a proud identification with humanity if he thought that his own threescore and ten represented something like 1 percent of the total period of mankind's history and experience. One cannot feel the same self-importance when informed of the skull of a human who lived a half million or more years ago. One's participation in the human pageant seems minuscule and negligible.

If he did wear his name by a fluke Julius Africanus resembles "The Nubian Geographer," Edrisi. Edrisi was born in Morocco, but he never saw Nubia in his life, nor did I get the impression when reading his book that he overemphasized Nubia. Why he was given the nickname is a puzzle. The famous geography which he, "the greatest of Arab geographers" and "the most brilliant geographical author and cartographer of all medieval times," wrote (I quote Bernard Lewis and Hitti) had the title *The Pleasure of Him Who Desires to See Different Countries Revealed to Him,* and is prosaically called *Description of Africa and Spain* in the partial French translation.

His career was of the highly appreciated sort that authors dream about. His sponsor, Roger, the Norman king of Sicily, was passionately curious about the world which lay outside his own knowledge, called in Edrisi and supplied him with silver from which to make a model showing what it was like and financed the sending of investigators to far parts to collect data. The silver tablet when finished weighed 450 pounds, and Edrisi had left over two thirds of the silver supply which his lavish employer had given him. "Keep it for yourself!" said the munificent Roger.

To the modern reader or to the student seeking information about medieval Africa, Edrisi's method of presenting geography is irritating. He employs the "climate" system, slicing the world as he knew it into stripes and then splitting the stripes into sections, each piece described separately and without consideration of the outlines of countries or regions—a bit of Nubia, for example, in one section, more Nubia in a later passage in another section. He treated the world as if he were some giant cutting it up into portions to serve to guests. The system does not appear to have primarily concerned climates, as we understand the word, and it was not an annoying device invented by Edrisi, but was a Moslem arrangement based on the oldest geographical science we of the Western world know, that of the Greeks. (The Orient can offer a lengthy mythical geography, the Chinese *Chan-Hai-King,* which may have been composed, the translator says, two thousand years before Christ.) But Edrisi used the climate system with peculiar insistence. Beazley complains about "his rigid climatic system, treating *terra habitabilis* under seven zones from equatorial to polar regions and ignoring all divisions whether physical, political, linguistic or religious."

Despite the fact that Edrisi's work, intended for the pleasure of the reader who desired "to see different countries revealed to him," had been sponsored by a European king, it gave little pleasure to Europeans, being practically ignored by the Christian public of the day, though later translated (mid-nineteenth century) and recently published in two countries of Europe. Europe was then isolationist, rigidly separationist intellectually from Islam. It would be almost two hundred years before the teaching of Arabic was countenanced.

Another Moslem geographer came along four centuries afterward whose writing had just the reverse experience. His book became a European best seller, one of the most successful books by an African author of all time in the European market, but cut no figure in his home continent. He, like Edrisi, had a European sponsor, the great Medici Pope Leo X, who bestowed upon the Moslem his own name when the Moslem shifted to Christianity, Leo. "Leo Africanus," as Hassan Ibn Mohammed al-Wazzan al-Fasi now became, wrote a geography of Africa which promptly ran into eight editions in Italian within fifty years, was put into English (the Pory edition, 1600), had already been put into Latin and into French (the Temporal edition, 1556) and attained the tribute of being openly plagiarized by at least three authors and supplying unacknowledged material to Marmol. All this, plus other translations and certain modern reissues.

But I have no corresponding indications of interest in Leo's geography in Leo's land, the land with which it deals. I do not know anything about its publication in Africa, even if ever there was such publication. It is of record that the original Arabic manuscript was lost. In the rewritten version Leo revealed himself as a religious renegade who dealt with Africa objectively for the delectation of Christian Europe. This would not make for popularity at home.

Leo Africanus was "The Father of Colonization." His book gave the European world the only account of Inner Africa—the imitative Marmol excepted—it was to possess until Mungo Park, two and a half centuries later. His enticing representation of Africa's wealth roused ravenous appetites, which would for a long time be gratified only by window-shopping. Then came those adventures of explorers, the bridge across which colonization passed.

Leo's account of Timbuctoo was dazzling. "In the whole annals of literature there is not another passage which has conducted more materially to the progress of geography," wrote Robert Brown, who edited in 1896 a reissue of Pory's Leo. In addition to some lustful passages about girls to be had at bargain prices and people walking about in the nude, Leo told of gold . . . gold . . . the gold that Europe craved then even more than now.

The king had along with various golden objects, a rod of gold that weighed thirteen hundred pounds. People came to market with more gold than they could spend. In Bornu he found horsemen with golden spurs and horses with golden bits and dogs with golden chains. Leo's book also contained observations of less avid appeal. Several pieces of the varied information he offered are cited in this book.

Leo's travels were wide and his adventures and religious experiences make by comparison the diversified careers sometimes claimed by their publishers for modern authors seem mild pap. His birth date (variously given) was just before or just after his natal town of Granada was conquered by Christian Spain in 1492. His Moslem family fled to Fez. In his teens he went across the Sahara with his uncle, who was ambassador to the Negro personage we know as the powerful first Askia. He also traveled in northern Africa and in the Near East.

He wrote a book of his travels. He and his book in manuscript were in a ship off the Tunisian coast which was captured by pirates— Christian pirates. Those were the golden days of piracy, the days of the spectacular Barbarossa, and "The Scourge of Christendom" had a counterpart in "The Scorge of Islam." The Christian pirates carried Leo, still a young man, to Italy and, impressed by his intellectual standing as an author, gave him to the Pope instead of turning him into a slave laborer or a galley slave. Leo tactfully accepted conversion to Christianity, accepted a new name as offered by Pope Leo X, became teacher of Arabic at Bologna University—for by then Christian Europe had overcome its shrinking from the language of the Moslems—and had a cardinal as one of his pupils. Also at the Pope's encouragement he rewrote his book about Africa.

He had lost the original manuscript, which had been pirates' booty. It had quite as adventurous a career as its author. It was being transported by sea as part of a valuable library from one Italian port to another. The ship was taken by Moslem pirates, who tossed the manuscript into the water.

Leo's rewritten *Description of Africa* was duly published and enthusiastically received, as has been stated. Leo presently returned to Africa and, we are told, resumed the religion of his youth. I do not know this, but one can well fancy that he lived out his days in nerve strain lest the *Description* in one of its European versions come to the attention of a local Moslem able to translate it into Arabic. It contained phrases such as "the damnable Mohammedan sect," "the wretched doctrine," "the false prophet, Mohammed," and dwelt in vituperative fashion on the shortcomings of Africans, all this written for policy's sake during his non-adhesive Christian period.

All in all, the African author Hassan Ibn Wazzan, remembered in innumerable reissues of his book as Leo Africanus, had a remarkable writing career.

Africa held books in high esteem, even reverence. I have told about the hundreds of booksellers' shops in Marrakesh. When Sultan Aby Yusuf of Fez negotiated with one of the Sanchos of Iberia at the end of the thirteenth century, he demanded that there be delivered to him all the Arabic books which had fallen into the hands of Sancho's people. Accordingly Sancho gave up thirteen loads of manuscripts, titles of many of which are mentioned, and they were sent to Fez. It is significant that this part of the reparations payment, the return of the books, is the only item specifically named by the historian in his account of the peace settlement.

The historian in question is the problematical author of the *Roudh el-Kartas*, which I have frequently cited. This is a book with too many authors. The uncertainty about its authorship has led to much learned argument and to confusion in bibliographies, some crediting this important source to one and some to another: to "Ibn Abi Zar [with alternate prenames offered] of Fez" or to "Abd-el-Halim," variously described as "of Fez" or as "of Granada," and some even combining the two into one long name. Professor Levi-Provençal, one of the big figures in Arabic study, has discussed the question with care in his *Islam d'Occident*, but leaves the personality of the author still up in the air. His translation of the full title of the book is quaint and provocative: *The Friend Who in the Garden of the Svelte Young Girl Finds Joy in the History of the Kings of Maghreb* [western North Africa] *and in the Annals of the City of Fez.*

It is customary to refer to the book simply as *Kartas* and it is prudent to dodge indicating its author. It is a book of high value to students and of interest to anybody, being full of human interest and spicy episodes; it covers the events of about five hundred years in and around what is now Morocco, has been translated into many European languages, though not into English, so far as I know, and in the French translation is nearly six hundred pages long. The French translator, Beaumier, favored Abd-el-Halim as author.

Africa made a contribution during the period when Arabic culture led the world, most especially in the rediscovery, the study and the translation of Greek wisdom and science. Our vanity cannot deny the comparative Arabic brilliance of those days. We admit that Moslem contacts in the Crusades were an education for Europe. Hitti tells us that while Baghdad rulers were "delving into Greek and Persian philosophy their contemporaries in the West, Charlemagne and his lords, were dabbling in the art of writing their names." Baghdad and Cordova were the earlier intellectual centers. Cordova is said to have possessed a royal book collection so big that it needed forty-four volumes to catalogue the library. Later, as Islam faded in Spain and Baghdad fell, Islamic culture moved to Cairo. Northern Africa benefited by the services of literature's handmaiden—paper. In Morocco there were, *Kartas* says, four hundred papermakers. It was from Morocco that the industry, Oriental-born, passed over to Moslem Spain and then to Christian Europe.

Europe's earliest introduction to Arabic cultural discoveries came, oddly, through a Carthaginian, he being the first to translate, via the hyphen of Arabic, classic texts from the Greek Europeans had long since forgotten into their accustomed Latin. Twelve centuries after Hannibal and the Carthaginians invaded Italy, Constantinus Africanus came not with elephants but with knowledge, and at the now very old and then very young University of Salerno translated from the Arabic medical and other works which included much from the Greek.

Of the man himself we have no knowledge. We can assume, since he was a monk and Carthage-born, that he came from one of those hide-out pockets of Berber Christians. He was one of three writers from Africa to receive the nickname "Africanus": Julius, who helped preserve the records of Egypt, Leo, who told of inner Africa, and Constantinus, the Carthaginian monk who taught Europe about Greek wisdom. Constantinus died at Salerno in 1087.

Another, the famous Averroes, invaded Europe—not in person but by his startling line of thought. He was born in Cordova in 1126 and spent much time in Africa. It is possible he may even have been of African Berber descent. Such was the suggestion often propounded about Moslem personalities, and the uncertainty and arguments as to Arab or Berber ancestry came up often, sometimes acrimoniously. There was prestige in the possession of forebears who were Arabs, of the land of the Prophet. Even Ibn Khaldun, who himself stated definitely that he was of Arab blood, has been by some called Berber and his claim attributed to snobbery.

The original name of the philosopher who jolted Europe was Ibn Rushd, which as his ideas penetrated into Christian Europe and gained notoriety was rather clumsily repronounced and finally completely altered to Averroes and became, as Sir Hamilton Gibb says, "a battle cry for the first assailants on the medieval Catholic philosophy of Europe." This Europeanizing of his name was a sort of backhanded tribute, indicating how thoroughly Christians adopted, criticized and quarreled about him. He impressed them even more deeply than he did his own people, as is proved by the long-time violent discussions, notably "the great Paris Condemnation of Averroes," which Dr. Gordon Leff speaks of in his book *Medieval Thought*.

Africa and Moslem Spain both petted and persecuted Averroes. For a time he was the intellectual playfellow of the Almohade sultan, to whom he revealed Aristotle. Later, held to be a dangerous free-thinker, he was disgraced and his books were burned.

Long after he had gone to his rest at Marrakesh in Morrocco, Averroes helped in the discovery of America. Columbus, who read widely before he tackled the voyage into the mysterious blank spaces of the West, is said to have given credit to Averroes as one who inspired in him a belief in the existence of a world beyond the seeming emptiness.

Just as Arabs transmitted to Europe the wisdom they had acquired from the Greeks they bestowed on Europe the numerical system they had learned from the farther East, but which we call "Arabic." It would seem that the gift passed along to Europe via Africa. But the new and efficient system dragged its feet as it slowly moved into the daily business of Christian Europe.

An Italian merchant mathematician named Fabonacci, often called Leonardo of Pisa, who had traveled and studied in North Africa and been shown the Arabic numeral system, invitingly revealed in a book the simple charm of Arabic numbers and zero. His book was written in 1202. A more romantic tale gets the Arabic style to Europe at an earlier date. This is often cited by serious writers, but admittedly as an improbability. It is that Pope Sylvester II had in his pre-papal youth "stolen" the secret of Arabic numerals from an Arab in Spain. Gerbert, his name before he became Pope, was for the time and place— tenth-century Rheims—an outstanding intellectual. He wrote books, including a work on mathematics, and he designed an abacus. A variant tale about Gerbert is that he was a student at the then brand-new University of Fez and had learned about Arabic numbers and carried the news of them to Europe.

Fez probably did not endow Christian Europe with this convenient substitute for the almost unmanageable Roman numbers. But there seems no doubt that the city of Bougie in Algeria did do so, for it was at Bougie, then a great place for foreign trade, that Leonardo of Pisa was educated.

The culture of Moslem Africa reached its peak in those days when Africa had knowledge to spare and exported it across the Mediterranean. But gradually northern Africa began to slide down, to slide in culture, to slide in power. Moslem culture, its roots in the East, had crossed Africa like a vine to breed a fine flower in Spain. The roots weakened. The Spanish flower withered and the vine was squashed under the feet of history.

Across northern Africa came rough riding the disruptive second Arab invasion, tribes whose inherited taste ran rather to brigandage than to culture; they were a destructive rowdy lot.

There was disintegration of Moslem Spain under Christian attacks. Many disheartened refugees drifted across the Strait to Africa and brought disheartenment with them.

Africa's shores were feeling Europe's attacks. Africa shifted and quivered; dynasties snarled and snapped at one another. The Turks took Egypt, took all North Africa to the Moroccan frontier.

The social atmosphere was changing. It was another aspect of the isolation of Africa. It seems as if a delayed Middle Ages, such a period from which Europe was emerging and which Moslem North Africa had to a large degree dodged, was moving across the Mediterranean.

So we see the greater days of Africa's literature failing. In many quarters piracy would supersede culture. But certain fine figures still stood up along the way.

In Morocco at Tangier and in the city of Tunis there grew up almost simultaneously two of these fine figures, two unique boys. One —the Tangier boy—became "perhaps the greatest land traveller who ever wrote his travels," in the estimation of Burckhardt, who first introduced his narrative to English readers in a short fragment. The other was the most remarkable of all the Arabic historians. They were Ibn Battuta (1304–78) and Ibn Khaldun (1332–1406).

"The Marco Polo of Islam," certain people have called Ibn Battuta, and some have ventured to reverse the phrase to run that Marco Polo was "The Ibn Battuta of Europe." But Ibn Battuta's story having been till recently unavailable to us, a comparison has been beyond the power of most of us. Ibn Battuta's full narrative came into European hands only with the French conquest of Algeria. It was later put into French with learned care, but in a fashion without appeal to the ordinary reader: four volumes of Arabic and corresponding French passage on the same page. Now at last Ibn Battuta is being gradually set before us in a translation with generous notes by Gibb, who has already published a one-volume abridgment of Ibn Battuta's whole adventure.

Previous to the discovery of the complete manuscript several abridgments—or rather abridgments of abridgments—were issued, Burckhardt's being especially enticing. He found copies of a partial manuscript in Egypt. In pre-printing days books were very expensive and it was often the custom to procure copies of a portion or of an abridgment of a book. Burckhardt turned his partial manuscripts over to Cambridge. From these the Reverend Samuel Lee made a translation in 1829, which necessarily was thin in text and hampered insofar as it treats of Africa by the almost complete ignorance of the continent in pre-exploration days.

I go into these details to explain why "the greatest land traveller" is not so familiar to the general public as Marco Polo, whose story has been multitudinously published over the centuries and so frequently shown to us in motion pictures that he is a household word.

It has been estimated that Ibn Battuta covered seventy-five thousand miles in his almost thirty years of traveling, and since, as he said, "I made it a habit never so far as possible to cover a second time any road that I had once travelled," he saw so much of the world that the title *A Donation to Those Who Are Interested in the Curiosities of the Cities and Marvels of the Ways* is really a modest one.

He visited not only the lands of every Moslem ruler of the times but other localities less congenial. He even went to then Christian Constantinople, where he saw the Church of St. Sophia, and was told that it had been built by Solomon's cousin and that some of its official clergy were descendants of the Apostles.

His memory was prodigious, also his ear for variations in sounds. He tells of hearing a short speech about himself uttered in Persian which he did not then understand, "but the words stuck in my memory and when I learned the Persian language I found out their meaning." To the average reader a detriment to this wonderful memory of his is that his narrative is supercharged with the names of the immense number of persons whom he encountered. He could not be described as a name-dropper but rather as a name-pelter. This rather slows down the reader because Islamic names frequently take up a whole printed line or more.

Ibn Battuta, this aside, is lively. His narrative is bright with curious incidents and short stories of local association, sometimes laughable, sometimes startling. And he is so entertainingly frank about himself.

He reveals without embarrassment his greed for gifts and his complacent expectation of hospitality along the route. Early in the outset of his travels he profited from the kindly Moslem habit of aiding the stranger. The town governor of Constantine in Algeria gave him "a fine mantle in the corner of which he had tied two gold dinars." "This," says Ibn Battuta, "was the first alms bestowed upon me on my journey." Later in his adventurous career Ibn Battuta became a celebrity and regarded lavish presents and luxurious entertainment as his due. To receive a man who had seen so much and could tell about far and unknown countries was a privilege and was worth a high recompense. He was welcomed as a grand personage, feted and petted and given gifts to cover his travel expenses, and he was openly resentful if these gifts did not come up to the standard of his expectations.

At Mali, where his reception was skimpy, Ibn Battuta spoke out vigorously to the sultan. It was his last great journey, and he had by then acquired great self-confidence. "I have travelled through the countries of the world and met their kings . . . You have neither shown me hospitality nor given me anything. What am I to say of you before other rulers?" The niggardly sultan capitulated, and Ibn Battuta left his capital with "a gift of a hundred gold *mithkals.*"

Another and an even more surprising bit of frankness was Ibn Battuta's candid admissions of his uxorious longings and their frequent gratifications. He married and left behind him more women than any other historic personage whose autobiography I have read. He was a vigorous man. He survived travel hardships. He had an interest in food and studied its local variations. He wanted women and it was impossible to tug a wife and offspring across the world's spaces, so he married wives and left them behind. He traveled everywhere in the Eastern Hemisphere except Christian Europe, and everywhere he traveled he got married. He must have heard wifely endearments and other comments in all languages of the day, those of Christian Europe excepted.

For all his ardor, he was something of a prude. He worked himself into indignation because the women of the Maldive Islands, a Moslem locality which he was the first to describe at first hand, were semi-nude, wearing only a long apron. He says, "I tried to put an end to this practice, but I met with no success." At Mali he noted with great disapproval that girls, even the sultan's daughters, went about "in front of everyone naked, without a stitch of clothing on them." He held rigid ideas of sexual propriety. At Moslem Walata in the southern Sahara he was shocked deeply to discover that married women had male "friends" and that men had women "companions."

One man scandalized him, being a theologian who attempted to take his "companion" along with him on the Mecca pilgrimage.

When Ibn Battuta was in his sixth year of traveling he left Aden for a journey down the East Coast of Africa, being, as Freeman-Grenville says, "the only Moslem traveller of the Middle Ages to give an eye-witness description." Nor did the great Christian traveler of the Middle Ages, have in this anything of actual observation to offer. Marco Polo's account of this region is secondhand; he did not go to East Africa.

Any reader about old-time Africa will be likely to find Ibn Battuta cited more often than any other Arabic source, Leo excepted. He saw it all from the Mediterranean to the Niger and far down the East Coast, and he recorded what he saw. On Mombasa and Kilwa, I have repeated some of his comments. On his way he saw and smelled Zeila, "the most stinking town in the world because of the quantity of its fish and the blood of the camels they slaughter in the streets." He chose to spend the night at sea in spite of the extreme roughness rather than pass a night in the town, and he went on to Mogadishu in Somaliland, just above the Equator.

Mogadishu is still a capital city, but its amenities of the more elegant sort have shrunk since Ibn Battuta's visit. He lodged by the courtesy of the sultan at the "Students' House," to which meals were brought to him from the sultan's residence nearby. A handsome set of robes was given him: a silk wrapper which was tied around the waist in place of drawers, a tunic of Egyptian linen, a furred mantle of Jerusalem stuff and an Egyptian turban with an embroidered edge.

The meals served were excessively copious, and in commenting on his local tablemates Ibn Battuta says, "A single person of the people of Mogadishu eats as much as a whole company of us would eat, and they are corpulent and fat in the extreme." His detailed account of the very complex cookery is intriguing and appetizing. Those were the days of Africa's elaborate cuisine. His contemporary, Ibn Khaldun, generalizing about cookery, says, "We have on occasion counted forty different kinds of vegetables and meats in a single cooked dish."

Ibn Battuta's last and most arduous journey of all was also African. It was the forth-and-back crossing of the Sahara and the visiting of places on the desert's rim and places on the wheel of the Niger. Delafosse calls him "the first explorer of the western Sudan." He saw and told about Timbuctoo, Gao and the capital of the Mali Empire at its medieval apex, so proudly remembered by modern Africans that its name, after a long absence, reappears on the map as the Republic of Mali.

Ibn Khaldun at second hand—but good second hand—wrote a little later the first historic study of Mali we possess, so that between the two, the great traveler and the great historian, we have a contemporary picture of the civilization and strength of inner Negroland in its early vigor, quite uncontaminated or unimproved or uninfluenced. These two wrote long before Leo Africanus, the semi-Christian, long before the coming of the Portuguese and the other European explorers, and when the only intruders among the Negroes were Arabs and Berbers.

Ibn Battuta spent nearly two years in this, his hardest adventure, going southward across the desert via the western route, returning by the Hoggar region of the center. He was now fifty years old. He arrived at Fez, kissed the sultan's "beneficent hand," told his story, his many stories, and decided "to settle down under the wing of his bounty after long journeying." The Sultan Abu Inan caused a secretary to write down his travel record as he dictated it.

As well as dictating his memories Ibn Battuta very naturally talked to his Moroccan compatriots, probably talked volubly and picturesquely. He would have told them of Islam in far places, in magnificence in India, and modestly followed though locally respected at the very end of the earth, for China was to them, to most of them, the world's rim, beyond which nothingness. In China there were Moslems, much riches, many marvels.

One marvel from China of which he would tell them and which no doubt amazed Moroccans just as Marco Polo's similar report amazed Europeans was "the stone that burns like wood," as Polo called it. Ibn Battuta told how it was used twice over, the cinders kneaded with water, dried and used again for cooking. An equally surprising fuel item about which he may have told them—he mentions it in

his book—was that employed at a Persian banquet of ultra-preten-
tious luxury: the food was cooked with silk!

He told of a locality of Yemen where the flocks fed on small fish,
of the stone-deaf sheikh he had known at a place near the Black Sea
who could understand long communications, even stories, written
in the air with the narrator's finger.

Certainly he told them about his dizzy climb up the mountaintop in Ceylon where was the eleven-span-long footprint which
Adam had made when he fell to earth after he was thrown out of
Paradise. (This Marco Polo reports by hearsay.) To this, as a part
of Islam's tradition, they would have listened with respect. But
sometimes Ibn Battuta's travelogues roused incredulity at the Moroccan court. One of the incredulous was Ibn Khaldun.

Ibn Khaldun was then in his early twenties, a young man on his
own with a brain for sale in the confused political scene of North
Africa and Moslem Spain. Already he had left his native Tunis and
gone west, and now he was at the court of Abu Inan, of the dying
dynasty of the Merinids, as a minor item in the sultan's basket of
"eggheads." He heard Ibn Battuta with a young man's resentment at
the verbose boastings of the master's pet and with self-sufficient skep-
ticism. Later he recalls the lesson which the vizier read him, a lesson
illustrating the same idea John Masefield puts very neatly: "Travellers who see marvellous things . . . are seldom believed by those
who have stayed at home."

Said the vizier, "Be careful not to reject information because you
have not seen such things yourself," and then told a story about
a boy who grew up almost from infancy in prison with his father.
Presently he asked his father to tell him whence came the meat they
ate. The father tried to describe a sheep. "Why, that is just a rat!"
cried the boy. The vizier concluded his parable, "The only animals
he had seen in prison were rats, so he believed all animals were the
same."

It was Ibn Battuta's stories about Moslem India which had especially
roused incredulity, and most particularly his report of a magnificent
procedure quite outside North Africa's experience. The Indian king
whom Ibn Battuta knew was in his words, "of all men the fondest of
making gifts and of shedding blood"—the so-called "terrible Mo-

hammed ibn Tughlak" (a modern English comment, not Ibn Battuta's). Ibn Battuta told how this royal eccentric when he re-entered his capital, Delhi, after an absence would cause mangonels, mounted on elephants' backs, to catapult gold and silver coins among the people along his route.

Nowadays Ibn Battuta's record of travel, parts of which his countrymen doubted, is accepted as on the whole reliable, though some have been critical of a few items, such as his account of a visit to North China.

But Ibn Khaldun, so far as I have been able to note, never indicated in his own writings any appreciation of Ibn Battuta's study of the wide world of their day. The two were of different types of mentality and temperament.

The difference between the two, between the great traveler and the great Ibn Khaldun—one of the Pleiades of all-time historians, so named along with Thucydides, Xenophon, Josephus and some more modern, in the opinion of Toynbee, is easily discerned in the fashion in which each tells of one of earth's greatest dramas which occurred in their time and from which both suffered. The Black Death of 1348–49 destroyed an estimated third to half of the population of the world as our ancestors knew it: Europe, Asia, northern Africa. It killed both of Ibn Khaldun's parents and the mother of Ibn Battuta.

This sweeping giant among the scattered minor plagues which had before and have since tormented the world, this monster which rushed across the whole world of the day is only vague to us now. We all feel familiar with the Flood of Noah, though many may class it as myth rather than history, but the demi-deluge which was the Black Death has slipped into memory's shadows, just a shuddery name, although chronologically it is infinitely nearer than the tragedy of Noah and unquestionably real.

The effects which the Black Death had upon those of mankind who survived and upon their successors were both shock and inspiration. Afterward the world was like a person who had taken a strong dose of purgative. The world was weaker and stronger. By "something like general consent," wrote Coulton in his study of the Black Death and its consequences, "this catastrophy deeply affected the course of

European civilization . . . It contributed to hasten that impulse of independent research which we call the Renaissance and that religious revolution which we call the Reformation."

Here is Ibn Battuta's story. Going westward from China, he encountered in Syria the Black Death, which was also going westward, and like himself, coming from China, so it is said, and Ibn Battuta, ignoring the traditional instructions of Mohammed that one should not take flight from pestilence, made fast for another and distant city. He went to Damascus. But the Black Death was there too.

Damascus took steps. A crier proclaimed that the people should fast for three days. They obeyed. "At the end of this period the amirs, sherrifs, qadis, doctors of the Law and all other classes of the people in their several degrees assembled at the Great Mosque until it was filled to overflowing with them and spent the night there in prayers and lithurgies and supplications." In the morning they all went forth together on foot, carrying Korans in their hands and barefooted. "The entire population joined in the exodus, male and female, small and large, the Jews with their Book of the Law and the Christians with their Gospel, their women and children with them, the whole concourse of them in tears and supplications . . . They made their way to the Mosque of the Footprints." (This was two miles outside Damascus, deriving its name from prints impressed upon a rock there which were said to be from the foot of Moses.) "They remained there in supplication and invocation until near midday, then returned to the city . . . God Most High lightened their affliction, the number of deaths in a single day reached a maximum of 2000 whereas the number rose in Cairo to 24,000 in a day."

It is a story in the Ibn Battuta manner, picturesque, dramatic, unquestioningly pious.and personal: he says he witnessed the scene himself in July, 1348. Incidentally, by the inclusion of Christians and Jews, Damascus, a Moslem locality, evinced a wider mind than did Europe in the Black Death, where a rumor started that the pestilence was artificially produced by the Jews and an idea was advanced that God's anger might be appeased by their destruction. Thousands of Jews were killed.

Ibn Khaldun surveyed the Black Death, which had made him an

orphan, with the calm of an historian. His brief and impersonal passage early in his *Muqaddimah* is both solemn and spirited. He insists on the tremendous effects of this world disaster, dealing with it as an experience which befell all civilization. Then he says, "When there is a general change of conditions, it is as if the entire creation had changed and the whole world been altered, as if it were a new and repeated creation, a world brought into existence anew." He goes on to say that there is a new need to tell about this altered world, a task for the historian. It was a new aspect of a new chapter waiting to be written. He gives this as the great underlying motive for the work he sets himself.

Thus it seems as if Ibn Khaldun had found an inspiration and a reason for his great historical effort in the Black Death, which had butchered his boyhood by its sudden horror, had profoundly shaken his youth and evidently been deep and constantly in his thoughts.

But though he appreciated its importance as an element in the world's career he of course did not any more than others of the day divine from what and how it had come. All Boccaccio could say was that some mystery "seemed to transfer the disease from the sick to the sound in a very rare and miraculous manner."

The chain of death which rushed the Black Death along, the chain of the rat, the flea, the rat, the flea, the man, was still and for a long time thereafter unperceived. Yet there was a clue of a negative kind. A hint might have been discerned in the fact that the Black Death seems not to have crossed the Sahara and that beyond the Sahara there were no fleas. The "Sand Curtain" stopped that tiny vehicle which carried the greatest destructive force the world ever knew or dreamed of—until very recent years.

The Black Death reached Aswan, where, Maqrizi says, it killed twenty-one thousand. Farther up the Nile, Burckhardt discovered that the plague was unknown and declares that he had "reason to believe that it never passes the cataract of Aswan." Fernandes in the very early sixteenth century announced that pestilence was unknown on the western Sahara coast. In contrast we read in the Chronicles of Zara Yaqob of a plague outburst so violent that "there were not enough left alive to bury the dead" in Ethiopia, unprotected by the Saharan barrier.

The Black Death's little vehicle, fleas, were not known in the Sahara and the adjoining sub-Saharan lands. Early explorers noted their absence: Lyon, Duveyrier, Leo Africanus, who said, "A great quantity of scorpions, but one would not know how to find a single flea." And the recognized Saharan authority, Gautier, says, "The flea cannot live in the Sahara." Wildly exaggerated stories of the flea's malignancy were told in slave trade days, and frightened slaves who were driven across the desert shuddered in fear. Burckhardt, who tells of their flea apprehension, classes it as almost as bad as their fears of being castrated or of being used as food.

This little attempt to reconstruct inner Africa's escape from the disaster which shook the rest of the world concerns, of course, only the period in question, when the sole access to the sub-Sahara from northern Africa was via the Sand Curtain. Nor should we picture inner Africa as any health heaven, though naturally we have no detailed knowledge.

Shortly after northern Africa and the others met the great scourge the first news came from Negroland of an unknown mysterious mortal sickness. Ibn Khaldun revealed it in his passage about Mali history. It was a sickness which attacked especially persons of high degree. The victim about whom Ibn Khaldun had received information was the King of Mali. "The indisposition commences with periodic attacks and finally reduces the sick person to a state where he can scarcely keep awake for an instant. Then death follows." The King of Mali so died after two years of illness, in 1373.

This was a magic malady suitable to a region where magic and reality mingled so closely. Negroland saw sickness as supernatural and tried to cure it by supernatural means. One prescription can be taken as typical of many—an uncouth search for startling help combined with the native doctor's vain wish to make himself important. For a woman who had lost children stillborn and desired a child: the wearing of a small bell around the neck, also a shoulder bag containing fragments of a dog's face, a scrap of the meat of a pig and of an antelope, some locusts, the hairs of an albino and some of her own pubic hairs. I pick this up in a work of anthropology dealing with what was the Belgian Congo.

Along with these repulsive fantasies Negroland developed early an interesting idea of the association of bodily illness with the mind, an intuitive application of psychology to sickness and to its cure that used hypnotism and self-hypnotism. Of the latter is the remarkable legend of Sondiata, the great Mali ruler who fell in boyhood into a sort of paralysis of the legs and cured himself by will and ambition for power, so that he stood suddenly erect.

This, even if the legend lies, shows in itself a modernity of approach to medical problems—the sickness, perhaps imaginary; the self-cure.

As for the weird medicaments and charms, we have all passed that way. The mystic potency of a unicorn's horn—naturally a rarity! —which in England's plague crises several centuries subsequent to the Black Death was classed as a sovereign preventive and saved the lives of the soldiers of Charles V in the attack on Tunis, the emperor going about dipping a piece of this horn suspended on a green silk cord into the wells which the defending enemy had poisoned with blood and dead bodies and thus purifying the drinking water for his army. Marmol, one of Charles V's soldiers, tells this.

The mysteries of medicine which still befog us were then—in the days of Ibn Khaldun—very cloudy indeed. He himself writes, evidently as a report of other peoples' belief rather than as an expression of a conviction of his own, the theory that the conjunction of the two "unlucky planets," Saturn and Mars, is the precursor of pestilence.

There was, however, a more practical attitude. The most important hospital of Cairo—the city and its vicinity possessed five—had separate quarters for infectious diseases. So, maybe, had the others. Equally practical, and showing a consideration for civic safety, was Fez's locating of its community for the sick. It was situated outside of one of the gates, "so that the South wind might carry far from the city exhalations which might be harmful to the people. Furthermore the river did not pass through the place of the sick until after leaving Fez and thus there was no fear that its waters inside the city would be polluted by contact with the sick who bathed and threw their refuse into it." (*Kartas.*)

Another fashion of choosing a location for the sick was designed by the famous Dr. Razes (ninth–tenth centuries), called the greatest of Moslem physicians, who before he would pick an emplacement for the Baghdad hospital hung pieces of meat in various quarters of the city and picked the place where the decomposition showed itself to be the slowest.

The oldest of Moslem Egypt's hospitals, as well as many of the other African hospitals, had a section for the insane. This oldest hospital dated back to the ninth century and was built by Ibn Talun as a feature in the splendid capital called El-Katai, which he constructed not far from where Cairo was later to rise. It would seem that Ibn Talun had a morbid interest in mad people. His own end suggests he was himself incipiently mentally ill. He visited the hospital every day and inspected the quarters of the insane. A madman asked him for the gift of a grenadine, received it and threw it so violently at the royal visitor that it broke open and splattered Ibn Talun with seeds and red juice. It was Ibn Talun's last hospital inspection. He himself became very ill. He called in many doctors, but refused to follow their treatment. He sank toward his end. In fury he ordered that they be executed—beheaded or beaten to death—before he died.

A belief in contagion was reluctant for it was an element in the familiar discord of science and religion. A learned contemporary and friend of Ibn Khaldun's, a Spanish Moslem named Ibn al-Khatib, supported the heretical theory with courage. While admitting that "the religious law denies it" he declared that contagion was an indisputable reality. It was proved by the fact that "one who comes in contact with the afflicted gets the disease, whereas he who is not in contact remains safe, and how transmission is effected through garments, vessels and ear-rings." (I quote this translation of his argument from Hitti.)

But the wisest and most modern comment—a comment probably surprising in the fourteenth century but very close to the health reasoning of the twentieth—was made by Ibn Khaldun himself.

Here is my condensation of a passage in *Muqaddimah*, using largely Ibn Khaldun's own words as put into English by Franz Rosenthal: "The principal reason for pestilence is the corruption of the air through too large a population; corruption results from the putrification and evil moistures with which the air has contact. It is necessary to have empty spaces and waste regions interspersed between civilized [meaning closely populated] areas. This makes circulation of the air possible. Pestilences occur more frequently in densely settled cities, as for instance in Cairo and Fez."

Ibn Khaldun lived in the fourteenth century but his mind was ageless, and it is no wonder that he grasped the problem of the cities which confronts us today. I quote: "His sociological studies antedated modern European sociology by more than four centuries." He was "the greatest historical philosopher Islam produced and one of the greatest of all times . . . the real founder of social sciences." He was "the greatest historical genius of Islam and the first to produce a philosophical and sociological conception of history." He "conceived and formulated a philosophy of history which is undoubtedly the greatest of its kind that has ever yet been created by any mind in any time or place." I have quoted in this order from Gustave von Grunebaum, Philip Hitti, Bernard Lewis and Arnold Toynbee. In case that Toynbee and the rest may seem ultra-eulogistic to my reader, I can state that these are only typical medals which modern Europeans and Americans pin on the long-departed chest of the fourteenth-century Ibn Khaldun.

He invented a new approach to history, to telling the story of mankind. He saw it as a picture of men, not as the portrait and biography of men's rulers. This was a novelty in his day. It was at variance with history's established pattern, at variance with history's pattern until nearly our own times. "At the beginning of this century 'History is the biography of great men' was still a reputable dictum," writes E. H. Carr in *What is History?*.

Ibn Khaldun saw mankind not as bystanders and impersonal victims in a crowd scene, not as part of a remote vague background of people, animals and geography while the front interest concentrated on a few great figures—on kings and their battles with one another, on the intrigues and ups and downs of royal families and the rise and fall of dynasties. No wonder he has been called the originator of sociology.

A curious tribute to the modernity of Ibn Khaldun's way of thinking comes from his admirers who are Communists. The University of Leningrad recently issued a collection of studies dedicated to the memory of the great Russian Arabist Krackovskij, in which one article dwelt on Ibn Khaldun as "the champion of progress" and gave to *Muqaddimah* the descriptive subtitle "On the Nature of the Social Life of Mankind." (Russia, I mention in passing, has studied Arabic literature intently. The 1960 International Congress of Orientalists was held at Moscow, attended by many of the world's erudite, including, I read in *Arabica*, nearly a hundred French representatives.) Many of us have an offhand notion that Communism is a relatively recent form of theorizing. It is a surprise to see cause to look back upon this fourteench-century African as a sort of John the Baptist, a forerunner in the preaching—or rather an elucidator of the Communist point of view.

The Russian praise of Ibn Khaldun is generous, for it would seem that in a *Muqaddimah* geographical passage he passed along a horrid epithet about the Volga country. He referred to it as "The Stinking Land."

I have cited and quoted Ibn Khaldun often in this book, on many subjects. These subjects are in themselves so varied as to give a hint of the wide sweep of his work. Any attempt to sum up his writings would be silly, almost impossible. The table of contents and the careful index in this, the recently published first English translation of *Muqaddimah* (1958, by Yale Professor Rosenthal), show that, insofar as the knowledge of the times permitted, he told about every aspect of mankind's interests and activities and ideas.

Ibn Khaldun's history, a very long book to which he gave a long title, which for usual reference has been cut down to the one word *Ibar*, includes the far-spreading *Muqaddimah* (Introduction to History), a history of the Berbers of North Africa, an indispensable source but more along the conventional history model, plus the history of the world as he viewed it. *Muqaddimah*, or *Prolégomènes*, as it was called in the French translation, made a century ago by de Slane, who also translated the *History of the Berbers*, has been brought to the reader rather confusingly under a pair of titles which are both very difficult. Perhaps the subtitle offered by the Russian admirer, "On the Nature of the Social Life of Mankind," gives a more inviting notion of its contents.

The English translation of *Muqaddimah* runs to three volumes. The *History of the Berbers* in French runs to four volumes.

While Ibn Khaldun was planning, researching, writing, rewriting and revising he led an agitated life and an unhappy one. I have mentioned that the Black Death made him an orphan in boyhood. A shipwreck robbed him of wife and all his family. He mingled in the disorder of politics in northern Africa and Moslem Spain and was by temperament intrigue-prone and of slippery and shifting loyalties, sometimes unlucky in rousing suspicion. He met on occasion misfortune, disgrace, exile, a self-inflicted period of retreat, imprisonment and great dangers. For details one may see his autobiography, which de Slane has translated, and parts of which are included in *Histoire des Berbères*.

In later days, when he had removed, or rather succeeded in escaping to Egypt, he became involved in routine work, judgeships and teaching. At one time he taught at Azhar University. Again he was president of a Cairo college. Honorable, but not exciting. Toward the end of his life he was sent on a mission to Syria, where he showed vast shrewdness and played a characteristically dubious role and had a final brilliant adventure—all concerned in dealings with Tamerlane.

He escaped from Damascus just before the sacking of the city by letting himself down its wall on a rope. He presently fell into the hands of Tamerlane and cajoled and flattered him, and gave him questionable assistance. The aging Mongol conqueror, then involved in his last and, to himself, rather unsatisfactory campaign, looked westward with greedy eyes toward Ibn Khaldun's own homeland and, for military purposes, desired geographical details on Mediterranean Africa. Ibn Khaldun prepared a manuscript supplying information.

Ibn Khaldun, "eye witness to the siege of Damascus and its destruction gives us the first description of Tamerlan in Arabic literature," says Dr. Fischel in telling of "their historic meeting in 1401." Today Tamerlane features as one of history's shudders, who, for example, massacred at Aleppo near Damascus twenty thousand and built their heads into some mounds ten cubits high, with all the faces on the outside. The other party in the "historic meeting," Ibn Khaldun, is one of history's treasures.

He was over sixty-eight years old when he performed this adventure of combined athleticism on a rope and diplomatic self-interest. He returned to the humdrum of judgeship and to the continued revising of his great book—for, of course, in pre-printing days a book was never finished to a conscientious author. Five years later he died. In a troubled, lonely and rather disappointing life he did not have the uplift of guessing at the lasting importance of his writing, of guessing that six centuries after he had written his history a selected bibliography—that is one not seeking to be all-inclusive—as prepared by Dr. Fishel and included in *Muqaddimah,* made up of translations of his history for readers he never dreamed of, such as the people of America, and volumes and articles about him, would fill twenty-seven printed pages.

In the first one thousand years of Islam an old-time German, so Hitti tells us, calculated that there were 590 Arabic historians. Of the 590, Ibn Khaldun, the African, was to many minds the greatest, and to all of us he must stand as the most original.

ዘእንጮ ፋትክእኗ

THE DARKER WRITERS, MOSLEM AND CHRISTIAN · Books came into and across the Sahara and into Negroland with Islam. The written words and the power to write them, the exotic luxury of foreign wisdom, even the ability to record wisdom of their own came into lives that had been bookless. Here and there authorship budded and books bloomed on the Niger and beyond, and many sought and cherished imported and native volumes.

Books sold at higher prices than any other merchandise, Leo observed at Timbuctoo. No doubt it was the same at other centers of sub-Saharan Moslem culture, though Timbuctoo, at the terminus of a great trans-desert route, would have been more amply and easily supplied. The city's private libraries were astonishingly large. Ahmed Baba, the most celebrated of Timbuctoo's savants, said that he possessed sixteen hundred books and that his collection was one of the smaller ones of the city. Timbuctoo became one of the recognized centers of Moslem culture; it was not alone among sub-Saharan localities, but it is especially interesting to us today because about Timbuctoo's learning and its learned men we possess much detailed information.

There was a local proverb, "Salt comes from the north, gold from the south, but pious and learned things and pretty stories we find nowhere but in Timbuctoo."

The University of Timbuctoo ranked, or came near to ranking, with those of Cairo and Fez, or so it was said—to compare, or to attempt to compare, looking back over the years, the values of universities so foreign is impossible.

The universities of Azhar at Cairo to the east, Karaouine at Fez in the west, which were founded in 988 (date from Maqrizi) and approximately 860 respectively, the two elders, and Sankore at Timbuctoo to the south—these three universities made the educational triangle on Africa's map. Others, less renowned, were sprinkled about, including that of Tunis and perhaps a rabbinical college at ancient Sijilmassa on the northern fringe of the Sahara, of which Slouschz speaks, believing it was founded in the tenth century.

Sankore at Timbuctoo was mosque and university combined. The term "university" in its case indicates an intensive grouping of the upper-grade scholastic effort of the region, not a formal university building. Sankore was roughly the quarter where the learned lived, *san* was in the Songhai language a term applied to a person of high degree, hence a savant. The Sankore Mosque, according to one legend, was built to sacred measurements, a pious personage having while on pilgrimage to Mecca measured the Kaaba with a cord, marking the two dimensions, and having upon his return to Timbuctoo caused the Sankore to be built of exactly the same size. Legend number two has it that the mosque was built at the initiative of a woman, "a great lady, very rich and very desirous of performing good works."

It is rather surprising, since the public activities of females—if there were any—have not been emphasized in the histories of Islam, to read the definite statement that the Fez Mosque, seat of what has been called the world's oldest university, was also erected by a woman. Her name was Fathma Oumm el-Benin (Mother of Two Sons), and she came of a family from Kairwan—hence the name of the mosque, Karaouine—and was the heritor of a great fortune. This "saintly lady fasted during all the time of the building operations" (*Kartas*), which presumably meant fasting according to Ramadan rules: no food or drink while the sun shone.

Azhar Mosque at Cairo was built by a man. Maqrizi quotes an inscription therein that the construction had been "under the direction of the slave Jawhar, the scribe, the Sicilian." This was the slave general and ex-Christian who founded the city of Cairo.

Cairo's university and that of Fez, both older than any in Europe, are still active. At Cairo things are being modernized, we hear. Fez received wide notice in 1960 when it celebrated its eleven hundredth anniversary, internationally patronized, representatives of many foreign lands participating. But the University of Sankore is no more, though serious local schooling persists. I saw no signs of the Sankore University and never heard it mentioned at Timbuctoo, though a mosque called Sankore exists. The original edifice fell in ruins and was rebuilt. The reconstruction cost "600 blocks of salt, equal to about £200," according to Barth. Timbuctoo lost its prestige when trans-Saharan trade died. But some of its savants, the *san* of the old days, live on and give us by the writings they left behind the best picture we possess of events and of the ideas of the Negroes and dark Berbers before the alterations of colonialism.

Education was a stern business for these peoples who had books, just as it was for the bookless, whose harsh initiation systems for the young have been mentioned. Ibn Battuta when he traveled through Mali noted that "they put their children in chains if they showed backwardness in memorizing the Koran," and studying was so intense at Timbuctoo that there was no time for play. When the great conqueror Sonni Ali captured the city and certain of Timbuctoo's savants fled into the desert, these dignified gentlemen trembled with fear because they had to mount on camelback and fell off when the animal jerked to its feet. This was because all their lives they had been sedentary, shut-in students, "because when young they had never had the chance to play." So says the *Tarikh es-Soudan*.

Sonni Ali, the fifteenth-century conqueror, gave such of Timbuctoo's intellectuals as did not flee the city a rude time. He scorned them, for he classed them along with the ultra-pious and he—though he was supposedly a Moslem, as his name Ali indicates—was of a non-religious type. He ruined that idyllic calm and secluded scholarly life of theirs, which was a sort of monasticism without sexual deprivations. They who had been the elite of the town were snubbed and ill used, and their pious sentiments were shocked by his blasphemous behavior. Afterward one of them wrote stinging words about his indecent burlesquing of the Moslem prayers: "He would put off till nightfall the five ritual prayers [which he should have made at set times during the day with prostrations] and would then make gestures while sitting down and would merely mention the various prayers, saying 'You can split them up amongst yourselves!' "

The historians Sa'di and Kati, the authors of the two regional *tarikhs* (histories), tell about him in an almost frenzied tone, calling him "the tyrant, the débauché, the accursed, the oppressor," and "this scoundrel . . . unjust, bloody . . . who caused the death of so many that Allah alone can count them and persecuted the savants and the pious." In one passage after another they give the dark picture—perhaps unfairly dark—of the mighty ruler on whom they looked back with double hatred, because he had disturbed their way of life and because he scorned their religion. His attitude is understandable. He ruled a bi-religious empire. Even Timbuctoo was part pagan. Understandable also was their hatred, though it gives us what is probably an absurdly distorted view of a great African king.

It seems worth noting as a clear-cut example of that prejudice which must always sit on history's shoulder and which is especially forceful in the picture of pagan Africa. Islam wrote the African story. Christianity has interpreted it. Sometimes we wonder if the pagan has got a fair portrait. Walter Lippmann has said something to the effect that it is naïve to suppose that there can be just one genuine accurate version of events in history.

It was with dignified delight that the historians quoted above dipped their pens in golden ink to tell of the happy years for the intellectuals which followed the death of Sonni Ali and the down-fall of the Sonni dynasty and thenceforth endured for a century, until the Moroccan invasion of the country.

The new ruler, the "very orthodox" Mohammed, the first of the Askia dynasty who came to power at the end of the 15th century, appreciated the savants of Timbuctoo as a part of his great empire, headquarters at Gao, farther down the Niger. He brought back those who had fled. The learned became his pets. He gave them allowances. He is recorded to have visited a prominent savant who was sick, and it was his habit to stand up when he received an important learned man, a remarkable tribute in a part of the world where a ruler usually demanded a prostration and a self-sprinkling of dust from those who presented themselves before him.

Askia Mohammed made Islam his slogan. His pilgrimage to Mecca was magnificent. He received from the caliph the title of his lieu-tenant in the land of the Negroes. He came home with a legendary glory in that he had been proved to be a descendant of Mohammed. It was he who launched the first and for long the sole Holy War in Negroland. This was against the Mossi, and has already been men-tioned. Probably in this the Askia had a mixture of motives: a desire to Islamize a powerful pagan group, a desire to add their land to his empire and a desire to avenge Mossi attacks in the past on what were now his territories, notably on Timbuctoo. He was successful only in the third of these desires.

In the pre-colonial literature of Africa below the Sahara the *Tarikh es-Soudan* and Ahmed Baba are respectively the best-known book and the best-known author. But surprisingly it was not the best-known author who wrote the best-known book, although for about fifty years it was, in Europe's mistaken opinion, unhesitatingly as-cribed to him.

Ahmed Baba wrote works, more than forty of them, but not the *Tarikh es-Soudan,* which was written by Sa'di, also of Timbuctoo. It was an understandable confusion when the publishing business was young, when books were hand-copied manuscripts, and it happened in a region where the public able to read Arabic was scattered and where periods of general turmoil were frequent. It was just a mis-take, and one for which Ahmed Baba himself was certainly not responsible. He made no claim to have written the work in question, if only for a very good reason, as will be explained.

Let us consider the book and then its involuntary and innocent pseudo author. The *Tarikh es-Soudan* was evidently the joy of Negroland's intelligentsia. Ambitious tribal folk paid to be taught Arabic. To read a book, to be able to read a book written in Arabic, to read a book about the ancient and the recent importance and drama of their region—these gave them triple prestige and delight.

The *Tarikh es-Soudan* was therefore widely distributed, and even in the early days of African exploration Europe heard about it. So Barth presumably was looking for it, and in Gando in northern Nigeria, which is a considerable distance from Timbuctoo, he was able to examine a copy—"a respectable quarto volume," as he called it— and made some valuable historical notes "during the few days" that he had it in his possession. Barth must have been locally misinformed about its authorship, for without any question he attributed it to Ahmed Baba, repeatedly using in his abstract phrases like "as Ahmed Baba says."

Barth's abstract of Ahmed Baba gave Europe a new version of Inner Africa's past, Europe's first on-the-spot story, far more vital than the items which Cooley had collected from the sparse non-Negro sub-Saharan sources and published in a slim volume, *The Negroland of the Arabs*.

The *Tarikh es-Soudan* is still an essential source. But Ahmed Baba no longer gets the credit, for at the end of the last century, when France occupied Timbuctoo, a French Arabist, Houdas, had the opportunity to study the book and discovered that Ahmed Baba could not have written it. This did not demand intensive detective work but it did require that the investigator have leisurely access to the manuscript, which explorer Barth did not have. I find on page 374 of Houdas' French translation of the book itself the record of Ahmed Baba's own death! "On the morning of Thursday, 6 of the month of Cha'ban of the same year [just mentioned as 1627] died the illustration and benediction of his times, the cheik, the doctor, the very savant, the unique of his century, and the phoenix of his epoch, the jurisconsul Ahmed-Baba-ben-Ahmed-ben-Omar-ben-Mohammed-Aqit."

Houdas further discovered that the real author was the historian generally known as Sa'di, whose full name is in the usual fashion a rosary of "bens."

The *Tarikh es-Soudan,* which is a long book—it runs to nearly five hundred pages, translator's footnotes included in the original French translation (a reissue is announced)—is the history of the western part of that wide belt of sub-Saharan Africa to which the old-time Arabs gave the name of "The Land of the Blacks" (Sudan). The name became geographically associated with two regions: Sudan by the Nile and Sudan by the Niger. The latter is the *Tarikh*'s territory, and since decolonization it calls itself the Republic of Mali. Primarily the book tells about the Songhai of Gao, where reigned Sonni Ali and Mohammed Askia, and about the glories of Gao's neighbor and sometime dependence, Timbuctoo. But it gives also something of the history of surrounding regions: old-time Mali, Jenne, the Tuareg, etc.

It and the *Tarikh el-Fettach* are the outstanding historical works about true Negroland. They have been often cited in this book.

The manuscript of the latter, though known by repute, emerged from hiding long after the *Tarikh es-Soudan.* It was called by an early traveler, Dubois, "the phantom book," concealed—so local gossip had it—because it told how important regional families came of humble origin, sometimes of slave origin. In 1911 a French official procured a manuscript copy and in 1913 a French translation was published, running to just under 350 pages, of which 10 percent might be translator's footnotes. The title is usually abridged to *Fettach* (Searcher) or to *Fettassi.* In the complete thirteen-word Arabic form it means "A History for the Use of One Who Seeks Knowledge about Cities, Armies and Important Personages."

In its account of regional events the *Fettach* overlaps the *Tarikh es-Soudan* at both ends and it also outshines the other by occasional imaginative items; it was from the *Fettach* that I culled the account of the jinnee author Chambarouch and the strange adventures of Noah's giant assistant, Oudj. But the *Fettach* contains much definite information and many interesting legends.

The prime author was Mahmoud Kati, a friend of Mohammed Askia and one of the Askia's companions on his triumphant Mecca pilgrimage. Further passages were added by Kati's grandson. Kati himself had the chance to see a lot of history. He was born in 1468. He died in 1593. One hundred and twenty-five years—it is a confirmed fact.

Let us go back to Ahmed Baba, who did not write the history of the Sudan but was so renowned as an author that its authorship was automatically attributed to him. Ahmed Baba of Timbuctoo came of a learned heritage. He was a Berber. So was the actual author of that history book, Sa'di. The author of the other historical work, the *Fettach,* was a Negro.

It throws an interesting light on the question of interracial relationship in Africa that Timbuctoo, the center of sub-Saharan wisdom as well as that of cross-continental trading, should have been comfortably double racial—Negro students and students of the white race working together under double-racial professors. Ahmed Baba, the Berber, was in part taught by a Negro, a Mandingo, described as the leading professor of the day, and himself an author. When we speak of the Berber element as "white" the adjective is probably not to be taken literally. The desert's sun and the charms of Negresses had undoubtedly tinted complexions as time passed. On the right forearm of Ahmed Baba "the name of Mohammed was written in white letters naturally formed under the skin," says the *Tarikh es-Soudan,* which indicates that the rest of his arm was dark.

Ahmed Baba was a prolific author. His most important work was in the way of biographical dictionaries, a type of work then greatly esteemed, but since it records the careers of largely forgotten persons of the sixteenth century and earlier no more suited for present-day general reading than a very old copy of Who's Who.

But Ahmed Baba's own career has real interest. His contemplative learned existence among his personal library of sixteen hundred books and his coterie of admiring students and fellow savants crashed. When Morocco conquered Sudan-on-the-Niger, Timbuctoo suffered massacres, rapings, pillages and a group of citizens were forcibly carried away to Morocco as captives. One of the captives was Ahmed Baba in chains, which caused him to fall off camelback and break his leg. Seventy-five days of Saharan travel, driven by a heartless captor, several years' imprisonment at Marrakesh, then detention with liberty to teach. Some of Marrakesh's important intellectuals attended his courses.

A Moroccan source gives a dialogue between the Sultan of Morocco and Ahmed Baba, who scolded the sultan sternly, his greatest grievance that the invading Moroccans had pillaged his library, stolen his sixteen hundred books! Free at last, he returned to his home. El Oufrani in his history of the Saadian dynasty in Morocco gives a short poem Ahmed Baba wrote during his years of banishment (1594–1607): ". . . murmur my name to my friends and take them the perfumed greeting of an exile . . ."

His death at Timbuctoo and the panegyric by Sa'di in the *Tarikh es-Soudan,* which Ahmed Baba was wrongfully supposed to have written, have been quoted. He wrote many books. I have before me a list of some twenty-one of his titles.

There was considerable other authorship in the sub-Sahara, but it has seemed interesting to dwell on the writers of Timbuctoo at the period of its brilliance. They reveal a notion of the real Timbuctoo, which was the symbol of Africa's old-time mystery and continues today to be a sort of symbol for the maximum of earthly remoteness.

Much of the sub-Saharan pre-colonial writing, which was of course in manuscript form, was naturally lost or mislaid in the Moroccan sacking, in all the complex swirl of interregional tribal, racial and religious wars and conquests of pre-colonial days and in the altered local moods and conditions that came with colonization. The manuscript of what might be called books might yet turn up. Smaller manuscripts have.

Among the important pieces of authorship which survived was one which was translated into two or more European languages and has been widely read by the world outside Africa. This was an excerpt from a history book by the Sultan Bello of the family of Fulani Holy War conquerors. His father, Osman dan Fodio, Islam-inspired— with probably a high flavoring of ambition—changed history in the interior of what is now Africa's most populous nation, and was the ancestor of Sir Ahmadu Bello of independent Nigeria.

Bello's family was intensely literary. Bello, his father, his uncle, his brother, his son all wrote. It is stated that Bello and his father between them composed about two hundred recorded works. At a guess, much of this material would be what might be called state papers—official and argumentative discourses—or essays on Islamic questions.

But it was by a book, in the real sense of the term, that the Sultan Bello came to the reading public of Europe. It was at the time of the Denham-Clapperton-Oudney expedition (1822–24). Captain Clapperton, with whom Bello came in contact, was the first Englishman, the first white Christian he had ever seen. He confided to the captain a copy of a part of his book, and when Clapperton got home it was translated from the Arabic and published as an appendix to the expedition's book about their adventures, the first successful and recorded penetration into deeper Africa and trans-Saharan crossing by European explorers. An ampler translation of Bello's book appeared later.

Bello must have been pleased at the efficient effort of Clapperton as author's agent. In Bello's giving of his manuscript to his first white visitor we see a great change in the sub-Saharan state of mind, the budding wish of Africa to display herself to the world outside the continent, to see herself reflected in pleasant image in the foreign mirror. It is a wish which plays an increasing part in the sentiment of all of us—"What does the foreign press say?" In Inner Africa it was then something new. I do not suppose that Kati had any thought about Christian Europeans reading his *Fettach*.

Grim as it is, it was the European and American slave trade which apprised Inner Africa indirectly but forcibly about the outer world. Coastal Africa had been familiar with Europeans for this long time back. Now Europe and later the Americas had stuck their claws far into the interior with the slave traders' demands. Europe and Inner Africa had become acquainted.

Bello was probably fascinated by the prospect that his writings would be read in a far-off white Christian country. His book, which was one of the earliest literary efforts from sub-Saharan Africa to be translated and published in England, had a descriptive title meaning that "it cleared up and explained away difficulties to be found in the history of Central Africa." The introductory note announced that it was "composed by the ornament of the century, who had no equal among his contemporaries, Mohammed Bello, son of the prodigy of his times the noble Sheik Osman." Among its historical items was much speculation about a question over which people are still arguing: the origin of the Berber race. One of its bits of geography was a mention of a port, unnamed, where the Christians came to buy the slaves which Yoruba procured from Bello's countrymen.

The map supplied by Bello shows frankly what we all feel in our hearts: a big mark for the home town and minor, vaguely floating indications for other localities; the distance from Bello's palace at Sokoto to the leading local mosque is as great as the distance from Jenne to Timbuctoo, or as the whole of Dahomey. At the time when the inside of the continent was so mysterious and so curiosity-piquing, geographers in England and France (for the expedition's adventure, including the Bello appendix, was promptly put into French) studied it intently.

There has also been produced considerable literature without authorship in the sense that the word is applied to the works of a Bello or a Sa'di or an Ahmed Baba or a Kati. Kati, by the way, acknowledges in his preface that he wrote with the aid of information given him "by the hand and by the tongue"—the two helpers, directly or indirectly, of every historian.

Africa has supplied a crop of what are usually called "chronicles," our understanding being that these were originally verbally transmitted data about local happenings and fragments of tribal memories and legends. These verbal recollections were collated and recorded in written form, and across Negroland many chronicles of varying interest have been assembled and put into a European language. Sir Richard Palmer's Kano Chronicle is among the most familiar.

So many have said, "Africa has no history," sometimes modifying their statement to explain that Egypt and Mediterranean Africa are excepted, that the saying has become a proverb: "A continent without a history." It eased colonialism's qualms.

This has been very displeasing to Negroes who have lived in Europe and in America, who are in a way displaced Africans, especially displeasing now that de-colonization has given a new prestige—or at any rate dramatic value—to their place of origin and made every

Negro realize that he has two countries: that of his present residence and Africa.

"History" is one of those words with two meanings. It may mean not the record of events but the events themselves. To suggest that Africa, Saharan and sub-Saharan, has been eventless or non-conscious and forgetful of events in the way we attribute to animals is, of course, nonsense. Her peoples passed through a plenitude of history —"kings and battles" galore. And their system of oral recitations of their past, of which we have evidence in many regions, shows that they did not forget. But historians with paper and pens and a written language they did not have except when they were Moslems. The written history of such as were pagan and bookless has been necessarily composed by aliens, by disapproving Moslems in Arabic and later by Christians in various European languages, and later yet by no longer bookless Africans who, however much they revered their continent of origin, had soaked up and been influenced by a non-African point of view and attitude of mind.

So in one way and by one only of the two definitions of "history" the old and offensive proverb was right. History they had in bookless Africa. Historians they had not.

In her efforts to record her history and her literature Ethiopia was different. Ethiopia had always been insistently individual. Nowadays the introvert which she had been for so long has changed suddenly to the energetic extrovert.

Long isolated primarily by geography, Ethiopia has emerged and opened up. The reason is the airplane. For some two thousand years she clung to her gorge-cut mountains, dug her claws into her national and religious pride and survived a series of assaults from alien religions (Hebrew and Mohammedan) and from alien peoples, both neighbors and foreigners. She was never really colonized; the Italian interlude was rather an occupation (1935–41), one of the swiftest in-and-out jobs in the history of African colonization, and her misfortune and her escape, which put her back beside Liberia as one of the sole two self-governing lands in a continent of colonies, gave Ethiopia international advertising.

So far as either civilization from the outer world or any intimacy with the rest of Africa was concerned, she has joined these two clubs only very recently, and since she got wings. Her Negus took to touring a cordially receptive world. And in 1963 Ethiopia was chosen by independent Africans as the scene for what the world press called "the largest summit conference in history."

Her literature shows her unique character through the years. Africa below the Sahara was bookless, outside the Islamic influence. Ethiopia by contrast was very bookish. Ethiopia possessed in addition to the official language, Amharic, and a great many other languages, a book language not used for common communication but reserved for literary purposes only. It is called Gheez and Ethiopia produced in Gheez many books, including a translation of the Bible with apocryphal trimmings, a two-century-long piece of work begun in the fifth century.

Gheez as a form of writing was an intimate relative of a system coming from the South Arabian style of the family of Canaanite and Phoenician scripts. It was one of the older forms of writing, older than our own, older than the Arabic of the north, in which the Koran was written.

It was Ethiopia's literary tool until fairly recent times—a square-cut, stern-looking writing with two little dots, one above the other, separating the words. It resembled very old inscriptions still existing in South Arabia. Its appearance has little resemblance to the swift-flowing and feathery grace of what we know as Arabic. For example the Arabic edition of the *Tarikh es-Soudan* and the Gheez edition of a history of the wars of the Ethiopian King Amda Syon (both of which I happen to possess) look very different. Ethiopic was written as we write, from left to right, not as the Arabs do, from right to left—the latter, by the way, is said to be a better method. "To bring the pen from left to right the tendons of the thumb, those of the back of the hand and the muscles of the wrist are forced into uncomfortable contractions, while there is no effort when directing the pen from right to left," according to a Frenchman in Algeria, el Hadj Dinet, who—converted to Islam and the author of a life of Mohammed—was competent to compare the effort involved in the two scripts. Another Arabisant, W. Montgomery Watt, says, "Arabic can be written almost as fast as shorthand."

The Ethiopian people in general were not literate. But they were very proud of their books and boastful about them. To an early European traveler they displayed their royal library of ten thousand manuscript volumes, some of which, so they claimed, were the most ancient books in the world, having been written by the Egyptian sages in the time of Moses. Twenty-three copyists were constantly employed in the transcribing of such manuscripts as seemed to be falling into decay. The traveler who recounted all this was Gicome Baretti, "an Italian gentleman" who went to Ethiopia in 1655.

Their manuscripts were prepared with great and costly care. Ullendorff tells how for the more elegant presentation of a long work as many as one hundred to one hundred and fifty goats would have to be killed to provide the parchment required. The calligraphy and illustrations were of "a high degree of perfection." Much of the literature was translated material, the work of anonymous clerics and copyists, and much of the subject matter was pious. I have already given some details about the Ethiopian religious works in connection with the remarkable illustrations dealing with the miraculous accomplishments of the Virgin Mary.

The minority Jewish group in Ethiopia, the Falasha, were equally insistent on the religious theme in what they wrote, which, oddly, was also in Gheez, not Hebrew. In dealing with the Jews in Africa, I mentioned these peculiar people whose strange psychology supported through the centuries the strain of a double isolation, since they were an isolated group shut up inside an isolated country.

One of their pieces of religious literature which I have mentioned deals with the personalization, the idolization almost of the Sabbath. Surviving and translated along with this Falasha text is a Book of Baruch—I do not say *the* Book because there were many books so attributed or entitled. Leslau in his *Falasha Anthology* lists and gives the outlines of five different Books of Baruch, starting with the familiar Old Testament apocryphal title, and the studies of Grant and of Doresse tell of an agnostic Book of Baruch (text in *Gnosticism, an Anthology*, edited by Professor Grant).

The Book of Baruch which the Falasha revered—its full text is given by Leslau—was an item borrowed from their hostile encompassing neighbors, the Christian Ethiopians, and altered to accord with their own beliefs, as in cutting out mention of Christ and the

Trinity, but conserving the dramatic passages about the florid and shining heavenly dwellings of the departed good people and the ghastly horrors endured by the departed bad ones: for virgins "a golden bed of precious stones and garments and purses"; a place called The City of God, "brighter than the sun, the moon and the stars ten million times over, decorated with pearls and filled with fruit and plants," the residence of "the mighty of the earth who killed no one" and of others whose virtues are itemized. Then Baruch beheld the pits of fire where were punished those who had committed incest or "fornication with domestic animals and wild beasts," saw idolaters tormented by rocks of fire, "for they worshipped stones," and high priests who had taken bribes seated on thrones of fire.

Ethiopia produced historical literature. It consisted in part of separate chronicles of what happened or was said to have happened during the reigns of various emperors. The value of these, historically speaking, is sometimes uncertain since the documents, as they survive, may have been composed long afterward. The life of the famous Lalibela, builder of monolithic churches in series, for instance, was not set down till nearly two hundred years after his remarkable career.

The story of Amda Syon—date of composition subject of argument—is a particularly exciting piece of writing. It was composed by an ecclesiastic author, nameless, who evidently had forgiven or prudently forgotten the king's youthful misdemeanors, both moral and religious when—so it is said in sources other than the history in question—Amda Syon married or mated indecorously with his deceased father's concubine and with one or two of his own sisters, was excommunicated and violently avenged himself against the Church. With enthusiasm the ecclesiastic tells of the Christian warrior going forth to repel the Moslem enemy "who dared attack the Prince of Princes, the tail of a dog daring to fight the head of a lion."

Comes a spirited, vivid and victorious battle scene, concluding, "The combat had lasted from morning till sundown. The king had his hand so fast stuck to his lance by the blood of his enemies that it was needful to drag the weapon apart from him by force."

It is not often that we know the authors of Ethiopia's Gheez literature by name or personality. One exception is Zara Yaqob, the king.

Another is the thirteenth-century savant—himself a Copt—who compiled a work embodying the canon law and civil and penal legislation, later put into Ethiopic under the title *Fatha Nagast*, "which has retained its practical importance to the present day," says Ullendorff. Another is that written cornerstone of the country, *Kebra Nagast*, "The Glory of the Kings."

Zara Yaqob wrote seven books. The most important was *The Book of Light*, 117 chapters long and motivated by the desire to bring idolaters to Christianity. It is in this book that Zara Yaqob brought the charge of baby-eating against the Jews. His works were the fierce expression of the highly religious and stern king of a country seeking and destined to have unwavering and unchanging survival.

In this unwavering and unchanging survival the author of *Kebra Nagast* played and still plays a major part. We know the name of this author, or perhaps compiler and editor. The non-Ethiopian world calls *Kebra Nagast* a work of fiction. Its basic theme, the episode of Solomon's mating with an Ethiopian queen, seems to us fabulous. But to Ethiopia right down to modern times it has been the most revered and potent chapter in that national history which is so long that it makes all other surviving national histories seem like scraps.

As I have said before, the Ethiopian believes his emperor descends in a direct line from Solomon. This belief in an ancient, noble and sacred heritage has given Ethiopia uniquely obstinate self-confidence and vitality under difficult conditions. Solomon embraced their queen one night during the tenth century B.C. The child of their union was ancestor to the emperor ruling in A.D. 1955—their constitution of that date says so. It is the world's longest surviving dynasty or line of inherited power.

Nebura Ed (Chief Priest) Yeshaq of Aksum, sometimes referred to as Ishaq, who formulated the *Kebra Nagast*, pricked his pen into Ethiopia's destiny. Whether we call him author, compiler, translator, editor, he gave form to a glorious and inspiring legend, embellished with bits from the Old and New Testaments and from old-time writings of the Near East and of Egypt's Copts, and he did this at the moment when the grandchildren, a hundred times "great-greats," of Solomon, after generations of hiding from usurpers, came back to their throne, and when they and the people craved a fillip, a gloze of glory and a mystic message of continuing value. That its value was continuing is shown by the fact that in 1872 Ethiopia's royalty begged for the return of the *Kebra Nagast* manuscript, which had been part of the loot in the British expedition of 1868, saying, "My people will not obey my orders without it." Whatever part exactly he played in the composition of *Kebra Nagast*, Ishaq was one of the most influential authors in all secular literature.

THE AUTHORS WHO TALKED · Where some wrote so brilliantly but most could not write at all literature had two manifestations. In contrast with the authors who could and did write there were the non-writers who were the designers—the wise observers, the imaginers, the dispensers of praise and criticism—the revisers and editors, and the transmitters and repeaters through the centuries of traditions and history, legends and marvels—in short, the "writers who talked."

The oral literature which these nameless, non-writing and bookless authors have given us is both a record of the past and a picture of Africa's thought and fancy and desires and fears, and it has in both phases great value to us today. It was the essence of Africa's mind.

In the bookless regions and in the old pre-colonial days the recital by a specialist was a big element in popular life. These official talkers astonished early European travelers, who reported how the speaker or bard would deliver an historical discourse for days on end, his narrative interspersed with apropos songs and pantomimes.

Such performers had power. They were the press and the drama, the literature, the history, the libraries of the people, their inspiration and sometimes their criticism. Ibn Battuta tells how at the court of Mali he observed an old custom dating from the country's days before Islam displaced bookless paganism which permitted on certain feast days a bard in disguise—he wore a feathered dress and a mask like a bird's head—to deliver a hortatory address, almost a rebuke, direct to the king. The king was reminded of the fine actions of his predecessors, admonished and urged to live up to their high example.

Experts among the bards were said to carry along traditions of their tribe and its rulers for hundreds of years, trained by retired practitioners in the art and inheriting and embellishing their memories. They operated across sub-Saharan Africa, their caste variously named in regional languages. Laing in Sierra Leone heard the bard called a *jelle*; Major Gray, his near contemporary in Senegal, speaks of him as *jallikea*, or *joulah*. Elsewhere he was sometimes *dyeli*. The term *griot* was very common and covered the history teller, the entertainer and a lot of activities, including sometimes that of a blackmailer who threatened unless he received a bribe to recite details damaging to an individual or a family. The official talker was a big man in the community in the days when the glamour of tribal institutions was untarnished by foreign influence.

Now the authority and prestige of the recited has diminished, but what survives of the narratives of these picturesque historians has been the source indirectly for almost all of our history of pagan sub-Sahara. People who cannot write provide no documents or inscriptions. The detailed past of the wide sweep of bookless Negroland must be based on verbal information.

It is regrettable that modern historians and anthropologists could not hear the tribal reciters in their pre-colonial swagger and almost sacred power and conviction. It is an art and a tribal property which has dwindled and lost authority. Students who seek to draw memories from aged folk who remember the tales they used to hear or who listen to the younger folk who attempt to imitate the old professionals meet snags and disappointments. They meet the talker who consciously or unconsciously tries to tell a fine tale, the talker who artlessly introduces some item from general history that he has picked up under colonialism's teachings—a dashing deed or phrase pillaged from far parts which he hitches to a former local hero or regional drama.

Jan Vansina, expert in the method of sifting and evaluating oral history—especially in the Congo region—warns that "there is the possibility of conscious falsification [by the reciters] out of fear, prestige and other reasons." Meyer Fortes complains that in some cases "myths and legends counterfeit history; they do not document it." Captain Urvoy, who worked over the past of the central Sudan, which includes the Republic of Niger and Bornu—now in Nigeria— noted in the old recitals which are handed down orally that the career of a popular king would be garnished with all the fine deeds of his predecessors. I quote these remarks from some of Africa's thoughtful historians and anthropologists as revealing that the study of oral history under today's conditions is a hard one, and as J. D. Fage says, "There are limits to the value of oral traditions."

But for all that, Dr. Vansina repudiates with a snort the suggestion that "written sources are better than oral ones." He says, "This is the maxim of the non-historian." And despite the disappointments and snags oral history in bookless Africa is sometimes the only kind there is.

We can view with more ease that sort of Africa's oral literature which does not claim to recount the actual annals of kings and tribes but offers a revealing picture of Africa's thoughts and fancies and desires and deeper emotions through the ages. These help us far more than scraps of local history to an understanding of that puzzling continent now in the throes of rebirth. I wish to speak about a few of the mass of creations and revisings of Africa's talking authors—some items which seem especially characteristic of Africa's mentality—such as their imaginative handling of tribal origins, often associated with wicked reptiles and giant heroes, their revamping of the adventures of some personages made familiar by the Old Testament and the Koran.

These tales are not factually true, but they are truer than history in another sense. They show the sentiment of the people. Oral history has been a photograph considerably touched up. Tales and legends are a psychological portrait. Authors they surely had, some individual who invented or who gave circumstance to some instinctive longing or fear or vanity, or imported into the local setting some renowned name or personage.

Sprinkled across the continent one may find legends of Old Testament and Koran heroes who came in person to Africa. One was allegedly born there—Noah, in Nigeria—to say nothing of Moses, who was, of course, by birth an African.

Noah, who according to the myth cited by Ibn Khaldun first taught carpentry to the world, had presumably a post-Deluge residence in the western Sudan, while another legend lands him in Morocco, where he settled down and founded a town at Salé. Salé still stands. It is across the river from the capital city of Rabat. Two of Noah's children were buried in Morocco. His son Shem, who founded Ceuta at the Strait of Gibraltar, was buried in Cairo. One of the anchors of the Ark is a treasure, still displayed at Kairwan in Tunisia.

Thus Africa's imaginative storytellers scattered and conserved Noah's memory. These were not Deluge stories about the adventures and escapes of native heroes such as are distributed across the world. They were specific references to the African performances of the individual Noah and his family. And they are not post-colonial tales. They do not come from the Christian colonial influence.

Jonah also came to Africa, though not by intent. His first glimpse of Africa was the Atlantic coast of Morocco. It was on the beach where was located the ancient city of Massa that the whale spewed Jonah up and the people of Massa revered Jonah's memory. Upon that beach, says Leo, who was there (Massa is now extinct), was a particularly sacred mosque partially built of whales' ribs, such building material being abundant because great numbers of dead whales were washed ashore. Any whale which attempted to swim in the Atlantic along this special coastline was instantly and miraculously deprived of life. This was in punishment, we infer, because one of their ancestors had swallowed Jonah, an event which evidently affected local people profoundly and inspired very imaginative local authorship.

We are told that there is symbolism in the Jonah story which interests psychologists. The folk of Massa were probably moved simply by retroactive indignation against an animal which had misused a man. A contrasting and very domesticated monster figures in a Christian legend of Ethiopia. A saintly monk and some companions traveling on a pious mission mistook one night the open mouth of a gigantic boa serpent for a cave and went inside to sleep. The boa had a drink and swallowed them. Instinctively understanding the sacred mission of his passengers, the boa took them to their destination, spewed them up, waited and carried them home again and re-spewed them. This happened, according to a legend told by Doresse, to St. Abiya-Egzi.

King Solomon was the traditional grandfather of Ethiopian royalty, the supposed founder of a Moroccan Jewish colony and the creator of a hell on earth for disobedient jinn in Algeria. It was in this last locality that Ibn Khaldun shut himself away from distractions for four years and conceived the scheme for his great history. This coincidence must have delighted thoughtful Africans of his times. There was an Arabic literary tradition that great authors had been inspired by the jinn. Sir Hamilton Gibb in his *Arabic Literature* frequently speaks of this and cites by his name and its title a Spanish Arabic writer's work consisting of "a series of imaginary interviews with jinn who inspired [according to the ancient Arab conception] the great poets of the past." There at Kalaa, the jinn place of imprisonment, possibly impregnated by their influence, Ibn Khaldun the greatest of Africa's authors in Moslem times, was inspired.

Moses was naturally a pet of Africa's storytellers. He was African-born, traveled far in Africa—way up the Nile into Nubia and even, some said, across to Gibraltar. He was by marriage to an Ethiopian woman the legendary ancestor of Lalibela, the great Ethiopian church builder. And some even believed the tradition that he was himself a black man. It was from Gao on the Niger that the Pharaoh imported a troup of magicians he met competitively.

Africa's imaginative storytellers would so interpret the Koran as to have it that Moses traveled to the western extremity of Morocco. His companion was a mysterious unknown and immortal personage called El-Khadir, who had taken of the Fountain of Life and who enters into history as aid and counselor through the ages—he was the reputed vizier of Doul Karnein (the mythical Alexander the Great). His earliest appearance seems to be as traveling mate and adviser of Moses. They went to "the confluence of the two seas," which some in Africa have called the meeting of the Mediterranean and Atlantic, and they visited a city which was, so says an African legend, Tlemcen near the Algerian-Moroccan frontier.

We ask ourselves on what and how did the storytellers base these and many other tales about Old Testament and Koran heroes.

Was there even before the Arabs came the nucleus of parallel stories in Africa's mind which, under the influence, direct or indirect, of the Old Testament or the Koran, was amalgamated with some heroic name or circumstance in the books?

A very simple instance of how myths can shift their African dress is the story of the helpful ants, which was so old that Apuleius hitched it to Psyche and which reappeared later attached to the Virgin Mary. (The ants helped Psyche, the victim of Venus, to sort seeds of grain; ants helped the Virgin to find the needle with which she had been mending the clothes of the Baby Jesus and which she had lost in the sand.)

Did central Africans have a far older flood tradition which was subsequently mingled with the fame of Noah when they heard of his adventures and then combined with a giant of their own invention —Oudj, mentioned earlier in this book—who in his turn was combined with Moses and the Exodus from Egypt, which Oudj sought to impede and whom Moses killed?

Or did word of the adventures and heroes of Israel, of which yet more ancient counterparts have in some cases been discovered in the East and Near East, come into Africa originally from some yet earlier communications than the Jewish and Arabic book-based teachings?

There has been endless speculation, in which anthropologists, missionaries and Islamists have joined, about Africa's adoption of what we class as Old Testament or Koran heroes and Africa's rearrangement of their adventures.

If Africa's main source was the Koran some maintain that the

Koran had merely copied passages inaccurately from the Old Testament.

Islam responded that it was the Koran which first told the traditions correctly and that the Jewish book had previously botched them. Islam claims to be a restatement of the true religion revealed by God to Abraham "before Israel ever was." Moslem scholars using the term "Israelite stories" to indicate Old Testament narratives, looked upon them, as a rule, as "mere fiction presented as history." I quote from a note by Rosenthal on a passage in *Muqaddimah* where Ibn Khaldun cites an "Israelite story" as correct.

Bearing out Islam's confidence in the unique authenticity of the Koran is the tradition that Mohammed said, "If Moses were alive he would have no choice but to follow me."

That the Koran actually copied the Old Testament, albeit inaccurately, is impossible, for the compiler of the Koran, according to orthodox Moslem belief, could not read (some non-Moslems differ), and furthermore the Old Testament was not put into Arabic until some centuries after Mohammed's death. But Mohammed might have heard from Jews in Arabia stories about the careers of Jewish heroes, possibly garbled.

Goldziher tells that the Jewish Bible was a mysterious thing to earlier Arabs and offers a quaint item. According to a Moslem tradition the Jewish sacred books were made up of a thousand chapters of a thousand verses each, that was to say seventy camel loads of books. It took a year to read through one part, and only Moses, Joshua, Ezra and Jesus had studied them in totality.

Africa's storytellers absorbed in various ways about which we cannot tell, and accepted uncritically, altered and to their notions improved these tales from the East. All over Africa—Moslem northern Africa, Christian Ethiopia, sub-Saharan Moslem and semi-pagan localities—legends have been invented and retold about those familiar heroes.

The authors who adopted these heroes and combined them with romances of their own designing and imported these heroes in person into an African setting performed an interesting bit of unwritten authorship.

Another subject which these authors worked at was the problem of what had been the origin of the Berbers. They advanced at least a dozen differing answers, mostly with Old Testament associations. In view of the fact that modern anthropology has been able to put forward only uncertain and widely varying theories on the question, we must admit that the conflicting legends of the storytellers are just about as informative and more romantic.

Some of the launchers of legends even appreciated what we now recognize: that the Berbers were not merely a local group, not just the storytellers' neighbors and adjacent tribesmen in Tunisia, Algeria and Morocco, but a race distributed to the Red Sea and down into the Sahara.

One racial ancestor of their fancy was Abraham. It was naturally pleasing to believe that a single individual, and an individual of lofty importance, was the forefather of their group. They also liked to think that the name of the continent Africa, as it gradually became familiar to geography, was derived from one of Abraham's grandsons. This story of their origin was popular and got a wide distribution. Sultan Bello favored it in his history, although he mentioned as alternate possibilities some fantasies about the Berbers having been fathered by jinn or having proceeded from Gog and Magog.

Some of the oral anthropologists reached for another ancestry, in the family of Ham, the son of Noah, whose name is still preserved in the term "Hamite."

There were varied African versions in which sometimes Ham himself and sometimes members of his family figured, such as his son Canaan, or a descendant named Berr, or a great-great-grandson named Berber. It might have been Ham himself who went to northwestern Africa, where he lived till he was 443 years old, his family settling in various North African regions. The motive for his migration was that, being accursed, he turned black and fled to hide his embarrassment. His descendants and those of his family in northern Africa, however, were unaffected by Ham's color. The Berbers are a white race.

Another legend takes Ham to the Sudan and makes him the ancestor of the population by the upper Nile. Yet another tells how Ham's son married one Arteyt, from which mating came the Nubians, the Zenj and "all the tribes of the Negroes."

Thus we note that African weavers of legends early met a variation of that Hamite puzzle which students of racial matters today would like to dodge. The Hamites once meant a definite section of humanity believed to descend from Noah's son Ham. Anthropology inherited the name, if not the Biblical association and the old-time common meaning, but the term "Hamitic," both as a physical and a linguistic designation, is falling apart in anthropology's hands, is beginning to be used with uncertainty and reluctance, and seems destined to slip gradually onto the obsolete shelf.

Another and more exciting ancestor, and one who did not bequeath embarrassment to anthropology, was the subject of Berbers' imaginative storytellers. This was Goliath. It is said that there is still in southern Morocco a tribe carrying Goliath's name—the Ouled Jalout, "Jalout" being "Goliath" in Berber and Arabic. Goliath was understood to be of royal title, and presumably those of his family and their followers who migrated to North Africa after his downfall and founded there the Berber race brought the name along with them. No doubt they also brought with them the glamour and prestige of gianthood and gave to the Berbers, who told the story, a conviction of springing from an outsize ancestry.

To Africa in general a giant ancestor or local hero was an almost essential tribal heritage, for Africa held to a high degree the universal reverence for the gigantic. A giant represented strength. He was the early symbol of greatness and success in the days when the world seemed spacious. A ninety-two-foot statue of Ramses II overlooked Egypt. Even New York has its Statue of Liberty! This delight in the images of enormous males and females seems inherent in mankind. Jewish writings tell of an Adam of vast size. A Moslem tradition even caused his forehead to brush the skies. There seems to have been a belief even to relatively recent times that early humans were huge. The eighteenth-century Puritan divine, Cotton Mather, sent to the Royal Society, so Tylor tells us, an account of the discovery in New England of some bones which, he argued, were remains of antediluvian giants.

Africa expressed this fascinated preoccupation with giants in her oral literature, and the giants her storytellers invented made Goliath (six ancient cubits and a span tall—nearly twelve feet) seem like a pygmy. They use the familiar imagery of their homeland—giant heroes or villains who carried elephants with ease or who ate five hippos at a meal. There was one who carried four elephants suspended to a tree trunk and as he walked along ate another, which he held in his hand. There was one who bore several elephants on each shoulder, and when he sneezed uprooted the strongest tree.

These details delighted the listeners and caught attention. But beneath the grandeur of the giants was by implication the history of a people. As an example, giant episodes dealing with the Niger region are recorded by an interesting person—an ex-Catholic missionary father, part anthropologist and linguist, part lusty liver and part French colonial official—who spent almost all his life at Timbuctoo, by name Dupuis-Yakouba. (William Seabrook wrote a book about him, *The White Monk of Timbuctoo*, 1934; and I myself saw him when I was there.) Yakouba's legends take up almost seventy pages as appendix to Lieutenant Desplanges book about the same region.

A huge female called Fatimata Belle—no one had ever seen a woman so big, for her a year's sleep meant a night's rest—typified the Bellah, Tuareg vassals, who invaded the country of the Sorko, a part of what was to become the great Songhai Empire. The sandal of one of Fatimata Belle's giant sons was so heavy that a strong man could not lift it off the ground. The Sorko were dominated by Fatimata Belle until they, too, bred a giant, Farang, who slew her and her giant offspring. Farang was an immortal hero; the stories of his adventures and victories continue into the days when firearms came to the region—bullets had no effect on him. His name even became a synonym of power to such degree that in one of the Senegalese legends I find "Farang" given as the name of a Pharaoh who by insistent *corvées* drove to flight out of Egypt a group who became the original inhabitants of Senegal.

These pieces of oral literature, still unforgotten, are the overall, revised and improved repetition of history told by symbolism. Such is a legend included in the *Tarikh es-Soudan* about the beginning of the Songhai power. There came from a far place a savior who conquered the demon fish with a ring in his nose which tyrannized over them, the savior becoming the first king of an empire which endured for eight hundred years. The interpretation, albeit the pious author of the *Tarikh* gives it a religious twist, would seem to be that a vigorous newcomer vanquished the pillaging river folk—the fish with a ring in his nose—who had been the torment and ruin of the farmers and village dwellers.

Farang the giant personalized history. His adventures were the dangers through which they had passed; he himself was the surge of force with which over and over they had resisted. Deathless Farang fought giants and men and beasts and magic, each of these opponents a symbol of an enemy across the years.

It is a fine way to tell history, though it lacks the literal value of chronicles—no specified times or dates, no individual names, no definite localities. It thrilled the young and bred courage and roused patriotism.

The lively parts entertained the ribald element, such as the girl wife's lament at the physical discomfort she suffered from a giant husband who was extra-uxorious: "Do you think that a woman on whom rests a leg like his [and there the narrator attributed to her other plaints which are not printed] is not ready to die?" Or on account of Farang's attack on Fatimata Belle. He and his followers in a big pirogue traveled rapidly along the Niger and came so suddenly upon the huge woman straddling the river, one foot on each bank and bending forward to fill her water bucket, that they drove straight into "the noble parts of Fatimata." They entered into her belly without knowing it and reached the barrier of her heart. "We can go no farther!" they cried in amazement. "We have reached the end of the river!"

Eventually by nature's process the pirogue and its paddlers and the giant Farang emerged, Fatimata untroubled by the intrusion. Later Farang and the giantess battled and Farang won. Her surprising posture is supposed to signify that the Bellah invaders, whom she typified, held both banks of the Niger.

There was humor too: the giant suitor Farang stood back politely in the village street as an act of respect to the father of the girl and knocked down a house. And Farang as a decorous person was disturbed because his drawers, to the making of which had gone 333 measures of cloth (the measure equal to a man's forearm, say a generous half yard), would cover only one of his legs.

But to the sober, wise and proud old folks every detail had serious significance. They listened to the repetition of the Farang legends, which they had heard so often dramatically told and enacted by the professional storyteller, with head noddings and exchange of glances of comprehension. A color, a locality, Farang's precious guitar, which a hyena stole and died for his pains—cut into pieces with Farang's little fingernail—all this and the rest had important concealed meaning in their history. The giant was themselves. The animals which the giant fought were the tribal emblems of their enemies. The eel and hippo, the hyena, serpents, birds and the crocodile—all were associated with tribal groups and clans. It was jumbled, non-factual, non-chronological history, but very much their own.

It was a vision of history untrammeled by cold actuality, inaccurate but never sodden, quite non-photographic, but with a wider suggestion than the flat truth of the photograph and leading the listener into the past by a pathless route, the route of the emotions. Sometimes the art of pagan Africa has seemed to us similarly to possess power through its very disregard of the exact. And so perhaps the recital of these sweeping memories of a past that was nebulous but marked with their own character, vague in the habits of history—dates and names—and often supernatural, but true in its spirit, spoke to them directly and unhampered, and they understood as a person is carried along by his own identity, not the consciousness of his experiences, but the feel of himself, the "I am I."

I should imagine that one of those who listened to the legends of Farang or to many of such others in bookless Africa felt closer to the past of his people, though certainly without the slightest factual knowledge, than does any reader of history as it is written, closer than those who listened to the court recitals of dynastic chronicles. It was useless stuff as history, but rather fine art. It was history as bookless Africa sometimes knew it in pre-colonial days—not "a land without a history," as some have said, but a land where history could leapfrog facts yet mirror the truth.

Other stories were told besides those of the past. All over Africa there was a profusion of folklore and fables. Europeans listened, and many regional collections of such tales have been made and published in an assortment of European languages, also an anthology of the folklore of all Africa by René Basset, which has been called the only outstanding complete collection. (Delafosse says so in *L'Ame Nègre*.) Basset gives stories translated from ninety-eight different African languages plus a few African folk tales as imported by Negroes into the United States and West Indies, including the familiar Anansie spider stories. His anthology gives tales from all over the continent, from the Berbers and Arabs of the north to the Bantu, Hottentots and Bushmen.

Folk tales, though imaginative and sometimes containing wisdom and warning, were of limited scope and did not show the mind of Africa in its spaciousness, as did tribal oral literature. Folklore dealt with individual humans and animals, often with the interrelationship of the two. Perhaps in this regard it was the most revealing. As Rodney Needham has said, the social anthropologist when studying primitive peoples must, among other things, "accept a common nature of mankind and animals." Basset includes quaint tales about this animal-human relationship—such as the story of a Moroccan girl who lived with gazelles, a Tuareg boy who became the pet of the ostriches, an instance of a lion-human friendship in East Africa, the experiences of a woman in the upper Nile region who indirectly learned manners from a hyena, and many tales of animal-human marriages.

In the historic tribal stories animals appear not as mere individual beasts but as symbolic of important actions or emblematic of big human groups.

Animals in exalted or powerfully villainous situations, the newcomer from some far place who becomes the leader or savior, or else the coming of the whole tribe from some remote place—these elements seem to be the outstanding features in the legends of tribal origins. Often the three elements mingle in the same legend.

The conviction that they come from some far land is deeply planted in the African mind. It is said that few think their present location is their original home. Their migratory past was a proud heritage and they liked to say, "Once we came from afar off!" Alternately they celebrated the powerful personage who came from afar and organized the local people, often marrying a local female.

This was probably an idealized memory of an invasion. Perhaps he was a giant. Often there is mention of some animal either as hero or villain of the episode, or as a mystic influence.

Although groups took animal emblems indiscriminately it seems as if the animals upon which the imagination of Africa's legend builders fixed as heroes, villains or expressions of mystic force were often chosen from two extreme opposites in the social order of the animal world, either reptiles or that most respectable of beasts, the domestic cow.

Here are two tales about the legendary renown of individual cows. The sacred white cow came out of the Nile and gave birth to a male child. Such to the Shilluk on the upper Nile was the creation of the human race. The first conversion to Islam was brought to Sudan by the Niger by a mysterious couple, a cow behind which walked a man.

Cattle in some tribes had a mystic value. The so-called "Cattle Fulani," to distinguish them from those Fulani who were not pastoralists but preachers and conquerors, had a conviction almost of kinship with their herds. Neighboring Negro tribes would say, "When his father dies he does not cry, but oh what sorrow when he loses a cow!" and it was believed that the Fulani pastoralist could converse with his cow, could speak her language. There is a fable that a Fulani long ago rubbed his body against a newborn calf, was adopted and suckled by the calf's mother, since when the "Cow Fulani" and cattle are brothers.

In the upper Nile region there existed what Seligman called "almost religious esteem" for cattle, and between man and beast an attachment to which he gave the psychological term "identification." More recently Evans-Pritchard has carefully and sensitively described the same sentiment in his *Nuer Religion*. I like his phrase, "an enduring relationship between a social group and its ancestral herd."

The animal-human closeness in Africa may seem to us to show deplorable savage simplicity, a manifestation of that inability to distinguish between man and beast which is a characteristic of what older anthropologists like Tylor called "the lower races." It is contrary to the ideas of all three of the "book religions." To some of us it may seem to suggest, although crudely expressed, a great wisdom that we have lost.

Ancient Egyptians, who were no simple savages, attached religious significance to animals. An explanation of this which might be stretched to cover other Africans through the ages is in Henri Frankfort's *Ancient Egyptian Religion*. He wrote, "We assume that the Egyptian interpreted the nonhuman as superhuman, in particular when he saw it in animals—in their inarticulate wisdom, their certainty, their unhesitating achievement, and above all their static reality. With animals the continual succession of generations brought no change . . . The animals never change, and in this respect they appear to share—in a degree unknown to man—the fundamental nature of creation."

Africa's interest in animals centered particularly upon snakes, a preoccupation which goes against our taste but which we must view tolerantly, given our recognition of serpents in religious literature, in mythology and as an emblem of medicine.

Africa was snake land. Snakes appeared in her rock art. Her storytellers repeated tales with reptilian heroes and villains. To the snake was attributed in some parts of the continent a value akin to deification. And from antiquity her snakes were celebrated in classical literature.

Strabo told about snakes in what is now Morocco so huge that they grew plots of grass on their backs—possibly an honest report from an observer who saw the grass moving as a giant serpent slithered through.

A Latin poet who lived in the time of Nero and whose name was Lucan wrote a long account of what was to him recent history—the exploits of Caesar, Pompey and Cato—and offered a list of Africa's snakes which is said to have been "a celebrated passage," much studied by medieval readers. He lists by name and with frightening details nearly twenty varieties of serpents encountered by Cato in his march across what is now the Kingdom of Libya. Cato, seeking to protect his men, engaged members of the local tribe of Psylli, who were themselves immune to harm from snake bites and were able to cure others who had been bitten. The Psylli had in their bodies "by nature a certain kind of poison which was fatal to serpents and the odor of which overpowered them with torpor," says Pliny.

It is striking and rather puzzling that Pliny, writing about a day when Negro Africa was unknown, tells about a peculiar immunity claimed into modern days by certain sub-Saharans. Wilfred Hambly, who conducted a study of African snake beliefs on the spot in 1929–30, reports claims to such immunity as attributable to family heritage, or to membership in a secret society, or to self-immunization with an anti-venom, and lists localities where such claims are made in West Africa, northern Nigeria, among the Hottentots and Bushmen, in Rhodesia, Ethiopia and many other regions.

An African snake was the father of Alexander the Great, according to his mother's alleged confession to her husband, the snake being the physical guise worn by the god Ammon for the seduction. Alexander when he visited the Oasis of Siwa to check his supposed Ammon-via-snake parentage was led into the desert by two serpents "hissing as they went." This Arrian attributes to Ptolemy, later to be Egypt's king.

This story of the snake in the royal bedchamber is a recurrence of a very old myth about the snake's association with conception and the snake as a tempter of women. The snake which while a woman slept and was unaware had intercourse with her has been the innocent girl's fear and the guilty woman's excuse—the obvious reason, a phallic resemblance, to which add the instinctive morbid fascinations snakes have had for women ever since the birth of mythmaking. Hambly notes that there have been snake fecundity beliefs across the sub-Sahara: Mandingo, Ashanti, Yoruba, Swahili. Hottentot girls sometimes went to bed with a weapon at hand in snake fear, sexual fear.

An interest which Africans and others took in snakes and in which the serpent occupied a dignified intellectual position rather than one of lascivious suggestiveness was that of the Ophite sect, a Gnostic group already mentioned, which revered the memory of the snake in the Garden of Eden because it tried to introduce Adam and Eve to knowledge—the thwarted serpent-teacher.

The oral history of Africa dwells on the performances of individual snakes, often mentioned by name, tells sometimes of their malevolence, sometimes of their power and evident executive ability, sometimes of their helpfulness toward the humans they supervised. The supernormal activities of snakes writhe across space and time in Africa's story.

The earliest great snake—and he was doubly great, for he was so big that he shook the earth when he slithered across the country and he held absolute power as king of the land for four hundred years— was Arwe of Ethiopia. The father of King Solomon's famous sweetheart, the Ethiopian Queen of Sheba, deposed and destroyed Arwe. It is said that his memory was carried along into modern times by some of the pagan population.

The snake Ouagadou Bida made history in the modern sense in West Africa. Its actions had considerable influence upon colonization, for it was Ouagadou Bida who inaugurated and enriched one of the most renowned of West Africa's gold fields and thus lured early European penetration. This was Bouré near the upper Niger, tantalizing then, now forgotten, then sought as "a new source of wealth for our old Europe, weighed down with debts and over-population." (I quote from an enthusiastic comment on Bouré made by the geographer Jomard in 1830.) But the result was one of colonialism's disappointments.

This snake had an odd parentage. Its case is just the reverse of that of Alexander the Great. It was the son of a human father, who incidentally was a descendant of Job, and of a mother of jinn descent. All of her other offspring were normal human children. It promptly ran—or wriggled—away from home and became master of a section of what is now the Mali Republic, which section bore its name, Ouagadou. Would-be settlers were required to pay it a yearly tribute of their prettiest girl, entailing a grim sort of annual beauty contest.

One contest displayed as winner a beauty with whom a strange newcomer who "spoke only twice a year" was smitten, and the almost silent admirer slew the lustful serpent.

The serpent's severed head flew up into the air, talking as it flew, and predicted ruinous drought. "No rain water will fall for seven years. I shall turn the rain to gold!" The serpent's head shot across space for several hundred miles and came to earth near the Guinea border at the once renowned Bouré gold fields.

Beneath this story of the gold-giving serpent—it had once caused gold to rain down on the earth for fifteen days steadily—there is presumably something symbolic. The story by intent refers to the golden prosperity of the ancient land of Ghana. The drought refers to the trouble which came to the pagan country through the Moslem conquest. In the emphasis with which the legend was kept alive and insistently repeated one might see a cunning device: to dwell on the magic menace of the gold land and scare away intruders.

The snake called Sarki appears in the legends of northern Nigeria, playing a part which seems to have nuisance value rather than dignity. The legend deals with what is supposed to have happened one thousand years ago but which in its written form as included by Palmer in the Kano Chronicle is recent. Sarki controlled a well and allowed people to draw water only on Fridays. A newcomer to the region cut off its head, which was like that of a horse, and received as recompense the local queen as bride. From their union came a son, and presently grandchildren who became rulers of certain of the big states of Nigeria—Kano, Katsena and others.

Sarki was just a snake in a water hole—a very common item in African snake fables—but its name still lives. In Hausa language "Sarki" is synonymous with "King" or "Chief." A long series of rulers wore the title "Sarki" before their individual names. Osman dan Fodia, the Islamic conqueror, was locally called "The Sarki of the Moslems." The significance of Sarki the snake and the whole complex and confusing legend in which it plays a part offer racial, social and religious history put into code or cypher which it is difficult to interpret.

In the system of historic concealment, disguising happenings behind a veil which listeners were shrewd enough to see through, the serpent seems to have been a favorite device, and one often associated, as in the case of Sarki, with the rise to power of human kings. Sarki shared its name with royalty for a thousand years.

A kingmaker who was a kind snake operated on the borders of what is now Mali and Senegal, a benevolent and patient creature which submitted to indignities to encourage its protégés. It was a big and pampered boa which possessed a mane and tufted tail, and its abode was a cavern before which its devoted admirers placed fine food and big basins of milk and sherbet. When a ruler died the men of rank presented themselves for its inspection. The boa sniffed them one by one and tapped its choice for successor with its nose, then returned to its cave, the lucky man chasing after it and clawing bristles from its tail—the number of the bristles indicating the number of years he would reign as king. "It is claimed," says El-Bekri, "that the prognostic was infallible."

Certain members of a group of distinctly second-class reptiles were recognized as kingmakers or authenticators of kings in the neighborhood of Lake Chad. These were a select few of the large regional lizard. Their elevation to a post of such influence and authority was based on a tragic episode.

The legend runs: The population, at the advice of magicians, immured three princesses, Gara, Garé and Windé, in the city walls of Goulfeil near the lake. So far the legend might be true history. Children were sometimes immolated in walls as a macabre sort of good luck sacrifice, and this not alone in pagan Africa. What follows may have been not fantasy but a sincere expression of remorse and fear of magic reprisals, combined with the widespread idea that reptiles may really be the reappearance of dead humans. From the land of the Zulu to the borders of the Sahara was the belief that an ancestor can be reincarnated in a reptile. "Our ancestor has come to visit us!" said the Zulus.

The sacrificed princesses came back as lizards. Their father recognized them. They, presumably the same three, were henceforth accepted as masters of the city. A new king would present himself ceremoniously before the lizards' hole, and if the lizard of the day—an immortal lizard, which lived through the centuries!—was satisfied with the candidate it would emerge, the new king would be introduced to it, the lizard being addressed as "Gara, the king's daughter" (the name and the rank of the eldest of the pitiful little victims of a bygone day).

This ritual ceremony was re-enacted through the generations. Lebeuf, an archaeologist who worked extensively in the Chad region, says that as late as 1947 the ancient practice was carried out at Goulfeil, now a place of trifling importance, but perfunctorily, "in a pale sort of fashion." The ritual, which once perpetuated a childlike belief in a superhuman reptile and inspired confidence in their ruler, has become, as rituals sometimes do, a bit of the routine in a public parade.

The actualities of formal, officially recognized snake worship in some parts of pagan Africa gave to the reptiles a practical and less imaginative position than they held in legends, and to our notion, brought something commonplace and vulgar into an interesting symbolism. Similarly the snake-handling cult in some southern United States localities, of which one is reminded and about which Professor La Barre has written a psychological study, is not symbolism but a combination of the foolhardy with the eccentric.

Actual snake worship, that is the deification of the serpent, occurred in West Africa, especially in Dahomey, and in Uganda, where the individual snake, the physical, visible snake, usually a python, was revered and established in an honored home, a sort of chapel with the services of special priests and priestesses.

The "chapel" of the sacred snake was not an elegant place, indeed it could not have been, given the nature of its deified inhabitant. Burton describes the temple, as he calls it, at Ouidah in Dahomey as a small cylindrical mud hut with a thatched roof and roughly whitewashed inside and out, and a more recent writer, Parrinder, repeats Burton's observations with the rather quaint fact added that just across the way is the Roman Catholic cathedral. Hambly says that in Uganda were "sacred cows for supplying milk to the python."

Especially interesting is the part which women took in the matter of python worship. In the old legends powerful snakes demanded beautiful girls as tribute, for table or bedtime delicacies. The position of the python priestesses was less dangerous. The priestess who joined the python cult was put through a course of preparation at a "convent," learned to handle the snakes fearlessly and was taught to perform frenzied dances.

To some snake priestesses marriage was forbidden. They were "the brides of the sacred snakes." Other sects of the cult were more liberal. I read about the leader of one of the modern Christian offshoot groups in Ghana, the name of which was The Apostolic Revelation Society, who states that his father was a Christian but his mother was a *dasi* (literally "wife of a snake") that is, a priestess, who evidently could also be the wife of a man.

It was only natural that so much of the rites of serpent worship should be entrusted to their women. In many legends in which the symbolic serpent figured and which the cult of the serpent domesticated and carried along, female characters predominated—the rescued maiden, the girl sacrifice, the king's daughter for a hero's bride.

WOMEN

THE STRONG AND THE
REMEMBERED · WOMEN IN A
POLYGAMOUS CONTINENT ·
SURVIVAL OF THE
WOMAN SYMBOL

THE STRONG AND THE REMEMBERED ·
How did Africa esteem her women?

A significant fact partly answers this question. A considerable number of female individuals survive in Africa's history, a far larger proportion than is carried along in our own—Europe's and America's —if we disregard those women of our own who figure in our history pages as consorts or sweethearts of royalty and men of high degree, or queens who secured power solely by heritage, plus, of course, the familiar female Christian saints.

Africa's famous females attained renown and are remembered because of their own performances. Some are legendary rather than historic personages, but this is a greater indication of the public attitude. An actual historic woman of exceptional attainment might have been regarded as a freak, a human sport, whereas to invent or embellish the story of a female and build a legend around her showed a readiness to believe in the accomplishment and authority of the female.

Some of the important women of Africa have already come into the pages of this book, such as the two she-generals, the battling Jewesses, Cahena of northern Africa and Judith "The Fire" of Ethiopia. Also the fighting Mossi princess Yennenga. Three very ancient famous African females were Makedda, who dared the journey to the court of Solomon and returned to give birth to the ancestor of a long dynasty, Dido (Elissa), who was born in Phoenicia and died a suicide near the Carthage she had founded, and Tin' Hinan, the first ruler and "Our Grandmother," as say the Tuareg of the Sahara.

Here is a woman of more recent renown: Amina, or Aminatu, of what is now Nigeria, who became the mistress of the Hausa country in the sixteenth century, of Katsina and Kano, "and conquered as far as the shores of the Ocean," as Bello tells it in his history. She also figures in the Kano Chronicle and another local chronicle, that of the Abuja. She held sway for thirty-four years. Her love life was as spectacular as her warrior exploits, for at each town she conquered she chose herself a lover and murdered him before she rushed on to further military and amorous exploits. She also introduced into that part of Africa a new excitant, for it was she who imported as tribute from the west the delightful kola nut, also a novel abuse—the castration of eunuchs.

So recent as to have come to the experience of an early English missionary was the South African woman warrior Mantatisi of the Sotho tribe called the "Wild Cat People," whose peculiar feminine capacity was part of a supernatural regional report which came to his startled ears. The Englishman was "the father of African missionaries," Robert Moffat, whose daughter became Livingstone's wife. To Moffat the first rumors about Mantatisi seemed "like the reveries of a madman." She was reportedly "at the head of an invincible army, numerous as locusts, marching onward among the interior nations, carrying devastation and ruin wherever she went; she sent out hornets before her army"—and here stands a tribute, primitive yet proving a mystic confidence in their woman leader—"she nourished the army with her own milk!" This I quote from Moffat as transmitted by Peter Becker in *Path of Blood*. Moffat's life as told by his son describes Moffat's personal encounter with "the dreaded Mantatees," so known because of the name of their chieftainess.

One is struck by the readiness of African public opinion to carry along legends and history in which a woman is shown as the supreme commander over male soldiers. Across Africa and up and down from the Mediterranean to the continent's southern tip one finds such legends, which one might think would have been distasteful to men and puzzling to women. The woman soldier was a familiar fact in Africa, as elsewhere. The courage and endurance of the celibate corps of Dahomey impressed pre-colonial European visitors, and there were women soldiers in other African regions. This differs from a woman commanding general and conqueror, whose acceptance again indicates that Africa had a point of view of her own about women, as in so many other matters.

In a political sense a pair of women made Moroccan history. Kinza was the Berber concubine of Idris, that great-great-great-grandson of Mohammed who fled across the top of Africa to found a kingdom, and she collaborated brilliantly and bravely in the saving of her murdered master's dream and in establishing her son, the infant Idris II, on the throne.

Zeineb, reputedly a magician, was remembered as a sort of manageress at one of North Africa's finest periods. She was a woman of political skill, plus other charms and abilities—the concubine of one chief, the wife of another, and the consort successively of the two founders of that almost incredible Almoravid Empire, which stretched from beyond the Niger to the Pyrenees—Abou Bekr and Yusuf ibn Tashfin—slipping shrewdly and smoothly away at the right moment from the former into the arms of the second. "It was to the intelligence of this woman that Yusuf owed the establishment of his power. It was because he followed Zeineb's advice that he was able to secure supreme authority and overcome the resistance [of his rival, Abou Bekr]." So wrote Ibn Khaldun.

Feminine names—some of them very pretty, some very imposing—garnish the history of Ethiopia. The importance in which Ethiopians held women shows in their loyalty to a fundamental tradition which features a woman and in the supreme reverence they have chosen to pay to the Virgin Mary. In addition to Makedda and General Judith "The Fire," we meet, for example, Helena (Elini), who was an outstanding individual in three reigns and who, as his step-grandmother, secured the throne for a child heritor. It was she who dispatched to Portugal that emissary carrying a fragment from the True Cross whose mission eventually brought Europe into relation with the empire of the mysterious Prester John. "She was the father and the mother of us all," they told Alvares, who came with the Portuguese. "She governed for me," said Prester John, referring to his boyhood as king.

Helena was a name she acquired in maturity, for she was born a Moslem and her marriage to Christian Ethiopian royalty was for political reasons. Her original name was Golden Pomegranate (Romanie Ouarq). She became devoutly Christian, built a church to the Virgin's honor and observed the rigorous Ethiopian fasts, eating only every other day during Lent.

It was Taitu, the wife of the second Menelik, who founded Addis Ababa, Ethiopia's modern capital. Menelik II had fixed his capital on a mountaintop over nine thousand feet above sea level, where it was painfully cold, especially since wood for fires was lacking. Taitu, on a bathing expedition at a lower altitude, was enchanted by the softness of the air. "Let me build a house here!" she demanded of Menelik. In the back of her head was a project to transfer the nation's capital. Her house was built and her project gratified. A competent lady who could think for herself.

The Empress Woizero Zawditu—hers was a noble name, for the first word meant "Descendant of Solomon" and the second name meant "Crown"—was the daughter of Menelik II and was used as a bargaining piece in the consolidating of his empire. Menelik married her to the son of his rival when she was about six years old. Eventually and after disastrous interludes Zawditu, now a woman in the forties, was crowned empress beneath a crown which, as the official photograph shows, was at least a foot high, a basket upside down over her small face, and Ras Tafari, whom we know as Haile Selassie, was appointed regent and heir to the throne.

It was a difficult combination.

We can look back on the Golden Pomegranate Helena, who cut an opening in Ethiopia's isolation by calling to Europe. We can contrast the last woman ever likely to rule over Ethiopia (the Constitution of 1955 forbids female rule), who temperamentally sought to conserve the country behind walls.

Africa's queens under their own power, not consorts, are rare in the continent's story. In Moslem Africa there was only one. She was a violent and tragic figure who in her short reign issued her own coinage, one piece of which is in the British Museum, carrying a date corresponding to 1250, and a legend stating she was queen and the former slave of al-Salih. She was Shajar-al-Durr (meaning "Pearl-Spray").

Pearl-Spray was a human hyphen in history. She stretched between Saladin's fading dynasty and the rising Mamluks, so that her name figures in both dynastic lists—at the tail of the Ayyubids and at the start of the Mamluks.

Having borne a child to Sultan al-Salih, whose favorite slave she was, according to Maqrizi, she became a free woman and proved herself a shrewd and courageous one. Salih was dying. Joinville gives an account of how it came about: poison was put upon a mat upon which he was accustomed to squat while playing chess and an open sore in his leg was infected. Desperately ill, he was brought back to Egypt. Pearl-Spray kept his death secret until the return to Egypt of his successor, an incompetent who risked the disintegration of the country, already wobbling under Crusade attack, and gave her approval to his assassination. Again Joinville tells a spirited story, concluding with the ghastly picture of one of the murderers, who extended the dead Sultan's heart "in a hand all reeking with blood" under the nose of the prisoner St. Louis as a salable souvenir.

It is said that it was Pearl-Spray who got St. Louis and his people away in safety, in exchange for ransom, to be sure, when the Mamluks wished to massacre them.

Pearl-Spray was now queen, ruling over Egypt, but her time was short: Moslem opinion was against a woman ruler, a thing of which tradition said Mohammed had disapproved. A husband was assigned to her and called "Sultan," and an infant male of the Saladin family was associated to make a sort of tripartite government. The husband did away with the child. Pearl-Spray caused the death of the husband and Pearl-Spray herself was savagely killed. Then Mamluk power took over.

So ended the career of the human hyphen in history and Islam's only African queen.

Indeed African queens in their own right have been rare even in pagan Africa, where women have had a stronger role. One called Jinga was a short-time queen and a short-time Christian at the disordered period when the Congo region met simultaneously the Portuguese influence, the new religion of Christianity and the demands of the foreign slave trade. Female chiefs and paramount chiefs have been and still are numerous.

There were, even way back in the Middle Ages, female authors— these in northern Africa, of course. I have run across mention of only two of these: Nodhar, daughter of a learned Berber named Abou Hayyan, and Aicha, daughter of a lawyer of Bougie in Algeria, "who shone in the literature of the 14th century" and left several poetic works which have survived.

A very influential African woman religious leader lately startled the world press, the Prophetess Alice Lenshina of Northern Rhodesia, who inspired the destruction of some hundreds of people in 1964. She is outside the time of this book but worthy of mention as showing that the authority of women is as strong as in pre-colonial times.

Queen mothers often held places of high power. When a treaty was made in 1765 between the King of France and the Damel (king) of that region, where stands Dakar—then nothing, 320,000 inhabitants now—the document was signed first by "the mark of the queen mother," followed by "the mark of the king [Damel]." We also hear of queen consorts who shared power with the king, and of women who were members of a government head along with a male.

An exceptional case of woman's sole and supreme rule was developed with queer complications in a small kingdom of some forty thousand inhabitants, the Lovedu in the Transvaal, and is described by Annie Lebeuf in *Women of Tropical Africa*. The hereditary king decided 150 years ago to make his dynasty feminine. His daughter succeeded and the female line continued. The woman ruler's prime duty was to supervise and manage the weather. She had supernatural power and could "make rain" and determine the cycle of the seasons.

A complication was that the supreme female ruler was not permitted to marry in the usual way, although royal etiquette at Lovedu permitted her to become a mother. By royal rules she was obliged to keep a harem of other women, and if her "wives" had children they were regarded as belonging to the queen and might with propriety be her successors.

This system of woman marriage to another woman, which to us could carry but one inference, seems to have had another and a respected meaning and was practiced sometimes by women of rank or importance and was widespread in pagan Africa. I find it mentioned as of a certain Zulu woman, and as of women of importance in a Transvaal group, the Venda, where sometimes when she had lost her own progeny a woman would enter into an official marriage, after the usual payment arrangements with the bride's people, mate her with a suitable man and claim the resulting child as her own, thus securing a heritor of her own family.

On the far side of Africa similar marriages occurred. In Benin, Dennett tells of pre-colonization days: "The dowager Queen maintains a court of her own composed, as number one person, of the Amoma, her so-called wife," followed along in importance by "Amada, her naked boys," and by others, such as the medicine man and the official sacrificer of human beings, called the Ioba.

WOMEN IN A POLYGAMOUS CONTINENT ·

There was a multitude of African women who did not get into history, but there were very few who did not get married.

Almost invariably the African woman was a married woman. Africa had no old maids. There were no elderly virgins in the continent, or they were so few as scarcely to count. In Coptic Egypt, where the Christian population was a minor factor, there were some nuns who lived in austerity. Ethiopian Christians also had nuns, "some of them very holy women, and others not so," according to Alvares, who said that some of them had children. Ethiopian Jews, the Falasha, had nuns. In Dahomey the Amazon corps was supposedly celibate, but some broke the rules. The female priests of the snake cult were the same. Female celibacy, except under religious or other pressure, was so rare as to rouse open contempt, being attributed to some physical defect or mental derangement.

The African spinster of normal physique and character who had contrived to remain single from inclination was a curio so unusual as to gain renown. Ibn Khaldun interjects into his Berber history a note about the daughters of a North African notable who insisted on living out their lives manless and attained from this mere fact lasting fame, their home locally known as "The Chateau of the Girls." They all lived to a great age. Ibn Khaldun's father had seen one of them who was ninety-two years old and pronounced her to be "of all women in the world the most virtuous in conduct."

As well as having practically no spinsters and few nuns Africa is said to have had a minimum of prostitutes.

In Africa women got married. Some of them had sole title to their husbands. Some shared him with other wives.

Polygamy was all over the continent. (More correctly we should say polygyny, since the multiple was exclusively a male practice, but I shall stick to the more familiar word, polygamy.) Islam, of course, practiced polygamy, but Islam showed Africa nothing new. Sub-Saharan Africa was already polygamous. Among the Jews of northern Africa it was sometimes practiced, and we are told that it continued with them into modern times. The marriage customs of Punic Carthage are not clear, says Gsell, an accepted authority on ancient North Africa, suggesting polygamy may sometimes have been permitted there.

Even Christian Ethiopians were sometimes polygamous and, it is stated, still are. Alvares says he "lodged in the house of a man and he had three wives still alive . . . and they said he had had seven wives." The Ethiopian Church disapproved of departure from monogamy, but the civil government raised no objection. The warrior king Amda Syon had several wives.

Although it is outside the scope of this book, which aims to tell about the ways and thoughts of the continent before colonization, it is of interest to note the contest between Negro Africans and Christian missionaries when Europe came and to note that Africa's marriage habit has been hard to alter. Some of the new African Christian "Prophet" cults have laid down their own conduct rules and have specifically approved the old polygamous privilege, maintaining that polygamy was not forbidden in the Bible, but only by the Christian Church rules and reacting against the stern disapproval of the early missionaries—"One wife only if you want God!" was the typical admonition of a century ago. However, the noted Anglican Bishop Colenso was deposed in those same early days for favoring the baptizing of polygamists among the Zulus, says Dr. Sundkler in his study of the Bantu prophets of South Africa.

One of West Africa's "Prophet" Christian sects in Ghana, where various forms of prophetism have been carefully investigated by Dr. Baëta, himself an African, includes in its regulations that polygamy is "normal" and that "the idea that a man should marry one wife belonged to Europeans only," adding tartly that if the Europeans observed this rule at home "they were certainly not so doing in Ghana"!

The astronomical figures about some of the harems as reported by early travelers startled us. They were mostly the status symbols of pagan kings and chiefs in the sub-Sahara. Moslems were supposed to have a maximum of four wives at a time, though some exceptional royal personages were extravagant, like Sultan Moulay Ismail of Morocco at the turn of the seventeenth and eighteenth centuries, who reputedly had five hundred or more. On the kings of pagan Negroland here are some figures (not guaranteed correct): the kings of Benin, "a large number of wives, often more than a thousand" (Dapper, seventeenth century). The Benin king who died in 1933 had "some hundreds," according to a local historian. The Ashanti king felt it his official obligation to keep up a mystical number of 3,333 wives, the number "carefully kept up but never exceeded." Other localities: "more than 300"; "250 wives"; and the modest claim of thirty wives in Junod's report about a fairly recent chief among the Thonga of southern Africa. A contemporary of his had so many wives he hardly knew them and children so numerous that he lost track of their identities and, all unaware, married his own daughter.

Such marital statistics—some probably fanciful travel tales, some reliable—concerning kings and chiefs were presumably a display of prestige rather than a manifestation of maniacal lust and did not indicate, in fact could not indicate, the situation of the ordinary man. Nature was not so extra-prolific with girls nor were the fatalities of men in wars, hunting, and so on, numerous enough to provide several wives, let alone hundreds for every African male.

I suggest that polygamy, which we regard as a degradation of womankind, was better for the women, as it was practiced in the sub-Sahara, than it was for the men. Of course, those women who were inmates of the colossal harems of the notables had a poor deal. But for the ordinary women it meant security and a respectable position.

On men, ordinary men, it imposed a lifetime of restricted sex excitement and sex fun: a wife, two or three—that was all. No flirting, no occasional nights out with loose girls and none of the titillating pleasure of witnessing some questionable show where the sight of female performers displaying themselves without clothing before a number of men was not only provocative and comical but also gratified some perhaps unrealized sex antagonism. After all, no strip tease exhibition could have been a treat to the sub-Saharan man, many of whose women neighbors moved before their eyes nearly naked every day as they fetched water and wood and pounded grain.

It would seem that, given the usual understanding of the temperaments of women and of men, polygamy catered to the female side. But it was a dubious method for the management of sex cooperation, admittedly a difficult thing to manage. If one could put aside prejudice he would have to admit that no section of humanity has so far devised a comfortable, successful, smooth-running system for the mating, breeding and satisfaction of sex desires of men and women. Our own way is disfigured by woe and wrangling. And since legends began all the world has tangled the management of its sex life. We must accept it that any attempt to contrast various systems—pagan Africa's, our own and all the others—is but a comparison of inefficiencies.

There were some practical reasons to explain the multiple marriages of sub-Saharan pagan men.

One was that it was usually condemned as wrong and unwholesome for a woman to have sex relations with her husband while she was nursing a child, and the nursing process was prolonged until the child was of walking age—"until the child can carry upon its head unassisted a calabash of a certain size full of water to a certain distance without spilling it." Furthermore in certain regions intercourse had to stop during most of pregnancy.

These prohibitions deprived her husband of sex life over a period of several years or else tended to indiscreet rule-breaking and reprimand if detected or if another pregnancy betrayed the married pair. The nursing infant's health was said to suffer if the mother so misbehaved. The prohibitive rules could even tend to an attempt to avoid conception, a heinous action which would conflict with the profound desire for children, a sort of sacred obligation in them all.

It was therefore natural that the husband whose wife gave him a child should seek another wife—no simple process but one which involved careful study of a complexity of family considerations and certain property negotiations with the guardian of the young woman of his choice. It was no matter of beckoning to a suitable girl met on a forest path, as we might artlessly imagine.

Another practical advantage to polygamy from the native point of view was that it relieved the wife of a part of the arduous labor of housekeeping in primitive conditions, where the water supply was sometimes far off, wood for fires the same and grain had to be pounded almost interminably. In addition it increased the farm output. Wives in agricultural localities helped with farm work. The more wives, the more crops. Equally true in principle whatever the husband's occupation. I find in a book by Azikiwe, who became the Republic of Nigeria's first president, a quoted passage to the effect that polygamy is almost an economic necessity for the people of the interior, and Blyden, one of the very early Negro African intellectuals, in the Western sense, asserted, "Compulsory monogamy is for Africa a mistake, a crime, and worse than a crime, a blunder."

A wife overburdened was torn between natural resentment at the prospect of a newcomer and relief. Some wives, we are told, sincerely opted for the relief. Talbot tells about a woman who complained to the native court of cruelty because her husband refused to marry any other woman than herself! Jealousy between wives was inevitable. But it might be that we exaggerate the unhappiness of a wife who shares her husband by attributing to her the psychological reactions of the wife in a monogamous society. The wife in a non-monogamous society did not suffer hurt pride. She did not suffer prying suspicion or quiver under the gossip and pity of other people. Her husband's taking another wife was a normal happening. Let it be understood we are not discussing what marriage ought to be, but rather the sentiment of Africa's women.

The position of Africa's women and the detail and laws of married life varied so greatly that one cannot venture to offer any general picture. The variation depended on geography and climate, on the difference between the matrilineal and patrilineal systems and on the wide gap between Islam and paganism, also of course on tribal traditions and notions.

Speaking widely, I suggest that the pagan woman had the opportunity for an active and good life, given always that one appreciates that the marriage system under which she lived, the possibility of having to share her husband with others, was a long-established custom and to her a dignified one. Women in the Moslemized localities south of the Sahara and in the Sahara's habitable parts enjoyed in many regions equal opportunities. In northern Africa the women labored less and had less freedom.

Let me offer items from here and there that give a glimpse of women's lives in the pre-colonial period, some picturesque, some shockingly cruel, all characteristic and significant.

Take female adultery, that greatest misdeed in married life, since it plants in the supposed father's mind a doubt as to the fatherhood of his child. The ultimate ferocity I find in the report of the first European explorers to go to the Bornu region in Nigeria. Denham tells how a sinning woman and her partner if caught in the act were thrown to the ground, hands and feet bound together and beaten with a club by the injured husband till their brains spurted out of their skulls.

That was Moslemized Africa. In contrast the married ladies of Moslem Walata in the southern Sahara had unabashed satisfaction in gentlemen friends. In Moslem Mauritania it was the women who were masters of the tents. The first European who ever lived among them, René Caillié, reported with amazement that these women had more "empire" over their husbands than did "our ladies of France," and another observer tells how the wife eats alone, he serving her and waiting for his meal until after she has finished. The Tuareg of the desert, Moslem to a moderate degree, accepted as a romantic habit that their young women should participate without reproach in evening festivities of music and free love under the stars. These same women became respected and often unique wives, and were the intellectuals of the group, the readers and writers of the Tuareg script, called Tifinagh.

In the Mzab oasis cities in the northern Sahara, where a special form of Moslemism was intense, women lived in complete seclusion. When very rarely they left home they were wrapped and double-wrapped, and if a man approached in the narrow streets they would hustle into a corner and turn their backs till he passed. If a man attempted to address a word to a woman in the street he was fined and exiled from the Mzab for two years. A Mzabite wife guilty of adultery was flogged officially, the exact rules for her punishment being laid down by law—pitiable reading it makes: how, still veiled, she was to be whipped upon the shoulders, being caused to sit in a huge basket which covered her to her armpits, and how, "in order to avoid the spectacle which pain or fear might cause, the basket and the surrounding ground should be abundantly sprinkled. . . . Pregnant women not to be flogged until after the confinement."

Yet in this sternly moral community—almost a little nation until after the French conquest of Algeria—a Mzabite husband would accept with equanimity the pregnancy of his wife when he came home after an absence of several years on a far trading venture, the explanation being merely that the child had slumbered for an exceptionally long period in its mother's belly.

All the above reactions to female adultery concern Moslem localities where traditionally an adulteress was condemned to stoning, with the protective condition that her evil action had to have been seen by four witnesses! (The Koran, sura 24, says that anybody who defames a woman and cannot bring four witnesses shall be scourged with fourscore stripes.)

Pagan husbands, while naturally indignant at the faithless wife, did not in general demand such harsh punishment. Adultery was cause for divorce of a wife, and a wife seeking freedom had to have a clean sheet. A practical query in the land of few clothes would in some localities be put to a woman asking for a divorce: "Has any man caressed your breast or your buttocks with guilty intention?"

The seducer risked severe, even fatal chastisement from an angry husband, or the payment of fines which might be ruinously high if he interfered with the wife of a chief.

Divorce among the pagans was much complicated by finance. There were many variations of divorce customs across the sub-Sahara. Speaking generally, a divorce involved the repayment of all or part of the value in goods or cattle or other matters which had been given by the husband or his family to the father or family of the bride. This so-called "bride wealth" had been the suitor's outlay in order to secure a wife.

Such investment on the part of a wife-seeking male used to be called by critical and contemptuous Europeans "a purchase price."

Modern anthropologists say this is a wrong interpretation, that it is rather a pledge between the contracting families. One recalls the dowry system in Europe, under which a girl's father in order to marry her off suitably, often had to endow her with a sum of money or property.

In pagan Africa the preliminary "bride wealth" negotiations were sometimes a matter of very careful bargaining. A maiden was a creature of high value. Her value lay primarily in her child-producing capacity. I find this phrase attributed to a native source: "Women are like God because they bear children." The young man's family invested the needed property on his behalf to establish his future as a family man of his own. If he later had polygamous ambitions he himself had to pay the costs. Sometimes the marriage dealings, which might have been consummated between the two families when she was born, sought to turn a girl over to a man she disliked. There have been reported suicides. A West African explorer of long ago tells that rebellious girls, kicked out of home, turned to prostitution.

There was nothing haphazard about African pagan marriages, and pagan society appreciated in its own fashion the importance and dignity of the female partner.

There were elements and potencies in the status and behavior of the females which though surprising to our notions indicated the vigor and briskness of woman's brains. One which will make us smile is the stringent rule, very general but not universal, that the mother of the bride and the husband were to have no contacts. Sometimes the father-in-law (wife's father) was also a forbidden contact. "The son-in-law must never be in the presence of his mother-in-law or his father-in-law. He must dodge them. Even at a war council, where both men were obligatorily present, they must always keep themselves far apart." This ruling concerns the Moslems of Mauritania, indicating the custom was not exclusively pagan. Sometimes the other father-in-law (husband's father) was compulsorily avoided by the wife. "A woman is prohibited to enter the hut of her father-in-law" is cited as a marriage regulation among certain Bantu of Northern Rhodesia.

Some wise old matrons in the long ago, for it must have taken a long time to spread this custom across Africa, evidently noted the in-law problem which our modern marriage counselors report and took definite steps to avoid both awkward temptations and family quarrels.

It must have been the matrons who dictated a way of family management which seemed to them practical and to us shocking. This was the immediate destruction at birth of deformed babies. I find mention of this in various parts of Africa.

It seems significant that some of the old-time European explorers noticed the absence or rarity of deformed people. "In the whole of my peregrinations amongst savage tribes I never saw a deformed child," asserted John Petherick after sixteen years' travel, mostly in the upper Nile a century ago. To this there were some exceptions. Dennett describes a kinglet in the coastal Congo region who was a hunchback. Burton saw several hunchbacks, male and female, as a feature in a circuslike procession at the Dahomey "Customs," and at Benin, so Dapper says, dwarfs were used in a parade. The inference might be that these hunchbacks or dwarfs were displayed as show pieces in a parade, being rarities because they had escaped destruction at birth.

Newborn babies were formally examined by the midwife and attendant women—this is from a detailed account of the procedure among a tribe on the Ivory Coast. "Was it mute?" They slapped it, and if it did not cry it was condemned. "Had it the normal number of fingers and toes?" "Was it correctly formed—arms the same length, legs and eyes as they should be?" If anything was wrong the child must perish. It would be the cause of unhappiness. It was immediately drowned. "And the mother was forbidden to cry." Children who later revealed themselves to be feeble of brain or incurably sickly were destroyed. This from reports on the Mossi—now the Volta Republic—region.

There was in the system a cold-blooded yet courageous comprehension, for how could a woman raise a deformed or idiot child in primitive conditions? How could such an unfortunate be protected in adult life? What children might she or he breed? Out, and out quickly, was the matrons' answer.

For the child itself they felt no sympathy. Such inferior children were not classed as human beings. They were regarded—this, for example, was the belief of the Mandingos—as evil spirits. Or else by certain other tribes as serpents in disguise. Weak-witted or paralyzed young creatures would be thrown into a river. "If you hide by the water you will see that child lengthen into a snake," they would say. Hambly tells this of two tribes, living respectively in southern and northern Nigeria.

It is interesting to note that primitive females settled in a slashing fashion a much and unsatisfactorily discussed modern problem.

From quite other motives a sweeping and brutal form of birth control was adopted by the Jagas, a cannibalistic group which, intoxicated by the opportunities when the foreign slave trade's demands erupted into the Congo region, ravaged it for profit and helped push the budding Christian movement back into paganism. Jagas destroyed their children wholesale, tribal numbers being kept up by absorbing juvenile captives in the raids. It was a system which accorded with their special way of life at a special time of exultant violence, and a thing apart from the normal instinct of paganism. Women were pleasant to the Jaga roving bandits; babies and toddlers, an impossible handicap.

Horrid too, and not explicable by the temporary frenzy of a greedy savage gang, but attributable only to magic fears, was the frequent destruction of twins, or sometimes of only one of the twins. Pagan African society viewed twin births, although they were probably more frequent than among ourselves, as abnormal and disturbing events. Twins were weird. Some tribes welcomed twins excitedly as good omens. Far more common were distaste and dismay. Among such tribes few twins survived. Twins, they thought, brought misfortune to a community. In some villages the shocking event of a twin birth caused the neighbors to take protective medicines and to give the same to their cattle, convinced that otherwise the cattle would fall ill and they themselves would develop a sort of elephantiasis. This extreme superstitious alarm was among certain Bantu in the Lake Nyasa region, but the birth of twins was pretty generally deplored across the sub-Sahara.

Twins were evil spirits and a magic danger. Twins were not really human.

There is a choice of explanations as to why twin babies were said to be associated with evil magic. Magic association followed a primitive revulsion, or else magic might be artfully claimed to save the mother's good name. In the former case a double birth of children was, they felt, a non-human happening which shocked and disgusted them. It seemed like a litter. African pagans were intensely desirous to have children, but had a horror of having them supplied wholesale, as with the animals. On the other hand, the mother of twins was likely to be condemned as an immoral woman. One man could not be the father of two children; obviously she had committed adultery while pregnant. A loyal midwife might do away with the two or with one twin in the hope of dodging evil tongues. If tongues still wagged it was a good defense to say the twins had been a magic sending.

Magic was always in the minds of pagan Africans. It was a part of their daily lives just as much as machines are a part of our own. It was the great force. It explained the supernatural and it was a tool for the handling of the tangible, the unseen dangers and the joys of the spirit.

The forests and the rivers and the trees had magical spirits; the humans—some of them—also possessed or were afflicted with magical powers. Malinowski, speaking of primitive peoples in general, says that magic, human magic, was from the earliest times in the hands of specialists and "the first profession of mankind is that of a wizard or witch." African rock art shows magicians engaged in their mysterious work.

It is well worth noting in our attempt to size up woman's place in pagan Africa that, although the professional practical magicians, such as those whom we call by the misleading name of "witch doctors," were usually men, individual women were magic's mysterious agents. They themselves were magic.

They had been magic throughout the ages. The Koran (sura 113) warns against "the mischief of women blowing on knots," such act and the tying of knots in a special fashion being a form of evil enchantment which, tradition says, was performed against Mohammed himself, causing him to fall ill.

Magic power was a quality possessed or acquired only by some women, but the fact that a woman, any woman, might have magic at her call made all women objects of awe, suspicion and alarm, for to pagan African society witchcraft was "the most dangerous occult that can impinge on life" and the result of "a state of mind founded in universal human psychology." I quote these two phrases from Meyer Fortes and Malinowski respectively. What proportion of the population was actually witchlike is not known. The number so accused through fear or malice was large.

Female witches allegedly figured throughout the sub-Sahara. They occurred all along the West Coast, in East Africa and in South Africa. Male witches were comparatively rare. Some witches were normal women who had acquired witchcraft by intent. Some were born to be witches. We even hear of unfortunates upon whom had fallen the supernatural power to harm others and who sought to be rid of it, as a curse. Typical of those who voluntarily became witches might well be a frustrated woman of nervous or hysterical nature seeking to get even with her world and influenced and instructed by other women proficient in the malevolent art to do damage by thought and action. The women born to witchery were believed to be only semi-human. They had, tucked in their insides, an inherited physical peculiarity, a substance that could be discovered by native post-mortem, sometimes described as "a dark bloody-looking mass" in the abdomen.

But witches looked and at most times behaved just like other females. Nobody could be sure, could feel safe, lest neighbor or relative or wife might be a witch. Nerves quivered and gossip reveled. Accusations sprang both from sincere suspicion and from jealousy or quarrels. Sickness, accidents, deaths—especially the deaths of children—set folk to witch-hunting. A barren wife suspected a co-wife. A husband could ask divorce, citing as cause that his wife was a witch, and could obtain return of the bride wealth he had paid to her family.

The witch was a double peril. She could by her very conviction of her own malignant power shock the nerves of her victim. Sometimes this was her only weapon and her attack was purely psychic. To her victim her unseen power was frighteningly real. "The African belief in witchcraft," says Dr. Lucy Mair, "closely parallels the Christian belief in the Devil." In addition her attack upon her already nerve-weakened victim would sometimes be combined with the actual tools of her business.

The incidental equipment might include direct poisoning or the use of noisome stuff. And she was in various tribal rumors and accusations held capable of many fantastic acts. She had, for example—I offer two of the queerest items I have noted—an appetite and ability for remote cannibalism, the far-off witch eating the victim's inner force and causing death; or she performed night flights on strange steeds, even on the backs of flies.

Fatal poisonings were sometimes attributed to the mystic powers of witches when they were in reality routine crimes or the acts of feminine amateurs, usually women who wanted to get rid of their husbands.

Africa was a place of remarkably inventive and dexterous poisoning. There was the Nubian substance, "one grain of which was strong enough to kill ten men in less than a quarter of an hour, but if given to one man alone made him expire instantly." (From Leo Africanus.) There were in the center of the western Sudan villages in wartime poison arrows soaked in a hollow log in a concoction so virulent—it was made from the flowering vine *Strophanthus sarmentosus* and affected the heart—that a wound from the arrow might cause immediate death. Or the quick thumbnail flip of poison powder into an enemy's drink, or the finger, poison under the nail, that artfully slipped into the calabash as it passed along to the chosen victim. Or there was the knife used for splitting a fruit or carving a hunk of meat which had a fatal dose on one side only, the side served to the hated guest.

Women excelled in the discovery of poisonous plants. In ancient times women sought for edible growing things while the men hunted. They made experiments, sometimes disastrous, always instructive, and in the grim art of poison brewing, as well as in the jovial business of brewing native beer, the women were wise and accomplished.

"They are taught poisoning as a matter of course at the young girls' academies!" an old-time European colonist told me. He was referring irresponsibly but with sincere conviction to the female secret societies' instructions for girls. The anthropologist-nun, Sister Marie-André of the White Sisters, tells how poison information was passed in secret from knowing mothers to their daughters, and how some-times at night people may listen to the pestle thumping indicative of the pounding of noxious powder by some unknown and intended for someone of the village.

Leo Africanus mentions cynically that even the simplest woman is familiar all across Africa with the properties of the *addad* root, which can kill a man in less than an hour.

But these were normal criminals, killing for gain or revenge, not persons of the abnormal nature of witches. Poison was but a minor part of the witch's outfit. Primarily the great weapon and the weak-ness of the witch, her destruction of others and her own punishment, were both psychological. The witch traded on fear and was herself affrighted.

The development and growth of witchcraft in Africa were a mani-festation of Africa's imaginative reaching into the unknown, of the intense undisciplined thinking of people without books—for the writing down of thoughts is a laxative for the brain—which used women as the prime instrument. Indeed witchcraft, as it affected the witch and as it affected the bewitched, was a sort of dramatizing of social sentiment—the revolt of the unlucky, the underdog, and the tormenting of the fortunate—a sort of primitive attempt at equali-zation which called in as its aids not alone poison but a war of nerves, even hypnotism.

The mass of pagan Africa's female population were normal women, laborious wives, affectionate mothers and decent neighbors. But such exceptional activities of the African woman as I have mentioned—her occasional power as a war leader, her capacity for crime, her cold practicality toward handicapped children and the innate witchery sometimes attributed to her—do not present an all-over pretty aspect of dainty and romantic femininity. What they do give is an indica-tion of the attainment by women and their acceptance by society as a strong and vigorous element. They show that pagan Africa did not expect its women, as a matter of course, to be squashy, and that the women had no readiness to be squashed.

It is interesting to note and difficult to explain how different was the lethargic position imposed upon and accepted by women in northern Africa, where a woman passed her life cloistered within her home—or if she went outside its doors was obligatorily concealed behind a veil—and lived a purely domestic life, occupying rather the place of a house pet than that of a member of the general public.

Legally in Islam "women had no power whatever. Men control their actions." Judges, whose duties also included supervising the property of the insane and orphans, had the responsibility of "the marrying of marriageable women without guardians." These quotations are from Ibn Khaldun, who was for a time professor of Islamic jurisprudence at Cairo.

Mohammed loved women with a widespread enthusiasm which caused grins and frowns in the non-Moslem world, and traditionally asserted that he "liked best women, perfume and prayer" (listed in this order), but Mohammed did not set women free. And the women seem to have shown no disposition to try to free themselves, at least those who dwelt in cities. The country people and the very poor were of necessity less closely imprisoned. It was clearly impossible to cloister the womenfolk of tent dwellers, and some tribes ignored the veiling custom. All this refers to conditions in the pre-colonization days. The situation in northern Africa has changed of late.

The Koran has a sura entitled "Women," the tone of which is kindly but not encouraging to their self-confidence except in the matter of their sex desirability. Yet a very sympathetic understanding of women is traditionally shown by its author. The Islamic Paradise, where men enjoyed the company of beauteous damsels "whom no man shall have deflowered," is in the Koran and seems to depict a man's Heaven. To this Mohammed is supposed to have appended a consolation to Moslem's womenfolk. These beauteous damsels of Paradise were once dutiful wives on earth, perhaps elderly and ignored, but when admitted to Paradise "their gray hair and their watery eyes were wiped away and Allah remade them into virgins." So some patient old lady on earth could enjoy dreams. She could picture the return of beauty, a second and unending honeymoon in the ideal setting of luscious fruits and rivers of wine and clarified honey, with the satisfaction of displaying her charms to all and even the fun of chatting and flirting with pleasing strangers, which had been so sternly forbidden to her in her earthly existence.

The sura "Women" starts off by authorizing a man to have up to four wives. Just as among sub-Saharan pagans, there were in northern Africa many who married only once, or who had only one wife at a time. Divorce and repudiation were available but made difficult by Islamic legalities and by money complications—the discussions as to the return of the bride payment or the completion of gifts of marriage promised to the bride.

The breaking up of a Moslem marriage in northern Africa was not the simple matter of a husband saying three times a certain Arabic phrase, as it is represented by storytellers and sometimes by serious writers. It was a sober and lengthy business, as it is elsewhere, plus certain formalities as to her obligatory residence in his house for a set term, he forbidden to see her. There is a sura in the Koran entitled "Divorce," which outlines the rules of procedure. When France controlled so much of northern Africa there were learned studies made of the local repudiation and divorce rules—there is a difference between the two, although the Koran lumps the instructions under the sole title "Divorce." Particularly careful is a chapter in *La Condition de la femme musulmane dans l'Afrique du Nord*, which the esteemed historian Ernest Mercier published in Algiers in 1895.

Divorce at her desire was available to the wife for several causes and seems to have been rather generous toward her. Repudiation was exclusively the husband's perquisite, but a costly luxury to him since it entailed financial sacrifices with regard the dowry payable to the wife. The possibility of repudiation made a woman's position precarious. The Moslem law spoke loftily of her financial rights, but there must have been slips. The spendthrift husband, the deceased or non-responsible father, her own complete inexperience in life outside the home walls, her inability to work for her livelihood, the isolation which had deprived her of any male acquaintance who might have offered her aid or a chance to remarry—her prospect was sometimes bleak. We hear of repudiated wives who had to live on in what must have been friction, humiliation and even degradation in the ex-husband's house.

Life could offer more to a concubine than to a legitimate wife. This might disturb the moralist. But we must remember that the concubine was not a naughty girl, but the victim of circumstance. She was usually a girl captive, part of war's booty or a bought slave, perhaps a Negress, perhaps a European Christian maiden, prize of the Corsairs. She had no choice but to become her master's bedmate if he desired her.

Once she was chosen as his concubine there opened before the girl, black or white, pagan slave or European captive, interesting possibilities. If she bore her master a child her future was assured. She was no longer a salable slave. She was officially "Mother of the Child." At her master's death she was set free. Very naturally, pregnancy was her goal.

Judging by the number of northern African royal persons who are recorded in history as having been mothered by Negress slaves or captive Christian women, we can assume that concubinage was a wide and general habit. Among royalties was Mostansir, Egypt's ruler for sixty years, son of a Sudanese slave. The Idrisid dynasty of Morocco was physically continued and wisely upheld by Kinza, the Berber captive girl.

The exotic sweetheart was enticing. The African historian al-Marrakechi gives us an indication that she also had a practical appeal to the pocketbook. He tells about the contemporary Moroccan sultan who took the name of Al Mansur, meaning "The Victorious," after having gloriously defeated the Christians in the battle of Alarcos. (The sultan himself, by the way, was a concubine's child—some say of a Christian slave; some make her "a Negress who had been given to his father," which seems more likely since he is described as of dark complexion, with black eyes.) After Al Mansur's victory the Christian female booty was so numerous that Moslem parents were obliged to "gift wrap" their daughters, offering jewelry and treasure to catch a bridegroom. "Otherwise," says al-Marrakechi, "they could not marry off their daughters. So many Christian girls were available for purchase so cheap nobody would marry a free woman except she had a big dowry."

One of the Christian concubines later got herself and her name— "Habib, a woman of high class with great intelligence"—into Arabic pages (*Kartas*) by concealing the death of her royal husband and bribing the military to proclaim as sultan her son of fourteen. His half-brother and successor was also concubine-bred, son of "a Nubian slave," and was described as a mulatto.

A racial assortment of concubines presumably was enjoyed by such of non-royalty as could afford extensive harems. The dark skins sometimes observed among North Africans carry visible record of maternal importation from beyond the Sahara. We do not know what effect the pagan mother may have had on mind and spirit, and we can only guess what was the mental heritage from the Christian captive mothers.

The notion that a European girl captured by pirates could rise to harem majesty and mother sultans-to-be tickled Europe's fancy. The alleged experiences of one such victim-heroine, an eighteenth-century Irish girl named Betty Thomson, was told in the *Cork Examiner* not so long ago (condensed in *The Irish Digest*, 1940). I have not checked this story.

It would seem that the life of the concubine in Moslem northern Africa offered to a lucky concubine a certain security, and even the possibility of brilliant surprises not available to the legitimate wives, whose days were dull and sometimes insecure.

The contrast between this subhuman way of living cooped up indoors through a precarious lifetime and the laborious, occasionally violent life of the sub-Saharan and Saharan women is striking. The supine submissiveness on the one hand, their readiness to hide themselves from the outside world, is startlingly different from the brisk self-confidence of the others. It is a psychological puzzle, for the difference lay not only in the treatment society enforced but in the character of the women who submitted.

The position cannot be attributed solely to the Islamic attitude toward women.

Some of the sub-Saharan and Saharan women were Moslems and yet were lusty and vigorous. The Tuareg women were the unveiled sex, and I have mentioned the dominant position of the females of Mauritania. Many of the women in Moslem tropical regions were unveiled and non-secluded. They were quite free in practically all of West Africa except for the inland part of Nigeria. There in the latter part of the fifteenth century a powerful ruler of Kano began the custom of wife seclusion. He had theories of his own about the rightful status of women. He had a thousand wives, and he introduced the sport of girl-catching, sending messengers to dwellings in the neighboring countryside to capture "every first-born virgin for him." (From Kano Chronicle.) The custom of secluding women was followed locally, especially among groups of standing where slave labor made wives unnecessary in agricultural work and wives could be tucked away without economic loss.

It is interesting to read a violent attack upon the oppressive treatment of Nigerian Moslem women: "Men treat these beings like household implements," wrote Osman dan Fodio, the Fulani conqueror. He claimed education for them, not education in the reading and writing sense but instruction in Islamic matters: "the articles of the Law which concern them," so that they should no longer be "like beasts," knowing nothing but housework. In clamoring for the rights of women Osman dan Fodio may have been influenced by observing the vitality of womankind in other parts of the sub-Sahara. He had traveled and his forebears were from western regions.

In contrast at about the same time Lane noted in his widely read description of Egypt as he saw it (it was recently in its ninth edition) that the education of girls was practically nil and that few were even taught to say their prayers.

If the wide gap between northern Africa's female position and that of women in most other parts of the continent cannot altogether be laid to the influence of Islam, it is also clear it was not just a racial matter, the difference between the white and the Negro temperaments, for some of the Saharan and sub-Saharan people were white Berbers. Nor was it the result of invading Arab stock; a considerable proportion of the population in northern Africa remained Berber. The coming of the Arabs was a dramatic chapter, but it contributed only a part of the racial mixture.

It is true that northern Africa, according to the Arabic system, viewed the family as a fabric carried from father to son while the sub-Sahara often, but not always, employed the opposite, the matrilineal system, and that very naturally the matrilineal system gave women prestige. I cannot think this was a determining factor between female freedom and veil-wearing seclusion.

The matrilineal way was carried along from primitive times, when people did know for certain that women produced the babies but were still unaware that men also did their part in the process. Delafosse found that even in his day, in the early part of this century, there was "a fairly wide spread belief that women could conceive without having any dealings with a man," this artificial insemination being the work of a spiritual essence.

The matrilineal system was maintained by many tribes which had long since become too wise to ignore the facts of procreation. Common sense suggests that both the patrilineal and the matrilineal systems were in error, a child being the offspring of both parents.

In sub-Saharan Africa, which made an excessively severe business of family relations, the genealogical systems, like the tribal complications, greatly tangled with the rules as to who should marry whom.

We, who classify incest under a few simple heads and suffer only occasional interference from our relatives officially, do not guess what family restrictions, obligations and troubles can be.

The avoidance of what pagan Africa considered to be incest was a delicate problem, and the ramifications of family relationships which made this or this marriage improper—indecent—were almost unbelievably complex. Such inhibitions could scarcely go further than this instance, reported from the Dinka of the Sudan: "I have heard of a case in which a father, anxious to marry his daughter to someone else, argued that she could not marry the young man by whom she was already pregnant, since the pregnancy made them relatives." This is not a bit of whimsicality invented by a random traveler but an item in one of the contributions to *Studies in Kinship and Marriage*, published by the Royal Anthropological Institute of Great Britain in 1963, its author a careful student of the Dinka and author of a book about their religious psychology, Godfrey Lienhardt.

Usually less fantastic but very complex and weighty were the marriage prohibitions for family reasons across pagan Africa, where the family—ancestors, progeny and proper mating—was so close a part of life, most especially in pre-colonial times. The subject of kinship and its effect on marriage has been studied intensively and extensively by modern social anthropologists. It does not fit into the scope of this book. Some of the important writings about it are mentioned in my list of books read—and awe-inspiring reading it has been.

Sub-Sahara has largely conserved the old matrilineal system of tracing the family through the mothers. The patrilineal system of Moslem Africa is familiar to us in a simplified aspect, in the name each of us wears: the son and the daughter of the marriage of John Smith and Mary Robinson are known, he as Mr. Smith and she as Miss Smith until she marries and is called Mrs. Brown. North Africa's Moslem males carried the patrilineal sentiment more obviously in a string of their forefathers' names held together by "ibns."

The Moslem lady bore also her father's name, bore it behind a veil which to the public made her an anonymous phantom.

The use of the veil was of debatable value to the woman veiled. Mohammed's opinion was that "a veil which falls low [i.e. covered her bosom as well as her face] was a protection against affront." A woman might be delighted at the assurance that her charms so glowed that she must hide herself lest men at the sight of her would lose their self-control and violate her honor. The concealment of her face was regarded as especially important, more important than the hiding of her body. Lane says that in Egypt a woman "who cannot be persuaded to unveil her face in the presence of a man will think it but little shame to display the whole of her bosom." This presumably under special circumstances indoors. Indoors and in the family circle woman doffed her sex camouflage and wore flimsy garments.

The Koran gives carefully a list of such males as might be permitted to inspect her veil-less: her husband, of course, her father and her sons, the sons of her sisters, her husband's father, her husband's sons (by other marriages) her brothers and their sons. Mohammed considered it permissible for women who had passed the menopause to lay veils aside. However, if they retain them "it will be better for them." Perhaps few women cared to advertise their age and to admit that they were no longer provocative.

The careful packing of her form before a woman ventured abroad —in Egypt a black mantle to the ground over long trousers, in western North Africa a white full-length cover, sometimes leaving only one eye visible—amazed early European travelers. In Egypt under Turkish dominion no woman, not even a European woman, could appear out of doors uncloaked and unveiled. In the Middle Ages a scandal upset Cairo. There was an earthquake at the start of the fourteenth century, and women were imprudent enough to rush out into the streets unveiled.

Nowadays northern Africa, Egypt to Morocco, has changed. There are few veils. Women grow independent. This loosening of feminine restrictions and uprising of feminine energies must have been in the air since early colonization days. Several women stood out in the annals of Algerian resistance to the French conquest. One became famous. She was Lalla Fatima, who was "the soul of the insurrection against France" in the 1850's. (I quote from the historian Gsell.) But this happened in the Kabyl Mountains, where woman's lot differed from that in the cities.

Sometimes I wonder whether female bondage was as absolute as represented. Here and there we strike incidents that seem to contradict the idea of a completely downtrodden sex without self-confidence, whose only contacts—husband and close family members aside—were those they encountered when they streaked back and forth on rooftops to gossip with one another. Even Mohammed's own wife Ayesha, who had been a bride at nine, played an important public role.

I find one item which shakes our belief in the rigid Moslem feminine discipline. It concerns a familiar explorer, Vasco da Gama, and is recounted in a Portuguese record written shortly after it happened. On Vasco da Gama's second voyage (1502) to the Orient he visited Kilwa, which had been the ancient entry of Moslems to East Africa, Islam's Plymouth Rock on the Indian Ocean. At Kilwa, da Gama threatened the king and scared the population, and over two hundred of the local women, encouraged perhaps by sailors on shore leave, apparently turned traitor.

Here is what happened—I quote from the Portuguese narrative, *Lendas da India,* translated by Lord Stanley and included in Freeman-Grenville's anthology on East Africa: "In the city there were some beautiful women who, on account of having been shut up by the Moors, from their custom of being very jealous, were very captive and ill-treated. For this reason many fled and came to the Portuguese, who took them secretly on board the ships and kept them in strict concealment. All these women asked to be made Christians, as they would rather be captives of the Christians than wives of the Moors."

Vasco da Gama may have doubted the sincerity of their Christian longings. Certainly he doubted that two hundred beautiful women could ride upon his ships without destroying discipline. So he sent them ashore with a message to the already badgered king to the effect that should the Portuguese, upon their return voyage from India, ascertain that any injury had been done the women because of their escapade he, da Gama, would destroy Kilwa.

The king sent criers through the city to invite any man whose women were missing to come to the palace and fetch them away and not to punish them. All except forty husbands came and reclaimed their traitresses.

The story seems to show Moslem feminine discipline in a remarkable light. Even admitting that great pressure was put upon the Kilwa husbands, it seems to suggest that both in the facility and courage of their escape and in their re-establishment at home again this group of wives were indeed free and well treated. One doubts that, reversing the case, a group of sixteenth-century European women could have left home to embark on the ships of foreigners and non-Christians of a different race—say Mohammedans from black Africa—and have been subsequently received back and forgiven. But in considering the incident as a side light on Islam's attitude toward women, we must bear in mind that it all happened in East Africa and not in northern Africa.

In northern Africa women have been unlucky. It is a coincidence that an awkward and fussy attitude toward both women and sex relations existed in the same piece of geography since the days of early Christianity.

The Christian attitude was quite different from the attitude of the Moslems. We wonder what was the reaction of northern Africa's population—especially of the women, who were the more intimately affected—to the sudden social change when Islam almost overnight ejected Christianity and its theories.

Christianity had viewed idealistically and had tried to teach its followers to believe that the sex act was something of a misdemeanor and even that the sex difference was in itself an unfortunate heritage from the original sin. In Egypt monasticism was launched in a big way, holy men even castrated themselves to avoid temptation. Across northern Africa chastity, male and female, was advocated. From the time of Algeria's St. Augustine comes down to us a typical attitude toward women. If marriage—which in itself was not regarded with enthusiasm and was to permit sex relations for the purpose of procuring children—did not exist, so much sooner, offspring lacking, would come the miraculous and glorious end of the world.

Presumably only the most pious of the Christian flock were sincerely impressed by this lofty thinking, but it was a part of the social sentiment of the region, an atmosphere which must have created a certain antagonism toward women and caused a shaking of feminine self-confidence.

Sex, which they represented, was a naughty necessity, needful for procreation.

Came Islam with its openly expressed delight in the sex act and its indifferent acceptance of the partner as a negligible personality, so that again, all over again, women wore moral leg irons and again suffered a blow to human natural pride.

A brutal estimate of femininity was the Moslem interpretation that vessels in a dream mean women, "because they are receptacles." This was not a crude jest of the vulgar but an item by Ibn Khaldun on the science of dream interpretation.

This by no means meant that the males of the Moslem world despised sex and regarded sex relations as degrading. On the contrary, in their philosophical and psychological studies they exalted the sex act for its pleasure, its relief to male nerves and its benefits to morale and health. "He has been acclaimed as the greatest Moslem after Mohammed," says Dr. Montgomery Watt in his recent book about Ghazali, *Muslim Intellectual*. Ghazali declared that the satisfaction of what he called natural needs did not turn a man's heart from important or sacred things, instancing that a Revelation (i.e. a part of the Koran) came down to Mohammed while he was in bed with his wife Ayesha. The Prophet's "noble sense of justice and his virile powers," so Ghazali says, "caused him on occasion to have intercourse in swift succession with all his nine wives." Ayesha is cited as stating that he effected such a marital marathon in a single night, or one single morning.

In another passage Ghazali compares Mohammed and Jesus, who to his religious teaching was not God but an important prophet, wondering why Jesus abstained from marriage while Mohammed had multiple wives, and—if I correctly understand the meaning of the passage—finding in the comparison the indication of Mohammed's superiority. "What may trouble the brook cannot trouble the immense sea." (This and the previous Ghazali quotes are from *Ihya*. They are given at length in G. H. Bousquet's *La Morale de l'Islam et son éthique sexuelle*.)

The classifying of Moslem women as something like second-class humans caused Europeans to declare in the days of old that Islam denied women souls, meaning presumably that to Moslem women there was offered no prospect of immortal life. This was a misunderstanding. A traditional promise of Mohammed's, mentioned a few pages back, which the sura, "The Inevitable" seems to confirm was to the effect that good wives would go to Paradise and be again young and pretty companions in the male love life of the hereafter. So Islam's women did possess immortal souls, but in Paradise, as upon earth, the feminine function was sexually utilitarian.

The strip of geography of northern Africa, Egypt to the Atlantic, contrasted with the rest of the continent. It carried along throughout our era an atmosphere that was not favorable to women's vigor and self-confidence.

Pagan Africa and much of the sub-Sahara and Sahara that was Islamized gave women a good and a healthy life, granting always that we can swallow the pill—a bitter pill to us—of that polygamy, which all Africa shared.

One may reflect upon what may have been the progressive effects mental, physical and emotional, upon the respective offspring during many generations of maternal isolation from general society in contrast to the mother's free outdoor life.

SURVIVAL OF THE WOMAN SYMBOL · Two female qualities, physical qualities, influenced Africa from long before our era until yesterday.

One of these was typified by the very ancient representations of pregnant women, in whose ample form primitive people took an interest so great as to verge on reverence, and whose instinctive conservation would seem to show Africa's continued appreciation of woman's mystic import, which our civilization takes for granted.

The other preserves in the form of pagan Africa's favorite coinage what is in intent a tribute to the delights of love, a form whose charm suggests the open door to sexual joy.

Both offer themselves to our notice in a fashion almost grotesque, but if we reconsider them with gentleness we discern in them a tribute to woman, uncouth but far more profound than anything in art or poesy, something very real.

The primitive representations of pregnancy were often monstrous, showing sometimes a huge, squatting, legless body, or one with colossal breasts, or even garnished with a multitude of breasts in festoons. They were the first tangible expression of humanity's religious impulse, the adoration of fecundity, the bewilderment and awe before the mystery of birth, the cult of the Great Mother. They have been found almost everywhere in the world, and many in Africa. Leakey found them. Rock paintings show females with nobly borne bellies and buttocks. The art of Punic Carthage included bottle-shaped figures, which seemingly are the symbol of pregnancy. And most especially did these cult objects appear in Egypt, where Petrie found steatopygous figurines, which he dated to some seven thousand years B.C.

The cult as such waned in Africa, but survived across the ages as a delight in the amplitude of actual females. It was a continued recognition of the mystic image, the woman fat with child. Plumpness, a sort of pseudo pregnancy, enticed male admiration and desire. It was the symbolic woman, the prime passion rouser.

So Africa's females came to imitate what had been worshipped, women emulated in a modified form the ancient and long-forgotten idols. The idol became a fashion plate. In many regions of Africa women sought by special diets or even by drugs to put on billowing flesh or to develop protruding rumps, some were still so seeking into recent years.

It seems significant that the first fat actual female indiviual—not a figurine but a living woman—of whom we have knowledge should be the first of all Africa's women ever to appear by name in recorded history, Egypt's females aside. (Egypt's tastes then ran to leaner forms.) She was Eti, wife of King Perehu of that part of "The Divine Land" of Punt, which was probably situated in Somali, and an almost photographically convincing likeness of her was made by the Egyptian recorders who saw her, and was until not long ago an item in the remarkable series of reliefs portraying the Punt expedition. But an avid modern admirer of the voluptuous female form raided the Deir el Bahri Temple and stole the block in question off the wall. The Egyptologist Mariette saw it in its place and included it as one of the plates in his *Voyage dans la Haute Egypte* (1878), so that we know what Eti was like. She was plump all over and had immensely heavy thighs and calves and haunches, which show through a transparent skirt.

Twenty-eight centuries later and from farther down the East Coast, Marco Polo gives us a secondhand report of female fatness: "The women of Zanzibar have breasts four times bigger than those of other women." "The Marco Polo of the Arabs," Ibn Battuta, saw for himself the fat ladies of the Sahara: "Nowhere in the world have I seen any women to equal these in stoutness." They were, he says, "the most shapely in figure of all women." Another, El-Bekri, repeats what a traveler saw. It is a quaint and rather pretty picture of a young desert woman: "She was resting on her side—the position which they assume rather than to sit and thus compress the rounded part of their body—and a child amused itself by crawling under her waist and coming out the other side, so slim was her waist and so ample the lower part of her back." This young woman, given the local beauty standard, would have won the title of "Miss Sahara."

Some of the obesity tales which travelers told are rather horrifying. Two deal with females of rank, for fatness was in some regions a mark of status; it cannot have been the continuing adornment of a working woman, and was sometimes acquired temporarily by girls as a honeymoon charm. Speke in his search for the Nile source saw a princess so huge that she could not rise to her feet unaided. It took eight men to lift her. He offers the measurements which he himself took of one of these dames: 52-inch bust, 31 inches around the thigh. As far away across Africa as one can go, in Mauretania near the Atlantic, a French observer at the very end of the eighteenth century saw that the chief's wife required several strong men to hoist her to her kneeling camel and two men to support her when she walked.

These instances—and there are many others in Arabic geography and in the narratives of pre-colonization travelers—not only cover a wide spread of the continent but also mention variegated distribution of ampleness. Some, but not all, were of the steatopygous kind in which Bushmen took delight and which occurs frequently in the sub-Sahara. These fat females were called by Europeans by the ribald name of "Hottentot Venus," and were the subject of much jest. There was an alleged "Hottentot Venus" on show as a spectacle in England in 1810.

Various styles of obese women were noted among a variety of racial groups: Negro, Berber, Bushman, and even the Jewish women in northern Africa were "extraordinarily fat and deliberately so, for among them fat legs were considered a sign of great beauty." The Jewish consort of the ruler in eighteenth-century Tripoli was so stout that when she sat forth on muleback "five or six men always had to surround her to prevent her falling off."

So, as time passed, had an ancient cult merged into actuality, into a sensual image, the soft companion for nights of love. It was again a manifestation of Africa's art as performed upon the person—this was not scarification but aggrandizement, amplification.

The art carried its pains, but these were unavoidable. "Good-looking women were as nothing if they were not fat," according to a study of the social setup of the early nineteenth century, and on the Gold Coast of the same period one might see women "wearing a sort of cushion projecting from just below the small of the back, sometimes preposterously big." In Africa "thin women were discredited" was the cool judgment.

In coastal Nigeria there was the "Fatting House," which Mary Kingsley mentions, where damsels went through a course of pre-marital beautification by a heavy diet of greasy food, bodies covered with white clay to prevent perspiration. We read of other and cruel styles of altering nature's outlines by forcible feeding: "Little girls crying and rolling on the ground, even trying to throw up the milk they had been forced to drink," wrote Caillié in the Moslem Maure-tania part of his *Journal*. Speke witnessed "a sixteen-year-old girl sucking at a milk pot on which her father kept her at work by holding a rod in his hand."

Most startling of all was the risk of death taken by the Tuareg women. These Saharans felt a double delight in the plumpness of their women, for such not only pleased the eye and the touch but was also an outward mark of high prosperity, since to desert dwellers fattening food—in fact any food at all—was a luxury. So Tuareg women would absorb with precautions doses of the poison *falezlez*, a plant which if eaten greedily by an animal can blow it up like a balloon and kill it inside a few hours. The Tuareg woman would take it several times running with a meal and in very small quantities, with afterward a nap. After several treatments plumpness was attained, but at great risk.

In sub-Saharan Africa the attraction of the well-bolstered female still maintains. A Liberian newspaper advertised recently a patent medicine with the enticing words, "Would you like to increase your weight ten, twenty, thirty pounds or more?" Such is the genteel approach of today to an artificial procurement of the modified form of female fleshiness which has gradually emerged from the ancient fertility cult. It is Africa's atavistic recall and adaptation of wo-man's greatness, the inherent tribute to fecundity.

The other symbol of female charm has had a practical role in

African life from antiquity until quite lately. This is the cowrie shell, the Concha Veneris, which has been called mankind's "first religious emblem," the first gentle conception of femininity. It became in tangible tiny form the most important and long-enduring coinage in sub-Saharan Africa.

The cowrie is believed to have charmed the African fancy in the days before our era, coming to the sub-Sahara from Egypt, later from Morocco and in the early days of colonization via European traders. Old Ghana swapped its gold for cowries. Cowries were currency from Lake Chad to the Atlantic and along the Niger basin from source to sea. In addition to its associated charm it was easy to handle, unlike salt, iron bars, etc. As with other currency, its value fluctuated. In earlier colonial times it began to take many little shells to equal a shilling or a thaler. Native merchants had the knack of counting them with phenomenal speed. Explorer Soleillet claims to have watched a pair of market women count 130,000 in less than an hour. Even as lately as World War I, when currency ran short, it is said that the return of the cowrie system was seriously considered. Nowadays the cowrie is a rarity and has its value like any old coin. I bought about a half dozen at In Salah from a Tuareg woman just before World War II and paid a quarter of a franc for each one.

The cowrie is about a half inch long, oval and white and smooth as fine china or smooth skin, split lengthwise, with a neat opening. In prehistoric times people found the form a delight. It was a sex symbol, the Concha Veneris, a replica in miniature of the door through which a child comes out into the world. It was an emblem of fecundity and of femininity. The appeal of the cowrie was universal, but there was something especially and particularly Africa's in the enthusiastic adoption of the cowrie as a coin, and it made their money sweeter.

Some pages back I posed the question, "How did Africa esteem its women?" and in a quick survey of the continent's attitudes have sought an answer. I think that Africa, though expressing herself in this regard in a fashion different from our own, showed that her women were esteemed very deeply because of a perpetual awareness of woman's profound importance. I quoted a native phrase, "Women are like God because they bear children," and Africans never forgot woman's almost divine function. Marry she must and have babies. Africa was the fruit of her tree, some trees rooted in walled gardens, some free and wild.

These women, those who fought and those who toiled and those of endless patience who lived in dim dark rooms and went abroad in veils, none seeing them and they seeing so much, hearing so much—the observers whom none observed, who saw and noted and remembered, the Private Eye of Moslem Africa—these women in their separate ways carried along Africa's destiny. Africa seems to have possessed an acute realization of the peculiar value of the female sex; it was perhaps the most intimate and the most especially characteristic element in all of Africa's thinking.

It seems right to conclude this attempt to understand a continent's thoughts and emotions, what it was in former days and what it inherits and carries forward, with a review of Africa's women, who were the heart and the continuance of the continent's life.

PAST ENTERS FUTURE

AFRICA'S MOOD AND MIND ARE CONFUSED AS, after a period of enforced inactivity and non-responsibility, she assumes, or hopes presently to assume, the charge of her own national lives and futures.
From the Mediterranean to the Cape of Good Hope she is in a condition of mental miscegenation. Into each African group has come
the massive presence of another race, another language, another religion and another code of behavior. A stranger and master with
accomplishments, possessions and self-assurance has roused both awe
and resentment.

Some in seeking to imitate the stranger's thinking, to acquire novel
skills and a new learning, have lost spontaneity and in part forgotten or stuffed into the back of the mind the old thoughts of the

African heritage. These, the vigorous, the seekers, are the offspring of this mental miscegenation and carry a mind that is partly that of mother Africa, partly of foreign fathering. Others seem to have passed through the colonial period uninfluenced, supine to authority, tenacious of Africa's thoughts.

In them all, in the bright and vigorous and imitative as well as in the supine mass, the mental matrilineal strain must be a strong heritage. Mother Africa cannot have been outbred in a fewscore years, and will presumably grow more potent in the future.

I have tried to delineate something of this heritage, mother Africa's role, what Africa was before her interesting short mating with Europe.

Europe's sojourn in the continent as a whole—there had been an assortment of minor European presences through the centuries and major occupations at Africa's top and bottom—was a short and strange experience to Africa's people.

If a map were a sentient thing that of the African continent would have been amazed at its sudden new self, laid off in portions, each tinted with a color representing a European nation, in many cases inscribed with a newly invented and unfamiliar name and sprinkled over with cities and landmarks called after European explorers, royalties and persons of renown: Stanley and Brazza, Victoria and Leopold and Albert and Rhodes, etc., while tribal regions were often reduced to anonymity and the tribes themselves often split in two or three by the slicing frontiers Europe had outlined.

The discomfort which Africa felt at some of the names applied to parts of the continent is shown in the brisk series of alterations made by new nations: Ghana, Mali, Malawi, Zambia, Tanzania, etc. Some regions have been under three different names within the memory of the older inhabitants.

The colonization and decolonization of Africa was one of History's greatest oddities. Europe's sudden impulse to rush into the continent and Europe's sudden decision to rush out again—both reasonable enough to Europe—will be remembered by Africa, now becoming history-conscious and scholarly, as an experience resembling the marvelous, a sort of magic happening. Europe's backward glance seems bewildered and often sad at the memory of so much effort and so many lives thrown away because History took the bit in its teeth and made the race for Africa compulsory and inevitable. I suspect that as a whole, colonization affected and scarred the morale of the colonist more than it altered, helped or harmed that of the colonized.

Colonialism's almost complete occupation of the continent came at the latter part of the last century, became with the aid of colonialism's twin sister, the "protectorate," complete—Liberia excepted—and lasted until Africa, the non-combatant in the struggle, emerged as the real victor of them all in World War II. The cynical name given to colonization, "The Scramble for Africa," needs no amplification. This wholesale and concerted desire for Africa was new, the desire itself, very old. She was the problem continent, enticing and dangerous since antiquity, sometimes seduced in one region or another, sometimes the bride of a lasting union, as when the Arabs came, sometimes ravished—always the world's strange bedfellow, with a mind and character of her own, somewhat of an introvert, the Island Africa, separated geographically and by some innate wish from the rest of the world, except now and then, when she has been the world's brilliant magnet.

It was an isolation which Europe's presence increased rather than lessened. By freeing Africa from the responsibility of self-government, handling its own foreign contacts and mingling with the rest of us it put the continent apart from the reality of a changing world and into a sort of purdah or era of old-fashioned spinsterdom under parental management. No freedom. No responsibility. No errors. Nothing done except routine jobs. Very safe and very soporific. Learning many new tricks and trades and acquiring sometimes education, but in a perpetual childhood of the spirit, under a usually benign but always numbing direction.

Her peoples, once conquest merged into pacification and colonial government was organized, were benevolently restrained from war except sometimes as individual soldiers of the colonial master, and so without war's emotional and physical and nervous stimulus and relief, which came to Europeans during the same period (1914 and 1939) and to which Africans, like other humans, had been accustomed. War, much as we prefer peace, is a purging of the spirit, a tonic and a tranquilizer.

Interregional peace was imposed. There were no more raiding and slave-capturing. Tribes were side by side, like livestock in a barn. Yet despite the roads which colonialism built—along with the other valuable disciplines and benefits it inaugurated, the suppression of cannibalism and human sacrifice, the religious and other teachings—the colonial system, under which rival European nations controlled and segregated one region from another, held Africans apart, often even from fellow tribesmen, reduced Africa's cohesion and entity. Travel across and up and down and the displacement of groups was pretty well reduced to the far journeys of a few Moslem pilgrims, Mecca-bound, or the traveling of exceptional youths in search of education or even the chance at a foreign university. Almost lacking were the old-time intertribal and interregional contacts which would have kept each section apprised of the problems and new thoughts of the other and stirred competitive striving—those contacts which were the newspapers of the bookless.

So the period while Africa was a continent of colonies was a mixture of opportunity and inhibition and restriction from which Africa emerged to find that the independence she had longed for is not all easy and gay and that, though she has acquired new knowledges and accomplishments, she is herself both weighed down and invigorated by the legacy of her past, the old ways of thinking and feeling—for her past was long and colonialism only a fleeting passage.

Some, like myself, may find Africa's instinctive repudiation of our modern civilization significant. Certainly it is interesting. These peoples all over Africa who accepted reluctantly and partially the ways of the modern world as a part of colonialism's dose were on the whole no dull savages but peoples of character, peoples who had been through a long past, submissive yet brave, with an ability to learn and a readiness to forget, capable of imaginative thinking, of creating art we have found inspiring, of building and administering wider empires than contemporary Europe knew.

It was the air of Africa which seems to have brought earth's first human to fruition. Once Africa's civilization along with that of her Near East neighbors left the rest of the world crawling behind her. Then the "African Clock" was far in advance. The same was true in the days of Carthage's traders and explorers, of Alexandria's

scientists. In early Christian times Africa was a—perhaps the prime
—center of theology. In the early Middle Ages, Africa was brilliant,
more brilliant than Europe was. The "Clock" was still ahead.

Then Africa quit, manifested no wish to keep step with the world's
progress, seemed to sense an instinctive repugnance for modern civilization, which was then in its infancy and which many of us now
begin to admit is becoming pockmarked with flaws.

Africa—we have called it laziness or retarded mind—wilfully
clung to her familiar, distinctive mental equipment. Her laziness,
if such it was, was a protection and a deprivation. She preserved her
own way of thinking, kept new and sometimes good things away.
Thus hers—except for the colonial interlude—has been a mind
resting while we have throbbed and clanged and perhaps overtired
ourselves.

As we stand today Africa has lost a great deal. The "African Clock"
began to run slow some centuries back and it still runs slow. But
that "Clock" has been a capricious thing and might again run fast.
Who knows? This, should it happen, will not be today or tomorrow.
Someday in the future Africa—which once was precocious while our
world lagged behind, which later curled up into a sort of nap while
we surged forward and which dozed her way through the rise of
modern progress, the dazzling alarms of modern civilization, Africa,
which has indeed rested while we churned and toiled and horrified
ourselves with fears bred by our own genius—someday Africa may
rouse herself and amaze a tired world.

APPENDIX
SUBJECT INDEX

A LIST OF READINGS · This, as explained in the Foreword, is not a bibliography. To attempt to offer a bibliography on the various aspects of my wide subject would be absurd. What follows is a partial record of the writings from antiquity to now which have been helpful or have seemed to me apropos.

Because so many phases of Africa's thinking and feeling come into this book I have divided the list of titles into groups according to subjects, leading off with a section called "The Background" which includes what this covering phrase suggests and which is followed by two other groups dealing respectively with the effects upon the continent of the three great religions from without which came to Africa, and with the religion, magic and philosophy which Africa's native minds evolved for themselves.

Other sections list works on subjects as distinct as the bodily alterations, both sexual and allegedly ornamental, for which Africa has had
a penchant, and the legends spread over the continent about the supposed actual presence in Africa of many Biblical and Koranic heroes.
At the end is a list of works about women in a polygamous society.

Sometimes the same book has been useful to me in dealing with two
or more different subjects. In such cases the book, when it reappears,
is designated in abbreviated form followed by reference to the previous
list where it was first mentioned in detail.

The editions indicated are those I myself own or have used in one of
the large libraries of America, England and France.

The spelling of proper names accords with that used by the various
authors, translators or editors of the volumes listed.

I—THE BACKGROUND

a—ARABIC

Abd al-Hakem, "Traditions anciennes relatives à l'etablissement des
    Musulmans en Afrique septentrionale" (de Slane's appendix no.
    1 to *Histoire des Berbères* by Ibn Khaldun, See below)
Abou Zakaria, *Chronique de,* tr. and notes Masqueray, Emile, Alger,
    1876
el-Bekri, Abou-Obied, *Description de l'Afrique Septentrionale,* tr.
    de Slane, Alger, 1913
Sultan Bello, *History of Tekrour* (in Denham, See List I c)
Edrisi, *Description de l'Afrique et de l'Espagne,* tr. Dozy and de Goeje,
    Leyden, 1866
Abou'l Fèda, *Vie de Mohammed,* tr. Desvergers, Alger, 1950
Ibn el-Ahmar, *Rawdat en-Nisrin,* tr. Ghaoutsi Bouali and Georges
    Marçais, Paris, 1917
Ibn al-Athir, a portion of his general history which deals with North

Africa (de Slane's appendix no. 5 to *Histoire des Berbères* by Ibn Khaldun, See below)

Ibn Battúta, *Travels in Asia and Africa,* tr. (excerpts) Gibb, H. A. R., London, 1929, and his issue of full text in progress, Cambridge University Press, 1956, 1962 (Full French translation, Dufrémery and Sanguinetti, Paris, 1854–74)

Ibn Jubayr, *Travels,* tr. Broadhurst, London, 1952

Ibn Khaldun (Khaldoun), *Histoire des Berbères,* tr. de Slane, Alger and Paris, 1925, 1927, 1934, 1956

———, *The Muqaddimah,* tr. Rosenthal, Franz, New York, 1958 (called also *Prolégemènes,* tr. de Slane)

Ibn Selim Aswani, extracts in Maqrizi in "Notices on Nubia," appendix to Burckhardt (See List I c)

al-Jahiz, Le Turc en selle (in *Historiens Arabes,* anthology, ed. Sauvaget, Paris, 1946)

Kati, Mahmoud and One of his Grandsons, *Tarikh el-Fettach,* tr. Houdas and Delafosse, Paris, 1913

Abd al-Latif, *Description de l'Egypte,* tr. de Sacy (quoted in Roncière, See List I d, and Lane-Poole, *History of Egypt,* See List I d)

Leo Africanus, *Description of Africa* (many translations and editions. I have used principally Schefer, based on Temporal, Paris, 1896–8)

Maqrizi, *Le Traité des Famines,* tr. Wiet, Gaston, Leiden, 1962

———, La Mosque al-Azhar (*Historiens Arabes,* anthology, ed. Sauvaget, Paris, 1946)

———, appendix to Burckhardt (See List I c)

El-Marrakechi, "Histoire des Almohades" (in *Anthologie de la littérature marocaine,* ed. Duquaire, Paris, 1943)

al-Masudi, (el Mas'ud) *Meadows of Gold and Mines of Gems,* tr. partial, Sprenger, Aloys, London, 1841 (Maçoudi, *Les Prairies D'Or,* tr. de Meynard and de Courteille, Paris, 1861

al-Moqaddasi, "Description d'al Fostat" (in *Historiens Arabes,* See above)

En-Naciri, "Histoire du Maroc," tr. de Graulle (in *Anthologie de la littérature marocaine,* ed. Duquaire, Paris, 1943)

En-Noweiri, "Conquête de l'Afrique septentrionale par les Musulmans" (de Slane's appendix no. 2 to Khaldun, *Histoire des Berbères*)

Ibn Fadl Allah al-Omari, *Masalik el Absar,* tr. and notes Gaudefroy-Demombynes, Paris, 1927

al-Oufrani, *Nozhat-Elhadi,* tr. Houdas, Paris, 1889

Roudh el-Kartas, author uncertain, tr. Beaumier, Paris, 1860

Es-Sadi, *Tarikh es-Soudan,* tr. Houdas, Paris, 1900

Siré-Abbas-Soh, *Chroniques du Fouta sénégalais,* tr. Delafosse, Paris, 1913

al-Zawari (in al-Omari, *Masalik,* See above)

Ez-Zayani, "La Garde Noire," tr. Houdas (in *Anthologie de la littérature marocaine,* ed. Duquaire, Paris, 1943

b—AFRICA'S HERITAGE FROM ANTIQUITY AND BEFORE

Apuleius, *The Golden Ass*

Bates, Oric, *The Eastern Libyans,* London, 1914

Breasted, James Henry, *Ancient Records of Egypt,* University of Chicago Press, 1908

Clark, J. Desmond, *The Prehistory of Southern Africa,* Harmondsworth, Middlesex, 1959

Cole, Sonia, *The Prehistory of East Africa,* Harmondsworth, Middlesex, 1954

Emery, W. B., *Archaic Egypt,* Harmondsworth, Middlesex, 1961

Frankfort, Henri, *Ancient Egyptian Religion,* New York, 1961

Frankfort, Henri and H. A. and Wilson, John, *Before Philosophy,* Harmondsworth, Middlesex, 1959

Gardiner, Sir Alan, *Egypt of the Pharaohs,* Oxford, 1961

Gsell, Stéphane, *Hérodote, textes relatifs à l'histoire de l'Afrique du Nord,* Paris, 1916

———, *Histoire ancienne de l'Afrique du Nord,* Paris, 1913–1929

Hadas, Moses, *A History of Rome as told by Roman Historians,* Garden City, 1956

Harden, Donald, *The Phoenicians,* London, 1963

Heliodorus, *Ethiopian Story,* tr. Sir Walter Lamb, London, 1961

Herodotus, Rawlinson translation

Leakey, L. S. B., *Adam's Ancestors,* New York, 1960

——, *The Progress and Evolution of Man in Africa,* Oxford University Press, 1961

Mariette-Bey, Auguste, *Voyage dans la Haute Egypte,* Cairo and Paris, 1878

McBurney, G. B. M., *The Stone Age of Northern Africa,* Harmondsworth, Middlesex, 1960

Petrie, W. M. Flinders, *A History of Egypt,* 1884, 1896, 1905

——, *The Making of Egypt,* New York, 1939

Pliny, *Natural History*

Sallust, *The Jugurthine War*

Strabo, *The Geography of*

Warmington, B. H., *Carthage,* Harmondsworth, Middlesex, 1964

Wheeler, Sir Mortimer, "First Light" (in *Dawn of African History,* ed. Oliver, R., Oxford University Press, 1961)

——, *Rome Beyond the Imperial Frontiers,* Harmondsworth, Middlesex, 1955

c—PRECOLONIAL AFRICANA

EUROPEAN WRITINGS

"Ali Bey," *Travels in Morocco, Tripoli, Egypt* . . . , Philadelphia, 1816

Alvares, Father Francisco, *Prester John of the Indies,* tr. Lord Stanley, revised and edited Beckingham and Huntington, Cambridge, 1961

Barth, Henry, *Travels and Discoveries in North and Central Africa,* London, 1857–58

Binger, Capitaine, *Du Niger au Golfe de Guinée,* Paris, 1892

Bowdich, T. Edward, *Mission from Cape Coast Castle to Ashantee,* London, 1873

Brown, Robert, *The Story of Africa and Its Explorers,* London, 1892–95

Browne, W. G., *Travels in Africa, Egypt and Syria,* London, 1799

Burckhardt, John Lewis, *Travels in Nubia*, London, 1819

Burton, Sir Richard, *A Mission to Gelele, King of Dahome*, London, 1893

———, *First Footsteps in East Africa*, London, 1924

Ca' de Mosto, Alvise, *Relation des voyages à la côte occidentale d'Afrique*, ed. Schefer, Paris, 1895

Caillié, René, *Journal d'un voyage à Temboctou et à Jenné dans l'Afrique centrale*, Paris, 1830

Cooley, William Desborough, *The Negroland of the Arabs*, London, 1841

Denham, Le Major, *Voyages et decouvertes dans le nord et dans les parties centrales de l'Afrique*, tr. Eyriès and de Larenaudière, Paris, 1826 (French translation of Denham and Clapperton, *Narrative of Travels and Discoveries*, London, 1826)

Durand, J. P. L., *A Voyage to Senegal*, London, 1806

Fernandes, Valentim, *Description de la côte d'Afrique de Ceuta au Sénégal*, ed. Monod, Théodore, Paris, 1938

Gibbon, Edward, *The Decline and Fall of the Roman Empire*, Milman-Smith edition, 1872; Bury edition, Chapters 16–20 and 36–43, New York, 1958

Hakluyt's Voyages, vols. III and IV, London, 1926

Horneman, F., Journal of F. Horneman (in vol. II, *Proceedings of the Association for Promoting the Discovery of the Interior Parts of Africa*, London, 1802)

Jackson, James Gray, *An Account of the Empire of Marocco*, London, 1809

———, *An Account of Timbuctoo and Housa* (by El Hadj Abd Salem Shabeeny), London, 1820

Jobson, Richard, *The Golden Trade*, Teignmouth, Devonshire, 1904

Joinville, *Chronicle of the Crusade of St. Lewis*, London, 1957

Laing, Maj. Alexander Gordon, *Travels in Western Africa*, London, 1825; also Laing's letter from Timbuctoo in *The Quarterly Review*, 1829

Lander, Richard, *Records of Capttain Clapperton's Last Expedition to Africa*, London, 1830

Lander, Richard and John, *Journal of an Expedition to Explore the Course and Termination of the Niger*, London, 1832

Lane, E. W., *Manners and Customs of the Modern Egyptians*, London, 1957

Laugier de Tassy, *Histoire du Royaume d'Alger*, Amsterdam, 1725

Lenz, Oskar, *Timbouctou, Voyage au Maroc, au Sahara, et au Soudan* (French translation), Paris, 1886

Leyden, John, *Historical Account of Discoveries and Travels in Africa*, Edinburgh, 1817

Linant, Adolphe, "Journal of a Voyage on the Bahr Abiad or White Nile" (in *Journal of the Royal Geographical Society*, London, 1832)

Lull, Ramón, *Blanquerna* (translation from the Catalan), London, 1926

Lyon, Capt. G. F., *A Narrative of Travels in Northern Africa*, London, 1821

Marmol, *L'Afrique de*, tr. D'Ablancourt, Paris, 1667

Mollien, G., *Voyage dans l'interieur de l'Afrique aux sources du Sénégal et de la Gambie*, Paris, 1820

Monteil, P. L., *De Saint-Louis à Tripoli par le Lac Tchad*, Paris, 1895

Morgan, J., *A Complete History of Algiers . . . interspersed with many curious Passages and Remarks not touched on by any other writer whatever*, London, 1731

Nachtigal, Gustave, *Sahara et Soudan* (French translation), Paris, 1881

Park, Mungo, "An Abstract of Mr. Park's Account of His Travels" (in vol. II, *Proceedings of the Association for Promoting the Discovery of the Interior of Africa*, London, 1802)

———, *The Travels of*, London, 1932

Petherick, John, *Egypt, the Sudan and Central Africa*, London, 1861

———, Mr. and Mrs., *Travels in Central Africa*, London, 1869

Rankin, F. Harrison, *The White Man's Grave, a Visit to Sierra Leone in 1834*, London, 1836

Richardson, James, *Narrative of a Mission to Central Africa*, London, 1853

———, *Travels in the Great Desert of Sahara*, London, 1848

Schweinfurth, Georg, *The Heart of Africa*, London, 1874

Shaw, Thomas, *Voyage dans la Régence d'Alger* (French translation), Paris, 1830

Speke, John Hanning, *Journal of the Discovery of the Source of the Nile*, London, 1922

Tully, *Narrative of Ten Years' Residence at Tripoli* (letters written by Richard Tully's sister-in-law), London, 1817

Windus, John, *A Journey to Mequinez and the Residence of the Present Emperor of Fez and Morocco . . . for the Redemption of British Captives, in the Year 1721*, London, 1725

d—MORE RECENT WRITINGS

Arcin, André, *Histoire de la Guinée Française*, Paris, 1911

Arkell, A. J., *A History of the Sudan*, London University, 1961

————, "The Valley of the Nile" (in Wheeler, *The Dawn of African History*, See List I b)

Baumann, H. and Westermann, D., *Les Peuples et les civilisations de l'Afrique; Les langues et l'education* (French translation), Paris, 1957

Beazley, C. Raymond, *The Dawn of Modern Geography*, London, 1897–1906

Bovill, E. W., *The Golden Trade of the Moors*, Oxford University Press, 1958

Continuity and Change in African Cultures, ed. Bascom, William R. and Herskovits, Melville J., University of Chicago Press, 1959

Coppet, Maurice de, *Chronique du règne de Menelik II* par Sellassié Guèbrè, notes and appendices by de Coppet, Paris, 1930–31

Cornevin, Robert, *Histoire de l'Afrique*, Paris, 1956

Crowder, Michael, *The Story of Nigeria*, London, 1962

Davidson, Basil, *Old Africa Rediscovered*, London, 1959

Delafosse, Maurice, *L'Ame Nègre*, Paris, 1922

————, *Civilisations Négro-Africaines*, Paris, 1925

————, *Haut-Sénégal-Niger*, Paris, 1912

————, *Les Nègres*, Paris, 1927

Doresse, Jean, *L'Empire du Prêtre-Jean*, Paris, 1957

Dubois, Felix, *Tombouctou la mystérieuse*, Paris, 1897

Duffy, James, *Portuguese Africa*, Harvard University Press, 1959

Duveyrier, Henri, *Exploration du Sahara, les Touareg du Nord*, Paris, 1864

———, *Journal de route*, Paris, 1905

Egharevba, Jacob U., *A Short History of Benin*, Benin, Nigeria, 1953

Ellis, A. B., *The Tshi-Speaking Peoples of the Gold Coast of West Africa*, London, 1887

———, *West African Sketches*, London, 1881

Fage, J. D., "States of the Guinea Forest" (in Wheeler, *The Dawn of African History*, See List I b)

Freeman-Grenville, G. S. P., *The East African Coast* (an anthology), Oxford, 1962

Gautier, E. F., *La conquête du Sahara*, Paris, 1935

———, *Moeurs et coutumes des musulmans*, Paris, 1931

———, *Le Passé de l'Afrique du Nord*, Paris, 1937

———, *Le Sahara*, Paris, 1928

Greenberg, Joseph H., *Languages of Africa*, Indiana University Press, 1963

Guernier, Eugène, *La Berbérie, l'Islam et la France*, Paris, 1950

Guthrie, M. and Greenberg, J. H. (in *Journal of African Languages*, London, 1962)

Herskovits, Melville J. and Bascom, William, ed., *Continuity and Change in African Cultures*, University of Chicago, 1958

Herskovits, Melville J., *The Human Factor in Changing Africa*, New York, 1962

Hitti, Philip K., *A History of the Arabs*, London, 1961

Hodgkin, Thomas, *Nigerian Perspectives, an Historical Anthology*, Oxford University Press, 1960

Horrabin, J. F., *An Atlas of Africa*, New York, 1960

Huntingford, G. W. B., "The Peopling of the Interior of East Africa" (in *History of East Africa*, ed. Oliver and Mathew, Oxford, 1963)

Huxley, Elspeth, *Four Guineas*, London, 1955

Johnston, Sir Harry H., *A History of the Colonization of Africa by Alien Races*, Cambridge University Press, 1899, 1913

Julien, Ch. André, *Histoire de l'Afrique du Nord*, Paris, 1931

Keppel-Jones, Arthur, *South Africa, a Short History*, London, 1961

Kimble, George, H. T., *Geography in the Middle Ages*, London, 1938

Kingsley, Mary H., *Travels in West Africa*, London, 1897

Kingsnorth, G. W., *Africa South of the Sahara*, Cambridge University Press, 1962

Labouret, Henri, *Histoire des Noirs d'Afrique*, Paris, 1946

Lane-Poole, Stanley, *Cairo*, London, 1898

————, *A History of Egypt in the Middle Ages*, London, 1901

Language in Africa, ed. Spencer, John, Leverhulme Conference on the Language Problems of Tropical Africa, Cambridge University Press, 1963

Lebeuf, Jean-Paul and A. Masson Detourbet, *La civilisation du Tchad*, Paris, 1950

Lewis, Bernard, *The Arabs in History*, New York, 1960

Malinowski, Bronislaw, *The Dynamics of Culture Change, an Inquiry into Race Relations in Africa*, Yale University Press, 1961

Marsh, Zoe, *East Africa Through Contemporary Records* (anthology), Cambridge University Press, 1961

Martin, A. G. P., *Quatre siècles d'histoire marocaine au Sahara*, Paris, 1923

Mathuisieulx, H. M. de, *A travers la Tripolitaine*, Paris, 1913

Meniaud, Jacques, *Haut-Sénégal-Niger, géographie économique*, Paris, 1912

Mercier, Ernest, *La population indigène de L'Afrique sous la domination romaine, vandale et byzantine*, Constantine, Algeria, 1896

Migeod, Frederick W. H., *A View of Sierra Leone*, London, 1926

Milne, J. G., *A History of Egypt under Roman Rule*, London, 1898

Monod, Théodore, *Méharées*, Paris, 1937

Moorehead, Alan, *The Blue Nile*, London, 1962

Orr, Capt. C. W. J., *The Making of Northern Nigeria*, London, 1911

Présence Africaine, Africa from the Point of View of American Negro Scholars, France, 1961

Reade, Winwood, *The African Sketch Book*, London, 1873

Roncière, Charles de la, *La découverte de l'Afrique au Moyen Age*, Cairo, 1924–27

Seligman, C. G., *Races of Africa*, London, 1930

Slade, Ruth, *King Leopold's Congo*, Oxford University Press, 1962

Soleillet, Paul, *Voyage à Ségou*, Paris, 1887

Talbot, P. Amaury, *In the Shadow of the Bush*, London, 1912

Terrasse, Henri, *Histoire du Maroc,* Casablanca, Morocco, 1949

Thomson, Oliver, *History of Ancient Geography,* Cambridge University Press, 1948

Ullendorff, Edward, *The Ethiopians,* Oxford University Press, 1960

Urvoy, Y., *Histoire de l'Empire du Bornou,* Paris, 1949

———, *Histoire des populations du Soudan Central,* Paris, 1936

Westermann, D., *Les langues et l'education,* (part 2 of Baumann and Westermann, See above)

Willis, A. J., *An Introduction to the History of Central Africa,* Oxford University Press, 1964

Wright, Richard, *Black Power,* New York, 1954

II—RELIGION AS IT AFFECTED AFRICA: THE NEWCOMERS WITH BOOKS

a—JEWISH DISPERSION, ACTUAL AND LEGENDARY, AND JEWISH INFLUENCE

Adler, Elkan Nathan, *Jewish Travellers* (anthology), London, 1930

Bainville, Jacques, *Bonaparte en Egypte,* Paris, 1936

Box, G. H., *Conflict in the Pre-Christian Period between Judaism and Hellenism,* London, 1929

Chronique de Za'ra Ya'eqob, tr. Perruchon, Jules, Paris, 1893

Dio Cassius, *Dio's Rome,* (Roman History) Troy, N.Y., 1905

Eldad the Danite," "The Letter of (in Adler, *Jewish Travellers,* See above)

Epstein, Isidore, *Judaism, a Historical Presentation,* Harmondsworth, Middlesex, 1959

Freud, Sigmund, *Moses and Monotheism,* New York, 1959

Hirschberg, H. Z., "The Problem of the Judaized Berbers," (in *Journal of African History,* 1963)

Hoonacker, A. van, *Une communauté Judéo-Araméenne à Eléphantine en Egypte au VIe et Ve siècles av. J.C.,* London, 1915

Ibn Khordadhbeh, (in Adler, See above)

Josephus, *Jewish Antiquities*, vol. VII, London and Cambridge, Mass., 1963

——, *The Jewish War*, Harmondsworth, Middlesex, 1959

Leslau, Wolf, *Falasha Anthology*, translated from Ethiopic sources, Yale University Press, 1954

Malfante, Antonium (in Roncière, See List I d)

Noth, Martin, *The History of Israel*, London, 1960

Obediah Jaré da Bertinoro, Letters of (in Adler, See above)

Parkes, James, *A History of the Jewish People*, Harmondsworth, Middlesex, 1964

Philo, quoted by Box, G. H., *Early Christianity and the Hellenic World*, London, 1929

Schloessinger, Max, *The Ritual of Eldad Ha-Dani*, Leipsig, New York, 1908

Slouschz, Nahum, *Travels in North Africa*, Philadelphia, 1927

Williams, Joseph, S.J., *Hebrewisms in West Africa*, London, 1930

Za'ra Ya'eqob, "Le livre de la lumière" (in *Chronique de Za'ra Ya'eqob*, See above)

In addition to the above there are in List I, "The Background," and among the items about Ethiopia in List II c, which follows, titles containing references to the presence, power and misfortunes of the Jews in Africa.

See especially in List I a, "Arabic"

El-Bekri

Edrisi

Ibn Khaldun, *Histoire des Berbères*

Kati

En-Noweiri

b—CHRISTIANITY, ITS FALL, ITS SURVIVALS

Biblical:

Isaiah ("The Suffering Servant")

Acts of the Apostles (See also C. H. Rieu's notes to his translation, Harmondsworth, Middlesex, 1958)

Ammianus Marcellinus (See Hadas, List I b)

St. Augustine, *The City of God*, vol. II, London and Cambridge, Mass., 1963

————, *The Confessions of*, London, 1959

Aurelius Victor (See Hadas, List I b)

Basset, Henri, *Essai sur la littérature des Berbères*, Alger, 1920

Basset, René, Les règles attribuées à Saint Pakhome (in *Mélanges Africaines et Orientaux*, Paris, 1915)

Bazin, René, *Charles de Foucauld*, Paris, 1934

Belzoni's "Operations and Discoveries in Egypt" (in *The Quarterly Review*, London, 1821)

Berard, M. (in *l'Algérie traditionelle*, ed. Certeux and Carnoy, Paris and Algiers, 1884)

Bissuel, Henri, *Les Touareg de l'Ouest*, Alger, 1888

Bouquet, A. C., *Sacred Books of the World*, Harmondsworth, Middlesex, 1959

Bousquet, G. H., "Judaisme, Christianisme et Islam" (In *Studia Islamica, XIV,* Paris, 1961)

Bousset, Wilhelm, "Gnosticism" (in *Encyclopaedia Britannica*, 11th ed.)

Briggs, Lloyd Cabot, *Tribes of the Sahara*, Harvard University Press, 1960

Budge, E. A. Wallis, Preface to *Egyptian Tales and Romances*, London, 1935

————, *Legends of Our Lady Mary, the Perpetual Virgin and Her Mother Hanna*, Oxford, 1933

————, *The Wit and Wisdom of the Christian Fathers of Egypt* (Based on *Anan Isho of Beth Abhe*), Oxford, 1934

Bultmann, Rudolf, *Primitive Christianity*, London, 1960

Butler, Dom Christopher, *The Church and the Bible*, London, 1960

Butler, Dom E. C., (in *Cambridge Medieval History*, vol. I, Cambridge University Press, 1913–34)

Cook, Stanley, *An Introduction to the Bible*, Harmondsworth, Middlesex, 1956

Cross, F. L., *The Early Christian Fathers*, London, 1960

——, Preface to *Jung Codex*, New York, 1955

Cyril of Jerusalem, "The Story of the Finding of the Cross" (tr. from a Coptic text, See Budge, *Egyptian Tales* above)

Daniélou, Jean, S.J., *Primitive Christian Symbols*, London, 1964

Doresse, Jean, *L'Evangile selon Thomas, ou les Paroles Sacrètes de Jésus*, Paris, 1959

——, *Les livres secrètes des Gnostiques d'Egypte*, Paris, 1958

Drower, E. S., *The Secret Adam, a Study in Nasoraean Gnosis*, Oxford, 1960

Enslin, Morton Scott, *Christian Beginnings*, New York, 1956

——, *The Literature of the Christian Movement*, New York, 1956

Forster, E. M., *Alexandria*, Garden City, N.Y., 1961

Foucauld, Père and Motylinski, A. de C., *Textes Touareg en prose*, Alger, 1922

Gibbon, Edward, *Memoir of My Life and Writings*, London, 1837

Grant, Robert M., *Gnosticism, An Anthology*, New York, 1961

——, *Gnosticism and Early Christianity*, Columbia University Press and Oxford University Press, 1959

——, *The Secret Sayings of Jesus*, Garden City, N.Y., 1960

Greenslade, S. L., *Schism in the Early Church*, London, 1964

Girardin, St. Marc, L'Afrique sous St. Augustin (in Masqueray's Introduction to *Abou Zakaria*, See List I a)

Gough, Michael, *The Early Christians*, New York, 1961

Grégoire, Henri, "The Byzantine Church" (in *Byzantium*, ed. Baynes and Moss, Oxford, 1961)

Grevin, Emmanuel, *Voyage au Hoggar*, Paris, 1926

Hagemonius, *Acta Archelai* (quoted by Jonas, see below)

Harnack, Adolf, *What is Christianity?*, New York, 1957

Hatch, Edwin, *The Influence of Greek Ideas on Christianity*, New York, 1957

Herklots, H. G. G., *How the Bible Came to Us*, Harmondsworth, Middlesex, 1959

Hervieux, Jacques, *What are the Apocryphal Gospels?*, London, 1960

Ibn Abd al-Hakam, (quoted by Hitti, See List I d)

Jonas, H., *The Gnostic Religion*, Boston, 1963

Leff, Gordon, *Medieval Thought from St. Augustine to Ockham*, Harmondsworth, Middlesex, 1958

Macquarrie, John, *The Scope of Demythogizing, Bultmann and His Critics*, London, 1960

Marrou, Henri, *St. Augustine*, London and New York, 1957

Meer, F. Van der, *Augustine the Bishop*, London and New York, 1961

Monod, Théodore (in *Journal of African History*, 1961)

Paul the Deacon (See Hadas, See List I b)

Pistis Sophia, a Gnostic Miscellany, Englished by G. R. S. Mead, London, 1921

Procopius, *Secret History*, University of Michigan Press, 1961

Puech, Henri Charles, "The Jung Codex and Other Gnostic Documents from Nag Hammadi" (in *The Jung Codex*, New York, 1955)

Quispel, Gilles, "The Jung Codex and its Significance" (in *The Jung Codex*, See Puech above)

Rodd, Francis Rennell, *People of the Veil*, London, 1926

Russell, Bertrand, *Why I am Not a Christian*, New York, 1957

Sharpe, Samuel, *Egyptian Mythology and Egyptian Christianity*, London, 1863

Sundberg, Albert C. Jr., *The Old Testament of the Early Church*, Harvard University Press, 1964

Theodosius, "On the Position of the Holy Land" (in Beazley, See List I d)

The Gospel According to Thomas (See Doresse, See Grant above)

Van Unnik, W. C., "The 'Gospel of Truth' and the New Testament" (in *The Jung Codex*, see Puech above)

Virgin Mary, "The History of, as Told by Her to Theophilus, Patriarch of Alexandria" (See Budge, *Legends*, above)

Virgin Mary, "The Narrative of, as Told by Herself to Timothy, Patriarch of Alexandria" (See Budge, *Legends*, above)

Wallace-Hadrill, D. S., *Eusebius of Caesaria*, London, 1960

Weiss, Johannes, *Earliest Christianity*, New York, 1959

On the survival of Christianity in Ethiopia See List II c which immediately follows.

c—"PRESTER JOHN" AND PORTUGAL: CHRISTIAN-ITY IN ETHIOPIA AND IN OLD CONGO

Almeida, M. E. de, "Historia de Ethiopia" (in appendix to *Chronique de Za'ra Ya'eqob,* See List II a)

Alvares, Fr. Francisco, *The Prester John of the Indies,* ed. Beckingham and Huntingford, Cambridge University Press, 1961

Amda Syon, *Histoire des guerre de,* tr. Perruchon, Jules, Paris, 1890

Barros, Joao de, "Chronique" (in Castro e Almeida, See below)

Beazley, C. Raymond, *Prince Henry the Navigator,* New York and London, 1895

Boxer, C. R., "The Old Kingdom of the Congo" (in Wheeler, *The Dawn of African History,* See List I b)

———, *Race Relations in the Portuguese Colonial Empire,* Oxford, 1963

———, "V. S. R. Welch and His History of the Portuguese in Africa" (in *Journal of African History,* 1960)

Budge, A. E. Wallis, *Legends of Our Lady* (See List II b)

———, *One Hundred and Ten Miracles of Our Lady Mary,* Oxford, 1923

Camoens, Luis Vaz de, *The Lusiads,* tr. Atkinson, Harmondsworth, Middlesex, 1952

Carli, Padre Dionigi, "Viaggio nel regno del Congo" (cited in Leyden, See List I c)

Castro e Almeida, Virginia de, *Les grands navigateurs et colons portugais du XVe et XVIe siècles* (anthology), Paris, 1934

Childs, Gladwyn Murray, "The People of Angola in the 17th Century, According to Cadornega" (in *Journal of African History,* 1960)

Davidson, Basil, *Black Mother,* Boston, 1961

Doresse, Jean, *L'Empire du Prêtre Jean,* Paris, 1957

Du Casse, le Sr., "Memoire d'Angola" (See Roussier, below)

Gama, Vasco da, "A Journal of the First Voyage of Vasco da Gama," tr. Ravenstein (in *Portuguese Voyages,* ed. Ley, See below)

Girard, Capt. Alexandre, "Souvenirs d'un voyage en Abyssinie" (in Coppet, See List I d)

Johnson, Dr. Samuel, *Rasselas, the Prince of Abyssinia,* London, 1759

Labat, J. B., "Relation de l'Ethiopie occidentale" (in Leyden, See List I c)

Lewis, I. M., "The Somalie Conquest of the Horn of Africa" (in *Journal of African History*, 1960)

Ley, Charles D., *Portuguese Voyages 1498–1663* (anthology), London, 1953

Lobo, Father Jeronimo, "A Voyage to Abyssinia," tr. Samuel Johnson (in *Portuguese Voyages*, See Ley above)

Major, Richard Henry, *Life of Prince Henry of Portugal*, London, 1868

Pankhurst, Richard, *An Introduction to the Economic History of Ethiopia*, Addis Ababa, 1961

Penrose, Boies, *Travel and Discovery in the Renaissance*, Harvard University, 1952

Rattray, Achille, *Abyssinie*, Paris, 1880

Resende, Garcia de, "Le Chronique du Roi Joao II" (in Castro anthology above)

Ross, Sir E. Denison, "Prester John and the Empire of Ethiopia" (in Newton, *Travels and Travellers of the Middle Ages*, London, 1926)

Roussier, Paul, *L'Etablissement d'Issiny, 1687–1702, Voyages de Du Casse et al. à la côte de Guinée*, Paris, 1935

Sellassié, Guèbrè, *Chronique du règne de Menelik II*, notes and appendices by Maurice de Coppet, Paris, 1930

Ullendorff, Edward, *The Ethiopians* (See List I d)

Vansina, Jan, "The Foundation of the Kingdom of Kasanja," (in *Journal of African History*, 1963)

———, "Notes sur l'origine du Royaume du Kongo" (in *Journal of African History*, 1963)

Yule, Col. Sir Henry, "Prester John" (in *Encyclopaedia Britannica*, 11th edition.)

———, *Cathay and the Way Thither* (revised by Henri Cordier), London, 1915

Chronique de Za'ra Ya'eqob (See List II a)

d—THE NAME "ETHIOPIA" CONFUSION

Delafosse, Maurice, *Haut-Sénégal-Niger* (See List I d)

Duveyrier, Henri, *Exploration* (See List I d)

Herodotus

Homer, *The Iliad*

Ibn Khordadhbeh (in Beazley, See List I d)

Marco Polo, *Travels*

Marmol (See List I c)

Paniagua, A. de, *Géographie mythique*, Paris, 1911

Thomson, *Ancient Geography* (See List I d)

Trevelyan, G. M., *Illustrated English Social History*, Harmondsworth, Middlesex, 1964 (Shows a map dated 1558 where the Atlantic at the Guinea coast is called the Ethiopian Sea)

e—ISLAM AND AFRICAN MOSLEMS

Abel, Armand (in *Classicisme et déclin culturel dane l'histoire de l'Islam*, an International Symposium, 1956, ed. Brunschvig and von Grunebaum, Paris, 1957)

Abou Zakaria (See List I a)

Amat, Charles, *Le Mzab et les Mzabites*, Paris, 1888

Andrae, Tor, *Mohammed, the Man and His Faith*, New York, 1955

Benjamin of Tudela (in Adler anthology, See List II a, and in Beazley, See List I d)

Bivar, A. D. H., "A Manifesto of the Fulani Jihad" (in *Journal of African History*, 1961)

Blachère, *Introduction au Coran*, Paris, 1959

Brunschvig, Robert, *Un Aspect de la littérature historico-géographique de l'Islam*, Cairo, 1945

Burton, Sir Richard, *Personal Narrative of a Pilgrimage to al-Madinah and Meccah*, London, 1893

Contouly, François de (in *Bulletin du Comité d'Etudes Historiques et Scientifiques de l'A.O.F.*)

Dachraoui, F., "Contributions à l'histoire des Fatimides" (in *Arabica*, Leyden, 1961)

Dermenghem, Emile, *Mohammed and the Islam Tradition*, New York, 1958

El Hadj Nacir ed Dine (Dinet, E.), *Le pèlerinage à la maison sacrée d'Allah*, Paris, 1930

Evans-Pritchard, E. E., *The Senusi of Cyrenaica*, Oxford, 1954

Gaudefroy-Demombynes, *Une lettre de Saladin au Calife Almohade*, Paris, 1925

———, *Le pèlerinage à la Mekke*, Paris, 1923

Ghazali (quoted by Bousquet, G. H., in *La morale de l'Islam et son ethique sexuelle*, Paris, 1963)

Gibb, H. A. R., *La structure de la pensée religieuse de l'Islam* (French translation), Paris, 1950

Goldziher, Ignaz, "Etudes Islamologiques," tr. Bousquet (in *Arabica*, Leyden, 1960 and 1961)

Grunebaum, Gustav E. von, *Medieval Islam*, University of Chicago Press, 1958

Guillaume, Alfred, *Islam*, Harmondsworth, Middlesex, 1956

al-Hachaichi, Mohammed ben Otsmane, *Voyage au pays des Senoussia*, Paris, 1912

Hamdani, Husayn F., *On the Geneaology of the Fatimid Caliphs*, Cairo, 1958

Ibn Khaldun, "Histoire des Fatimides" (appendix II, vol. II *Histoire des Berbères*, See List I a)

Ibn Saghit, Chronique, tr. Motylinski (in *Actes du XIV Congrès Internationale des Orientalistes*, Paris, 1908)

Kano Chronicle, ed. Palmer, H. R. (in Hodgkin anthology, See List I d)

Kilwa Kisiwani," "The Ancient History of (in Freeman-Grenville anthology, See List I d)

The Koran, tr. Rodwell, J. M.; Blachère, Régis; Sale, George (with interesting notes and "Preliminary Discourse")

Levi-Provencal, E., *Islam d'Occident*, Paris, 1948

———, *La Fondation de Fez*, Paris, 1939

———, *Six fragments inédits d'une chronique anonyme du début des Almohades*, Paris, 1925

Marçais, Georges, *Notes sur lee ribats au Berbérie*, Paris, 1925

Margoliouth, D. S., *Mohammed and the Rise of Islam*, New York, 1905

———, *The Last Days of Fatimah, Daughter of the Prophet*, Paris, 1909

Marsh, Zoe (See List I d)

Massignon, Louis, *l'hyperdulie de Fatima*, Paris, 1955

———, *Les origines Shiites de la famille vizirale des Banu'l Furat*, Cairo, 1945

Mathew, Gervase, "The East African Coast Until the Coming of the Portuguese" (in *History of East Africa*, ed. Oliver and Mathew)

Meshullam ben Menahem, Rabbi (in Adler anthology, See List II a)

Morand, Marcel, *Les Kanouns du Mzab*, Alger, 1903

Motylinski, A. de C., *Guerara*, Alger, 1885

Naval Documents, *U.S. Wars with the Barbary*, vol. III

Poulet, Georges, *Les Maures de l'Afrique Occidentale Française*, Paris, 1903

Ritter, Hellmut (in *Classicisme et déclin*, See Abel, above)

Robin, Commandant, *Le Mzab et son annexion à la France*, Alger, 1884

Saunders, J. J., *A History of Medieval Islam*, London, 1965

Southern, B. W., *Western Views of Islam in the Middle Ages*, Harvard University Press, 1962

Sundkler, Bengt, *Bantu Prophets in South Africa*, London, 1961

et-Tidjany, Cheikh, quoted by Schefer (in Leo Africanus, See List I a)

Trimingham, J. Spencer, *Islam in East Africa*, Edinburgh, 1962

———, *A History of Islam in West Africa*, Oxford University Press, 1963

———, *Islam in West Africa*, Oxford University Press, 1959

Turner, H. W., "The Church of the Lord" (in *Journal of African History*, 1962)

Watt, W. Montgomery, *Islam and the Integration of Society*, London, 1961

Westermarck, *Survivances paiennes dans la civilisation mohamétane* (French translation), Paris, 1935

Yaqut (in Leo Africanus appendix, See List I a)

Zeys, E., *La legislation Mozabite*, Alger, 1886

III—UNWRITTEN RELIGION, MAGIC AND PHILOSOPHY

a—REGIONAL TREATMENTS

African Ideas of God, Symposium, ed. Smith, Edwin W., London, 1961

Christensen, James B., "The Adaptive Function of Fanti Priesthood" (in *Continuity and Change*, See List I d)

Cole, A. J., "Astrological Geomancy in Africa" (in Dennett appendix, See below)

Cremer, Jean, *Les Bobo, la mentalité mystique*, intro. Labouret, Henri, Paris, 1927

D'Aby, F. J. Amon, *Croyances religieuses et coutumes juridiques des Agni de la Côte d'Ivoire*, Paris, 1960

Dennett, R. E., *At the Back of the Black Man's Mind*, London, 1906

Dymond, G. W., "The Idea of God in Ovamboland, South West Africa" (in *African Ideas of God*, above)

Evans-Pritchard, E. E., "Nuer Religion" (in *Anthropology of Folk Religion*, ed. White, Leslie, New York, 1960)

Fourche, J. A. and Morlinghem, H., *Les communications des indigènes du Kasai avec les âmes des morts*, Bruxelles, 1939

Gaden, Henri, *Proverbes Peuls et Toucouleurs, Travaux et Memoirs de l'Institut d'Ethnologie XVI*, Paris, 1931

Godefroy-Loyer, R. P., "Relation du Voyage du royaume d'Issiny" (in Roussier, See List II c)

Guebhard, Paul, "Les Peuls du Fouta Diallon" (in *Revue des Etudes Ethnologiques*, Paris, 1909)

Hahn, Theophilus, *Tsuni-llGoam, the Supreme Being of the Khoi-Khoi*, London, 1881

Idowu, E. Bolaji, *Olódùmarè God in the Yoruba Belief*, London, 1962

Johnson, Bishop James, Yoruba Heathenism (in Dennett, See above)

Jones, C. I., "European and African Tradition on the Rio Real" (in *Journal of African History*, 1963)

Junod, Henri A., *The Life of a South African Tribe*, Neuchatel, Switzerland, 1912

Labouret, Henri, *Les Manding et leur langue*, Paris, 1934
Lebeuf and Detourbet, *La civilisation du Tchad* (See List I d)
Mangin, R. P., Eugène, *Les Mossi*, Paris, 1921
Messenger, John C., "Religious Acculturation Among the Anang Ibibio" (in *Continuity and Change*, See List I d)
Mouezy, Henri, *Assinie et le Royaume de Krinjabo*, Paris, 1953
Parrinder, Geofrey, *La religion en Afrique Occidentale* (French Translation), Paris, 1950
———, "Theistic Beliefs of the Yoruba and Ewe Peoples" (in *African Ideas of God*, See above)
Smith, Edwin W., ed., *African Ideas of God*, Symposium, London, 1961
Talbot, F. Amaury, *In the Shadow of the Bush* (See List I d)
Tauxier, Louis, *La religion Bambara*, Paris, 1927
———, *Moeurs et histoire des Peuls*, Paris, 1937
———, *Religion, moeurs et coutumes des Agnis de la Côte d'Ivoire*, Paris, 1932
Torrend, J., S.J., *Specimens of Bantu Folklore from Northern Rhodesia*, London, 1921
Westcott, R. W., "Ancient Egypt and Modern Africa" (in *Journal of African History*, 1961)
Wolfe, Alvin W., "The Dynamics of the Ngoma Segmentary System" (in *Continuity and Change*, See List I d)
Young, T. Cullen, "The Idea of God in Northern Nyasaland" (in *African Ideas of God*, See above)

b—SOME WORKS WHICH CLARIFY OR BEAR UPON BOOKLESS AFRICA'S THINKING: STUDIES BOTH AFRICAN AND GENERAL IN SOCIAL ANTHRO-POLOGY, PSYCHOLOGY, MYTHOLOGY AND THE-OLOGIES

Abraham, W. E., *The Mind of Africa*, London, 1962
Baumann (See List I d)
Bouquet, A. C., *Comparative Religion*, Harmondsworth, Middlesex, 1956

Campbell, Joseph, *The Masks of God in Primitive Mythology*, New York, 1959

Cumont, Franz, *Astrology and Religion Among the Greeks and Romans*, New York, 1960

Durkheim, Emile and Mauss, Marcel, *Primitive Classification*, tr. and intro. Needham, Rodney, London, 1963

Eliade, Mircea, *Images and Symbols*, London, 1961

———, *Myths, Dreams and Mysteries*, London, 1960

Evans-Pritchard, E. E., *Essays in Social Anthropology*, London, 1962

Fortes, Meyer, "Oedipus and Job in West African Religion" (in White, *Anthropology of Folk Religion*, See List III a)

Fraser, Sir James George, *The Golden Bough*, London, 1960

Freud, Sigmund, *Totem and Taboo*, Harmondsworth, Middlesex, 1936

Fromm, Erich, *Psychoanalysis and Religion*, Yale University Press, 1958

Gennep, Arnold van, *The Rites of Passage*, London, 1960

Hansberry, William Leo, "Indigenous African Religions" (in *Présence Africaine*, See List I d)

Hertz, Hubert, *Death and the Right Hand: a Study in Religious Polarity*, tr. Needham, London, 1960

Hubert, Henri and Mauss, Marcel, *Sacrifice, Its Nature and Function*, London, 1964

Jahn, Janheim, *Muntu*, London, 1961

James, E. O., *Comparative Religion*, London and New York, 1961

———, *La Religion Préhistorique* (French translation), Paris, 1959

———, *Sacrifice and Sacrament*, London, 1962

Jung, Carl Gustav, *Psychology and Religion*, Yale University Press, 1960

Levi-Strauss, Claude, *Totemism*, London, 1964

Lowie, Robert H., *Primitive Religion*, New York, 1924

Malinowski, Bronislaw, *Magic, Science and Religion*, Garden City, 1948

Parrinder, Geoffrey, *Worship in the World's Religions*, London, 1961

Radin, Paul, *Primitive Man as Philosopher*, New York, 1957

———, *Primitive Religion*, New York, 1957

Seligman (See List I d)

Seznac, Jean, *The Survival of the Pagan Gods*, New York, 1961

Smith, Homer W., *Man and His Gods*, New York, 1957

Smith, Huston, *The Religions of Man*, New York, 1961

Taylor, John, *The Primal Vision, Christian Presence amid African Religion*, London, 1963

Tylor, Sir Edward B., *Anthropology*, University of Michigan Press, 1960

——, *Primitive Culture: The Origins of Culture; Religion in Primitive Culture*, New York, 1958

Zaehner, R. C., *The Comparison of Religions*, Boston, 1962

——, *Mysticism, Sacred and Profane*, Oxford, 1961

INTER-RACIAL RELATIONS

Anân Ishô, tr. Budge, *Wit and Wisdom* (See List II b)

Avicenna (quoted by Ibn Khaldun in *Muqaddimah*, See List I a)

Cook, Mercer (in *Présence Africaine*, See List I d)

Dapper, Olfert, "Description de l'Afrique" (in Hodgkin anthology, See List I d)

Diodorus Sicilus (quoted in Gsell, *Histoire*, See List I b)

Heliodorus, *Ethiopian Story* (See List I b)

Ibn el-Faqik (cited in al-Omari, *Masalik*, See List I a)

Justin (quoted in Gsell, *Histoire*, See List I b)

Koran, Suras 3 and 30

Lincoln, C. Eric, *The Black Muslime in America*, Boston, 1960

Maspero, Gaston (quoted in Mahaffy, *A History of Egypt under the Ptolemaic Dynasty*, London, 1899)

Picatrix (quoted Seznac, See List III b)

Pliny, *Natural History*

Richmond, Anthony, *The Colour Problem*, Harmondsworth, Middlesex, 1955

Wasif, Ibrahim bin, "Book of Marvels" (in Ferrand, Gabriel, *Relation de voyages et textes géographiques Arabes, Persans et Turks* (anthology), Paris, 1913

SLAVERY, AFRICAN STYLE: NEGROES; EUROPEANS; TURKS AND NOTABLE SLAVES

Anonymous, *The Narrative of Robert Adams . . . . in the Year 1810*, London, 1816

Behagle, Ferdinand de, *Au pays de l'esclavage*, Paris, 1900

Bennett, Norman Robert, "Christian and Negro Slavery in the 18th Century in North Africa" (in *Journal of African History*, 1960)

Blyden, Edward W., *Christianity Islam and the Negro Race*, London, 1888

Brosnahan, L. F., "Some Historical Cases of Language Imposition" (in *Language in Africa*, See List I d)

Daumas, Eugène and de Chancel, Auson, "Code de l'esclavage" (Appendix to *Le Grand Désert*, Paris, 1848)

Davidson, Basil, *Black Mother*, Boston, 1961

Deny, J., "Chansons des Janissaires Turcs d'Alger" (in *Mélanges*, René Basset, Paris, 1925)

Faris, Nabih Amim (in *The Arab Heritage*, ed. Faris, Princeton University Press, 1944)

Fetha Nagast (résumé in appendix no. 10, de Coppet, See List I d)

Fyfe, Christopher, *A Short History of Sierra Leone*, London, 1962

Goody, Esther (in *Marriage in Tribal Society*, ed. Fortes, Meyer, Cambridge University Press, 1962)

Gordon, M. L., "The Nationality of Slaves under the Early Roman Empire" (in *Slavery in Classical Antiquity*, ed. Finley, Cambridge, 1960)

Général Gouraud, *Au Soudan*, Paris, 1939

Lane-Poole, Stanley, *The Barbary Corsairs*, London, 1896

———, *Turkey*, London, 1888

Mair, Lucy, *Primitive Government*, Harmondsworth, Middlesex, 1962

Newbury, C. W., *The Western Slave Coast and Its Rulers*, Oxford, 1961

Pamkhurst, Richard (See List II c)

Riley, James, *Loss of the American Brig Commerce*, London, 1817

Roblès, Emmanuel, "L'Algerie de Cervantes," *Algeria*, Algiers, 1859

Young, George, *Egypt,* London, 1930

Tuaillon, Georges, *L'Afrique Occidentale Française,* Paris, 1936

ART

Anonymous, *The Art of Ife* (brochure), Lagos, Nigeria, 1955

Clark, J. Desmond (See List I b)

Cole, Sonia (See List I b)

Cordell, Justine W., African Art (in *Continuity and Change,* See List I d)

Cortier, Maurice, *Mission Cortier,* Paris, 1914

Desplagnes, Louis, *Le plateau central nigérien,* Paris, 1907

Eydoux, Henri-Paul, *L'Exploration du Sahara,* Paris, 1938

Fagg, William (in *The Artist in Tribal Society,* ed. Smith, Marion W., London, 1961)

Fouchet, Max-Pol, *L'Art à Carthage,* Paris, 1962

Hardy, Georges, *L'Art nègre,* Paris, 1927

Harley, George W., *Masks as an Agent of Social Control,* Cambridge, Mass., 1950

Hassanein, A. M. Bey, *The Lost Oases,* New York and London, 1925

Jacquot, Docteur, *Expédition du Général Cavignac dans le Sahara algérien en avril et mai, 1847,* Paris, 1849

Lane-Poole, Stanley, *The Art of the Saracens in Egypt,* London, 1886

Lebeuf and Detourbet (See List I d)

Lhote, Henri, *Le Sahara,* Paris, 1937

———, *The Search for the Tassali Frescoes, the Story of Rock Art Paintings in the Sahara,* New York, 1959

Murray, R. C. (in *The Artist in Tribal Society,* See above)

Read, Sir Herbert (in *The Artist in Tribal Society,* See above)

Stow, G. W., *The Native Races of Southern Africa* (cited by Clark, J. Desmond, See above)

Terrasse, Henri, "Classicisme et décadence dans les arts musulmans" (in *Classicisme et Déclin,* Symposium, See List II e)

Tobias, Philip V., "Physique of a Desert Folk" (in *Natural History*, New York, 1961)

Van der Post, Laurens, *The Lost World of the Kalahari*, Harmondsworth, Middlesex, 1962

Willett, Frank, "Ife and Its Archaeology" (in *Journal of African History*, 1960)

AFRICA'S LITERATURE

In the List headed "Arabic" (I d) the larger part of the authors named are of African birth or residence.

In the List entitled "Christianity: Rise, Fall and Survivals" are mentioned the sources for some early Christian, Gnostic and heretical writings of African association.

The following anthologies contain excerpts from African authors:

Biographies of 360 North African intellectuals, most of them writers (in *Actes du XiVe Congrès International des Orientalistes*, Paris, 1908)

Duquaire, Henri, *Anthologie de la littérature marocaine, arabe et berbère*, Paris, 1943

Ferrand, Gabriel, *Relation de voyages et textes géographiques arabe, persans et turks*, Paris, 1914

Freeman-Grenville, G. S. P., *The East African Coast, Select Documents from the 1st to the 19th Centuries*, Oxford, 1962

Hodgkin, Thomas, *Nigerian Perspectives, an Historical Anthology*, Oxford University Press, 1960

Levi-Provençal, E., *Extraits des historiens arabes du Maroc* (text in Arabic, preliminary study of the authors in French), Paris, 1948

Sauvaget, J., *Historiens arabes*, Paris, 1946

Sedillot, L. A., Tableau de la civilisation arabe (in Bousquet, G. H., *Classiques de l'Islamologie*, Alger, 1950)

I have not found any inclusive study of the pre-colonial literature of the African continent.

The following works offer information on some African authors writing in Arabic:

Delafosse, *Haut-Sénégal-Niger,* Paris, 1912
Gautier, E. F., *Le Passé de l'Afrique du Nord,* Paris, 1937
Gibb, H. A. R., *Arabic Literature,* Oxford, 1963
Lane-Poole, Stanley, *History of Egypt in the Middle Ages,* London, 1901
Terrasse, Henri, *Histoire du Maroc,* Casablanca, 1949

On two individual African writers in Arabic there are many studies—Ibn Khaldun and Ibn Battuta. See some detail in my text, and, on Ibn Khaldun see also:

Fischel, Walter J., "Ibn Khaldun's Use of Historical Sources" (in *Studia Islamica XIV,* Paris, 1961
Muhsin Mahdi, Ibn, *Khaldun's Philosophy of History,* London, 1957
Toynbee, Arnold, *A Study of History,* Oxford University Press, 1940–61
On Ibn Khaldun in Russia (Review by Canard, M., in *Arabica,* Paris, 1960)

NON-ARABIC AFRICAN WRITING

Amda Syon, *Histoire* (See List II c)
Apuleius, *The Golden Ass*
St. Augustine, 2 titles and Marrou's study of his writings (See List II b)
Basset, Henri, *Essai sur la littérature des Berbères* (See List II b)
Cross, F. L., *The Early Christian Fathers,* London, 1960
Eldad the Danite, Letter of (in *Jewish Travellers* anthology, See List II a)
Fatha Nagast (See List "Slavery")
Grant, Robert, *Gnosticism, An Anthology* (See List II b)
Guernier (See List I d)

Juba II (in Pliny, *Natural History*)

Leslau, *Falasha Anthology* (See List II a)

Za'ra Ya'eqob, "Le livre de la lumiêre" (See List II a)

The following concern my text about Africa's literature in Chapters entitled, "In Arabic and Other Scripts" and "The Darker Writers, Moslem and Christian."

Comments on catalogue of Arabic MSS at Rabat (in *Journal of African History*, 1960)

Coulton, G. G., *The Black Death*, London, 1929

Hitti, Philip K., "America and the Arab Heritage" (in *The Arab Heritage*, See List "Slavery")

Jurbi, Edward J., "The Course of Arab Scientific Thought" (in *Arab Heritage*, See List "Slavery")

Nohl, Johannes, *The Black Death* (including a long passage from Boccaccio), London, 1961

Polo, Marco, Translations by Latham; Everyman's edition and (from text by Benedetto) Aldo Ricci.

Smith, H. F. C., "The 19th Century Archives of West Africa," (in *Journal of African History*, 1960)

BIBLICAL-KORANIC PERSONAGES ADAPTED INTO AFRICAN MYTHS AND LEGENDS

EVE—Monteil, C., *Contes Soudanais*, Paris, 1905

NOAH, FAMILY AND ASSOCIATES—Basset, Henri (See List "Africa's Literature")

Bousquet, "Judaisme" (See List II b)

Ibn Khaldun, *Muqqadimah* (See List I a)

Jackson, *Timbuctoo* (See List I c)

Kati, *Tarikh el-Fettach* (See List I a)

Lebeuf (See List I d)

(on Shem) Goldziher (in *Arabica*, 1960–61)

(on Shem) Slouschz (See List II a)

El-Bekri (cited by Ibn Khaldun in *Histoire des Berbères,* See List I a)

(on Ham and his family) Ibn Khaldun, *Histoire des Berbères* (See List I a)

Masudi (cited by Maqrizi in Appendix to Burckhardt, See List I a)

● GENERAL DELUGE REFERENCES IN MY TEXT—*The Epic of Gilgamesh,* ed. Sanders, N. K., Harmondsworth, Middlesex, 1960

Eliade, *Images* (See List III b)

Kramer, Samuel Noah, *History Begins at Sumer,* Garden City, 1959

Liu-Chai-Lien, *The Arabian Prophet,* Shanghai, 1921

Muller, Max, *History of Ancient Sanskrit Literature* (quoted by Ragosin, *Vedic India,* London and New York, 1895)

Plato (quoted in *Atlantis,* Donnelly, Ignatius, ed. Sykes, Egerton, London, 1960)

JONAH—Leo Africanus (See List I a)

Doresse, Jean, *L'Empire du Prêtre-Jean,* Paris, 1961

Eliad, *Myths* (See List III b)

SOLOMON—Basset, Henri (See under Noah above)

Basset, René, *Melanges africains et orientaux,* Paris, 1915

Slouschz (See under Shem above)

Williams (See List II a)

See also sources on Solomon and the Queen of Sheba in the list "Jewish Dispersion," II a.

ABRAHAM—Bello, *History of Tekrour* (See List I a)

Ibn Khaldun, *Histoire des Berbères* (See List I a)

(on Abraham's wife, as of excision) Monteil, *Contes* (See under Eve above)

MOSES—Basset, Henri (See under Noah above)

Doresse (See under Jonah above)

Ibn Khaldun (See under Abraham above)

Kati (See under Noah above)

Maqrizi (Appendix to Burckhardt, See List I a)

Es-Sadi (See List I a)

Slouschz (See under Shem above)

GOLIATH—El-Bekri (See List I a)

Ibn Khaldun (See under Abraham above)

Justinard, Lt. Col., *Un petit royaume Berbère, le Tazeroualt*, Paris, 1954

VIRGIN MARY—Basset, Henri (See under Noah above), for the fable of the ants

Budge, *Legends of Our Lady* (See List II b) for myths about the Virgin Mary, sometimes involving Jesus.

On alteration of biblical stories see also titles dealing with Gnosticism in List II b.

• WHAT WAS THE FIRST SOURCE OF THE ABOVE LEGENDS?

Goldziher, *Etudes Islamologiques* (See List II e)

Ibn Khaldun, *Muqaddimah* (See List I a)

Lewis, Bernard, *The Arabs in History* (See List I d)

Watt, *Islam and Integration* (See List II e)

Zaehner, R. C., *The Comparison of Religions*, Boston, 1962

ORAL HISTORY AND SIGNIFICANT LEGENDS

a—THE PROFESSIONAL HISTORY RECITER AND THE VALUE AND WEAKNESSES OF ORAL HISTORY

Abraham, V. E., *The Mind of Africa*, London, 1962

Ibn Battuta (See List I a)

Carr, Edward Hallett, *What is History?*, London and New York, 1961

Delafosse, *Haut-Sénégal-Niger* (See List I d)

———, *Civilisations* (See List I d)

Dupuis-Yakouba, *Industries et professions des habitants de la region de Tombouctou*, Paris, 1921

Evans-Pritchard, E. E., *Anthropology and History*, Manchester University Press, 1961

Herskovits, *Human Factor* (See List I d)
Laing (See List I c)
Taylor (See List III b)
Urvoy, *Histoire des populations* (See List I d)
Vansina, Jan, *Oral Tradition, a Study in Historical Methodology*, London, 1965
————, also articles in *Journal of African History*

b—SIGNIFICANT LEGENDS

Daumas, *Grand Désert* (See List "Slavery")
Delafosse, *Haut-Sénégal-Niger* (See List I d)
Dupuis-Yakouba, "Légendes de Farang" (in Desplagnes, See List "Art")
Evans-Pritchard, E. E., *Nuer Religion* (See List III a)
Frankfort, *Before Philosophy* (See List I b)
Gaden, *Proverbes Peuls* (See List III a)
Holt, "Funj Origins" (in *Journal of African History*, 1963)
Lebeuf (See List I d)
Es Sadi (See List I a)
Seligman (See List I d)
Siré-Abbas-Soh (See List I a)
Tylor, *Religion in Primitive Culture* (See List III b)
Vieillard, Gilbert, "Notes sur le caractère des Peuls," *Outre Mer*, 1932

c—LEGENDS INVOLVING SNAKES AND THE AFRICAN RESPECT FOR SNAKES

Arrian, *Life of Alexander*, tr. Sélincourt
el-Bekri (See List I a)
Delafosse, *Les Nègres* (See List I d)
Hahn (See List III a)
Hamby, Wilfrid, *Serpent Worship in Africa*, Chicago, 1931
Lebeuf (See I d)
Lucan, *Pharsalia*, Book IX

Parrinder, *Religion en Afrique Occidentals* (See List III a)
Pliny, *Natural History*
Strabo, *The Geography of*
Tauxier, *Religion Bambara* (See List III a)
Urvoy (See above)

• ON ARWE, THE FIRST KING OF ETHIOPIA (SERPENT)

Coppet (See List I d)
Doresse (See List I d)

●ON OPHILITES (OR NAASSENES) see titles dealing with
   Gnosticism (II b)

• ON SNAKE WORSHIP IN THE UNITED STATES

Barre, Weston La Barre, *They Shall Take up Serpents,* University of
   Minnesota Press, 1962

d—FOLKLORE

Basset, René, *Contes populaires d'Afrique,* Paris, 1903
Certeux, A. and Carnoy, E. Henry, *Algérie traditionelle,* Paris and
   Algiers, 1884
Delafosse, *Ame Nègre* (See List I d)
Dubouloz-Laffin, Marie-Louise, *Le Bou-Mergoud, Folklore Tunisien,*
   Paris, 1946
Foucauld-Motylinski (See List II b)
Torrend (See List III a)

BODILY ALTERATIONS; INITIATION; SECRET SOCIETIES

Baumann (See List I d)
Binger (See List I c)
Dapper (in Hodgkin anthology, See List I d)

Delafosse, *Haut-Sénégal-Niger* (See List I d)

Dos Santos, Father Joao (in Freeman-Greenville anthology, See List
I d)

Egharevba, Jacob (See List I d)

Eliade, *Myths* (See List III b)

Gennep (See List III b)

Hahn (See List III a)

Harley, George W., *Native African Medicine*, Harvard University
Press, 1941

Herodotus (Bk. II)

Mair, Lucy (See List "Slavery")

Masudi (in Freeman-Greenville anthology, See List I d)

Monteil, Charles, *Contes Soudanais* (See List "Biblical")

Monteil, Lt. Col. (See List I c)

Pistis Sophia (See List II b)

Seligman, C. G., *Races of Africa* (See List I d)

Sintra, Captaine Pierre de, Navigation de, (in Ca de Mosto, See List
I c)

Soeur Marie-André du Sacré-Coeur, *La Femme Noire en Afrique Occidentale*, Paris, 1939

Vansina, J., "South of the Congo" (in Wheeler, *Dawn of African
History* (See List I b)

Westermarck, *Survivances paiennes* (See List II e)

Windus, John (See List I c)

Women of Tropical Africa (collection), ed. Paulme, Denise, London
1963 (contains an 8-page bibliography of studies on the initiation practices and sex operations upon girls)

Za'ra Ya'eqob, Chronique de (See List II a)

WOMEN: INDIVIDUAL WOMEN IN LEGEND AND HISTORY; MARRIAGE; THE FAMILY; WITCHES; FECUNDITY CULT

The following collections deal exclusively with women or contain papers about women. Specific papers from these collections are mentioned below.

African Systems of Kinship and Marriage, ed. Radcliffe-Brown, A. R. and Forde, Daryll, Oxford University Press, 1960

Marriage in Tribal Society, ed. Fortes, Meyer, Cambridge University Press, 1962

Studies in Kinship and Marriage, ed. Schapera, I., London, 1963

Women of Tropical Africa, ed. Paulme, Denise, London, 1963

a—WOMEN IN LEGEND AND HISTORY

Alvares (See List II c)—Helena

Bello, *History* (See List I a)—about Amina

Brooke, G. C., in *A Literary and Historical Atlas of Africa,* Everymans, shows on Plate v-7 coin of Shajar-al-Durr—Pearl Spray

Chronique d'Abuja, from the Hausa, Lagos, Nigeria, 1962—Amina

Coppet (See List I d)—Helena

Delafosse, *Haut-Sénégal-Niger* (See List I d)—Yennenga

Gautier, E. F., "Anciennes voies du Commerce transsahariens," *Geografiska Annaler,* 1935—Tin Hinan

Kano Chronicle (See List II e)—Amina

Maqrizi (in *L'Itineraire de Saint Louis en Egypte,* Paris, 1900)—Pearl Spray

Moffat, John S., *The Lives of Robert and Mary Moffat,* New York, 1888—Mantatisi

Moffat, Robert (quoted in Becker, Peter, *Path of Blood,* London, 1962)—Mantatisi

Sellassié, Guebre (See List II c)—Zawditu and Taitu

Wheeler, *Rome Beyond* (See List I b)—Tin-Hinan

On Judith "The Fire," Cahena and Makedda (The Queen of Sheba) See List II a

b—WOMAN AND THE FAMILY; AS A SYMBOL; AS THE WITCH

Abraham, *Mind of Africa* (See List III b)

Azikiwi, Nnamdi, *Liberia in Work Politics,* London, 1934 (on polygamy)

Baeta, C. G., *Prophetism in Ghana,* London, 1962

Barbet, Charles, *La Femme musulmane en Algérie,* Alger, 1903

Beattie, John, "Sorcery in Bunyoro" (in *Witchcraft . . . in East Africa,* See below)

Beidelman, "Witchcraft in Ukaguru" (in *Witchcraft . . . East Africa,* See below)

Bousquet, G-H., *La Morale de l'Islam et son ethique sexuelle,* Paris, 1953

Breasted, James, *Ancient Records of Egypt* (See List I b)

Caillard, Mabel, *A Lifetime in Egypt,* London, 1925

Delafosse, *Civilisations Négro-africaines* (See List I d)

Dorjean, Victor R., "The Factor of Polygyny in African Demography" (in *Continuity and Change,* See List I d)

Evan-Pritchard, E. E., "Heredity and Gestation as the Azande See Them" (in *Essays,* See List III b)

Faure, Claude, *Histoire de la Prèsqu'île du Cap Vert et des origines de Dakar,* Paris, 1914

Fortes, Meyer, "Kinship and Marriage Among the Ashanti" (in *African Systems,* See above)

Freeman-Grenville anthology (See List I d), "An Arabic History of Kilwa Kiswani"

Fouchet, Max-Pol, *L'Art à Carthage* (See List "Art")

Gama, Vasco da, Second Voyage (from "Landas de India" in Freeman-Grenville anthology, See List I d)

Ghazali, *Counsel for Kings* (Nasihat al-Muluk), tr. Bagley, Oxford University Press, 1964 (chapter on women)

———, Ihya (quoted in Bousquet, above)

Gluckman, Max, "Kinship and Marriage Among the Lozi of Northern Rhodesia and the Zulu of Natal" (in *African Systems*, See above)

Hawkes, Christopher and Jacquetta, *Prehistoric Britain*, Harmondsworth, Middlesex, 1958

Huntingford, G. W. B., "Nandi Witchcraft" (in *Witchcraft . . . East Africa*, See below)

James, E. O., *Comparative Religion* (See List III b)—on primitive adoration of the cowry

———, *Religion Préhistorique* (See List III b)—on the primitive adoration of the cowry

Junod (See List III a)

Koran, Sura 55 (about women in Paradise; comments of Tabari cited by Andrea, List II e)

———, Sura 113 (about witches; comments of al-Beidawi, cited by Sale)

Kuper, Hilda, "Kinship Among the Swazi" (in *African Systems*, See above)

Laurentin, Anne, "Nzakara Women" (in *Women of Tropical Africa*, See above)

Lebeuf, Annie, M.D., "The Role of Women in the Political Organization of African Societies" (in *Women of Tropical Africa*, See above)

Lee, Rev. Samuel, *The Travels of Ibn Batuta*, London, 1829—on the cowry, "concha Veneris"

Lenz (See List I c)—on the distribution of cowry currency

Lethbridge, T. C., *Witches: Investigating an Ancient Religion*, London, 1962

Levine, Robert A., "Witchcraft and Sorcery in a Gusii Community" (in *Witchcraft . . . East Africa*, See below)

Lienhardt, Godfrey, *Social Anthropology*, Oxford University Press, 1964

———, "Dinka Representation of the Relations between the Sexes" (in *Studies in Kinship and Marriage*, See above)

Malinowski, Bronislaw, *The Dynamics of Culture Change* (See List I d)

Mariette-Bey, *Voyage dans la Haute Egypte* (See List I b)

Meeker, Odin, *Report on Africa*, New York, 1954

Mercier, Ernest, *La condition de la femme musulmane dans l'Afrique septentrionale*, Alger, 1895

Mitchell, J. C., *Tribalism and the Plural Society*, Oxford University Press, 1960

Mongait, A. L., *Archaeology in the USSR*, Harmondsworth, Middlesex, 1961

Murray, Gilbert, *Five Stages in Greek Religion*, Garden City, N.Y., 1951

Murray, M. A., *The Witch Cult in Western Europe*, Oxford, 1962

Nadel, S. F., "Dual Descent in the Nuba Hills" (in *African Systems*, See above)

Neumann, Eric, *The Great Mother*, New York, 1955

Parrinder, Geoffrey, *Witchcraft, European and African*, Harmondsworth, Middlesex, 1958

Parsons, Robert T., "The Kono of Sierra Leone" (in *African Ideas of God*, See List III a)—on post-mortem on witches

Petrie, Flinders, *The Making of Egypt* (See List I b)

Richards, A. J., "Some Types of Family Structure Amongst the Central Bantu" (in *African Systems*, See above)

Schwab, George and Harley, George W. (editor), *Tribes of the Liberian Hinterland*, Cambridge, Mass., 1947

Scott, Anna M., *Day Dawn in Africa*, New York, 1858

Soeur Marie-André (See List "Bodily Alteration")

Wilson, Monica, "Nyakyusa Kinship" (in *African Systems*, See above)

Witchcraft and Sorcery in East Africa (a collection of papers) ed. Middleton, John and Winter, E. H., London, 1963

SUBJECT INDEX

art (cont.)
207–10; in Morocco, 208; Bushman art, 206–7, 225; of Punic Carthage, 209–10; Mohammedan antagonism to representations of people and animals, 118, 211, 212; Ethiopian art, 6, 211, 213–16; art of Benin, Ife, Nok, 217, 218; lost wax method, 216, 218; influence of Africa's art upon the world, 216–18; iron workers' position, 219–21

St. Augustine, 4, 13, 14, 48–49, 62, 65–67, 117, 193, 337

authors of African birth or domicile or close association:
See St. Augustine; see Origen
Apuleius, 4, 48, 244
Eratosthenes, 5, 246
Philo, 19
Zara Yaqeob, 91, 92
Maimonides, 245
Cosmas, 245–46
Julius Africanus, 247
Edrisi, 247–49
Leo Africanus, 249–51, 264
the author of the Roudh el-Kartas, 251–52
Constantinus Africanus, 252–53
Ibn Khaldun, 253, 255, 258, 260–63, 264, 265, 266–70; and Tamerlane, 269
Averroes, 253
Ibn Battuta, 255–61, 262
Ahmed Baba, 271, 274–75, 277–78
Es-Sa'di (author of Tarikh es-Soudan), 273, 274, 278
Mahmoud Kati (author of Tarikh el-Fettach), 273, 276–77, 279

Sultan Bello, 183, 278–80
Nebura Ed Yeshaq (Ishaq), 285–86
two woman authors, 312
Osman dan Fodio, 332

Bantu languages, 177–79
Bible, 12–13, 14, 51, 291–94
Biblical and Koranic personages in African myths and legends: 7, 21, 22, 30–35, 128–30, 288–94
see Solomon
Adam, 128, 294
Eve, 128
Noah, 129, 289, 291
Jonah, 289–90
Moses, 290–91, 292
Abraham, 293
Ham, 293–94
Goliath, 294
See also under Christianity: myths and legends about the Virgin Mary and (in some cases) Jesus
Black Death in Africa (1348–49), 261–64, 265

Cahena, 27–28, 308
Candace, 43, 88
cannibals, 7, 158–61; Jagas, 160, 323; cannibalism in Egypt, 213; Ethiopian cannibal miracle by the Virgin Mary, 215–16
Cat (or qat; Tshat; kat), 239
children: desire for, 321, 339–40, 343–44; destruction of the deformed, 322–23; twins distrusted and sometimes destroyed, 323–24
Christianity, 6, 8, 12–14, 27, 28, 39–55, 103, 104, 105, 125

hospitals and treatment of the insane and of infections in medieval northern Africa, 265–66

Idris I and II, 99–100
incest rules, 163, 333
initiation and the instruction of youths and girls, 227–28
inter-racial relations in Africa, 7, 113–14, 137–65; inter-racial marriages and matings, 164–65
intoxicants, Africa's attitudes, 7, 231–35; Islam's rules, 231–33; wine in ancient Egypt, 231; date wine, 232, 234; native strong drinks, 233, 234; discovery of palm wine, 234
Isis, possible influence on Christianity, 14, 69–70
Islam, 6, 8, 12, 13, 70–71, 95–134
    see Mahdis; see Fatima, importance of; see Ali, the almost cult of; see Fatimids; see Man on the Donkey; Shiites, 98, 99; Kharijitism, 98–99, 112; see Mzabites
    see Idris I and II; see Kinza; see Almohads
    Sherifs, 100–1, 108, 109, 127; baraka, 100–1
    see Almoravids; see anthropomorphism; Ghazali's book burnt in a doctrinal dispute, 117
    Islam in the sub-Sahara, 119–25; Islam mingling with paganism, 125–27, 128, 130–31
    see Art, intoxicants; tobacco
    Islam's attitude toward women and the sex act, 164, 336, 337; Ghazali cited on, 337

Jews and the Jewish influence in Africa, 6, 8, 12–14, 17–37; Dispersion historically recorded and in legends and myths: Egypt and northern Africa, 18–21, 26–27; Elephantine, 19, 30; Sahara, 22–23; sub-Sahara, 23–24, 130; East Africa, 35–37; suggested Jewish origin of Fulani, 25; Maimonides, 245
    see under authors: Philo; see Cahena; Solomon; Judith of Ethiopia; Falashas; Sheba, Queen of; Eldad the Danite; see Biblical and Koranic personages in African myths and legends
jinn, 22, 129–30, 290, 293
Judith of Ethiopia, 28, 30, 308

Kinza, 100, 309
kola (or cola), 235–36
Koran, 13–14, 110, 119, 121–22, 154, 231, 324, 328–29, 334, 337; see Biblical and Koranic personages in African myths and legends

languages of Africa, 177–79
Lokman, 141–42

Mahdis, 96–97, 102, 103, 109–10, 111, 112
Man on the Donkey, 111–13, 140
Mandaeans (or Sabaeans or Nasoraeans), 58
Manichees, 57, 66–67
masks, 222
matrilineal system, 332–34
monastery system, debut of, 50, 52–55

sleeping sickness, the first case of record in Africa, 264
Solomon in African legends and myths, 21, 30–35, 88, 214, 290

tobacco, Africa's attitudes about its use, 7, 231, 235–38, 239–40
Prester John of Ethiopia and the tobacco riot, 236–37
and Ethiopia's hatred of tobacco, 240; indigenous tobacco, 236–37; tobacco as aphrodisiac, 238
various rules as to tobacco, 239, 240
Tuareg, 76–79, 319; were they once Christians?, 76–79; men's veils, 76; writing system, 78; Tin 'Hinan, 308; risks taken by women to achieve plumpness, 342
Turkish power and influence in northern Africa, 147–49; in Egypt, 149–51

universities and schooling, 7–8, 271–73; Cairo (Azhar), 271–72; Fez (Karaouine), 271–72; Timbuctoo (Sankore), 271–72
see initiation and instruction of youths and girls

witches, 77, 324–27
women, 6, 307–38, 339–44

women of importance in African history and legends, 307–13
see Yennenga; see Judith; see Cahena; see Sheba, Queen of (Makedda); see Kinza; Amina, 308; Mantatisi, 308–9; Zeineb, 309; Helena of Ethiopia, 310, 311; Taitu, 310; Woizero Zawditu, 310; "Pearl Spray," 311–12; Jinga, 312
polygamy (polygyny), 314–38
adultery punishments, 319–20
divorce and repudiation, 320, 329
"bride wealth" or preliminary payment by the husband, 320–21
in-law avoidance custom, 321–22
see children
Moslem women's position, 319–20, 328–29, 331–38; in Paradise, 338
concubine's position and rights, 329–31
veils, 331, 333–34
delight in female fatness, 339–42
women's magic powers, 324–25
women's capacity with poisons, 326–27
see matrilineal system; see Christianity's attitude toward women and sex; see incest; see cowrie

Yennenga, 171–72, 308

A Note About the Author

Galbraith Welch was born in Dakota Territory and now lives abroad. She is a former contributor of articles and reviews to *The New York Times*.

Mrs. Welch has traveled extensively in Africa, and is deeply involved in its history and culture. Two previous books, *The Unveiling of Timbuctoo* and *North African Prelude*, demonstrated her erudite and skillful treatment of the complex that is Africa. *Africa Before They Came* is her most recent portrait of that fascinating continent.

The text of this book has been set in 11 on 13 Gara-
mond Linotype with Garamond and Weiss Initials
used for display.